Day by Day through the Old Testament

C. E. HOCKING
M. HORLOCK

PRECIOUS SEED PUBLICATIONS

First printed 1982
Reprinted 1992, 1998

© Copyright by Precious Seed Publications 1982

ISBN 1 871642 04 3

The illustrations on the cover are
by courtesy of Alan Linton
Front cover: i) River Jabbok ii) Jezreel
iii) The Menorah iv) Valley of Baca
Back cover: a well preserved water tower

Printed by Redwood Books, Trowbridge

Preface

Day by Day through the Old Testament was first issued in 1982, and as a Committee we are delighted that the continuing demand for it has called for its re-issue in 1992. We thank God for His answer to this prayer, with which the original preface concluded, that He might 'graciously use this book to promote the joy and spiritual profit of His beloved people, for whom, by His Holy Spirit, He has provided such a rich library concerning His beloved Son'. May the God of revelation continue to extend its influence for His own glory through this reprint.

The size of the Old Testament, covering as it does approximately 3/4 of the total text of the Bible, may have contributed to so few believers giving the time and place to it that God has done, to the impoverishing of their spiritual understanding and experience. The Old Testament was the Bible used by our Lord when He was here; it was also the Bible of the early church as it spread the gospel of the grace of God across the Near East. This Day by Day, though necessarily *selective* in the text considered, is intended to promote a wider reading, and a more fruitful understanding of *the whole* of the Old Testament. The 365 passages treated here, out of the total of the 929 chapters it contains, are listed in the index on pages 415f.

To encourage further reading, we have included an introduction to the Old Testament as a whole, reviews of the contents and emphases of the books, along with five maps illustrating some of the geography and topography involved. Additionally, we have included a suggested reading syllabus to direct the reader through *the complete* Old Testament in one year.

Daily Bible reading may be varied using our Day by Day Old Testament and Day by Day New Testament providing the following schemes in one year:-

1. selected reading from every book of the Old Testament using this guide;

2. the complete Old Tetsament in one year using the reading syllabus on pages 411–414. These portions could be divided to provide morning and evening readings if desired.

3. selected readings from the Old Testament in the morning, and

the complete New Testament in the evening using both guides.

4. the complete Bible, using our New Testament guide in the morning, and the reading syllabus of the Old Testament in the evening.

With the addition to our library of 'Day by Day through the Psalms', yet another stimulus to daily Bible reading and meditation is now available. These books are issued to encourage your enjoyment of the Word of God with all its attendant spiritual benefits. To derive maximum help from this you will need to set apart time, to seek prayerfully God's light and blessing upon your reading, to read carefully the scripture portion for the day, to read the daily comments provided, crowning your own quiet meditation with thanksgiving and prayer that you might be a doer and not reader only.

Again we wish to record our indebtedness to our contributors for their ready and rich co-operation, and to the Committee whose skills and sacrificial support have made our burden light.

C.E. HOCKING
M. HORLOCK

Oh, how I love thy law! It is my meditation all the day.
Thou, through thy commandments, hast made me wiser
    than mine enemies; for they are ever with me.
I have more understanding than all my teachers; for thy
    testimonies are my meditation.
I understand more than the ancients; because I keep thy
    precepts.
I have refrained my feet from every evil way, that I might
    keep thy word.
I have not departed from thy judgments; for thou hast taught
    me.
How sweet are thy words unto my taste! Yea, sweeter than
    honey to my mouth.
Through thy precepts I get understanding; therefore, I hate
    every false way.

Psalm 119.97–104

List of Contents

	Page
List of Contributors	7
Introducing the Old Testament	8
Map 1. The Fertile Crescent	11
Genesis	12
Exodus	43
Leviticus	64
Numbers	80
Deuteronomy	93
Joshua	109
Map 2. The Inheritances of the Twelve Tribes	118
Judges—Includes Introduction to Ruth	119
Ruth	130
1 Samuel—Includes Introduction to 2 Samuel	133
2 Samuel	149
Map 3. The Kingdoms of David and Solomon	162
1 Kings—Includes Introduction to 2 Kings	163
2 Kings	178
Map 4. The Assyrian and Babylonian Empires	190
1 Chronicles	191
2 Chronicles	205
Ezra	223
Nehemiah	229
Esther	236
Job	240
Psalms	247
Proverbs	278
Ecclesiastes—Includes Introduction to Song of Songs	291
Song of Songs	295
Isaiah	300
Jeremiah—Includes Introduction to Lamentations	331
Lamentations	346
Ezekiel	347
Daniel	359
Map 5. The Persian and Greek Empires	371
Table. Kings and Prophets of Israel and Judah	372
Hosea—Includes Introduction to Amos	373
Joel—Includes Introduction to Micah	379
Amos	382

DAY BY DAY THROUGH THE OLD TESTAMENT

	Page
Obadiah	386
Jonah—Includes Introduction to Nahum	387
Micah	391
Nahum	394
Habakkuk—Includes Introductions to Zephaniah and Obadiah	395
Zephaniah	398
Haggai—Includes Introductions to Zechariah and Malachi	399
Zechariah	401
Malachi	410
Old Testament Daily Reading Syllabus	411
Index of O.T. Passages Treated in the Daily Readings	415

List of Contributors

R. V. Court	*Isle of Wight*	Exodus, Leviticus
S. Emery	*Workington*	Joshua, Judges, Ruth
J. Heading	*Aberystwyth*	Ezekiel, Daniel
C. E. Hocking	*Penarth*	Introduction to the O.T., 1 & 2 Samuel, 1 & 2 Kings O. T. Reading Syllabus
M. Horlock	*Cardiff*	Genesis, Table of Kings and Prophets
D. J. Lawrence	*Ammanford*	Isaiah 1-39
K. T. C. Morris	*Southampton*	1 & 2 Chronicles
J. Boyd Nicholson	*St. Catherines, Ontario, Canada*	Hosea, Joel, Amos, Obadiah, Jonah, Micah, Nahum, Habakkuk, Zephaniah
B. Osborne	*Dinas Powis*	Ezra, Nehemiah, Esther, Proverbs, Ecclesiastes, Song of Songs
J. B. D. Page	*Harrow*	Numbers
A. E. Phillips	*West Moors*	Haggai, Zechariah, Malachi
A. T. Shearman	*Worcester*	Deuteronomy, Jeremiah, Lamentations
T. E. Wilson	*Sea Girt, N.J., U.S.A.*	Job, Psalms, Isaiah 40-66

All Introductions are supplied by the contributors

Introducing the Old Testament

IN THE BEGINNING GOD. These majestic words conduct us into the vast inheritance of **divine revelation** which we call the O.T., 2 Cor. 3. 14. Here we have the very oracles of God, a part of the many entrusted privileges of Israel, Rom. 3. 2.

In it **the progress of history** may be traced, from what is termed pre-historic to post-exilic times. First place is given to *God and Creation*, Gen. 1-2. The *entrance of sin* and death into the world follows, Gen. 3, the story moving on from the *fall of man to the flood*, under which the earth was deluged in the judgment of God, Gen. 4-9. The *new start* made after the flood led to man's fresh departure from God, the development of the nations and the confusing of their tongues, together with the call of Abraham with its more immediate family ramifications, Gen. 10-45. Next it is *Jacob and his family in Egypt*, the emergence of Israel as a nation, and their *deliverance and exodus* from Egypt, Gen. 46 to Exod. 15. Then they journeyed to Sinai, received the first (old) covenant revelation there, and commenced their *pilgrimage and wilderness wanderings*, Exod. 16 to Josh. 2. Passing over the Jordan, *Israel entered into the land* under the leadership of Joshua. This time of victories was followed by the sad defeats and cries for divine deliverances during *the times of the judges*, Josh. 3 to 1 Sam. 7. The period of *the monarchy* follows when the 12 tribes were united under one king, 1 Sam. 8 to 1 Kings 11, and afterwards when the nation was divided into two kingdoms, 1 Kings 12 to Kings 25. Much of this history is paralleled in the Chronicles, the sad decline of the nation leading to *the captivities in Assyria/Babylonia*. Finally, part of the nation *returned to the homeland* when Cyrus of Medo-Persia made this open to them, the majority, however, choosing to remain in their more auspicious, if foreign surroundings, 2 Chron. 36. 22f; Ezra-Esther.

Throughout this record of salvation history **the unfoldings of prophecy** are interspersed, Isa. to Mal. Here the foundations of eschatology and apocalyptic are laid, with their contrasting moods of optimism for the believer, and pessimism for the world empires and earth dwellers at large. Beyond the prospect of Gentile world empires removed by climactic divine intervention, lies the establishing of the kingdom of God on

DAY BY DAY THROUGH THE OLD TESTAMENT

earth, when Zion will be named Jehovah-Shammah, "The Lord is there", Ezek. 48. 35. The prevailing mood is one of *yearning for future glory*. It must not be overlooked that the voice of prophecy is not confined to the books of the prophets, for even the O.T. histories are all too often anticipations of events greater and more dramatic than themselves. Neither are the prophets and their prophecies absorbed only with future events. So much of their ministry takes the form of challenge and correction for their contemporaries, and their introduction of future events is to provide yet another spur to the nation to return to God and a wholehearted commitment to Him.

Wise counsel, songs and sighs for the mind and the heart, add their own contribution, too, through **the Wisdom and Poetry** of the O.T., Job to Song.

This unique collection of inspired writings forms *the Bible for the Jewish people*. They use the mnemonic "Tanach to describe it. The consonants of this word are the initial letters of the three divisions of their Bible. The letter $T = Torah$, *the Law*, Gen. to Deut., while $N = Nebi'im$, *the Prophets*, including the former prophets, Josh. to 2 Kings, and the latter, Isa, Jer, Ezek, the Minor Prophets (Hos. to Mal), and $CH = Chetubim$, *the writings*, embracing the rather peculiar combination, to us, of the poetic books Psa, Prov, Job, the five scrolls, Song, Ruth, Lam, Eccles, Esther, then the historical/apocalyptic Daniel, and finally the historical books Ezra, Neh, and 1 and 2 Chron. Reference to this **arrangement of the O.T. canon,** the law of Moses, and the prophets, and the psalms, is made by our Lord in Luke 24. 44. The English Versions of the O.T. follow generally the Greek translation's arrangement of contents, where the literature may be broadly classified under the categories of 1. *Law*, Gen. to Deut; 2. *History*, Josh. to Esther; 3. *Poetry*, Job to Song, and 4. *Prophecy* (see breakdown of O.T. Reading Syllabus, p. 411-414).

But the importance and lasting value of the O.T. is demonstrated further by the **profuse quotation** of it in the N.T. Here its permanent place in a *progressive divine revelation* is stated, Heb. 1. 1, *the stages of its history* are drawn upon, Acts 7; 13, *its prophecies* are seen either as "fulfilled", Matt. 1. 22f; 27. 9f, or are endorsed as yet to be fulfilled, Matt. 24. 15; 26. 64, while *its psalms and poetry* are shown to be laden with deep significance, Acts 2. 34f; 13. 33, and practical direction, Rom.

12. 20. The differing subjects and emphases of Matthew, Romans, and Hebrews are all interpenetrated and supported by an array of O.T. evidence. The N.T. writers handle with great facility many O.T. verses in N.T. contexts.

The O.T., from what we have seen, then, is *a major part of the Bible for the believer in Christ*. Yet further, it is the initial aid to the understanding of Biblical Theology. The O.T. is **the theological word book**, facilitating our grasp of such great truths as election, redemption, justification, salvation, holiness, sin, sacrifice, etc. How much of the N.T. teaching adopts these much worked theological terms familiar from, and profusely illustrated in, the O.T.

The believer is also led into the richness of the past, present, and future ministries of the Christ by the Spirit's unfolding of the **typological significance** of the O.T. How impoverished we should be when meditating on, or worshipping the great God of our salvation apart from the heart warming help drawn from both *sanctuary and sacrifice*, which so perfectly foreshadowed that substance which we now enjoy. The range of the ministries of our great High Priest is fully and suggestively presented in the O.T. priesthood. What detailed portraits of *the Servant of the Lord*, and *the Shepherd of the sheep*, are found in the O.T. gallery. These and other O.T. motifs, such as the *liberating movement of God at the exodus*, the N.T. has clearly identified with the Person and work of our Lord Jesus. Lord, unfold Thyself to us in all the Scriptures, Luke 24. 27.

Let us seek the ready and authoritative help of the Holy Spirit so that we may truly "understand the scriptures", Luke 24. 45ff. For these are not only able to make us wise unto salvation, but are "profitable for doctrine, for reproof, for correction, for instruction in righteousness: that the man of God may be perfect, throughly furnished unto all good works", 2 Tim. 3. 16f. We must read and heed the O.T. Scriptures, being both warned and instructed by them, 1 Cor. 10. 11; Rom. 15. 4.

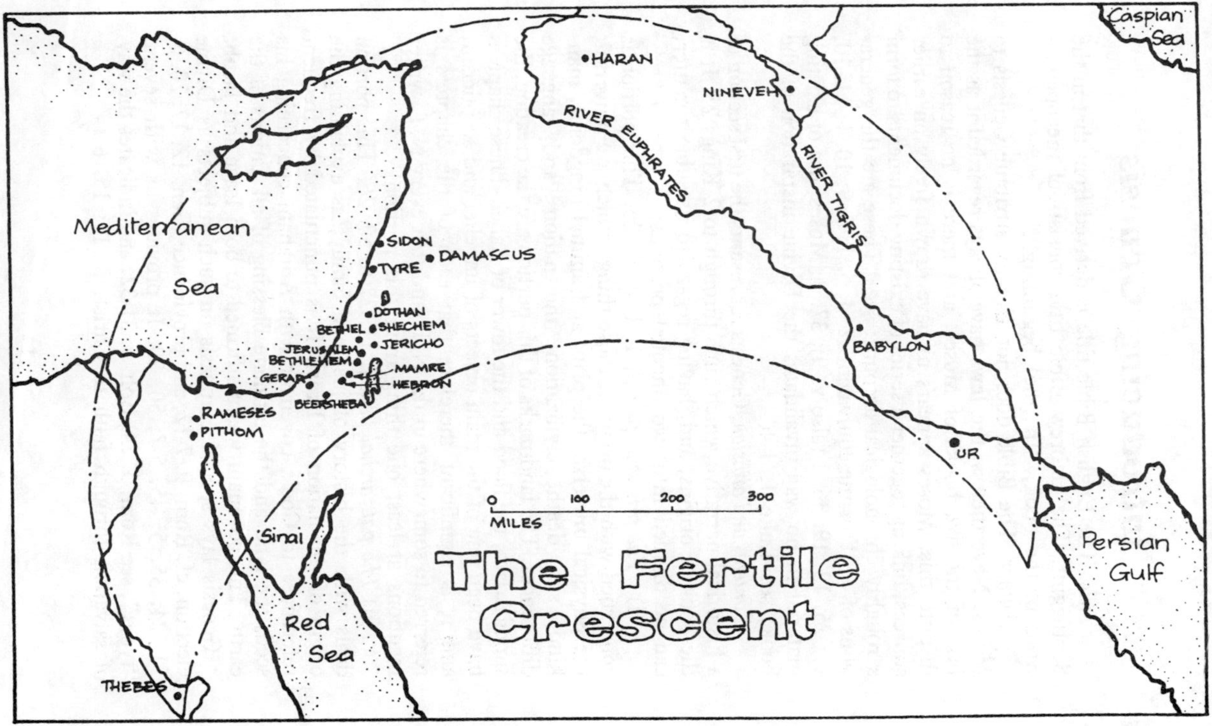
Caspian Sea
HARAN
NINEVEH
RIVER EUPHRATES
RIVER TIGRIS
Mediterranean Sea
SIDON
DAMASCUS
TYRE
DOTHAN
BETHEL
SHECHEM
JERUSALEM
JERICHO
BETHLEHEM
MAMRE
GERAR
HEBRON
BEERSHEBA
BABYLON
UR
RAMESES
PITHOM
0 100 200 300
MILES
Sinai
Persian Gulf
The Fertile Crescent
Red Sea
THEBES

Introducing Genesis

Title. The English Bible title is derived from that in the Septuagint. The Hebrew Bible title consists of the opening word of the book, "In (the) beginning".

Author. The Bible does not directly attribute Genesis to Moses. Nevertheless, the Jews have always regarded it as the first of the five books of Moses, and there is no reason to dispute this. Moses appears to have drawn freely on earlier sources, linking together a series of existing documents to form a roughly chronological account; see "These are the generations of . . ." or the equivalent, 2. 4; 5. 1; 6. 9; 10. 1; 11. 10, 27; 25. 12, 19; 36. 1 (also v. 9); 37. 2. Moses' use of existing material in no way invalidates the Divine inspiration of the book; see Luke 1. 1-4.

Contents and division. Genesis represents the first section of a historical narrative which runs through to 2 Kings 25. It is the book of origins, and, having regard to its subject matter, can be divided into two unequal portions:

(i) *The primeval period*, 1. 1 to 11. 26. This portion is concerned with the origin of those things which are universal; the physical universe, the plant and animal kingdoms, mankind, sin, death, civilization, the nations and language differences. The landmarks of this portion are the creation, the sin of Adam, the flood and the tower of Babel. These chapters have been one of the main objects of unbelief and scepticism, and it is significant therefore that each of the chapters is referred to somewhere in the N.T. and that every N.T. writer mentions at least one thing from this portion!

(ii) *The patriarchal period*, 11. 27 to 50. 26. This portion deals with the history of just one family, as explaining the origin of the nation of Israel. It is punctuated by frequent references to God's covenant with Abraham concerning his seed, the land and the ultimate blessing of all nations of the earth. This covenant was reaffirmed to both Isaac and Jacob.

Genesis lays special emphasis on such subjects as Divine election, cf. Rom. 9. 7-12, and providence, Gen. 12. 17; 20. 6; 31. 24; 35. 5; 45. 5-7; 50. 20. It provides us with several "types", see Rom. 5. 14; Eph. 5. 31-32, and indicates the way of salvation through faith in Christ, 3. 15; 15. 6.

Jan. 1st
READING : **Genesis 1. 1, 26 to 2. 3**

THE CREATION

THE TITLE OF DEITY used throughout the opening section of the Bible, Gen. 1. 1 to 2. 3, is "God" (Heb. Elohim, the root meaning of which is "power"). Creation was indeed a work of immense, divine and sovereign power, displayed for the most part in God's creative word. Note the recurring "and God said", 1. 3, 6, 11, 14, 20, 24; cf. Psa. 33. 6, 9.

The whole work was accomplished in just 6 days, Gen. 1. 31; Exod. 20. 11. These 6 days can be regarded as made up of two sets of 3 days each. The narrative clearly distinguishes "the heavens and the earth" from "all the host of them", Gen. 2. 1. The first 3 days are concerned with the formation of "the heavens and the earth"; the second 3 days are concerned with the "host" which fill them. This can be seen from the following summary of events. *Day* 1 saw the initial creation of the heavens and the earth, together with the origin of light, while *Day* 4 saw the creation of "lights" in the heavens, namely sun, moon and stars. *Day* 2 saw the making of a firmament with waters above and below, while *Day* 5 saw the creation of birds to "fly in the open firmament" and of fish to "fill the waters". *Day* 3 saw the formation of dry land and the beginnings of vegetation, while *Day* 6 saw the creation of animals and of man and woman, all being vegetarians, to live on the dry land.

How favoured man is! He is formed last, as the pinnacle and climax of God's creatorial achievement. He is king of the earth, 1. 26, 28; Psa. 8. 3-8. Indeed, we learn elsewhere that man was the object of Divine counsel before his creation, Eph. 1. 4; 2 Tim. 1. 9. Well may we marvel that the plan to save sinful men was formed *before* man was! To give effect to this salvation, the One who had made all things was required Himself to become a man, John 1. 3, 14. For man to be made in the image of the Creator, Gen. 1. 26, was an evidence of His *creative power;* for the Creator to be "made in the likeness of men", Phil. 2. 7, was an evidence of His *condescending grace*.

For a clear statement of God's purpose in creating, we need to look, not to the first book of the Bible but to the last. "All things" were created *for His pleasure* and will, Rev. 4. 11. Let us begin the new year with the determination to live in accord with that purpose.

Jan. 2nd

READING : **Genesis 2. 18-25**

BODY AND BRIDE

EVE CAN BE REGARDED as a type of the Church in at least two ways. In one sense she was part of Adam's *body*. Adam described her as "bone of my bones and flesh of my flesh", Gen. 2. 23. Relating this verse to Christ and believers, the apostle Paul wrote, "we are members of his body, of his flesh and of his bones", Eph. 5. 30. Clearly the union between Christ and the Church is so real that the language of Adam concerning Eve can be applied to it. God had the Church in His mind when he formed Eve. In origin she was unique. Adam and the animals were taken out of the ground, Gen. 2. 19; 3. 19, but she was not. She came into being as the outcome of Adam's deep sleep, an apt picture of death in a world where there was none. Similarly, it is on account of the death of Christ that the Church has her existence. Eve derived her physical life from Adam; we owe our spiritual life to the Lord. Contrast, however, the passive role of the first Adam, Gen. 2. 21, with the voluntary self-sacrifice of "the last Adam".

Eve was also Adam's *bride*. Genesis 2 emphasizes that, though man could exercise authority over the animal kingdom (expressed in his naming all living creatures), he could have no fellowship with them, vv. 19-20. The man found no helper suited to him. The animals had been made male and female; only man had no companion. God had pronounced "good" all that He had made thus far, but He recognized that man's isolation was "not good", 2. 18. It was only after a helper like man had been found for him that God could say that "everything" was "very good", 1. 31. The Church, which is Christ's body, is said to be "the fulness (i.e., complement) of him that filleth all in all", Eph. 1. 23. Reverently we may therefore say that the Lord would have been no more complete in His resurrection glory without the Church than Adam would have been without Eve. She was blessed because of Adam; as his bride she shared his dominion over the earth, Gen. 1. 28. All our blessings are "in" Christ, Eph. 1. 3; He who is to reign will not reign alone! Yet it is not so much His kingdom for which we wait, as for Himself, Rev. 22. 17. Let us praise the Lord today for the matchless grace which has made us part of His body and bride.

Jan. 3rd

READING : **Genesis 2. 16-17; 3. 1-6**

THE WILES OF THE DEVIL

It is apparent from the words of the serpent that he had been aware all along of the precise terms of the Divine prohibition. We find that he could quote the very words which God had used — "of every tree of the garden", 2. 16; 3. 1, "surely die", 2. 17; 3. 4, "in the day" and "eat thereof", 2. 17; 3. 5. It follows, then, that he asked Eve whether God had said something which he knew God had *not* said, v. 1. Satan (Rev. 12. 9) realized that it was inevitable she would give him a negative answer, but he was reasonably confident that, in doing so, she would refer to the restriction which God had made. That is, he wanted *Eve to tell him* about the fruit which God had withheld from Adam and herself. In this way he prompted her to fix her mind on that which God had denied them, thereby sowing the first seeds of doubt as to God's goodness.

Alas, Eve's answer betrayed clear indications of the effectiveness of the devil's strategy. When describing the provision God had made, she dropped the words "freely" and "every", 2. 16; 3. 2, thereby understating the bounty He had given. At the same time she added, without any warrant, the words "neither shall ye touch it", 3. 3. thereby exaggerating the limitation which He had imposed. Satan was quick to take full advantage of Eve's suspicion that perhaps God had not been as generous as He could have been. He proceeded to deny both God's *truthfulness*, v. 4, and His *goodness*, v. 5. As so often since, the devil's doctrine was a mixture of truth and error. Firstly, he flatly contradicted what God had said, v. 4. In this he lied. He then offered an alternative motive for God having placed the restriction, audaciously attributing to God the very self-seeking which had led to his own fall, v. 5. There was, however, an element of truth in his claims that her eyes would be opened, v. 7, and that she would be as God, knowing good and evil, v. 5 r.v., v. 22. What Eve "saw" seemed only to reinforce Satan's argument, and she took and ate the fruit, v. 6, allowing herself to be guided by appearance rather than by God's word.

Satan may accuse God to *you* as One who seeks other than your highest good. Direct him to the same Person and place where God directs him when Satan accuses you to Him—to the Lord Jesus and the cross.

Jan. 4th

READING : **Genesis 3. 7-24**

THE SEED OF THE WOMAN

THE SERPENT had triumphed; man had sinned. But within hours of Satan's victory God declared the circumstances and certainty of his final defeat, v. 15. The phrase "Seed of the woman" stressed that this final conquest would be achieved by One out of the human race. How fully and how gloriously the Saviour has retrieved for men all that Adam lost!

In a garden the first man was responsible for a decision which amounted to "Not Thy will, but mine, be done". This decision was carried into effect by one act of disobedience, performed at a tree, with far-reaching and unhappy consequences for all who came of his line. This act (i) brought about man's estrangement from God; "He drove out the man", v. 24. It (ii) lost man his access to the tree of life, vv. 22, 24. It also (iii) alienated nature from him. Man would have known satisfying activity and employment if he had not fallen, 2. 15. As a result of sin, however, he experienced sweat and hard labour in tilling the ground, with its prolific growth of thorns and weeds, until at last that same ground claimed him, 3. 17 - 19, 23. Finally, as a result of his sin, man (iv) found what the words "death", "sorrow" and "curse" meant, 2. 17; 3. 16-17.

In a garden the "second man", the Lord Jesus, resolved "not my will, but thine, be done", John 18. 1; 1 Cor. 15. 47; Luke 22. 42. This determination was expressed in one act of obedience, performed at a tree, which has had the most far-reaching and blessed consequences for all who are of His line, Rom. 5. 19; 1 Pet. 2. 24. The Lord (i) has brought us to God, 1 Pet. 3. 18. He has (ii) secured for us access to the tree of life, Rev. 22. 14; cf. 2. 7. One day He will (iii) liberate creation itself from its present bondage to corruption and decay. It is destined to enter into the freedom which will accompany the glorification of God's children, Rom. 8. 20-22; cf. Isa. 11. 6-9; 35. 1-2. Finally, the Lord (iv) will banish words like "death", "sorrow" and "curse" from man's vocabulary. "There shall be no more death, neither sorrow" and "there shall be no more curse", Rev. 21. 4; 22. 3. Happy day!

For the glory of God and our blessing, the woman's Seed suffered the bruising of His "heel" at Golgotha. Praise Him!

Jan. 5th

READING : **Genesis 4. 1-16, 25-26**

CAIN AND ABEL

ALL OUR SINS can be categorized as either being against God directly or against our fellow men. Adam's sin was against God alone; Cain's sin was against his brother.

Having regard to the name which Eve gave to her firstborn son, she evidently thought that he would be the one to bruise the serpent's head, 4. 1. How wrong she was! Far from being Satan's vanquisher, Cain "was *of* that wicked one", 1 John 3. 12. The devil is described by the Lord as (i) a "murderer" and (ii) a "liar", John 8. 44. Cain was both of these. (i) Whereas Eve was "the mother of all living", 3.20, her firstborn violently took a life. The first man born turned out to be a murderer! (ii) When God had confronted Adam with his sin, although he had attempted to excuse himself, he had responded truthfully, 3. 12. Cain aggravated his murderous deed with a blatant lie, 4. 9. In a special sense, therefore, Cain partook of the character of the devil. Knowing their Satanic origin, let us "put away" *all* malice and deceit, Eph. 4. 25, 31.

God is just. Even Cain could not deny this. He claimed that his punishment was greater than he could bear, Gen. 4. 13; he could not claim that it was greater than he deserved! Abel was a God-like man, distinguished by his righteousness. *He* "was righteous", Heb. 11. 4; his *works* were "righteous", 1 John 3. 12; his was "righteous *blood*", Matt. 23. 35. Cain was able to silence the voice of the righteous man but not the voice of his blood! God heard Abel's blood calling to Him from the ground, Gen. 4. 10; cf. Job 16. 18. It called to God for *vengeance* on his murderer, and was responsible for Cain's sense of despair, Gen. 4. 13, and loss of God's presence, v. 16. Praise God, the blood of Jesus, the mediator of the new covenant, "speaketh better things than that of Abel", Heb. 12. 24. One of the terms of the new covenant is that "their sins and iniquities will I remember no more", 10. 17. The blood of Christ calls for our *forgiveness*, Matt. 26. 28, fills us with hope and invites us into God's presence, Heb. 10. 19. In an attempt to prevent the fulfilment of God's word, Gen. 3. 15, the serpent struck at the seed of the woman, corrupting her first son and slaying her second. But God raised up Seth, appointing Eve "another *seed* instead of Abel, whom Cain slew", 4. 25.

Jan. 6th

READING : **Genesis 4. 17-24; 5. 1-6, 21-24**

THE SEVENTH FROM ADAM

ADAM HAD MANY SONS, 5. 4, but the Bible lists the descendants of only two of them, namely, Cain, 4. 17ff, and Seth, 5.6ff. It so happened that the seventh generation of both lines furnished exceptional men. *Lamech*, 4. 19-24, is notable for his *godlessness*, and *Enoch*, 5. 21-24, for his *godliness*.

Lamech was the first man to practise bigamy, in defiance of the Divine order which had applied "from the beginning", 2. 24; Matt. 19. 4-8. It was to his wives that he boasted of the way in which he had requited, with death, a mere wound inflicted on him by a young man, Gen. 4. 23. Lamech manifested in an intensified form the readiness to shed blood which was first found in Cain. God had earlier promised that sevenfold vengeance would be taken on any one who murdered Cain, v. 15. Lamech boastfully threatened a seventy-times-sevenfold retribution in his own case, v. 24 LXX. He would do better than God! He said, in effect, "for me it is not until seven times, but until seventy-times-seven". Contrast the teaching of the Lord Jesus concerning the reaction of His people to those who sin against them. The offending party is to be forgiven. He said, "not . . . until seven times: but, Until seventy times seven", Matt. 18. 22. Over against the craving of the natural man for a 70 times 7 revenge, the Lord set the duty of the spiritual man to extend a 70 times 7 forgiveness.

Throughout chapter 5, two words are used in connection with almost every man mentioned; namely "begat" and "died". There are, however, two exceptions. Reference is made to one man (Adam) who died, never having been born, v. 5, and to one (Enoch) who was born but who never died, vv. 21-24. *Enoch* is one of the two men who have left the world without dying, 5. 24; Heb. 11. 5; cf. 2 Kings 2. 11. (The Hebrew verb for "took", Gen. 5. 24, is used of Elijah also, 2 Kings 2. 3). The same privilege awaits those who "are alive and remain unto the coming of the Lord", 1 Thess. 4. 15. Enoch prophesied about the second advent of Christ, Jude 14, when two other men will leave the world without dying, Rev. 19. 20, yet their destination will not be the presence of God but the lake of fire! Faith enabled Enoch to walk with God and thereby please Him, Heb. 11. 6; cf. Mic. 6. 8; 1 Thess. 4. 1.

Jan. 7th

READING : Genesis 6. 5-14; 7. 1; 8. 1-5

NOAH AND THE ARK

ENOCH AND NOAH are the only two men of whom Scripture says that they "walked with God", 5. 22; 6. 9. *Enoch "prophesied"* about the Divine judgment which will befall the "ungodly" at the second advent of Christ, Jude 14. *Noah "preached"* about the Divine judgment which would befall the "ungodly" in the form of the great flood, 2 Pet. 2. 5. In that the coming of the flood caught the people of the day unawares, it provides an apt illustration of the coming of the Son of man, Matt. 24. 38-39.

Noah was a remarkable man. Apart from his immediate family, he stood alone in his witness for God. The society around him was altogether "corrupt" and "violent", Gen. 6. 11-13. Yet God saw that Noah was righteous "in this generation", 7. 1. Noah could have said correctly what Elijah said erroneously—"I, even I only, am left", 1 Kings 19. 10. There were no hidden 7000! What havoc sin had wrought. "God looked upon the earth, and, *behold, it was corrupt*", Gen. 6. 12, stands in marked contrast to the earlier comment, "God saw everything that he had made, and, *behold it was very good*", 1. 31. The moral pressures must have been enormous for Noah. Yet he stood out as different. In contrast, for example, to the prevailing disobedience, 1 Pet. 3. 20, we read four times that he did as God had commanded him, Gen. 6. 22; 7. 5, 9, 16. His example proves that it is possible to live an untainted life in a godless society. Paul wrote of "a crooked and perverse generation, *among whom* ye are seen as lights", Phil. 2. 15 R.V.

The passage of the ark through the water furnishes a type of *Christian baptism*, 1 Pet. 3. 20-21. Baptism is, of course, our identification with the Lord Jesus in His death and resurrection. It is perhaps fitting that the ark seems to have come to rest on dry ground on the same date in the year, Gen. 8. 4, as that on which the Lord rose from the dead. The pre-flood world, with its wickedness, represents our pre-conversion way of life, and the cleansed earth represents our new life in Christ. The flood cut off Noah completely from the old world, for all he knew of it was totally destroyed, 7. 23. If we are dead, buried and risen with Christ, let us "seek those things which are above", Col. 2. 12, 20; 3. 1.

Jan. 8th
READING : Genesis 8. 20-22; 9. 18-29
A SIN COVERED

NOAH soon showed that the flood had not changed or improved his Adam-like nature. The very first thing mentioned of him after the record of God's gracious covenant is the incident of his drunkenness, 9. 20-21. His sad fall only served to confirm God's assessment that the thoughts of man's heart were still naturally evil, 8. 21; cf. 6. 5. Noah may have built an altar on a *clean* earth and offered *clean* sacrifices, 8. 20, but his heart still carried within it the *evil* principle of sin. The seriousness with which God regards drunkenness can be gauged from its inclusion, along with the most shameful and degrading sins, among the works of the flesh, Gal. 5. 19-21. Noah's drunkenness was the first recorded sin of his life, and took place after he had walked with God for about 600 years! Let us learn from this that, no matter how far a person has advanced in spiritual experience, the possibility of a lapse always remains. "Let him that thinketh he standeth take heed lest he fall", 1 Cor. 10. 12.

Noah's sin resembled that of Adam, in that they both fell as the result of partaking of the fruit of a tree. Whereas, however, Adam's sin led to the realization that he was naked, the sin of Noah rendered him oblivious to his nakedness. But his son, Ham, saw what Noah's stupor hid from his own eyes. Alas, Ham not only failed to cover his father's nakedness; he went so far as to draw his brethren's attention to it. In contrast, Shem and Japheth discreetly covered their father. How do we react to the discovery of sins in our brethren. Do we enjoy giving publicity to their failings? Old and New Testaments unite in proclaiming that love *covers* a multitude of sins, Prov. 10. 12; 1 Pet. 4. 8. Joseph carefully avoided telling the Egyptians that it was his brethren who were responsible for his troubles, Gen. 40. 15; 46. 31-32. In a similar vein David met the news of Saul's death with the plea, "Tell it not in Gath, publish it not in the streets of Ashkelon", 2 Sam. 1. 20. It is our duty to attempt the restoration of a brother "overtaken in a fault", Gal. 6. 1. In so doing, we are to "consider" ourselves, lest we "also be tempted", for none of us is immune to the possibility of sin. How wise, therefore, for Shem and Japheth to proceed as they did, Gen. 9. 23; Ham "saw", v. 22, but "they saw not".

Jan. 9th

READING : **Genesis 11. 1-9, 26 to 12. 3**

MAKING A NAME

GENESIS 11 OPENS with the men of Shinar who set out to build a great city, and closes by introducing us to the man who turned his back on one.

The men left God out of all their plans, vv. 3-4: Abram was prepared to trust God for all, Heb. 11. 8-9. In attempting to avoid being scattered, Gen. 11. 4, they set out to *disobey* God's command, which was to multiply "in the earth", 9. 7: in leaving Ur, Abram *"obeyed"* the command of God, Heb. 11. 8. As a consequence of these actions they brought on themselves God's *judgment*, Gen. 11. 7-9; while Abram secured for himself God's *blessing*, 12. 2. Theirs was a city *"which the children of men* builded", 11. 5: the city for which he looked had *God* for its builder and maker, Heb. 11. 10. Their city was *never finished;* "they left off to build the city", Gen. 11. 8: for him, God *"has prepared"* a city, Heb. 11. 16. *They* wished to make their name great, Gen. 11. 4: to him God gave the promise that *He* would make his name great, 12. 2. For today's meditation we will link together three brazen challenges to God's authority in the Old Testament. (i) Lucifer stated his ambition, "I *will exalt* my throne", Isa. 14. 13. (ii) The men of Shinar set out to *make themselves a name*, Gen. 11. 4. (iii) Ahab and Jezebel attempted to compel *every knee* in Israel to bow to Baal, 1 Kings 16. 31-33; 18. 4; 19. 18. Each venture failed. Lucifer is "to be brought down to hell", Isa. 14. 15. The only name acquired by the men of Shinar was that of "Babel", that is, Confusion, Gen. 11. 9. God reserved himself 7000 in Israel, whose knees never "bowed to Baal", 1 Kings 19. 18. The apostle Paul directs us to Another, Phil. 2. 9-10. "God also has (i) highly *exalted* him, and (ii) given him *a name* which is above every name: that (iii) at the name of Jesus every *knee* should bow". Satan will not be exalted at all; the Lord is *highly* exalted! The men of Shinar have only a name of which they should be ashamed: the Lord has a name *above* every name! Seven thousand never bowed their knees to Baal; to the Lord *every* knee will bow! Let us remember that all these honours have been bestowed on the One, who for the sake of "others" took a series of downward steps from "being in the form of God" to "death, even the death of the cross", vv. 5-8.

Jan. 10th

READING : Genesis 12. 1-9

THE TENT AND THE ALTAR

ABRAHAM WAS a man of great faith and it is not surprising, therefore, that more is said about him in Hebrews 11 than about anyone else. His spiritual exploits are there summed up in three statements; "By faith Abraham . . . *went out* ", v. 8, "By faith he *sojourned in* ", v. 9, and "By faith Abraham . . . *offered up*", v. 17. Abram's life of faith began when "the God of glory" appeared to him and called him to leave his idolatrous surroundings, Acts 7. 2-3; cf. Josh. 24. 2. Abram came from Ur (i.e., "light") of the Chaldees, Gen. 11. 31; 15. 7. Ur's largest temple was known as "the house of the great light" and its chief deity was Nannar, the moon-god. But for Abram "the God of *glory*" totally eclipsed the brightness and splendour of Ur, its temple and its god! In response to the call of God, Abram exchanged his villa in Ur for a tent of goat's hair, and the impressive temple of Nannar for simple altars to the Lord. The two expressions which characterize Abram's life are "pitched his tent" and "builded an altar", 13. 8. By these he witnessed that he was a *stranger* to the world, cf. 23. 4; Heb. 11. 13, and a *worshipper* of the true God. Abram never had any regrets about leaving the glories and comforts of Ur; "If indeed they had been mindful of that country from which they went out, they would have had opportunity to return", Heb. 11. 15 R.V. Abram wanted no more to do with either Ur or Haran, Gen. 24. 6. He looked for a better city, Heb. 11. 10-16.

We possess the full-orbed revelation of *the God of glory*, made known to us as the Father, the Lord and the Spirit of glory, Eph. 1. 17; 1 Cor. 2. 8; 1 Pet. 4. 14 R.V. As with Abram, we have been *chosen*, Neh. 9. 7; Eph. 1. 4. and *called*, Heb. 11. 8; 1 Pet. 2. 9. We too are *pilgrims and strangers*, 1 Pet. 2. 11; and *worshippers* of the living God, able to offer up spiritual sacrifices, v. 5. Like Abram, "we have an *altar*", Heb. 13. 10, yet "here have we *no continuing city*, but we seek one to come", v. 14. We should not be *"mindful"* of—yea, we should altogether renounce—those things which belonged to our unregenerate days, Eph. 4. 22; 1 Pet. 4. 3. Having put our hands to the plough, let us not look back, Luke 9. 62. The restored prodigal ought not to crave swines' husks again! Abram "went out", and he never wanted to go back.

Jan. 11th

READING : **Genesis 12. 10-17**

WHEN FAITH FAILED

GOD WOULD LATER point out to Moses one very important difference between Egypt and Canaan, Deut. 11. 10-15. The land of Canaan was largely dependent for its fertility on the rainfall which normally fell during two periods of the year. The land of Egypt, however, had no great need of rain, on account of its highly developed irrigation system, which was fed from våst reservoirs filled by the annual rise of the Nile; cf. Ezek. 29. 9-10. When the rains failed and famine came to Canaan it was *natural*, therefore, that Abram should turn to Egypt. But Abram's resources were not merely "natural"! The "land" in which there was a famine, v. 10, was the very "land" to which God had called him, vv. 1-4, 7. Surely the place of Divine appointment would have been the place of Divine provision. But Abram was not equal to the test. He took matters in his own hands and went down to Egypt.

One false step soon led to another, and Abram's concern for his *sustenance* became concern for his *safety*, vv. 11-13. But God had promised Abram both a *land* and a *seed*, v. 7. In the strength of His promise about the land he ought not to have gone down to Egypt, and in the strength of the promise about a seed he ought not to have feared for his life. His words, "thou art my sister", v. 13, contained an element of truth, 20. 12, but they were clearly intended to deceive. Half-truths are untruths; God's standard is always "speak every man truth with his neighbour", Eph. 4. 25. Abram, playing the part of a tempter, also involved his wife in his sin. Ironically, the very precautions he took left the way open for Pharaoh to act as he did.

Abram's plans had certainly landed him in a fine predicament. Sarai was beyond rescue in Pharaoh's harem, v. 15, through whose guards no earthly power could hope to penetrate. Circumstances were now entirely out of Abram's control. The partriarch was well and truly helpless, but to his relief he was to discover that his God was not! The Lord plagued Pharaoh that he would let Abram's wife go, just as He was later to plague another Pharaoh to let Abraham's descendants go, Exod. 2. 24; chs. 7-12. How often God intervenes, in grace, to save us from the consequence of our own plans and actions.

Jan. 12th

READING : **Genesis 12. 18 to 13. 4**

BACKSLIDING HEALED

HAD ABRAM and Sarai been a worldly couple, no doubt they would have felt rather pleased with themselves as they "went up out of Egypt", 13. 1. Naturally speaking, everything had turned out well in the end. They had escaped the effects of the famine in Canaan, 12. 10, had gained a substantial increase in goods, 12. 16; 13. 2, were both unharmed, free and together again. But how *did* they feel? They were meant to be God's witnesses; through them "all families of the earth" were to be blessed, 12. 3. Yet their testimony as far as the Egyptians were concerned was worthless. In God's kind providence they had been spared the full consequences of their own folly, but they had *not* been spared a well-deserved, humiliating rebuke from Pharaoh, 12. 18-20. Pharaoh and his people clearly felt that they could no longer trust or respect the patriarch: "they sent him away", 12. 20. The writer to the Hebrews counted Abram and Sarai among those "of whom the world was not worthy", 11. 38. At the end of Genesis 12, however, they were considered unworthy of the world!

The Spirit of God reveals something of Abram's real frame of mind by stressing the route which he chose, vv. 3-4. He headed straight back to "the place where his tent had been *at the beginning*", "unto the place of the altar, which he had made there *at the first* ". It seems clear that in so doing Abram recognized that his visit to Egypt had been a sad mistake. He must now have realized that if God had been able to protect and provide for him and Sarai in Egypt, He would certainly have been able to have done so in the land of promise! Wisely Abram returned to the place where he had made his first mistake. The path of repentance and contrition is the only way to full recovery. The Lord's promise to wayward Israel is that He will give her "the valley of Achor for a door of hope", Hos. 2. 15. That is, she must be brought back, in heart at least, to the place of her first sin in the land, Josh. 7. 26, before she can be restored to the Lord, Hos. 2. 15-23. The erring believer must trace his backsliding to its source and judge it there. The Lord's message to the backsliding church of Ephesus was "*repent* and do the *first* works", Rev. 2. 15. His requirements have not changed.

Jan. 13th
READING : Genesis 13. 5-18

TRUSTING GOD

ABRAM'S RECENT EXPERIENCE had taught him that it did not pay to trust in himself. God had proved that He was *better* able to look after Abram's material needs and physical wellbeing than ever Abram was. It was not long before Abram was tested on this very issue again. The goods accumulated in Egypt soon provided the source of fresh trouble, vv. 6-7. It seems to have been a common thing for herdsmen to strive on account of restrictions of space and facilities, 26. 20. But strife between the servants of Abram and Lot was not acceptable. They were "brethren", 13. 8. The mention of the presence of the Canaanites, v. 7, stresses how sad and humiliating it is for "brethren" to strive before unbelievers. Abram regarded it better to separate in habitation than in heart, and proposed a geographical division, vv. 9-10.

On several grounds Abram could have laid claim to the first choice of territory. He was the older man, he was the head and leader of the clan, and it was to him that God had promised the land—all of it. But he had learned in chapter 12 that he could trust God for all his material needs. Because he had faith in God he could afford to offer Lot the unqualified choice of where he wanted to settle.

In spite of Abram's prior claim, Lot accepted his offer and, in spite of the character of the people there, 13. 13, he "pitched his tent towards" (*lit.*, as far as) Sodom, v. 12. The attraction of Sodom perhaps lay in its affluent society with plenty of ease and material prosperity, Ezek. 16. 49. Notice the progression: he "*beheld* . . . the plain", he "*chose* . . . the plain", he "*dwelled in* . . . the plain", vv. 10-12. Sight led to desire, which in turn led to action; cf. Josh. 7. 21; 2 Sam. 11. 2-4. Beware, then, the lust of the eyes! But if Lot "lifted up his eyes", v. 10, the Lord invited Abram to lift up his, v. 14. Abram was not going to be the loser by leaving all in God's hands! Lot had gone east, v. 11, but Abram was promised all he could see to the four points of the compass, and was encouraged to walk through the land as a conqueror, v. 17. Faith was to claim and to take possession of the land. Abram was now willing to rely on God alone to meet his needs—but this confidence was soon to be tested again.

Jan. 14th

READING : **Genesis 14. 1-24**

PREPARED BEFOREHAND

ABRAM REACTED WELL to Lot's plight. He did not respond as many would have, "Serve him right. He shouldn't have been in Sodom". He raced to Lot's rescue. Lot was Abram's "brother's son", v. 12, but in the hour of need he is described as Abram's "brother", vv. 14, 16. When one of our "brethren" is overtaken in a fault we should restore him, Gal. 6. 1.

Abram gained a great victory over Chedorlaomer's army and slaughtered the confederate kings, vv. 15, 17. Some idea of the size and power of their army is given by their earlier victory over the three tribes of giants, v. 5, and over the king of Sodom and his four allies, v. 10.

But Abram had one more king to overcome. It was Bera, king of Sodom! Bera "went out to meet him", v. 17, armed with a very attractive proposal, v. 21. In some ways Bera represented a bigger danger than Chedorlaomer. To defeat the latter required a *military* victory; to defeat Bera would require a *spiritual* one. Chedorlaomer "took", v. 12; Bera was going to offer. Having faced the lion, Abram was about to face the serpent. But of this he knew nothing as he returned from Dan. Happily for Abram, his God knew all about the forthcoming temptation and was going to prepare him for it through the ministry of Melchizedek.

The priest-king spoke of the most high God as (i) possessing heaven and earth, v. 19, and (ii) having delivered Abram's enemies into his hand, v. 20. This twofold message prepared Abram to refuse Bera's tempting offer. If Abram's God possessed heaven and earth then he did not *need* Sodom's goods, and if his God was responsible for his victory then he did not *deserve* them! The Divine titles Abram used when speaking to Bera show that he benefited from these words of Melchizedek. Confident that God was able to meet all his material needs, Abram would not have it said that he owed anything to the king of Sodom, vv. 22, 23.

Abram soon had his decision vindicated. God revealed Himself to him as his shield and exceeding great reward, 15. 1. With such a *shield* he would not need to fear men like Chedorlaomer, and with such a *reward* he would not need to accept the patronage of the likes of the king of Sodom.

Jan. 15th

READING : **Genesis 17. 1-8; 18. 9-15**

TOO HARD FOR THE LORD?

SARAH'S INCREDULOUS laugh, 18. 12, occasioned one of the great rhetorical questions of Scripture, "Is anything too hard for the Lord?", v. 14. That nothing is too difficult for the Lord is the claim not only of the historical section of the O.T., but also of the poetical and prophetical sections, Job. 42. 2; Jer. 32. 27. The same glorious truth is explicitly stated in the N.T. as well, Matt. 19. 23-25; Mark 14. 36; Luke 1. 37. To the Lord, only that is impossible which is contrary to His nature. Abraham had, therefore, at least a twofold reason for believing God's promises: (i) his God was omnipotent, and (ii) "it was impossible for God to lie", Heb. 6. 18. In Abraham's case, God bound Himself by a covenant; see Gen. 15. 18. Note the sevenfold "I will" of *the Almighty God*, who affirmed His covenant, 17. 1-8, and compare the sevenfold "I will" of *Jehovah*, Exod. 6. 2-8, of *the Lord of hosts*, 2 Sam. 7. 8-14, and in connection with the new covenant, Jer. 31. 31-34 R.V.

Abraham's wife had always been barren, 11. 30, but, in any case, it had now "ceased to be with Sarah after the manner of women", 18. 11. But Abraham and Sarah proved that it was not *too hard* for the Lord to give them a son, 21. 1, for He was able to bring life out of "death", Gen. 17. 17; 18. 12; Rom. 4. 19; Heb. 11. 12. Nor was it *too hard* for Him to cause that the promised seed should be born exactly to time, Gen. 17. 21; 18. 14; 21. 2. Earlier Abraham and Sarah had attempted to hurry things along, 16. 1-4a. Just as Abraham had once been willing to share Sarah with other men to save his life, 12. 10-16; cf. 20. 2, so she had been willing to share Abraham with another woman to secure a child. But God did not need human schemes to help Him accomplish His purpose. It is significant that, after Abraham had attempted to *run* before God, he was told, "*walk* before me, and be thou perfect", 17. 1.

Abraham also discovered that it was not *too hard* for God to deal with the "very grievous" sin of the cities of the plain, 18. 20; 19. 24-28. Nor was it *too hard* for the Lord to save His own, for, when He turned "the cities of Sodom and Gomorrah into ashes", He "delivered just Lot", 2 Pet. 2. 6-9. As we pray today, let us take encouragement from Jeremiah's words, ". . . there is nothing too hard for thee", Jer. 32. 17.

Jan. 16th

READING : **Genesis 22. 1-12**

FAITH TESTED

OUR READING records the last reported testing in Abraham's life. It was undoubtedly the severest. When God spoke to him, v. 2, He left Abraham in no doubt as to what He wanted. Every detail was explicit; God left no loopholes. He told Abraham *when to obey*. "Now"—not at some unspecified time in the future, or when he had many more children; cf. 25. 1, 2. God told him *whom to take*. "Thy son, thine only son Isaac, whom thou lovest". Each word sank as a knife, deeper and deeper, into the heart of the aged patriarch. Ishmael had been sent away some time before, 21. 14, it was unlikely that Sarah would have any more children now, and, in any case, God's promise and covenant centred in Isaac, 17. 19; 21. 12. God told Abraham *where to go*. "The land of Moriah . . . upon one of the mountains which I will tell thee of"; cf. 2 Chron. 3. 1. Finally, God told him *what to do*. "Offer". Abraham was not only to slay Isaac but to reduce his body to ashes!

Abraham therefore knew when, whom, where and what. The only thing he was not told was "why". No word of explanation was given. The man had already proved that he could trust God when he did not know *where*, Heb. 11. 8, and when he did not know *how*, Gen. 15. 5, 6. Could he trust God when he did not know *why?* Often in the past he had raised questions with the Lord when he had felt it necessary, 15. 2, 8; 18. 23. Now he remains silent and, with tremendous faith, meekly submits to the will of the God he loves.

His obedience was complete, v. 3. God had said, *"now";* so Abraham "rose up early in the morning"; see Psa. 119. 60. Note that though his obedience was prompt, it was not shortlived. He continued a three day journey without turning aside, Gen. 22. 4. God had said, *"Isaac ";* so "Isaac his son" he took. God named *"Moriah ";* so he "went unto the place . . .". God demanded that he *"offer"* Isaac; so he "clave the wood". His trust in God was total. He believed that both he and Isaac would return, v. 5, accounting that God was able to raise Isaac from the dead, Heb. 11. 19. In the event, he was not required to slay him, Gen. 22. 12. God wanted, not the offering of a human sacrifice, but the surrender of a human will. And this He had. Does He have mine?

Jan. 17th
READING : **Genesis 24. 1-27**

THE LORD'S LEADING

IN OBEDIENCE to the command of Abraham, his servant had journeyed to Nahor's city, vv. 2-4, 10. Being thus "in the way" which his master had directed, he needed the Lord's leading; see v. 27. His prayer for guidance was strikingly brief and to the point, vv. 12-14. Underlying his request was the confidence that God had a specific will about the matter in hand; "let the same be she that thou hast *appointed* ", v. 14. The choice of a bride for Isaac was particularly important because it would be through her that the chosen line was to be continued. Nevertheless, we must remember that *all* marriages among believers are regarded as important by the Lord. How encouraging for the young believer to realize that, when it is the will of God for him or her to marry, the Lord always has an "appointed" partner in view. Note in this connection that the Holy Spirit had Rebecca in mind two chapters before the one in which she first met Isaac, 22. 23. It is reassuring to know that the Lord has our futures in His control. Let the young, unmarried Christian trust in the Lord and seek His guidance.

In the circumstances, the servant felt justified in asking for a tangible sign and indication of God's will. The requirement he laid down was a very demanding one; for a young woman to draw, with a pitcher, sufficient water to satisfy ten tired and thirsty camels would require no small effort, vv. 19, 20 with v. 10. When circumstances clearly suggested that Rebecca was the one the servant sought, we discover him *"wondering whether* the Lord had made his way prosperous or not", v. 21. In spite of the inevitable joy that he must have felt at having received, so speedily, the possible answer to his prayer, he was wisely cautious. He still needed to ensure that the young woman met his master's stated requirement, "my kindred", v. 4. Apart from that, he would have had to attribute Rebecca's arrival and kindness to coincidence and not to the leading of God. We must learn that circumstances in themselves are not an infallible guide to God's will; ct. Jonah 1. 3. God will never lead us, in marriage or anything else, to do anything inconsistent with *our* Master's teachings!

May *we* prove the truth of the promise, "In all thy ways acknowledge him, and he shall direct thy paths", Prov. 3. 6.

Jan. 18th

READING : **Genesis 24. 12-52**

ANSWERED PRAYER

ABRAHAM'S servant's prayer for guidance was inaudible; see "in my heart", v. 45. Yet God heard it; cf. Neh. 2. 4-5.

The servant was not kept waiting long for the answer to his prayer. Rebecca arrived, "before he had done speaking", v. 15. Daniel's experience was similar, "Whiles I was speaking in prayer . . . Gabriel . . . said, . . . At the beginning of thy supplications, the commandment came forth", Dan. 9. 21-23. Again, it was immediately following his prayer against Ahithophel that David met the man through whom his prayer was to be answered, 2 Sam. 15. 31-32; 17. 1-14. God, however, does not always grant our petitions so quickly. Even when our requests are in line with His will, we may be required to make them many times; cf. Luke 11. 5-9. It is, nevertheless, a great encouragement to know that God *can* act according to the word of the prophet, "while they are yet speaking, I will hear", Isa. 65. 24. Rebecca's arrival provided the servant with clear evidence that God had sent His angel *"before"* him, to prepare his way, v. 7, as well as *"with"* him to prosper it, v. 40!

As soon as the servant was satisfied that his prayer had been answered, he bowed his head in worship, vv. 23-26. It is clear from his later comments to Rebecca's family that he felt a great sense of urgency about his whole mission; see vv. 33, 56. Notwithstanding this, he took the time to give thanks to God immediately for His guidance, v. 27, as later he bowed himself in worship straight after Rebecca's father and brother had given their agreement to her departure; *"when* Abraham's servant heard their words, he worshipped the Lord", v. 52. In similar fashion, Daniel took the time to bless God for His timely revelation, even though his life was in jeopardy and every moment was precious, Dan. 2. 13-23. Again, Gideon took the time to worship when God provided him with some much-needed encouragement before his battle with the army of Midian, Jud. 7. 9-15. We can benefit from such examples. Alas, too often we are hot in prayer and cold in thanksgiving; we are quick to ask and slow to give thanks! For every indication of God's guidance (Gen. 24), every timely deliverance (Dan. 2), every means of encouragement (Jud. 7), yea for everything, let us *"give thanks"*, 1 Thess. 5. 18.

Jan. 19th

READING : **Genesis 25. 19-34**

JACOB AND ESAU CONTRASTED

GENESIS 25 provides several points of contrast between the sons of Isaac. Apart from the difference in their appearance, v. 25; cf. 27. 11, there are at least four important contrasts to be noted. These arise out of:

(i) *The purpose of God*, v. 23. "The children being not yet born, neither having done any good or evil, that the purpose of God according to election might stand, . . . it was said . . ., The elder shall serve the younger", Rom. 9. 11-12. God's choice of Jacob was not influenced by any merit in him or fault in Esau; ct. Gen. 9. 26-27.

(ii) *Their different ways of life*, v. 27. Jacob was a "plain" (Heb., perfect, blameless, upright) man. He dwelt in tents, thereby witnessing that he was a sojourner and stranger; see Heb. 11. 9-10. On the other hand, Esau was a hunter; cf. 10. 9. By occupation Jacob was a shepherd, more concerned with caring for animals than killing them, 31. 38-40; 33. 13. Note his appreciative reference to "the God which fed (*lit.*, shepherded) me all my life long", 48. 15.

(iii) *The affection of their parents*, v. 28. Both Isaac and Rebecca were spiritual people, who brought their problems to the Lord, vv. 21-22. Although God had promised that Isaac would have a seed, 17. 19, yet, when Rebecca remained barren for 20 years, vv. 20, 26, "Isaac intreated the Lord". Sometimes God delays His gifts to teach us greater dependence upon Him. Whereas Isaac and Rebecca were united in their love for the Lord, they were divided in their love for their children. They should have both loved their sons equally, while recognizing Jacob's God-given precedence. Instead, their home was divided by their partiality and favouritism, v. 28; cf. "his son", "her son", 27. 5-6. Such division was a recipe for disaster.

(iv) *Their attitude to spiritual things*, vv. 29-34. In spite of his many failings, Jacob had his priorities right. He set great store by the birthright, with all its spiritual privileges. Esau, however, treated it lightly and was willing to part with it readily and cheaply. He was a "profane person . . . who for one morsel of meat sold his birthright", Heb. 12. 16. Contrast his "What profit . . .?" with Mark 8. 36. What about us? Is our affection set on things above or things on the earth?

Jan. 20th

READING : **Genesis 26. 1-33**

ISAAC TESTED

ALTHOUGH Isaac lived longer than Abraham, Jacob or Joseph, there is far less recorded of his life than of theirs. Indeed, chapter 26 is the only chapter of Genesis exclusively devoted to his experiences. The chapter records three incidents.

(i) *The famine*, vv. 1-11. This is linked with the earlier famine in the days of Abraham, v. 1; 12. 10, thereby stressing that Isaac was subjected to exactly the same testing as his father. Abraham had failed the test, but had been characterized mainly by obedience, 26. 5. Isaac imitated his father's obedience for he did as God commanded, vv. 2, 6. Alas, he also imitated Abraham's lack of faith, cowardly fear and cunning deception. Isaac's fear was altogether unfounded. God had promised to be with him, v. 3, so he should not have feared what men would do to him, Heb. 13. 15-16. As it was, nobody attempted to touch Rebecca, even though the couple were in Gerar for "a long time", v. 8. Isaac should have learnt from his father's mistake, for God had earlier shown Abraham's deceit to be unnecessary. Do *we* learn from others' mistakes?

(ii) *The wells*, vv. 12-25. On the basis of this section, we may associate Isaac's name with wells, as we do Abraham's with altars, and Jacob's with pillars. The herdsmen of Gerar contested Isaac's right to the new wells dug by his herdsmen, and he withdrew to fresh pastures, vv. 19-22. In view of the offer made to his father, 20. 15, Isaac could have claimed the right to dwell where he wished in Gerar. To avoid trouble, however, he waived his rights. This was meekness, and not weakness; see 26. 16. The Lord requires that we follow Isaac's example in turning the other cheek, Matt. 5. 39, and has left us His own example, Luke 9. 56. "Let your moderation (gentleness, sweet reasonableness, yieldingness) be known unto all men", Phil. 4. 5. Where the Lord's interests are at stake we must yield nothing, Gal. 2; where our interests are at stake we must yield all, 1 Cor. 8 and 9.

(iii) *The covenant*, vv. 26-33. Recognizing that the Lord was with Isaac, Abimelech sought and made a non-aggression pact with him; cf. 20. 22-32. Truly, "When a man's ways please the Lord, he maketh even his enemies to be at peace with him", Prov. 16. 7.

Jan. 21st
READING : **Genesis 28. 10-22**

BEHOLD, I AM WITH THEE

THE WORD "behold" occurs four times in Jacob's dream.

"Behold a ladder", v. 12a. The ladder symbolized unbroken communication between earth and heaven. It reached from Jacob, in his need and loneliness (for his only companion was his staff, 32. 10) up to God's immediate presence. Jacob was taught that, though his home was over 50 miles away—and would soon be much further—heaven was very near!

"Behold the angels", v. 12b. Jacob saw the angels of God as he journeyed away from home, and he met them as he returned, 32. 1-2. They "excel in strength, . . . do his commandments, hearkening unto the voice of his word", and minister to His people, Psa. 103. 20; Heb. 1. 14.

"Behold, the Lord", v. 13. Jacob owned, "The Lord is in this place", v. 16. He was more important than the ladder or the angels, and consequently He alone is mentioned whenever reference is later made to this incident, 35. 1, 7; 48. 3.

"Behold, I am with thee", v. 15. Jacob was not only given the security of God's *promise* of future blessing, vv. 13-14, and the assurance of His *protection* "in all places", v. 15b, but the guarantee of His *presence* to go with him, v. 15a,c. The guarantee was emphasized, being expressed both positively, "I am with thee", and negatively, "I will not leave thee". "Happy is he that hath the God of Jacob for his help", Psa. 146. 5. Jacob expected to be away from home for only "a few days", 27. 44, but it was over 20 years before he went back, 31. 38. The most important thing, however, was that, whether for a few days or 20 years, he was guaranteed the presence of the God of his fathers. He later witnessed that, as He had promised, God had been with him, 31. 5; cf. 35. 3, and had saved him from being further exploited by Laban, 31. 7, 41-42. God renewed the guarantee when Jacob headed home, 31. 3, and when, later, he left Canaan for the last time, 46. 4.

Jacob's response to the dream was a vow. Since God had promised (i) to be with him, (ii) to keep him, and (iii) to bring him back again, Jacob made a vow to the Lord, vv. 15, 20-22. In the light of the guarantee which the Lord has given us of His unfailing presence, Heb. 13. 5, let each of us ask today, "What shall I render unto the Lord . . .?", Psa. 116. 12.

Jan. 22nd

READING : **Genesis 32. 1 to 33. 4**

GROUNDLESS FEARS

JACOB'S reactions to the news of Esau's approach, with his 400 men, reveal a curious and sad mixture of trust in God and trust in himself. He had never been recalled by Rebecca, 27. 45, and had every reason therefore to expect a hostile reception. Nevertheless, he ought not to have been unduly alarmed by the news of Esau's coming. He knew that God had already preserved him miraculously from the evil intentions of Laban, 31. 24. 29. Apart from this, he had just met "the angels of God", 32. 1-2, and, with his eyes opened to see *God's host,* he should not have feared *Esau's host;* cf. 2 Kings 6. 16-17. Yet "he was greatly afraid and distressed", and took what steps he could to meet the emergency, vv. 7-8. Having made his *plans,* he made his *prayer,* in which (i) he reminded the Lord that He had led him into his present predicament, v. 9, (ii) he pointed to the blessings already bestowed, in themselves a pledge of more to come, v. 10, and (iii) he pleaded God's explicit promise to do him good, v. 12. At the heart of his prayer lay the admirably concise and specific request for deliverance, v. 11. All was well with Jacob while he was in God's presence, but when he emerged he continued to act as if he had never prayed at all! He was willing to "commit" his way to the Lord, but not to "trust also" in Him, Psa. 37. 5!

Jacob further resolved to "appease" Esau with a present of 580 animals. His servile messages, 32. 18; cf. v. 4, fell ill from one of whom God had said that his brother would serve him, 25. 23. Jacob fully expected to see Esau's face next, 32. 20, but was required to see the face of God first, v. 30. At Peniel, Jacob "had power over the angel, and prevailed: he wept and made supplication", Hos. 12. 4. There he was taught that "power *with God*" came before power "*with men*", Gen. 32. 28. There he clung to God for blessing, and obtained it, vv. 26, 29. Come the morning, however, he proceeded to act as if God's blessing was no protection from Esau, 33. 1-3. In the event, all Jacob's plans proved unnecessary, for his fears had been groundless, 33. 4. Not only had he seen *God's face* and been preserved, 32. 30, but he saw *Esau's face* and suffered no harm, 33. 10. Do not fear things which may never happen, or worry about difficulties which may not exist, Isa. 51. 13; Mark 16. 3-4.

Jan. 23rd

READING : **Genesis 37. 1-36**

THE GREEN-EYED MONSTER

THE BITTER hatred which the brothers of Joseph felt towards him was occasioned mainly by his coat and dreams. His coat "of many colours" (*lit.*, "of extremity", suggesting that it reached to his wrists and ankles) was a mark of special favour and distinction. It indicated to his brethren "that their father loved him more than" them, v. 4. Rachel had been Jacob's most loved wife, 29. 18, and his unique affection for Joseph was probably due to the fact that Joseph reminded him of her, both Rachel and Joseph being described as "beautiful and well favoured", 29. 17; 39. 6 *lit*. Joseph's two (signifying certainty of fulfilment, 41. 32) dreams only served further to alienate his brethren, vv. 5, 8, 11, 19, 20. The underlying cause of their animosity towards Joseph was *envy*, v. 11. What havoc envy has caused through the ages! It was responsible for the rebellion of Korah, Saul's attempts to kill David, Daniel being cast to the lions and, humanly speaking, the crucifixion of our Lord. "Who is able to stand before envy?", Prov. 27. 4. The hearts of Joseph's brethren were totally hardened against him by their envy. While he was in the pit, "they sat down to eat bread" and, though they "saw the anguish of his soul when he besought" them, they "would not hear", 42. 21. Their callous indifference became a byword in later generations, Amos 6. 6. Truly, envy is an awful thing. Beware the green-eyed monster!

Genesis 37 ends on a dismal note. Joseph was enslaved in Egypt, without one friend in the whole land, without any knowledge of the language, 42. 23, and without a trade acceptable to the Egyptians, 37. 2; 46. 34. What price his dreams now? Stephen briefly summarized the whole chapter, "The patriarchs, moved with envy, sold Joseph into Egypt" and then added, "*but God* was with him", Acts 7. 9. "But God"—what wonderful words! The Lord was at work in Joseph's life. He used the very action, taken by Joseph's brethren to frustrate the fulfilment of his dreams, to secure their fulfilment! Joseph's brethren helped bring about the very thing they wished most to avoid; cf. Gen. 11. 4b, 8a. Later, Joseph explained to them, "*Ye meant evil* against me; but *God meant* it for *good*", 50. 20 R.V. The Lord is able to overrule the wrongly motivated actions of men; see Isa. 10. 5-7.

Jan. 24th

READING : **Genesis 39. 1-23**

JOSEPH TEMPTED

JOSEPH GAVE a twofold reason for refusing to obey the command of Potiphar's wife. *First*, he was conscious of a duty to his master, vv. 8, 9a, and believed that to have yielded to her demand would have been a breach of trust. Potiphar had previously showed absolute confidence in Joseph's fidelity, v. 4. There was something about Joseph which told others that he was trustworthy; cf. vv. 22-23. Is the same true of us? *Second*, he was conscious of a duty to his God, v. 9b. He saw immorality as sin against God; cf. 2 Sam. 12. 13; Psa. 51. 4.

Potiphar's wife continued her line of attack: "she spake to Joseph *day by day*", Gen. 39. 10. Repeated temptation is hard to overcome. Many who resist at the first, succumb at the last. But Joseph was resolute! As far as possible, he refused even to "be with her". This was true wisdom. "Make not provision . . .", Rom. 13. 14. The man who does not wish to hear the church bell should not play with the rope! Avoid temptation if you would avoid sin; cf. Matt. 6. 13a. At the last, Joseph was forced to flee, v. 12. When tempted, flight is often the best line of resistance. Paradoxically, fleeing from temptation can lead the devil to flee from you, James 4. 7.

Joseph next suffered the trial of false accusation and slander. On an earlier occasion his coat had been taken from him and used to deceive his father into believing that he was dead, 37. 31-33. Now his slave's tunic was taken from him and used to deceive his master into believing that he was guilty. There is no suggestion, however, that Joseph attempted to vindicate himself. He probably wished to spare Potiphar any trouble and shame in his house. But the silent endurance of wrong was hard. Joseph was unjustly condemned by the man whose goodwill he prized above any other in Egypt. He had to bear the punishment meted out for a crime which he had nobly refused to commit. "*But* the Lord was with Joseph", v. 21; cf. vv. 2, 3, 23. Here lay his compensation. His victory over temptation secured for him the continued sense of God's presence and blessing, which a fall into sin would have lost him. The Lord was not yet ready to lift Joseph *out of* his sad predicament, but He would be with him *in* it. His grace would be sufficient; see 2 Cor. 12. 7-9.

Jan. 25th
READING : Genesis 40. 1-23
IN GOD'S TIME

SOMETHING TOLD Joseph that the dreams of Pharaoh's officers had meaning, and he was confident that God could provide him with the required interpretations, v. 8. After giving the interpretation of the butler's dream, Joseph attempted to use his brief association with the butler to good advantage, v. 14. He regarded the butler's dream not only as a Divine revelation to put the butler's mind at rest, but as a possible means of escape for him from his unhappy predicament. He was alive to God's providential ordering of his life, and was quick to detect the Lord's hand behind his contact with the butler. The chief butler was an important man, occupying the same position of responsibility in Egypt which Nehemiah was to occupy later in Persia, Neh. 1. 11 (where "cupbearer" is the same Hebrew word as "butler" in Gen. 40). Only Pharaoh himself would have the authority to over-rule Potiphar's action, 39. 20, but the butler was well placed to speak to Pharaoh on Joseph's behalf. Joseph had served the butler well, v. 4, and had interpreted his dream for him, vv. 12-13. Making a point of protesting his innocence, Joseph therefore requested that the butler return his kindness and speak for him to Pharaoh.

In spite of Joseph's plea, the butler forgot all about him for "two full years", 40. 23; 41. 1. Joseph's desire for an early release was understandable, and it may well have seemed unfair and frustrating to him that his ability, kindness and innocence should have been forgotten. At a later date, however, he would come to realize that God knew best. The very providence which introduced him to a man who could put his case to Pharaoh, caused the man to forget to do it! The butler's forgetfulness formed an essential part of God's purpose for Joseph. If the butler had immediately remembered Joseph and mentioned him to Pharaoh, the most that Joseph could have expected was to have been released, v. 14. Certainly Pharaoh would have had no reason at that time to confer on him the dignity which God had planned he should receive. The dream of the butler *was* going to play an important role in Joseph's later life — but it would be in God's time and not in his. Let us remind ourselves that God's timing is always better than ours. His clock always keeps strict time.

Jan. 26th

READING : **Genesis 41. 14-46**

NOT ME—GOD

WHEN JOSEPH stood before Pharaoh he must have realized that he was in a strong position to negotiate his release from Potiphar's prison. The haste in which he had been brought out of the dungeon, 41. 14, suggested the great importance which Pharaoh attached to his services, and Pharaoh's first words had revealed that Joseph was his only hope, v. 15. Joseph wanted his freedom as much as Pharaoh wanted his dreams interpreted, 40. 14. Yet, instead of offering his cooperation in exchange for his liberty, he disclaimed any personal ability to interpret Pharaoh's dream, v. 16. He boldly insisted on giving all the glory to God, "It is not in me: God shall give"; cf. Dan. 2. 28. The heathen monarch accepted the correction and later gave the due credit to God, Gen. 41. 39; cf. Dan. 2. 47. Let us remember that we *possess* nothing which the Lord has not given us, 1 Cor. 4. 7, we *have done* nothing for which He has not enabled us, John 15. 5, and we *are* nothing which His grace has not made us, 1 Cor. 15. 10. Joseph had been put into prison at the first because he had refused to sin against God, Gen. 39. 9, 20; he was not willing now to secure his release from prison by sinning against God, in robbing Him of His glory!

His testimony, "*God* will give", was entirely in character, for the name of God was often upon his lips — note the seven recorded occasions, 39. 9; 40. 8; 41. 16, 51, 52; 42. 18; 45. 5-9; 50. 24. Joseph possessed an acute God-consciousness. He had not experienced the personal manifestations of God which his fore-fathers had received, but nonetheless he enjoyed a profound awareness of God at all times. This may well explain the fact that, as far as the record goes, Joseph never uttered any words of complaint, suffered any fits of depression, or shed any tears through his many years of affliction. (The seven references to his tears all occur *after* his exaltation, 42. 24; 43.30; 45. 12, 14; 46. 29; 50. 1, 17). Happy indeed is the man who is habitually conscious of God in his life!

The thirteen years spent in Potiphar's house and prison, 37. 2; 41. 46, were not wasted. They were the years of Joseph's preparation for reigning. In them he demonstrated his fidelity, patience and capability, 39. 4-6, 22-23. Luke 16. 10a states the principle. Today is *our* "training for reigning"!

Jan. 27th
READING : **Genesis 42. 18-23; 44. 1-34**

TRUE REPENTANCE

JOSEPH WAS lord of all Egypt, and his brethren were at his mercy. But he had no intention of exploiting the situation to avenge himself. All his dealings with them were dictated by the desire to witness their genuine and wholehearted *repentance* for their past sin, that he might be reconciled to them. His younger brother Benjamin was crucial to his plans. Joseph could safely assume that, as a son of Rachel, Benjamin would be the special object of Jacob's favour and affection; cf. 44. 20. His absence during his brethren's first visit confirmed this. Joseph was determined to learn how his brethren reacted to Benjamin's privileged position. Did they feel the same envy and malice towards Benjamin as they had to him?

Their *first visit* to Egypt, 42. 5-26, resulted in the pricking of their consciences and the acknowledgment of their sin, v. 21. Joseph remembered his dreams, v. 9, but they remembered what had followed his dreams! During their *second visit*, Joseph skilfully tested his other brothers' true feelings towards Benjamin by favouring him with a five-fold portion, 43. 34. This "favouritism" would certainly have exposed any resentment on their part. The acid test of their repentance, however, came after they had left for home, and during their subsequent return to Joseph's house, 44. 3-34. They were told that they were free to return to Jacob but that Benjamin must remain — enslaved! They were thus given the golden opportunity to be rid of Jacob's favourite son, as once they had rid themselves of Joseph. Would they again prove heedless of a brother's plight and of a father's grief? Their reaction would tell Joseph whether or not they had undergone a change of heart. They replied that they preferred to share Benjamin's slavery than to leave him alone, v. 16. Judah began his plea as spokesman for his brothers, but ended it with a personal request — that he be allowed to take Benjamin's place, v. 33. There could be no doubt about the reality of his repentance. Once he had been glad to see one of Rachel's sons go into slavery, regardless of the sorrow it would bring to his father. Now he was willing to go into slavery himself instead of Rachel's other son, to spare his father further sorrow! True repentance means a complete change; it means my forsaking sin.

Jan. 28th
READING : Genesis 45. 1-11
THE CHAIN WITH TEN LINKS

JOSEPH'S EXALTATION and eminence in Egypt was a remarkable proof of the quiet yet sure working of Divine providence. He recognized that *God* had "sent" him there, vv. 5, 7, 8, and "made" him lord of all Egypt, vv. 8, 9. There were at least ten links in the chain of events which had established Joseph as "governor over the land", 42. 6.

(1) *The envy of his brethren*, 37. 1-11. The story started here. (2) *The anxiety of his father*, 37. 12-14. Jacob was apprehensive about his sons at *Shechem*, and sent Joseph to see if all was well with them. Jacob had good grounds for concern, 33. 18 to 34. 30. (3) *The friendly enquiry of "a certain man"*, 37. 15-17. The man's casual meeting with Joseph was needed to direct him to Dothan. (4) *The intervention of Reuben and Judah*, 37. 18-27. Reuben's good intentions and Judah's mercenary motives both proved essential. (5) *The journeying of the Arabian tradesmen*, 37. 25-28. How crucial were the timing, route and destination of their business trip! (6) *The domestic needs of Potiphar's household*, 37. 36. With so many homes and slaves in Egypt, Joseph ended up in the right house. (7) *The wickedness of Potiphar's wife*, 39. 7-8. The temptation she provided and her spite when rejected both had a part to play. (8) *The injustice of Potiphar's decision*, 39. 19-20. Although not deserved at all, Joseph's punishment was relatively light. Potiphar was "chief of the slaughtermen, or, executioners", 37. 36 marg. Yet God restrained his wrath within bounds; see Psa. 76. 10. (9) *The fall from favour of Pharaoh's officers*, 40. 1-4. This led to the all-important meeting between Joseph and the chief butler. (10) *The forgetfulness of the butler*, 40. 20-23. The last link!

A chain is only as strong as its weakest link. Every one of these 10 links played an essential part in Joseph's path to glory in Egypt. God accomplished His purpose through human agents without their knowledge, and often against their wishes. He overruled not only Reuben's attempt to save Joseph, the helpfulness of the "certain man" and the forgetfulness of the butler, but also the lust and spite of Potiphar's wife and the hatred of Joseph's brethren. All things were worked for Joseph's good, cf. Rom. 8. 28, and, with hindsight, he could see this. Trust God — He makes no mistakes!

Jan. 29th

READING : **Genesis 48. 1-22**

JACOB WHEN HE WAS A DYING

TAKING JOSEPH'S two sons, Jacob effectively adopted them as his own, and granted their descendants full tribal rights along with the descendants of his other sons, v. 5. The double portion was the right of the first born, Deut. 21. 15-17. Reuben, Jacob's natural firstborn, had forfeit his birthright when he "defiled his father's bed", and the birthright passed to Joseph and his sons, 1 Chron. 5. 1-2; cf. Ezek. 47. 13. It seems that Jacob had originally intended that Rachel should have been his only wife, Gen. 29. 15-20, and then Joseph would have been his natural firstborn. It was only the deception practised by Laban which had robbed Joseph of his birthright. Israel's eyes "were dim", and consequently he could not distinguish by sight between Joseph's two sons, 48. 10. His father's eyes also had been dim when he had come to give his blessing, 27. 1. In the event, both men gave the blessing to the younger. Isaac, however, did this without realizing it, whereas Jacob knew full well what he was doing, 48. 14, 19. "By faith Jacob . . . blessed both the sons of Joseph", Heb. 11. 21.

When first reunited with Joseph, Jacob had earlier exclaimed, "Now let me die, since I have seen thy face", 46. 30; cf. 45. 28. But God had reserved an even greater blessing for him and now Israel could testify that God had exceeded his highest expectations, "I had not thought to see thy face: and, lo, God hath shewed me also thy seed", 48. 11. Let us link this verse with 1 Kings 3. 5-13. Solomon prayed for "an understanding heart" to enable him to govern God's people. The Lord was pleased with his unselfish prayer and granted him also that which he had "not asked, both riches and honour". Truly, then, our God "is able to do exceeding abundantly above all that we *ask* (Solomon) or *think* (Jacob)", Eph. 3. 20.

Among Israel's last words was the statement, "I die, but God", Gen. 48. 21; which expression was later repeated by Joseph, 50. 24 R.V. Let us take these words to heart today, for they give us the assurance of God's unfailing presence when others of His servants pass on to glory. We treasure and respect the memory of many men of the past whose valued help is no longer available to us; see Heb. 13. 7. Yet the Lord Himself remains, "the same yesterday, and today, and forever", v. 8.

Jan. 30th
READING : Genesis 50. 14-26
A BACKWARD AND A FORWARD LOOK

IN TODAY'S reading Joseph is found looking backwards and forwards. (i) *By faith he was able to review God's unerring providences in the past.* Joseph's brethren were fearful that the death of their father would herald a drastic change in Joseph's attitude towards them, cf. 27. 41, and consequently sent to him a message of confession which was soon followed up by a personal offer of servitude. Once they had been willing to make Joseph a slave, 37. 27-28, but now they were willing for him to make them his slaves! Joseph's tears, v. 17, reveal how keenly he felt their doubts as to the genuineness of his forgiveness and goodwill. There are few things more trying and upsetting for a man than to be misunderstood and doubted by those he loves most. Joseph's feelings towards his brethren were in no way soured, however, by their unfounded concern. He made it clear that he had no wish to take revenge on them, recognizing that he was not "in the place of God", cf. 30. 2; 2 Sam. 5. 7, to whom alone vengeance belongs, v. 19 with Rom. 12. 19. He perceived that God had overruled their intended evil against him for the good of many, v. 20; cf. 45. 5-9. The knowledge that the sovereign Lord can always turn "the curse into a blessing", Neh. 13. 2, should fill our hearts with confidence and peace.

(ii) *By faith Joseph was able to rest in God's unfailing promises for the future.* Although holding high office in the most powerful nation on earth, Joseph did not regard Egypt as the right place for him to be buried. He had spent only the first 17 years of his life in Canaan and was now aged 110, and his recollections of the land would therefore have been faint and few. Nevertheless, to Joseph Canaan was the land of the Divine promises made to his fathers! In confident expectation that God would be true to His covenant, "by faith Joseph . . . gave commandment concerning his bones", Heb. 11. 22; cf. Exod. 13. 19; Josh. 24. 32. The beginning of Genesis records the entrance of death into the world, cf. Rom. 5. 12; it is perhaps fitting that the end should refer to a coffin! Let us rejoice today that, whereas the first book of Scripture ends with mention of a coffin, towards the end of the last book we have the promise, "and there shall be no more death", Rev. 21. 4.

Introducing Exodus

IT HAS BEEN said that Exodus (the word means a 'going out') is one of the most familiar and popular books in the Bible, although it may be more true to say that this judgment applies only to certain selected parts of the book.

The purpose of the Book is to record the deliverance, by blood and by power, of an enslaved people, who were the subject of Divine promises, e.g. 6. 2-9. The Book opens in darkness and gloom, and ends in glory. As it opens it tells of God coming down in grace to deliver an enslaved people, 3. 8, and it ends by declaring how this same God came down in glory to dwell in the midst of a redeemed people, 40. 34-35.

Its distinctive message is one of redemption, and the historical record pictures the outworking of Divine grace in the redemption and recovery of man to Himself by Christ Jesus. The story of Exodus is repeated in every soul that seeks complete deliverance, especially from sin and the world, seen as a virtual Pharaoh and house of bondage; cf. Rom. 6. 14-18. It shows that redemption is wholly of God.

In giving the Ten Commandments we see that this God of grace and mercy is a holy God, who must set standards for His people. Yet in the word "ye shall love the Lord your God" we see He desires the will and affection of His people.

God gives direction for the making of the tabernacle, and all the furniture connected with it, chs. 24ff, in order that He may have a centre of worship where a redeemed people can meet with Him, and have communion with Him.

A realized relationship with God is the fruit of redemption. The provisions of the Tabernacle, a very detailed foreshadowing of the Christ and His many ministries, cf. Heb. 9-10, ensure that this may be truly experienced consistent with the character of God.

An outline of the Book: **1.** Bondage, chs. 1-2. **2.** Redemption, chs. 3-15. (**a**) Israel's awful bondage, (**b**) Call and Commission of Moses, (**c**) Plagues on Egypt, (**d**) The Passover, (**e**) The Exodus. **3.** The Journey to Sinai, chs. 16-19. (**a**) Marah, (**b**) Sin, (**c**) Rephidim, (**d**) Sinai. **4.** Civil and Moral Laws, chs. 20-23. **5.** Worship, chs. 24-40. (**a**) Ceremonial Law, (**b**) Tabernacle and Priesthood.

Jan. 31st
READING : Exodus 1. 6-14; 2. 11-25
ISRAEL IN EGYPT

"GOD MOVES in a mysterious way His wonders to perform". As we commence our meditation on the book of Exodus, the book of redemption, the truth of these words meets us immediately. In relation to the affairs of Israel we are shown the change from honour to bondage and contempt. All was black, yet behind the sad record of chapters 1 and 2 we see this heartening truth that God was in control. Verse 7 of chapter 1 shows a fulfilment of God's promise to Abraham, Gen. 15. 13-16, and to Jacob, Gen. 46. 3, but verse 8 introduces Satan's efforts to block God's purpose. Although persecution followed, notice verse 12 "But . . . . ". The enemy said in effect "I will destroy", but God had said, "as the sand", Gen. 22. 17.

The next attempt to destroy the Messianic line in the killing by the midwives of every male born was frustrated by the firmness of the midwives, who feared God and disobeyed the king, v. 17. Then came the dread decree, v. 22.

God directs our attention to one family in which the purposes of God through Israel were understood, 2. 1-4. A baby boy! What a problem, what a challenge to trust. Hebrews 11 tells us that the parents of Moses acted "in faith" when they hid him, and then placed him in the ark in the river, v. 23, and this pre-supposes God's revelation to them concerning the child, for "faith cometh by hearing", Rom. 10. 17. We see God still in control as Pharaoh's daughter takes and cares for the future deliverer from Egypt, and obtains the services of the child's mother to care for him and teach him, Exod. 2. 5-10.

The years pass and the day comes when Moses "in faith" (how well he had been taught by his mother) renounces his position in the royal household, and takes his place with his own people, 2. 11-12, "choosing rather to suffer affliction with the people of God", Heb. 11. 25. Through a hasty action, Exod. 2. 11-15; Acts 7.23-29, Moses leaves the land of Egypt and goes to Midian where he is to be taught by God for 40 years, Acts 7. 29-30. While he is there God is still in control, and His people are not forgotten, v. 23. "God heard . . . God remembered . . . God looked . . . God had respect", Exod. 2. 24-25; cf 6. 5. If "none eye pitied thee", Ezek. 16. 5, God's eye did, and His covenant faithfulness guaranteed everything.

Feb. 1st

READING : **Exodus 4. 1-31**

MOSES' OBJECTIONS

IN SPITE OF God's positive statements concerning what He was going to do, Moses is still doubtful, and in verse 1 we hear him expressing his unbelief. God had said "they shall hearken to thy voice", 3. 18, but says Moses "they will not believe me, nor hearken unto my voice". Probably fear prompted this attitude. Very graciously God gives three signs which Moses was to use to convince the people of the omnipotence of their God, signs intended to assure them that God had sent His servant.

There are many suggestions as to the meaning of these signs. It is suggested in relation to the first, vv. 2-4, that God has in mind the history of the people. The rod symbolizes power and authority. God is showing that Israel had been held in the hand of God, and had come to a position of honour and rule through Joseph; but there came a time when another ruler arose (and behind him, Satan). The time would come when their rule would be re-established, and the power of Satan would be broken. They would become the head and not the tail.

The second sign, vv. 6-7, was a humbling one. Lest Moses and the people should become exalted by taking and controlling the serpent, they had to be taught that there is a corrupt heart within. All the power and worthiness is God's.

The third sign, v. 9, was to be used if the first two were rejected. It spoke of judgment. The river was the life of Egypt, see Ezek. 29. 1-12. God can turn a nation's (and an individual's) blessings into a tragic curse.

In verse 10 unbelief is still operating—"I am not eloquent . . . I am slow of speech, and of a slow tongue", possibly referring to an impediment. God gently reminds Moses of His sovereignty in relation to the use of speech, vv. 11-12. Far better the teaching of the Lord, and His control of the tongue, than the gift of eloquence. What a word for the preacher! Paul "came not with excellency of speech".

With verse 15 compare 2 Peter 1. 21 where Peter writes "holy men of God spake as they were moved by the Holy Ghost". We see this operating in the case of Moses to whom God said "I will be with thy mouth".

Verse 31 confirms the truth of God's word in 3. 18, and His intervention drew out their worship.

Feb. 2nd
READING : Exodus 6. 1-30
GOD'S PROMISES

CHAPTER 5 tells of the first approach of Moses and Aaron to Pharaoh. It is probable that they had high hopes concerning the outcome, although God had already warned them about this, "I am sure that the king of Egypt will not let you go", 3. 19. They were not prepared for the immediate response of Pharaoh, a hardening of the people's condition, an increase in their cruel burdens, 5. 4-14. Moses wisely told the Lord all about it, vv. 22-23. God's response in chapter 6 is very gracious. In verse 4 we have Him saying in effect "I have made a promise, I am going to keep it". In verse 5 His words are "I have also heard . . . I have remembered". The recurring reminder of the Lord's pity and covenant promise is another indication of His knowledge of the needs of our hearts.

Seven promises follow, vv. 6-8, prefaced by the announcement "I am the Lord". What guarantees there are in Him! Each of the promises are introduced with "I will", and who can withstand His will? Three of the promises in verse 6 relate to their slavery in Egypt, and they reveal that this slavery was to become a thing of *the past*. "I will bring you out from under the burden . . . I will rid you out of their bondage, and I will redeem you". This last word indicates that their deliverance is going to cost something. The still mightier exodus accomplished by the Lord Jesus at Jerusalem is suggested here, Luke 9. 31. How beautifully Paul treats the work of the Father, "who hath delivered . . . translated us", Col. 1. 13.

Two promises in verse 7 are in connection with *present* relationship. "I will take you to me for a people, and I will be to you a God". They were a complaining, doubting people, but He identifies Himself with them, and deigns to call them His own. Praise God, "I am His, and He is mine for ever".

Two more promises follow in verse 8, now referring to *the future*. "I will bring you in unto the land, and I will give it you". Again God says "I am the Lord". Why should they be fearful with such assurances? God was going to be their God, and they were going to be His people, and He pledged Himself to lead them and bring them home. This God is our God, and as He has brought us out of bondage, so he will bring us into the place prepared for His people, 1 Pet. 1. 4.

Feb. 3rd

READING : **Exodus 10. 1-29**

HE PATIENTLY WAITS

THE JUDGMENTS continue, and yet in them the longsuffering of God is seen. The quickness with which He terminated the different judgments, although Pharaoh's declarations were suspect, make it clear that judgment is His "strange work". The fact that a series of judgments were inflicted, and not one dread overthrow, shows that they were intended to lead Pharaoh to repentance, 2 Pet. 3. 9. This longsuffering is highlighted in 9. 20-21, but, as today, only a few believed.

The protection of the Israelites continues as the judgments progress, and we see God acting in accord with the implications of "my people", 9. 13. There is a delightful note in 10. 23, "all the children of Israel had light in their dwellings". The darkness could be felt all around, but within was light. Beloved we are "of the day", and although "the whole world is lost in the darkness of sin", because we are His people, we have the light of His written word, the warmth of the Father's love, the light of the bright and morning star, and even the sun of righteousness, in our dwellings. Praise His name!

Already Pharaoh has offered alternatives to God's declared purpose for His people, 8. 25, 28. In chapter 10 we have two more attempts at compromise proposed: "go now ye that are men," i.e., leave your children in the land, vv. 10-11, and "let your flocks and your herds be stayed", i.e. leave your property in Egypt, v. 24. These compromises are still with us. Some believing parents do everything to ensure that their children make headway in the world, often, alas, at the expense of their spiritual well-being; and questionable investments are made because they are profitable. How heartening to read the word of Moses "there shall not an hoof be left behind", v. 26; cf. v. 9. Since God has said "my people", on the basis of redemption, 8. 23 marg, our response should be "*all* for Thee".

Pharaoh had been steeling his heart against God throughout the history, 7. 14, 22; 8. 15, 32; 9. 7, 34, 35. All is now brought to a sad climax with the statement that "the Lord hardened Pharaoh's heart", 10. 27; cf. 4. 21; 7. 13; 9. 12; 10. 1; 14. 4, 8, 17, (note the different words used), and see Rom. 9. 17, 18. Matching Pharaoh's final note of defiance, v. 28, is the shutting of the door of grace.

Feb. 4th

READING : **Exodus 12. 1-20**

I WILL PASS OVER

As WE MOVE into the night of deliverance, we are reminded that what was going to happen that night would introduce them, as a nation, to a new beginning, v. 2. A lamb was going to be slain, and its blood sprinkled in the sight of all, and from this event they were to move out into freedom, with God! Stop for a moment and quietly consider, I am free because my Saviour has died, 1 Cor. 5. 6, and stand fast in that liberty.

The references to the lamb are interesting—"a lamb", v. 3, "the lamb", v. 4, and "your lamb", v. 5. A Saviour, the Saviour, my Saviour—this is the right order, Luke 2. 11; John 4. 42; Luke 1. 47.

On that solemn night death entered into every home, either by the lamb, or the firstborn of the house. Does this seem to be an unnecessary procedure? Could not God have determined the position in every home without this elaborate ritual? Indeed He could, but as God spoke to Moses, and through him to the people, He looked on to another Lamb, the Lamb of God. His finger was pointing onwards to the Lamb who should bear away the sin of the world, John 1. 29, 36. What a wonderful Saviour He is. If the lamb in Egypt had to be tested to ensure that it was without blemish, Exod. 12. 5, so this Blessed One was tested by man, by Satan, by God, and God opened His heaven to declare His pleasure in the One who always did the things that pleased Him.

Central to the family gathering round the table is the lamb whose blood has been sprinkled outside. The firstborn would gaze at it, for to him it was a very personal and precious thing. So we, as we gather around the table of the Lord, can say with deep gratitude and joy, "He did it for me."

They ate the feast with loins girded—because of what happened that night they were to become pilgrims. God had said "I will bring you out . . . and I will bring you in", 6. 6, 8. They were heading for a prepared inheritance. They were to keep the feast of unleavened bread, with the passover, 12. 14-20; 13. 3-10. Leaven, which in Scripture speaks of evil, was to be put away, then as now, 1 Cor. 5. 6-8. How can I permit sin to dwell in my life, let alone to have dominion over me, Rom. 6. 12-14, if the Lamb of God has died to deliver me?

Feb. 5th

READING : **Exodus 14. 1-31**

AT THE RED SEA

IN CHAPTER 13 God 'led the people about", v. 18. They were to learn that this round about way was "the right way", Psa. 107. 7. In His sovereignty, God brings them to a place of extreme peril. There is the sea, Pharaoh, the mountains around—they are hemmed in, and God brought them there. Yes, He knew what Pharaoh would say, v. 3, and do, vv. 8-9. In Israel's case, as in our own, "Blind unbelief is sure to err and scan His works in vain". They did not lift up their eyes high enough, v. 10. Such unbelief robs of confidence and joy, and in this case brought fear, v. 10. But extremities are to further spiritual education. Learn therefore:—

1. *The need for trust,* vv. 13-14, "Stand still, and see". How trying to human nature, which must be doing something! But what could they do at the Red Sea? Could they dry the waters, could they level the mountains, could they defeat the Egyptians? No! They must stand still, and let God work.

2. *The Lord's faithfulness,* v. 14. "The Lord shall fight for you". This is not now a conflict between Israel and Egypt, it is between the Lord and Egypt, and against all the gods of Egypt the Lord is going to execute judgment, vv. 4, 17-18. This should bring peace to their troubled hearts. O to prove in experience that "Thou wilt keep him in perfect peace, whose mind is stayed on thee", Isa. 26. 3! King Asa said "we rest on thee, and in thy name we go"—yes, to battle against a vast army, 2 Chron. 14. 11.

3. *God's enabling.* Israel was to "go forward", v. 15. This was no contradiction of His "stand still", but rather its sequel. The impossible become possible. Whenever God commands He enables. We do not know if the way across the sea was made all at once, or if it was divided as they went, but faith is now in operation. "By faith they passed through the Red Sea", Heb. 11. 29. Note the Egyptians "assayed" to do so and perished, Exod. 14. 23-28. This is not the pathway for the flesh.

4. *God's protection,* vv. 19-20. God places Himself between His people and the enemy. To touch them the enemy had to pass Him. How safe they were, even though they might still be trembling. Does He not say concerning Israel, "thou art mine"?, Isa. 43. 1.

Feb. 6th

READING : **Exodus 15. 1-27**

THE SONG OF REDEMPTION

THIS SONG is a logical sequel to the close of chapter 14. "Israel saw . . . the people feared the Lord, and believed the Lord", so "Then sang the children of Israel", 14. 31; 15. 1. This inspired song of Moses recognizes the grace and might of Jehovah, and looks forward to the culmination of the work of redemption which had commenced for them in Egypt. Truly, by faith Israel sang; see Psa. 106. 12. The song is taken up with God, and what *He* has done, "thee, thou, thine, thy", and finds no place for self. The people are "thy people", v. 16.

All enemies are seen to be destroyed, not only Egypt but those they are yet to meet, v. 15. What has happened is the guarantee of what is to happen, cf. esp. Rev. 15. 3.

God communicated to Moses the reasonings of Pharaoh away in the palace. "The enemy said, I will", v. 9. Six things (the number of man in all his failure) the enemy declared he was going to do to Israel, concluding with a statement that could be rendered "I will repossess them", v. 9 marg. The utter impossibility of such a thing coming to pass is seen in chapter 6 where God had already said "I will" seven times (no failure here). If God says "I will", Satan can do nothing about it. Israel was safe, not because of their faithfulness, but because God had declared "I will". His purpose cannot be thwarted. We think of the words of our Lord, "of all which he hath given me I should lose nothing", John 6. 39; cf. 17. 12. Satan might sift the apostolic band, but the Lord had prayed for Peter, Luke 22. 31-32. His power preserved him, and will us.

Israel was "the people which thou hast redeemed", "which thou hast purchased", vv. 13, 16. What a triumph of might, vv. 3-12, what a display of mercy, v. 13a! Over the foe "he hath triumphed gloriously", v. 1. To His people He "is my strength and song, and he is become my salvation", v. 2. There is no room here for unfelt truth. "I will praise him", v. 2b R.V.

The future is all assured, both "thine inheritance", and "the sanctuary, O Lord, which thy hands have established", v. 17, together with the throne, for the Lord "shall reign for ever and ever", v. 18.

Yet another fitting response to this is "to do justly, and to love mercy, and to walk humbly with thy God", Mic. 6. 8.

Feb. 7th

READING : **Exodus 16. 1-36**

BREAD FROM HEAVEN

WE RECALL the words, "God led them about", 13. 18, and are justified in concluding that the pillar of cloud had led them into this wilderness situation. Listen to the whole congregation murmuring in unbelief. Where are the triumphant strains of the song in chapter 15 now? Lack of food caused them to doubt that God was able and willing to provide. God heard their murmurings and said "Behold I will rain bread from heaven" — not fire and brimstone, but bread, Gen. 19. 24; Exod. 16. 4. "He hath not dealt with us after our sins", praise His name!, Psa. 103. 10.

Verse 6 suggests that the daily provision of this special food from heaven would be a constant confirmation of God's working for them in their deliverance from Egypt. They were brought out by Divine purpose. And having saved them God was going to preserve them. God knew that 40 years would pass before they came into settled conditions, and the people "did eat manna forty years, until they came unto the borders of the land" v. 35. For the Psalmist, too, He prepared a table, Psa. 23. 5, and is still able to do this. The Lord taught His disciples to pray "Give us this day our daily bread", Matt. 6. 11; not a month's supply in advance, but "daily bread".

There was no failure with Him. As they gather daily God's unfailing supply for them, God would "prove them, whether they will walk in my law, or no", v.4. Here there was failure, as with us, despite His gracious provision that it might not be so.

When the people saw the manna they exclaimed "what is this?", v. 15 marg. The description in verses 14 and 31, cf. Num. 11. 8, goes some way to help us. Its use was manifold, Num. 11.7-8. It really was supernatural food, Psa. 78. 24; 105. 40; 1 Cor. 10. 3, pointing on to the incarnation of our Lord Jesus. He is "the true bread", "the bread of God", "the bread of life", "the living bread", "the bread which came down from heaven". He is God's provision for a starving world. He is the food of a pilgrim people on the way to heaven, through meditation on the Word of God. Without Him we starve. For the overcomer there is the promise of "the hidden manna", Rev. 2. 17, antitype of "the golden pot that had manna" in the ark of the covenant, Heb. 9. 4.

Feb. 8th

READING : **Exodus 17. 1-16**

AMPLE WATER AND AMALEK'S WARFARE

AS WE COMMENCE our reading we see a strange combination of words — "according to the commandment of the Lord", and "there was no water", v. 1. But the rock is spoken of as being in Horeb, v. 6. Through it, the camp would be supplied as the water flowed down from higher ground, and as they moved on to nearby Sinai, where they would be encamped for many months, a perpetual supply was guaranteed.

God says to Moses "take . . . thy rod" — the rod of judgment; "I will stand . . . upon the rock . . . and thou shalt smite the rock", vv. 5-6. Although the rod was actually in Moses' grasp, the Psalms are consistent in saying that it was God who smote the rock, 78. 15-16; 105. 41; 114. 8. This is solemn as we know "that rock was Christ", 1 Cor. 10. 4. We are faced with this tremendous thought that in Exodus 17 we see Deity smiting Deity. "Jehovah lifted up His rod, O Christ it fell on Thee", cf. Zech. 13. 7.

The giving of the Holy Spirit as the direct result of the cross work of the Lord Jesus is emphasized here; "there shall come water out of it" — living water, ever fresh and sufficient. On the Day of Pentecost, the day when the Holy Spirit came, Peter declared concerning Christ, "he hath shed forth this", Acts 2. 33; cf. John 7. 39. The link in our passage between the smiting of the rock and the coming of the Amalekites was the sudden new supply of fresh water, vital for a nomadic people. It is a fact of experience that when the Spirit comes the battle begins. Amalek becomes a picture of the flesh which resists the Spirit all along the way, v. 16. Let us be certain of these two truths, (1) on conversion the flesh is *not* eradicated, and (2) the continual indwelling of the Holy Spirit does not gradually change the old nature into a new one. This means conflict as there can be no agreement between the flesh and the Spirit, Gal. 5. 17.

Beloved, bear in mind that although Egypt (the world) has been overthrown and Pharaoh (Satan) defeated, Amalek (the flesh) follows us into the desert and makes his presence known. But also bear this in mind that the indwelling Spirit of God is the guarantee of victory if we yield ourselves to Him, v. 14.

Feb. 9th

READING : **Exodus 19. 1-25**

ISRAEL AT SINAI

WE NOW COME to a very important point in the history of Israel (see the time note, v. 1) where God reveals Himself to them, first of all in grace, and then in terms of law. Before the law was introduced pure grace operated. Israel's murmurings up to this time are heard, but grace replies. Now they declare their willingness and ability to do all that God requires of them, v. 8. The promise of verses 5-6 was subject to "if ye will obey my voice indeed", and as we read its terms we learn what was in the heart of God for them. How much better for them had they acknowledged their inability to do all that was required of them, and had left themselves in the hands of God to work out His gracious purposes. God will not be frustrated, however, and in a new age where "grace reigns" Peter speaks of these blessings, which could not be achieved through human failure, becoming the portion of a heavenly people, who have been called "out of darkness into his marvellous light".

As God prepares to reveal His law to them, there was a terrifying display of divine power, a "thick cloud", v. 9, "set bounds", v. 12, "there shall not a hand touch", v. 13, "thunders and lightnings", v. 16, and "the voice of the trumpet", v. 16. Contrast this with the closeness and gentleness of verse 4, where the same God says "I bare you on eagles' wings and brought you unto myself ". How He loved them!

Grace has removed the fear associated with a law we cannot keep, and brought us to "mount Sion . . . the heavenly Jerusalem", see Heb. 12. 18-22, with the invitation "draw near with a true heart", 10. 22. How can this be, for our God is still "the Judge of all", 12. 23. Acts 7. 38 tells us that the Lawgiver was the Lord Jesus Himself, and even as He gave the law, He knew that He was to suffer the curse associated with the breaking of it, Gal. 3. 13. In His Own Blessed Person He was going to abolish the distance and the terror, that we might be redeemed, Gal. 4. 4-5, and justified, Rom. 6. 20-21. It is "to Jesus the mediator of the new covenant, and to the blood of sprinkling, that speaketh better things than that of Abel", that we come, Heb. 12. 24. Not that we are to refuse Him that speaks to us. Rather "let us have grace, whereby we may serve God acceptably with reverence and godly fear", v. 28.

Feb. 10th

READING : **Exodus 20. 1-26**

THE TEN WORDS

ALTHOUGH COMMUNICATED by an obscure people, until recently a nation of slaves, the ten commandments, as all areas of morality in the Hebrew Scriptures, are far superior to the ethical standards of other nations. If men discount their Divine origin how do they account for them at all? Of Israel alone God said "I have talked with you from heaven", v. 22. God again draws attention to the redemption from Egypt, v. 2. Redemption is a reason for obeying.

The first four of the commandments deal with direct responsibility to God, vv. 3-11; the remaining six have to do with conduct in relation to man, vv. 12-17. The Lord Jesus' summary is "Thou shalt love the Lord thy God . . . This is the first and great commandment. And the second is . . . Thou shalt love thy neighbour as thyself", Matt. 22. 37-39. God seeks the love of His people, a love shown in obedience. The Lord Jesus said "If ye love me, keep my commandments", yea even "my words", John 14. 15, 23.

As we listen to these laws we discover what is in the flesh, and the Lord Jesus made it clear that it is not only the act which makes us guilty, cf. Matt. 5. 28, and verses 17-48.

All of these requirements, except that relating to the sabbath day, are insisted on in the New Testament, although not as a ground of salvation, for what the law could not do, God has done, Rom. 8. 3-4. There is a sense in which these commandments go full circle, because what we covet in verse 17 will be our god, v. 3, which we will serve.

It is suggestive that the chapter concludes with the altar, which was to be of earth or stone, vv. 24-25. Nothing elaborate or attractive was to distract from the stark fact of man's shortcomings before God. No steps were to form an ascent to it, for man cannot make a way up to God without revealing his nakedness, v. 26. Remember, too, that this altar is made by a redeemed people, aware, by the light of God, how they fail Him in their most devoted moments. For such there is the burnt offering, representing the perfect obedience, even to death on a cross, of the Lord Jesus. In the good of this, fellowship may be enjoyed with the God of Peace through the sweet-savour offering of the Lord of Peace.

Feb. 11th

READING : **Exodus 25. 1-40**

I WILL DWELL AMONG THEM

THE BASIC PURPOSE of the tabernacle was that God might have a dwelling place among His people, v. 8. How a holy God can dwell among an unholy people is explained by the provision of a brazen altar in the courtyard, and the mercy seat in the most holy place. God hereby provides the righteousness in which He can meet with His own, while safeguarding His own holiness and righteousness. Offerings for the project were to be received "of every man that giveth it willingly with his heart", v. 2. There was no constraint here, it was not an act of duty, but all was out of a heart touched with the sense of God's goodness, and a recognition that all was His, Matt. 10. 8.

A Divine pattern is provided, vv. 9(2), 40; Heb. 8. 5; 9. 23, to which their building must conform, and it did as the closing chapters of Exodus prove by the repeated refrain "as the Lord commanded Moses". Even if, humanly, Moses thought another method would be better, "the pattern" was his authority, and to the pattern he adhered. Let us remember this when alternative methods of service are freely advocated—let us not depart from what is written.

God begins in the innermost place, the place of His presence, with the ark, and moves out to the confines of the outer court, as from heaven itself to earth. In His grace He inaugurates the movement towards men.

How full of relevation of Him the ark is! It was made of wood overlaid with gold: shittim wood (the incorruptible wood of the desert) speaking of the perfect humanity of the Lord Jesus, and pure gold, speaking of His Deity. He is Man, the Man: He is God, profound mystery, John 1. 14. The lid of the ark, made of pure gold, was called the mercy seat, the place of covering. Upon it, on the day of atonement, blood was sprinkled, Lev. 16. 14, which had been shed at the brazen altar in the courtyard. Because of that sprinkled blood the mercy seat became a meeting place between God and men, v. 22. Within the ark, covered by the mercy seat and the blood, were placed the tables of the law, 40. 20, and later a pot containing manna, and Aaron's rod that budded, Heb. 9. 4. We see a holy law, so sadly broken by Israel, but kept by the Christ, Psa. 40. 8, a blood-stained mercy seat, Rom. 3. 25.

Feb. 12th

READING : **Exodus 26. 31 to 27. 8**

MOSES WROTE OF ME

WE SHALL LIMIT our comments to one item from each chapter, the veil within the holy place, and the brazen altar in the courtyard outside. As we stand within the tabernacle and look around, all speaks of His glory, Psa. 29. 9.

The veil was a barrier "the Holy Ghost this signifying, that the way into the holiest of all was not yet made manifest", Heb. 9. 8. Beyond, in the Holiest, was the ark of the covenant and the presence of God, where entry was permitted only to the high priest on one day a year, as he took in the blood of atonement to sprinkle on the mercy seat. The Hebrews epistle interprets "the veil, that is to say, his flesh", 10. 20. When the Lord Jesus died on the cross the veil in the temple was "rent in twain from the top to the bottom", Matt. 27. 51. The way into the holiest of all was suddenly flung open. It was not the incarnation which brought salvation and nearness to God. His human body prepared for Him had to be rent in death. Because of that death God now says, "draw near".

In the courtyard we see the brazen altar, 38. 30. As we consider its purpose we see God's hatred of sin, and yet "where sin abounded, grace did much more abound", Rom. 5. 20. For consider the sacrifice offered, taking the place of the guilty one. It is described also as the altar of burnt offering, 31. 9, the altar which is by the door, Lev. 1. 5. That sweet savour offering wholly consumed upon it was the divinely appointed means of making it possible for man to draw near to God. As God gazed at that altar, with its repeated and varied sacrifices, He looked ahead and saw another sacrifice, not of bulls and goats, but of His beloved Son, Heb. 10. 1-10. He was to come to put away sin by the sacrifice of Himself, and to offer Himself up for us, "an offering and a sacrifice to God for a sweet smelling savour", Eph. 5. 2. The cross is central, Heb. 9. 26.

In the courtyard outside, the brazen altar spoke of sin dealt with according to Divine judgment, and access established, the finished work of the Christ. The golden altar inside, where the fragrant incense arose, spoke of the perfections of the Christ, and His continuing work on our behalf, 30. 1-10; Heb. 7. 25. One showed the fire of wrath quenched and holiness satisfied, the other the fire of worship kindled, holy service.

Feb. 13th

READING : **Exodus 28. 1-43**

WE HAVE A GREAT HIGH PRIEST

SOME MAY THINK that the minute detail in the description of the high priest's apparel is unnecessary, but we must ask why it is there? When we accept that God had His Own Son in mind as He spoke of the high priesthood, our difficulties vanish v. 3.

The high priestly garments are listed in verse 4, and described in verses 6-38. There is an ephod, vv. 6-14, a robe, v. 31f, a broidered coat, v. 39, a mitre, vv. 36-38, and a girdle, v. 8; Lev. 8. 7. All were essential that Aaron (and his sons) might "minister unto me in the priest's office", v. 41, cf. vv. 1, 43; 29. 44. The holy garments "for glory and for beauty", v. 2, suggest to us the personal and official glories of the ascended Christ, "crowned with glory and honour", Heb. 2. 9; 7. 26.

Consider the materials used, v. 5. Apart from One glorified (gold), who came from heaven and has now returned there (blue), who has been given universal authority (purple), the fulfiller of God's promises in David's royal line (scarlet), yet perfected in a humanity holy, harmless and undefiled (fine-twined linen), we would not be sufficiently supported for the present life, Rom. 8. 34-39. The ephod, vv. 6-14, is seen as the most important garment that was worn, the first item to be put on. It was of fine twined linen, speaking of His perfect humanity.

On the shoulders, as part of the ephod, were placed two identical onyx stones, one on each shoulder, each having engraved on it the names, of six of the tribes. The twelve tribes, represented by their names, were borne on the high priest's shoulders, the place of strength. So the glorified Lord today carries His people on His shoulders. But we also read that "Aaron shall bear the names of the children of Israel in the breastplate of judgment upon his heart", v. 29. The people are here seen, not as a company, but as individuals. The twelve stones, not two, were all different, each bearing the name of one tribe. The Lord Jesus bears each of us upon His heart, nothing can separate us from His love. Each was borne when Aaron went into the holy place, the place of worship and intercession, "for a memorial before the Lord continually", v. 29. Our High Priest has gone in to the true tabernacle, Heb. 9. 24, and there makes intercession for us, 7. 25.

Feb. 14th

READING : **Exodus 30. 1-38**

WORSHIP

GOD SEEKS the worship of His people. We see this in the provision of the altar of incense in the holy place of the tabernacle. The altar speaks of the Person and office of the glorified Christ as our Great High Priest. The incense speaks of His personal perfections as they bring delight to God.

We have meticulous instructions as to who shall approach this altar, and how. No strange incense was to be offered, v. 9. It must be that which was made according to the Divine specification, vv. 34-35. Beloved, our worship must not be corrupted by the flesh, or in self-will, but be prompted by Christ, its theme and delight. It must be Divine in origin. The fire to consume the incense was taken from the brazen altar, indicating the close connection of worship with the work of atonement. Hence, our worship must not be formal, but out of an appreciation of what happened outside at the altar, for God and for us. It will not be difficult to bring pure worship when prompted by the Spirit of God.

Linked with the instruction concerning the altar of incense is the instruction concerning the redemption money, v. 11-16. Is the Holy Spirit saying that only those who are redeemed can worship? But we remember that our redemption is not by silver or gold but by the precious blood of Christ, 1 Pet. 1. 18-19. Then follows the direction concerning the laver, vv. 17-21, — suggesting that cleansing by the water of the Word is another vital preparation for worship. The examining of oneself, and the adjusting of the life are essential preliminaries.

This constant burning of incense is seen, under the law, to be symbolical of prayer: "Let my prayer be set forth before thee as incense" says the Psalmist, 141. 2. In the heavenly temple too, the angel was given much incense to be offered with the prayers of the saints, Rev. 8. 3-5. Also the incense contained in the golden vials held by the twenty-four elders is said to be "the prayers of saints", 5. 8. Thus the unceasing wafting of the sweet perfume, made to yield its fragrance by the heat of the fire brought from the brazen altar of burnt offering, represented worship presented in Christ's perfections in communion with God, together with that loftiest and noblest expression of the life of prayer, which is intercession for others.

Feb. 15th

READING : **Exodus 31. 1-18**

GOD'S WORKMEN

WE ARE SHOWN here the kind of workmen needed. God says in relation to Bezaleel, "I have called by name", v. 2. He knows us all by name, and in His sovereignty He makes known to us His will and desire. How do we respond? When the call came to Moses his reply was 'Who am I?", Exod. 3. 11. Does it matter who I am if He calls? God has chosen the "nobodies" to do Him service, 1 Cor. 1. 27-28, and in the service of the nobodies He is glorified. "I have filled him with the Spirit of God"—what an endowment! What comfort there is in the words "I have given", v. 6. God not only provides a companion to work with Bezaleel, but all needed enabling for the vital work to be done. This he would promote by teaching, 35. 34.

Note the reference to the "wisehearted" in verse 6. These are those whose affections are controlled, and to whom is given the ability to handle Divine things. After all, the things they were to be associated with are the things necessary for the establishment of the witness to God in the wilderness, vv. 3-5. In Acts 6. 3 also we see men being chosen for a special task, and they were to be "full of the Holy Ghost and wisdom".

In the New Testament we see apostles chosen, and the necessary ability given to them. They taught to others what was first written in their own hearts, precious views of Christ put together in Divine order.

"I have put wisdom, that they may work", v. 6. He chooses and equips His workmen, yet they are responsible too. They are to make: there is to be no slacking on their part, they are to stir up the gift in them, 2 Tim. 1. 6; cf. 1 Tim. 4. 14. Further, they are to make "all that I have commanded", vv. 6, 11. The work to be done is all prescribed by Him, it is obedient workmen God needs. We must note, however, that it was not only the brethren who were called to this ministry in relation to the tabernacle. Special reference is made to the devoted work of the sisters, 35. 25-26, and we are told that they engaged themselves in spinning and weaving—how much better than pulling apart. In the assembly today the sisters may not be permitted to minister the Word, but they do much to draw together the strands of Divine teaching.

Do we know what God has given us to do? Are we doing it?

Feb. 16th
READING : Exodus 32. 1-35

THE GOLDEN CALF

As we read this chapter let us keep in mind the warning "let him that thinketh he standeth take heed lest he fall", 1 Cor. 10. 12. Why is this sad and tragic scene brought before us? To show us what men in the flesh are. The flesh has not changed, though these people "saw the God of Israel", and "the sight of the glory of the Lord", Exod. 24. 10, 17.

What a contrast with the previous chapter. There men are seen making all things as commanded by God, led by the Spirit of wisdom, not human imagination. Here we see them led by fleshly desires, making a visible idol form, led by another spirit. How quickly the change is effected. How subtly Satan works. In the mount, the tabernacle is revealed as the Divine system about to be introduced, while elements of idolatry, and that which is pleasing to man are introduced below and greedily seized, 32. 1-6. "Neither be ye idolaters, as were some of them", warns Paul, 1 Cor. 10. 7.

We should note here that the proneness of Israel to idolatry, seen so often in their history, indicates that a revelation superior to all that they knew will alone account for their loftier faith.

Note the boldness of Moses when confronted by God with the situation. He dares to argue with God, and as he does so he does not point to the people who had sinned and seek to find in them some ground of forgiveness. In faith he reminds God of His Own promises, and puts the whole matter back into the Divine hands, pleading His faithfulness to His Own word, vv. 11-13. In speaking to Moses about them, God has said "thy people", v. 7. No, said Moses, they are "thy people", v. 12. With all their failings they were still His. Praise God, our relationship with Him does not depend upon our faithfulness. Moses also prayed specifically for Aaron, who had been so weak and failing in the matter, Deut. 9. 20.

As we see the tribe of Levi, in response to Moses' "Who is on the Lord's side?", taking the sword against the offenders, some of whom were their own kindred, we recall the words of the Lord Jesus, "He that loveth father or mother more than me is not worthy of me", Matt. 10. 37.

Feb. 17th

READING : **Exodus 33. 1 to 34. 7**

GOD'S PRESENCE AND GLORY

CHAPTER 33 has much to say about the presence of the Lord. But how can Israel still experience that presence in view of their sinfulness and rebellion? God declares that He will send an angel before the people as they resume their journey, and this suggests that the immediate presence of God Himself has been withdrawn—a shadow has come between, v. 2. Israel mourns, regarding the news as "evil tidings", v. 4.

The "tent of meeting" (not to be confused with the tabernacle yet to be constructed) was now pitched outside the camp, vv. 7-11. Clearly before this it had been inside. What a solemn thought—communion with God is so disrupted that God is outside the camp, instead of dwelling among His people. Who will now identify himself with God in the place of separation? "Everyone which sought the Lord went out unto the tabernacle . . . without the camp", v. 7. Others worshipped at a distance, still within the camp. The New Testament challenge is "Let us go forth therefore unto him without the camp, bearing his reproach", Heb. 13. 13. If our Lord is outside that is our place. The presence of the Lord establishes the truth of separation from all that belongs outside, Exod. 33. 16.

Moses makes a staggering request to God—"show me thy glory", v. 18. Is this a man hungering and thirsting after God? God gently reminds His servant that no one can see His face and live, and promises to reveal His "goodness", putting him in a place of safety while He did so. In chapter 34 we see the Lord doing this, vv. 5-7. What a wonderful revealing of the character of God. Men gazed at Jesus Christ and saw God "manifest in flesh", His mercy, grace, longsuffering, His abundance in goodness and truth, forgiving yet by no means clearing the guilty. In the Lord Jesus, and His crosswork, we discover the perfect harmony in the character of God.

Moses came back to the camp as the man with the shining face, shining with the reflected glory of God. Alas, his was a fading glory. Let ours be a developing glory through occupation with the glorified Lord, in whose face we see "the light of the knowledge of the glory of God", 2 Cor. 3. 17-18; 4. 6.

Feb. 18th

READING : **Exodus 35. 20-29; 36. 1-8**

MORE THAN ENOUGH

IN CHAPTER 35 and 36 the construction of the tabernacle gets under way. The first stage, in chapter 35, records the people bringing their gifts to the Lord. We are struck by the *variety* of what they brought. Some brought small things, some large. Some brought things which, of themselves, were of little value; some brought that which was costly and precious. The controlling motive in the bringing was the willing heart, 35. 21, 22, 29. We judge that, in their giving, there was an appreciation of what their God had done for them, and how He had borne with them. This being so, the thought would not be "can I afford this", but "how much can I give?", 2 Cor. 9. 7.

The giving was *voluntary*, "a freewill offering", v. 29 R.V. It would have been valueless otherwise. We wonder how many of the people really appreciated the greatness of what they were doing. God was determined that in the wilderness, as they journeyed homeward, there should be a place of constant witness, a meeting place between Him and them. Did they realise that in a very large measure this was dependent upon them and their offerings? God was indeed to inhabit the praises of Israel, Psa. 22. 3. Again, we read that the men and women became involved enthusiastically, they were *warm-hearted*, 35. 21, 26, 29; 36. 2. They not only gave things, but first gave themselves to the Lord, cf. 2 Cor. 8. 1-5.

Chapter 36 opens with a picture of *abundance*. Not often in the history of God's people has it been necessary to restrain further giving because every need has been met, but such was the position here. "Let neither man nor woman make any more work for the offering of the sanctuary", they proclaimed throughout the camp, v. 6, "for the stuff they had was sufficient for all the work to make it, and too much", v. 7.

The work of construction begins and the workers are guided by the pattern shown in the mount. As they work we find references to wise-hearted men and women, 35. 25; 36. 1, 2, 8, and we realise there may have been a large number engaged in the work. Yet as we read down chapter 36 the refrain occurs frequently "he made", as though there was only one doing the work. This is the kind of co-operation needed in the Lord's work. Let us work as one man.

Feb. 19th

READING : **Exodus 40. 1-38**

AS THE LORD COMMANDED

THIS MUST HAVE BEEN an exciting time for Moses and the people of Israel. During the preceding months the work of preparation had gone steadily forwards, the workers being guided all the time by the instruction, "look that thou make them after their pattern, which was showed thee in the mount", 25. 40. There would have been occasions when individual workers wondered why they were doing a certain job in a particular way — left to themselves they would have chosen another way. The Divine edict however was "the pattern showed thee". This is a lesson for us in our service — we may be tempted at times to try methods which, in the eyes of the world, appear to be reasonable, and indeed more effective, but are not in accord with the pattern in the Word. We will enter into the joy of the Lord if what is said concerning Moses in verse 16 can be said of us, "according to all that the Lord commanded him, so did he". He accepted no responsibility for the formulation of the plan, but he did recognize his responsibility to carry out the plan. Seven times in succeeding verses is found the refrain "as the Lord commanded Moses", vv. 19, 21, 23, 25, 27, 29, 32. This is embraced within the comprehensive commendation in Hebrews 3. 2.

It is interesting that the only worker seen in the final erection of the tabernacle is Moses. Is this because he is intended to be seen as a picture of Christ? He is seen setting up the tabernacle, putting everything in its right place, and inaugurating every feature of service. If He is the One seen, we can understand verse 33 "So Moses finished the work".

It was the Lord Jesus who told out what God is, who declared the Father's name, who sanctified His brethren, who anointed with the Holy Spirit, cf. vv. 9-11, 15, and was minister of the true tabernacle. So as we would expect, "the glory of the Lord filled the tabernacle". The fulness of this points on to a coming glory, and yet was appreciated in part by the people even then. So, now, we have "the light of the knowledge of the glory of God in the face of Jesus Christ", 2 Cor. 4. 6, while we await "the glory which shall be revealed", Rom. 8. 18. Until then God's presence and guidance are assured, Exod. 40. 36-37.

Introducing Leviticus

WE READ repeatedly in the book that God spoke to Moses, and we are given details of what God commanded him, see 1. 1; 4. 1; 5. 14; 6. 1, 8, 19, 24, etc. The corollary of this is that Moses was to "Speak unto the children of Israel", e.g. 1. 2; 4. 2; 6. 25; 7. 23, 29, etc. We are not dealing with Moses' own views. These are the words of God communicated to him.

A good key-word for the book of Leviticus is holiness. God is here concerned with a people whom He has redeemed from bondage and brought into covenant relationship with Himself. In view of all that He has done for them, it is reasonable to expect that they will do what He requires of them, that is that they should live as a holy people. The demand that the people should be holy does not rest alone, however, on the fact that He has redeemed them, but also that He is holy — "be holy; for I am holy", 11. 44. Among Israel's pagan neighbours consecration to their deity involved often-times immoral rites. For Israel, God's requirements were obedience and faith, and a reflection of God's own holy character in their daily life. The standard of the New Testament is the same, 1 Pet. 1. 16.

The Lord Jesus is foreshadowed in the book. Various facets of His Person and atoning work are seen in *the offerings* of the early chapters, cf. Heb. 10. 5-10. Aaron *the high priest* points to Him as the *great* "High Priest of our profession", Heb. 3. 1; cf. 4. 14-16. *The feasts* of the Lord speak of the triumphs, the facets and phases of His work, 23. 1-44.

Sin is brought before us in all its ugliness as we contemplate the leper, chs. 13 and 14, but at the same time we see that God makes provision for *cleansing*. The work of Christ is focussed upon as we see blood being shed.

An Outline of the Book

1. Access, chs. 1-10
   (*a*) The five offerings, 1. 1 to 6. 7, (*b*) The law of the offerings, 6. 8 to 7. 38, (*c*) The priesthood, chs. 8-10
2. Holiness, chs. 11-27
   (*a*) Purity; (i) Pure Food, ch. 11, (ii) Pure Bodies, 12. 1-14. 32, (iii) Pure Homes, 14. 33-57, (iv) Pure Habits, ch. 15, (v) Constant resort to Blood, ch. 16
   (*b*) Sundry Laws, chs. 17-27

Feb. 20th

READING : **Leviticus 1. 1-17**

THE SWEET SAVOUR OFFERINGS

THE PRINCIPAL OFFERINGS were five in number, divided into two classes. The first three are classed as "sweet savour" offerings, speaking of God's delight in the perfections of Christ, and His voluntary submission to the Father's will in the work of atonement. The remaining two are "sin offerings", in which are seen God's fierce judgment upon sin in the Person of the divinely provided substitute. Our reading today deals with the burnt offering only, but the comments will embrace briefly the meal offering and the peace offering as well.

The Burnt Offering could be a bullock, a ram, or doves or pigeons. This was probably to accommodate the poor as well as the rich, but, typically, we see offerers with varying appreciations of Christ. The bullock was more costly than a ram, and the ram more costly than the birds, but God saw Christ in them all, and they were a sweet savour to Him. We can bring to God what we have learned of Christ, but all the time our knowledge of Him should be increasing so that the quality of our worship will move from the birds to the ram to the bullock.

The Meat (Meal) Offering, Lev. 2. 1-16. This is a bloodless offering, and the fine flour speaks of the perfect humanity of our beloved Lord. The offering of it on the altar suggests the culmination of that perfect life among men which was fully to the glory of God. The offering could be prepared in three ways: (i) Baked in the oven; (ii) Baked in a pan; (iii) Baked in a frying pan. These may suggest the different trials and testings to which the Lord was subjected: "in the oven", out of sight,—the suffering of mind and spirit known only to God, v. 4; "in a pan"— the public testings in the world, v. 5; cf. Matt. 16. 21, "suffer many things of the elders" etc.; "in the frying pan"—still more intense, including even the cross, v. 7. In them all the Lord was perfect.

The Peace Offering, Lev. 3. 1-17. This is a thanksgiving for peace already made, and assumes more spiritual appreciation of what has been accomplished for us. In Christ, God and the sinner meet in peace. Other Scriptures tell us that He *made* peace, Col. 1. 20, also that He *is* our peace, Eph. 2. 14. There can be no peace with God other than on the basis of what Christ did for us on the cross.

Feb. 21st

READING : Leviticus 4. 1-35

THE SIN OFFERING AND THE TRESPASS OFFERING

INSTRUCTIONS concerning these two offerings are found in chapters 4 to 6. 7. Many offerings were provided because no one offering could adequately set forth the various facets of the sacrificial work of Christ. The "sweet savour" offerings considered previously were brought to God voluntarily by one in communion with God. Now we see the approach of the sinner who is conscious, in the sin offering, of his sin against a holy God, or, in the trespass offering, of sin against his neighbour.

With the sin offering the actual offering depended on the status of the offerer(s), see 4. 3, 13, 22, 27. This illustrates the truth that in the sight of God sin is in proportion to one's privilege which brings with it increased responsibility and increased guilt, Matt. 11. 20-24. But the overriding truth is that all, irrespective of position, need Christ. In the ritual we see the guilty bringing the guiltless, 4. 3. This reminds us of the words of Peter, "the just for the unjust", 1 Pet. 3. 18. Thank God for the One without blemish who met all of God's requirements. The guilty one lays his hand in identification on the guiltless substitute, v. 29. The penalty for sin must be paid but the victim pays it, John 1. 29; 2 Cor. 5. 21. The offerer slays the victim, and as he gazes upon the dead body he could say "that death is my death". Note that the fat was burnt on the altar, and in this we see God's pleasure in the One who put away sin.

In thinking of the trespass offering we note that, although a sin-offering, it is concerned not so much with the guilt of sin but the effects of sin, and in chapter 6 the element of restitution is brought in. In its supreme sense our Lord made restitution on our behalf. He restored that which He took not away, Psa. 69. 4. An Emmaus Bible Course puts it like this—"God not only received through Christ all that He lost, but much more. He has gained by redemption more than He ever lost by the Fall. Think of the harvest of glory, honour and praise that shall be His for ever from sinners saved by grace".

Practically, it is well to note that God expects that we should make good with our brethren that in which we have trespassed against them if we want His forgiveness, Matt. 6. 14, 15.

Feb. 22nd

READING : **Leviticus 6. 8-30; 7. 37-38**

THE LAW OF THE OFFERINGS

FROM LEVITICUS 6. 8 to 7. 38 we have the laws relating to priestly action concerning the various offerings. The establishment of a detailed ritual was a safeguard against the introduction of error, and the entrance of idolatry. Chapter 7. 37-38 makes it clear that these laws did not originate with Moses or with Aaron the high priest, but came direct from God Himself. He did not leave it to His people to decide the processes of worship and communion.

The order of the sacrifices in these chapters differs slightly, but significantly, from the order given in 1. 1 to 6. 7. It has been suggested that in 1. 1 to 6. 7 we have the offerer's approach to God, but in 6. 8 to 7. 38 God's revelation of Himself to the offerer. In the latter revelation, the burnt offering comes first—the offering of Christ in all His wondrous perfection, and the peace offering is moved from its central place to the end. This suggests that the climax for the offerer is his entering into what has been obtained for him, the removal of all enmity, and the enjoyment of peace. It should be noted that in the peace offering, exceptionally, leavened bread was offered, 7. 13. This reminds us that, however grateful we may be, even our thanksgiving is tainted by sin.

We are not, of course, governed by these laws today, because Christ and His work are the end of such sacrifices and laws, having fulfilled them. The offerings of old time could not make the offerers perfect, Heb. 9. 9; 10. 1, but what they could not do Christ has done, 10. 10. As a fruit of the salvation He has brought to us, we now bring spiritual sacrifices, not governed by rules and regulations, but which are the outflow of love from redeemed hearts. Three such sacrifices are mentioned in the New Testament. (i) Our bodies, Rom. 12. 1. These are to be a living sacrifice in contrast with dead animals. We must use all our faculties in devoted service to the One who died for us. Our hands, feet, intellect, all are His. (ii) Our praise, Heb. 13. 15. Our conversation, the fruit of our lips, should witness to Christ, not only in church gatherings, but in everyday speech. (iii) Our money, our goods, Heb. 13. 16. Note this giving is a sacrifice, it will cost something, but others will be blessed.

Feb. 23rd

READING : **Leviticus 8. 1-36**

THE CONSECRATION OF THE PRIESTS

IN THIS CHAPTER Moses, in obedience to the command of God does what was laid down in Exodus 28-29. The tabernacle had been newly set up, and in our previous readings we have been concerned with the ritual relating to the offerings: none of this could operate without the priesthood. The high priest is now being set aside for his special work, but we must note that frequent reference is made also to Aaron's sons, who are closely associated with him in his priestly work.

It is not difficult to see in the high priest a foreshadowing of the work of our "great high priest", Jesus, the Son of God, Heb. 4. 14. There was a special work that only Aaron could do, and there were features in the ritual of consecration which were appropriate to him only, and which mark him out as being unique. For example, with the high priest the anointing oil was poured on Aaron's head before blood was shed, but with the priests blood was shed first, and the oil was sprinkled later. This is the order of salvation. There may be significance in that with the high priest alone the oil was "poured", v. 12, whereas with him and the priests it was "sprinkled" along with the blood, v. 30.

We look closer at the sons of Aaron as priests, and we realise they were priests because of relationship with him. That is our position exactly. Believers form a "holy priesthood" offering spiritual sacrifices to God, and also a "royal priesthood" to show forth to men the praises of God, 1 Pet. 2. 5, 9. We are this by virtue of our relationship with the great high priest through grace, and as we represent the royal, Melchisedec character of His priesthood in anticipation of a future day of glory. When Aaron's sons were consecrated as priests, the ram of consecration, v. 22, was killed, and the blood was put upon their right ears, the thumb of their right hands, and the great toe of their right feet, v. 24. From then on the whole body belonged to God in the great work of priesthood. The privilege and responsibility given to us is that we should be a spiritual link between others and God. We go to God on behalf of others — we go to others on behalf of God.

Feb. 24th

READING : **Leviticus 9. 1-24**

AARON TAKES UP HIS DUTIES

IN CONSIDERING the details of this chapter we must beware of trying to force a spiritual meaning from every detail given.

Moses had carried out the work of consecrating the priests, ch. 8. Now we see Aaron and his sons taking over the responsibilities planned for them. Only consequent on what is now to be done will the glory of the Lord be revealed, v. 6, 23. It is significant also that, before this could come about, there had to be sacrifices which recognized sin on the part of the offerer (the sin offering), v. 7, and obedience to, and delight in, the will of God (the burnt offering), v. 7. Both of these offerings direct us to the finished work of Christ.

Note that Aaron the high priest offered these offerings for *himself* as well as for his sons. It is important to remember that, however exalted by God we may be, we are still sinners. Indeed, the nearer we are to the Lord in fellowship, the more conscious of our sinfulness we shall be. Contrast Aaron's greater Antitype, Heb. 7. 26 ff.

Following Aaron's offering for himself and his sons, he offers again on behalf of the people. What we are seeing is God laying a righteous foundation, on which He can come out in mercy and grace to reveal Himself. After all the ritual has been completed, Aaron is seen blessing the people with uplifted hand, v. 22. (This is how the disciples last saw their Lord as He left them to return to heaven, Luke 24. 50-51). It is probable that Aaron used the lovely words of blessing that we find recorded in Numbers 6. 24-26. If so, the wealth of God's blessing is seen flowing from the work at the altar. Verse 23 may indicate that at this stage Moses handed over to Aaron full responsibility for the ordering of the tabernacle and the offerings. As they came out of the tabernacle the glory of the Lord was revealed, as was promised, and the fire of the Lord consumed on the altar the burnt offering, v. 24. The selection of this offering, rather than the other offerings, indicates God's pleasure in that which spoke to Him so clearly of His well-loved Son, and which reminded the Father of that Son's determination to do fully and completely all that would please Him. There are requirements to be met for God to be so manifestly among His people.

Feb. 25th

READING : **Leviticus 10. 1-20**

STRANGE FIRE

THE OPENING VERSES of this chapter present a great contrast to the closing verses of chapter 9. There, because all things had been done as the Lord commanded, the fire of the Lord fell and consumed the offering, and the people "shouted, and fell on their faces", v. 24. The tragic event of 10. 1-2 follows immediately, and mars the day of rejoicing. How could such a thing happen? We may compare the giving of the law with all its solemn accompaniments in the mount, while "a golden calf" is set up below.

Possibly these men, sons of Aaron, were inspired by a fleshly enthusiasm caused by drinking strong drink. This is suggested by the prohibition of verse 9. They snatched their censers excitedly, and acted as the Lord "commanded them not", v. 1. They took their own fire, that is, not that from the brazen altar, which had been kindled by God, ct. 16. 12, and probably their own incense, which had been forbidden, Exod. 30. 9. Also, they did not act according to divine precept.

These men had been privileged to see the glory of the Lord in the mount, Exod. 24. 1, 9-11, but alas that vision has been lost, and now self-will controls. The Lord acts in judgment, for great privilege brings great responsibility. Weigh for yourself the searching words, "I will be sanctified in them that come nigh me", v. 3.

Surely "our God is a consuming fire", Heb. 12. 29, and we see this operative in our passage. Previously we see God's fire coming out to consume the burnt offering, acceptable to Him, 9. 24, but now we see the fire coming to consume the rebel.

Aaron's response to this tragic event within his family is significant. "Aaron held his peace", v. 3. With a heart gripped with sorrow, he recognized the rightness of what God had done, and submitted to it. We recall the words of the Lord Jesus, "he that loveth son or daughter more than me is not worthy of me", Matt. 10. 37.

How necessary it was for the nation, so recently delivered from Egyptian idolatry and license, to be forcefully taught that "holiness becometh thine house", Psa. 93. 5. For the believer now there is the same insistence upon holiness; cf. 1 Pet. 1. 15-16.

Feb. 26th

READING : **Leviticus 11. 1-47**

CLEAN AND UNCLEAN

THE LAWS outlined here are mainly sanitary, and have in mind wilderness conditions. But although they may have served only a temporary purpose, it is clear that God has an interest, not only in the spiritual life of His people, but also in their social life. He is even interested in *what they eat!* The purpose of the legislation was "to make a difference between the unclean and the clean", v. 47, and surely the tenor of Scripture shows this vital matter to be of constant importance. But note that God is interested also in *what they touched.* The very carcases of the creatures listed were unclean and were to be avoided.

Truly, "I am the Lord your God . . . ye shall be holy", and "I am the Lord that bringeth you up out of the land of Egypt . . . ye shall . . . be holy", vv. 44, 45. The message is plain—our God is holy, and He has delivered us from that which is unholy. This places upon us the moral obligation to be as He is. What we feed upon, and what we touch, are formative in this connection. Believers today have been redeemed by precious blood also, and our God is holy, so "be ye holy", 1 Pet. 1. 15-19.

Do *we feed* upon that which is clean? What do we read? Of course the Word of God is pure, but what about our other reading? Is it "clean" or "unclean"? Much of today's literature is unfit for "holy ones", and cannot strengthen the spiritual life. Do *we touch* with impunity the "unclean" thing, do we get as near to it as we can, or do we shrink from it as defiling? Concerning such things the apostle says "flee", 1 Tim. 6. 11, "touch not the unclean thing", 2 Cor. 6. 17; cf. Jude 23.

The order of this legislation is significant. Following immediately the laws of the offerings, and the consecration of the priests, God brings the principles governing these to bear upon daily life. Ter Steegan has written:

    Man, earthy, of the earth, an hungered feeds
On earth's dark poison tree, . . . And as his food is he.
    And hungry souls there are that find and eat
        God's manna day by day;
    And glad they are, their life is fresh and sweet
        For as their food are they.

Feb. 27th

READING : **Leviticus 14. 1-20**

THE CLEANSING OF THE LEPER

THE LORD JESUS said to a cleansed leper "Show thyself to the priest, and offer the gift that Moses commanded", Matt. 8. 4. Our reading tells us of what would have happened when the man did this. These instructions in the event of a leper being cleansed, indicate that that happy state might be brought about, but the number of times this happened was so few that the disease was regarded as incurable, something with which only God could deal.

Note the leper was healed first, and subsequently "cleansed", vv. 3-4. This suggests just how vile and corrupting leprosy was, leading to despair and separation. It would illustrate that, "Vile and full of sin I am"—a moral leper.

On news that a leper claimed to be healed, the priest left the camp to go out to inspect him—he "came where he was", Luke 10. 33. In the ritual that followed God again points us to His Son, whose blood "cleanseth us from all sin", 1 John 1. 7. Two birds are taken. One is slain, the other released. The one released flies back to the heavens with blood of the slain one upon it, vv. 4-7. Both birds are needed to set forth the truth that Christ "was delivered for our offences, and was raised again for our justification", Rom. 4. 25. Not only was the released bird dipped in the blood of his fellow, but the blood was also sprinkled on the cleansed leper. Later the close link between this cleansing and sacrifice is emphasized. A lamb is offered as a trespass offering, v. 12. Some of the blood is taken, and put on the right ear, on the right thumb, and on the right large toe of the man, v. 14. His whole being is secured for God by blood, no longer to be used for sinful purposes. Further, oil, representing the ministry of the Holy Spirit, is taken and applied to those very same places. Where there is no blood, there can be no oil. But all those redeemed, and cleansed, have divine enabling in the use of their members for Him. The sin-offering, the burnt-offering, and the meal-offering, vv. 19-20, combine to bring out the many facets of the work of the Christ for the cleansing of a leper! If as priests we need setting apart by blood and oil for service in the sanctuary, as cleansed sinners we need the same blood and oil to set us apart in the world.

Feb. 28th

READING : **Leviticus 16. 1-34**

THE DAY OF ATONEMENT

BEFORE CONSIDERING the day itself, notice that when the year of Jubilee came, it was the day of atonement, Lev. 23. 27, 28 (*lit.* = atonements), that ushered it in, 25. 9.

We shall concentrate on the central feature of the day, the setting aside of two goats for a sin-offering, Num. 29. 11. One would not have depicted adequately Christ's work in atoning for sin. Atonement, an important topic in the book, is specially prominent in this chapter, the Hebrew word occurring 16 times (once translated "reconciling", v. 20; cf. too "mercy seat", 7 times, from the same root).

Two goats were taken, and presented to the Lord at the door of the tabernacle. Lots were then cast to decide which should die, and which should become the scapegoat—the sin-bearer. At the brazen altar one goat was killed as a sin-offering, the blood being taken into the most holy place by Aaron and sprinkled before, and on the mercy seat. On Aaron's return to the court, he placed both his hands upon the head of the scapegoat, confessing all the iniquities and transgressions of the nation over it, after which it was taken out of the camp and driven away.

What does it all mean? Isaiah tells us concerning the Saviour "he hath poured out his soul unto death (the goat at the altar) . . . and he bare the sin of many" (the scapegoat), 53. 12. This was for Israel and for us, cf. Matt. 20. 28; Acts 8. 32-35. For Israel, the effect of that day was that their sins of ignorance, and omission, were "covered" for another year, but this had to be repeated yearly. The antitype was an offering which needed no repetition, an offering which did not merely "cover", but "put away sin" completely. Not until the Christ appears "the second time without sin unto salvation", will Israel as a nation enter into the good of that salvation we already enjoy, see Heb. 9. 24-28. The psalmist, in the enjoyment of this, wrote "As far as the east is from the west, so far hath he removed our transgressions from us", 103. 12. One has written, "the tender shepherd seeks each straying sheep. He never rests till all be found. But no search finds His people's sins", Law. God's loving nature delights in being able to cleanse the sinner, and effect complete removal of the sin.

Mar. 1st

READING : Leviticus 21. 1-24

SEPARATION OF THE PRIESTS

WE HAVE THOUGHT, in a previous chapter, of the believer as a priest, a member of the "holy priesthood", and the "royal priesthood", 1 Pet. 2. 5, 9. It was God's work to set us aside into this privileged position. This thought is stressed in our chapter with the recurring words "I the Lord do sanctify" (set apart), vv. 15, 23; cf. v. 8. One purpose of this setting apart is "that ye may teach the children of Israel", 10. 11. Our present chapter emphasizes that this teaching must be supported by a life of separation — not a popular word today. The Scriptures clearly insist that many things the world can do with impunity are not for the priests, and Israel knew this, and expected an example from them. They looked for a higher standard than they had themselves, ct. Hos. 4. 9.

Defilement caused by death, and the touching of the dead, was forbidden except for certain very close relatives, Lev. 21. 1-4. It is clear that every possible step must be taken to avoid that which defiles. There is also a prohibition of practices which are associated with idolatry.

Verse 7 deals with the marriage of a priest, and certain links are forbidden. How lightly, today, some of the Lord's "priests" disregard the teaching "Be ye not unequally yoked together with unbelievers", 2 Cor. 6. 14. Such a yoke is not only grieving to the Lord Himself, but it is also the presage of disaster in the spiritual life.

Verses 16-21 are concerned with physical disqualification — in the priestly family there were those with blemishes which unfitted them for the public service. Because of these, they were forbidden approach to the altar of sacrifice, and the altar of incense, v. 23. Matthew Henry has a pertinent comment here — "We ought to infer hence how incapable those are to serve God acceptably whose minds are blemished and deformed by any reigning vice. Those are unworthy" who, though believers "are spiritually blind and lame and crooked, whose sins render them scandalous and deformed". But note they are not excluded from the priestly family because of the defect, v. 22. They may be unfit to serve, and to take part in public service, but the relationship remains, and they are still entitled to share in the sacrificial feasts. This is grace.

Mar. 2nd

READING : **Leviticus 23. 1-44**

THE FEASTS OF THE LORD

ALL THE FEASTS of this chapter, except the day of atonement, were to be joyous: on that occasion "ye shall afflict your souls", as the removal of their sin was being emphasised, v. 27. All the feasts pointed forward. They are:

1. *Passover,* v. 5. It was a constant reminder of redemption; Israel had been brought out of bondage. Here, it is to Christ our Passover, who was to be sacrificed for us, we are pointed. It is with the Lamb all commences. Following immediately was

2. *Unleavened bread,* vv. 6-8. All leaven was "put away" from the house for seven days. Deliverance from bondage is to issue in holiness. Today, God's people are to put away the leaven of evil from their lives, 1 Cor. 5. 7-8. The demand is for a holy life in keeping with the sacrifice of Christ.

3. *Firstfruits,* vv. 9-14. This could only be observed in the land. Bringing the first fruits spoke of gratitude, and a realization that all belonged to God. It was the guarantee that later there would be the full reaping. The resurrection of Christ is before us, "the firstfruits of them that are asleep", 1 Cor. 15. 20, 23 R.V.; cf. John 14. 19. He will soon raise the remainder.

4. *Weeks,* vv. 15-22. This was held on the fiftieth day after firstfruits, in Greek known as Pentecost, see Acts 2. 1 R.V. marg. Two leavened wave-loaves were offered. It was at Pentecost that the Church was born, the Spirit was poured forth, and Jew and Gentile were brought together in one body.

5. *Trumpets,* vv. 23-25. At the sound of trumpets the people came together, and offered special sacrifices. We listen for the trumpet sound gathering the church when the Lord returns, "and so shall we ever be with the Lord", 1 Thess. 4. 17. When the Son of Man later returns in glory Israel will be gathered, "with a great sound of a trumpet", Matt. 24. 31.

6. *Atonement,* vv. 26-32. Here Israel mourned for her sins, as they are to do uniquely when "they look upon me whom they pierced", Zech. 12. 10. But this leads to joy in the

7. Feast of *Tabernacles,* vv. 33-36, 39-43. Joy at last replaces all sorrow. The Lord reigns over the whole earth, Zech. 14. 16. All these feasts speak of Christ, and God's programme through Him.

Mar. 3rd

READING : **Leviticus 24. 1-23**

OIL, BREAD, BLASPHEMY

CONCERNING the seven-branched lampstand Thomas Newberry writes, "The golden lampstand, with its seven lamps and centre shaft, is the type of ministry according to God in the power of the Holy Ghost, in its various branches of testimony, having Christ for its centre, source and subject". In our chapter we see that this testimony is to be maintained by an unremitting supply of oil, an emblem of the Holy Spirit's ministry, vv.1-4. The light from the branches of the lampstand fell on the lampstand itself, "that they may give light over against it (Heb. the face of it)", Exod. 25. 37. It is God's design, in our Spirit inspired testimony, to manifest the glory of Christ; cf. Rev. 1. 12-13. John 16.14-15 highlights another point. The ministry of the Holy Spirit will focus on the Lord Himself. It is as we are thus helped by the Spirit, seeing the glory of God in the face of Jesus Christ, that we become more like Him too, 2 Cor. 3. 18; 4. 6. Verse 3 speaks of the light burning continually. It was the only light in a place which would otherwise be in complete darkness.

Also standing in the holy place was the table of showbread. As the light was to shine continually, so the showbread was to be on the table continually, Lev. 24. 8; Exod. 25. 30. The bread speaks to us of Christ Who not only gave His life for us, but also gives His life to us. We feed on Him. The twelve loaves representing the tribes, speak of what God's people are to Him, as seen in Christ. It is necessary that our feeding upon Him be not allowed to become "stale", for there was a renewal of the loaves every sabbath day, v. 8. For God, as for His saints, there is food, rest, fellowship, and satisfaction in Christ.

Outside the holy place, we are introduced to the reality of sin, even among God's people, vv. 10-23. In Exodus 20 the penalty for blasphemy was not stated, only that the person involved would not be "guiltless". Now a decision must be given, and God decrees death. Remember, blasphemy was treason, as it was speaking against their sovereign. In this day of grace, speaking against the Lord is not dealt with immediately, but the guilt is there. The principle of "an eye for an eye" is then enunciated, and we see strict justice being commanded. The penalty must not be greater than the offence.

Mar. 4th
READING : Leviticus 25. 1-24

REST AND LIBERTY

GOD is no hard taskmaster. Our chapter shows that He has more consideration for His people than we have one for another.

Verses 2-7 tell of *the sabbatic year,* every seventh year being set aside for rest, v. 4. The land was to be left fallow, and no agricultural operations were to be carried out. In Exodus 20. 10 a weekly sabbath was appointed for men and animals; now during this seventh year the land is included. The very natural question "What shall we eat the seventh year?", v. 20, is answered by God's bountiful provision in the sixth year, when the ground brought forth sufficient to cover three years, v. 21. This reminds us of a similar provision in relation to the supply of manna, Exod. 16. 22. Law writes "Faith has the richest board. It works when God says work. It rests when God says rest, and in obedience thrives". In practice, the sabbatic year was largely ignored by the people, and this was one reason for the 70 years of captivity, 2 Chron. 36. 21. The year of rest was to be used in gaining a greater knowledge of God's law, Deut. 31. 10-13—did this fall into disuse too?

The year of jubilee, vv. 8-24, followed seven successive sabbatic years. It was introduced by the day of atonement, v. 9, which involved mourning for sin, and the putting away of the sins by atonement. A proclamation of "liberty" was made, v.10, and the process of buying and selling property was related to the nearness to the trumpet sound on the day of atonement, v. 16. Does the expectation of the trumpet affect us in our home and business ventures?, 1 Thess. 4. 16. As, too, the presence of the Lord Jesus inaugurated a veritable year of liberty, Luke 4. 18, 19, so, at His second coming in glory, the earth will celebrate its jubilee.

Consideration of our chapter impresses upon us the following thoughts: (i) "The earth is the Lord's", Psa. 24. 1. He has not given it wholly into the hands of men. (ii) God is able to provide. For the year of jubilee followed a sabbatic year, and for two years in succession no agricultural pursuits would be followed. His bounty is proved by the obedient. (iii) The jubilee relaxed the ties of bondage, and "If the Son therefore shall make you free, ye shall be free indeed", John 8. 36.

Mar. 5th

READING : Leviticus 26. 1-13, 27-46

GOD'S FAITHFULNESS

GOD LOVES to bless. But His faithfulness demands that, where occasion necessitates it, He must chasten. To Israel the word comes "If ye walk in my statutes, and keep my commandments, and do them; then . . . ", v. 3. Consequent upon such obedience, there is a sixfold divine promise, "I will", vv. 4-12. "I will give you rain", v. 4; "I will give peace", v. 6; "I will rid evil beasts out of the land", v. 6; "I will have respect unto you", v. 9; "I will set my tabernacle among you", v. 11; "I will walk among you", v. 12. These promises were to be fulfilled literally for Israel, but we must not forget the spiritual application that we can enjoy today. For "He that spared not his own Son, but delivered him up for us all, how shall he not with him also freely give us all things?", Rom. 8. 32. The "all things" include blessing rained from heaven, His peace, His control of circumstances, His loving-kindness towards us, His presence, and His companionship. Israel, and we also, can rely on God's "I wills"; they are guaranteed by His "I am", v. 13.

God speaks of blessing first, then moves on to chastisement, when that is needed. "Here God adjoins paternal counsels to a sovereign's command. He shows what blessings crown obedient paths—what miseries beset the rebel way", Law. His very chastisement is a plain indication that He is concerned about His people's welfare, and that He must deal with that which is proving a hindrance to them, and leads to a rupture of communion. If He withheld chastisement we might well ask the question, "Doesn't He care?".

Pay special attention to verses 40-46. God knew that all the chastisement spoken of in the previous verses would prove to be necessary, and that His people would be scattered among the nations. But He had made promises to Jacob, Isaac and Abraham. The unusual order here, Jacob appearing first, emphasizes God's grace, as does the repeated "my covenant", v. 42. How could He break His word? How gracious, too, that, after referring to their disobedience, and their dispersion, He says "Yet for all that . . . I will not cast them away, neither will I abhor them", v. 44. He also knew the nation would turn: "And they shall confess", v. 40 R.V. This God is our God, and He has said, "they shall never perish", John 10. 28.

Mar. 6th

READING : **Leviticus 27. 1-34**

PROMISES

HERE we are concerned with a requirement that has no parallel in the New Testament. It is legislation to define the conditions under which persons and property could be dedicated to Divine service. Verses 2 to 8 speak of the dedication of persons and our minds go to Jephthah's vow, which involved his daughter, Jud. 11. 30-31, and Hannah's vow concerning Samuel her son, 1 Sam. 1. 11. Redemption of an animal, vv. 9-13, and of one's house, vv. 14-15, and even of one's land, vv. 16-25, are each separately treated. These are examples only of what might be dedicated to the Lord, but it is clear from these examples that the devotion to the Lord of the person himself, or of his personal property, was a token of gratitude.

It was a solemn matter, and although it was no sin to vow or not to vow, once made a vow was as binding as an oath, Deut. 23. 21. There was to be no change of mind or duplicity, v. 10. The Lord Jesus condemned the man who professed to have dedicated his money to the Lord so that he should be relieved of his responsibility to his parents, Mark 7. 11. This standard could well be considered in these days of loose speech. God wants us to mean what we say, Matt. 5. 37.

Vows could be discharged by giving the cash value of what had been dedicated, so individuals were assessed according to their age and sex. All those who are the Lord's are precious to Him, but He nonetheless recognized distinctions among them. These affect male and female, e.g. vv. 3, 4, and various phases of spiritual strength and maturity, vv. 3, 5, 6, 7. There is a Divine value set upon the youngest in the faith, and upon the eldest too. The silver of redemption, vv. 3-6, and the shekel of the sanctuary, vv. 3, 25, were alone acceptable. Only a priest could rightly assess the worth of the poorest saint. Nearness to God develops a truly Divine evaluation of His own.

Our chapter insists that all is to be done "unto the Lord", whether involving our persons, v. 2, animals, vv. 9-11, houses, v. 14, or land, vv. 16, 21-23. Assessment of the land was according to sowing, for the more that is sown of the good seed of the gospel and the Word of God, even of deeds of kindness, the greater the harvest. All that we are and have should be weighed in the light of the coming of the Lord, vv. 17-18.

Introducing Numbers

Title. This fourth book of the Pentateuch derives its name "Numbers" from the Septuagint Version. It was so called owing to the numbering of the people in the Sinai wilderness, chs. 1-4, and again 38 years later on the plains of Moab, ch. 26.

Writer. "Moses wrote their goings out", 33. 2.

Connections. The book is not isolated from other books. Exodus describes the *way out* of Egypt, and the foundational truth of redemption. Leviticus tells of the *way in* to God, detailing the principles of worship. Numbers relates the *way through* the wilderness, with lessons for our conduct in this world.

In Leviticus, the *priests* are prominent. In Numbers, the *Levites,* and later the *people,* are foremost.

Analysis. W. G. Scroggie sees two broad divisions:

1. *The Encampment at Sinai,* 1. 1 to 10. 10. There, the people were organized and prepared for the journey.

2. *The March to the Plains of Moab,* 10. 11 to 36. 13. Upon reaching Kadesh, unbelief halts the journey. After years of wandering, the march is resumed, but not without complaints.

Spiritual Instruction. Referring to several experiences of the Israelites in Exodus and Numbers, Paul says, "all these things happened unto them for ensamples (or, types, marg.); and they are written for our admonition". We need to study the book.

As Leviticus 1. 1 opens with the phrase "out of the tabernacle", so Numbers 1. 1 does with the words "in the wilderness". From "out of the tabernacle", where believers worship the Lord on the first day of the week, we go forth "into the wilderness" to serve the Lord. As priests, we worship in the sanctuary, and as Levites we work in the world bearing witness to the Christ.

Essentially, Numbers records the many vicissitudes of the people's wilderness life, which illustrate the numerous trials that believers encounter in the world. Primarily, it is not a Book of conflict with enemies from *without,* as Joshua is, but it relates attacks from enemies *within,* such as murmuring, unbelief, and insubordination, during our sojourn in the world. The grace of God does not fail, and our resources are found in Christ.

Mar. 7th

READING : **Numbers 3. 5-39**

THE LEVITES

THE LEVITES, whom the Lord had claimed for Himself, 3. 12, camped, not with the twelve tribes, but separated, and around the tabernacle, vv. 23, 29, 35. Spiritual instruction is to be obtained from them.

The Levites were, of course, the progeny of "Levi", whose name means "joined". The first requirement for us is to be "joined unto the Lord", 1 Cor. 6. 17, through the regenerative work of the Holy Spirit. The meanings of the names of Levi's three sons, and their sons, are also significant.

The *course* of a believer's life is suggested in Gershon, the eldest of Levi's sons, and his two sons. "Gershon", Num. 3. 17, means "exile", and we, as believers, should be as exiles, that is, separated from the world; cf. 1 Pet. 1. 1; 2. 11-12. Gershon's elder son was "Libni", v. 18, meaning "white", which is emblematic of the purity of a separated people. The younger son, "Shimei", which means "my report", hints at the time when every one of us shall give account of himself at the judgment seat of Christ, Rom. 14. 10-12; 2 Cor. 5. 10.

The *character* of an assembly is apparent in Kohath, and his sons. Kohath, meaning "assembly", the second of Levi's three sons, Num. 3. 17, reminds us of the local assembly. The eldest of Kohath's four sons was "Amram", v. 19, which means "people of the exalted One", indicating that believers, both individually and collectively in an assembly, should acknowledge the Lordship of Christ. "Izehar", his second son, means "anointing of the Holy Spirit", something essential for serving the Lord. The meaning of "Hebron", his third son, is "union", suggestive of union with Christ and true assembly unity. The fourth son's name was "Uzziel", "the power of God", upon which we are dependent in the Lord's work.

A warning regarding *concord* between one believer and another is suggested in Merari, Levi's youngest son, and his sons. "Merari" means "bitter", and he had two sons, called "Mahli" and "Mushi", v. 20, meaning "sick" and "yielding" respectively. Bitterness in spirit towards a fellow-believer or even the Lord leads to spiritual sickness, but healing comes from submission to the Lord, Eph. 4. 31, 32. A Christ-like attitude toward one another promotes harmony, Phil. 2. 2-5.

Mar. 8th

READING : **Numbers 4. 1-33**

THE LEVITES' WORK

THE LEVITES were involved solely with the tabernacle, both in the camp and during transit. Preparation for the latter aspect of their work is described in today's reading. It was a God-given work, and each task was settled for them with Divine precision, so that every man knew his work, and did it. The same principle should apply to us.

When movement of the camp was signalled, the Kohathites' work was to cover the furniture of the tabernacle, 4. 1-15. First, the ark was covered with the veil, next with badgers' skins and then with a cloth wholly of blue, vv. 5, 6. These coverings speak of the *Person of Christ* in His Manhood and humiliation, Heb. 10. 20; Phil. 2. 5-8, whilst the "blue" cloth, which alone could be seen, was a constant reminder that He was "the Lord *from* heaven", 1 Cor. 15. 47.

The table of shewbread, the lampstand of the light, and the golden altar were next covered, vv. 7-12, and only coverings of badgers' skins, normally used for footwear, Ezek. 16. 10, were visible. These articles symbolize *the ministry of Christ*, needed throughout the wilderness walk.

The altar, having had the ashes removed, was covered with a cloth of purple, and a covering of badger skins, Num. 4. 13, 14. This directs us to *the work of Christ*. If the outer badger skin covering is emblematic of the depth of His humiliation, then "purple", a colour of dignity amongst royalty, Jud. 8. 26; Esth. 8. 15, tells how for the crucified Lord of glory, 1 Cor. 2. 8, there was glory to follow, 1 Pet. 1. 11.

The laver, not mentioned, was omitted from the Kohathites' burden. The furniture symbolized God revealed in Christ. The laver catered for the purification of priests as they served.

The Gershonites were responsible for the curtains and the covering of badger skins besides the hangings of the court, 4. 24-26.

The charge of the Merarites was the boards, for the walls of the tabernacle, and the pillars of the court, 4. 29-32.

With their precious burdens, the Levites were ready to go forth into the wilderness. In the power of sanctuary worship on the Lord's day, we should go forth to serve the Lord. First *worship*, then *work*, is the Divine order, Matt. 4. 10.

Mar. 9th

READING : Numbers 8. 5-26

THE LEVITES' CONSECRATION

AFTER the tribal princes had brought their offerings on twelve successive days at the setting up of the tabernacle and Aaron had lit the lampstand, 7. 1 to 8. 4, the Levites were set apart and consecrated for the service of the sanctuary. There were three parts to the ceremony.

Their *Purification*, vv. 5-7. For this, the divine command was "Sprinkle water of purifying upon them", v. 7; cf. Exod. 30. 19, 20, which foreshadows "the washing of regeneration", Tit. 3. 5. Next, they were to "shave all their flesh" (i.e. not part of, but their whole body was shaved), indicating that that which is of nature must be removed, and that "our old man is crucified with" Christ, Rom. 6. 6. Then they were to "wash their clothes", for even our habits must be purified by, and be in accordance with, the Word of God.

Their *Presentation*, vv. 8-14, was associated with the offering of "a young bullock, and its meal offering", and "another young bullock . . . for a sin offering", v. 8 R.V., both of which speak of Christ's perfect sacrifice.

At the tabernacle, where all the assembled Israelites put their hands upon the Levites, Aaron offered them as an offering before the Lord "that they may execute the service of the Lord", v. 11. *Figuratively*, the Levites were presented as "a living sacrifice", but we should *actually* present ourselves as such to the Lord for His service, Rom. 12. 1.

After the Levites had put their hands upon the heads of the two bullocks, which were offered to make atonement for them, Moses "set the Levites before Aaron, and before his sons . . . for an offering unto the Lord", and so they were dedicated "to do the service of the tabernacle, vv. 12-15, but they were precluded from entering the tabernacle itself, 18. 2-7.

Their *Possession*, vv. 15-19. "For they are wholly given unto me . . . instead of the firstborn", the Lord said, v. 16. Initially, the firstborn were claimed by the Lord for judgment in Egypt, Exod. 11. 4-7, but later the Levites took their place in Divine service; cf. Num. 3. 12, 13, 40-51.

The Levites belonged to the Lord, but they were given back to the priests to serve. We, too, are not our own but the Lord's, 1 Cor. 6. 19, 20, and we should serve our Great High Priest.

Mar. 10th
READING : Numbers 10. 11-36

THE MARCH FORWARD

UP TO 10. 10, the Levites are prominent, foreshadowing the Lord's servants at *work*. From 10. 11 to 36. 13 the subject is Israel on the march, illustrative of the *walk* of believers.

The "cloud was taken up from off the tabernacle", 10. 11, the signal for the priests to blow "an alarm" on the two silver trumpets. Then each of the four camps of the encampment were to move forward in turn, 10. 2, 6.

For the march, the eastern camp of Judah was first, 10. 14-16, followed by the Gershonites with the Merarites "bearing the tabernacle" (i.e. the structure), 10. 17, on six wagons drawn by twelve oxen, which were given by the princes of Israel, 7. 1-8. The southern camp of Reuben was next, 10. 18-20, followed by the Kohathites "bearing the sanctuary" (i.e. the furniture), 10. 21, "upon their shoulders", 7. 9, for their burden was sacred. The western camp of Ephraim was third in position, 10. 22-24, and the northern camp of Dan, 10. 25-28, formed the rearguard, v. 25.

When the camp of Judah had taken "the first place", then each of the remaining three camps "set forward" at the sound of the silver trumpets, 10. 18, 22, 25. Before we "go forward", we should wait upon the Lord, and be led by Him.

Before leaving Sinai, Moses unwisely said to Hobab, his Midianite brother-in-law, "be to us instead of eyes", 10. 29-32. He turned to a son of the wilderness for guidance into the unknown. How easy it is to seek the help of man and forget that our resource is in the Lord!

The ark was not in the middle of the human column on the march, but "went before them", 10. 33, to lead them. Alluding to this scene, the Psalmist saw the ark symbolizing the "Shepherd of Israel", who dwelt "between the cherubim", leading "Joseph", figurative of the nation, "like a flock" through the wilderness with others following behind, Psa. 80. 1, 2; cf. Gen. 49. 24; Num. 10. 22-24. For us, Christ, as the good Shepherd, is the all-sufficient Leader.

With the experience of Sinai *behind* them, the ark going *before* them, and "the cloud . . . *upon* them", 10. 34; cf. Psa. 105. 39, they went forth with the ever-abiding presence of God, after Moses had prayed, 10. 35.

Mar. 11th

READING : **Numbers 11. 1-9**

THE PEOPLE'S COMPLAINT

THE ALL-WISE God, organizing and providing for His people in the wilderness, pervades the first ten chapters, but man and his miserable ways are manifested from chapter 11 onwards. This chapter opens with the first of the people's four murmurings from Sinai to Moab.

In the sun-scorched and sterile desert, the Lord fed His people miraculously every day with manna, said to be "the corn of heaven", Psa. 78. 24. Weeping, the people complained and said, "Who shall give us flesh to eat?", recalling the fish and six different vegetables that they ate in Egypt, vv. 4, 5. Not mentioning the lashes of the task-masters, and the burden of brick-making, they craved for Egypt's food. This attitude illustrates unsanctified human nature, with its worldly tastes and tendencies. With us, when the warmth of our first love wanes, and the freshness of Divine life decreases, we hanker for the fleshly things of the past.

Still complaining, the people said, "there is nothing at all, beside this manna", v. 6. They had become weary of the Lord's wonderful provision. How terrible! The manna is a type of Christ, John 6. 31-59, and so, figuratively, they spoke against Christ. It is possible for worldly pleasures and appetites to take the place of Christ in our lives and then we complain. When this occurs, Christ ceases to be the satisfying and precious portion for the soul, and as the Israelites complained openly "our soul is dried away", v. 6, so is our experience inwardly, owing to spiritual starvation. For nourishing the inner man, the fish and fruit of Egypt are no substitute for "the corn of heaven".

The reason for the people's failure was probably "the mixt multitude that was among them", v. 4. This mixed multitude, who joined the Israelites at the Exodus, Exod. 12. 38, would have been not a nondescript rabble, but, more likely, Egyptians inter-married with Hebrews. Here in the wilderness they "fell a lusting", v. 4, causing discontent, which resulted in disaster for the people. As a principle, mixture, which God abhors, causes spiritual weakness. On the other hand, separation from a mixed multitude is a source of strength, as discovered centuries later by Israel, Neh. 13. 3.

Mar. 12th

READING : **Numbers 11. 10-35**

MOSES' RESPONSIBILITY SHARED

THE SEQUEL to the people's murmuring, vv. 1-9, was Moses' displeasure of it.

As the people failed, so Moses faltered. This is detected in Moses' words addressed to the Lord "wherefore . . . layest (Thou) the burden of all this people upon me?", v. 11. He felt the immense burden of leading over two million people. Sometimes, you and I may feel "the burden and heat of the day", but the Psalmist says, "Cast thy burden upon the Lord, and he shall sustain thee", Matt. 20. 12; Psa. 55. 22.

Displaying their dissatisfaction with the manna, the people wept and said, "Give us flesh, that we may eat". So, in his complaint to the Lord, Moses said, "Whence should I have flesh to give unto all this people?", Num. 11. 13. In a barren desert, Moses was not able to supply food for that vast company for one single day, but the Lord did so every day for forty years! Even in an affluent society, it is possible to be discontented with our lot. The lesson to be learned is "in whatsoever state I am, therewith to be content", Phil. 4. 11, and "godliness with contentment is great gain", 1 Tim. 6. 6.

Giving expression to human frailty, as we all do sometimes, Moses said: "I am not able to bear all this people alone", Num. 11. 14; cf. Deut. 1. 9, 10. The burden was too heavy for human shoulders. Graciously, the Lord said to Moses, "Gather unto me seventy men of the elders of Israel . . . and they shall bear the burden of the people with thee . . .", vv. 16, 17; cf. Deut. 1. 13. From this juncture onwards, the responsibility of leading the people was to be shared with seventy elders, who would be fitted for the task because the Lord would "take of the spirit" which was upon Moses and would "put it upon them".

The principle set forth is collective responsibility, and each Israelitish elder was divinely fitted for the work. This is equally applicable to elders of an assembly. The Lord's words to Moses were "bear it not thyself alone", v. 17, and they apply to any man who attempts to do likewise in the Lord's work. The Scriptural pattern for an assembly is not one elder, but always a plurality of elders, and the elders share the responsibility of shepherding an assembly, Acts 14. 23 R.V.

Mar. 13th

READING : **Numbers 13. 1-33**

THE SPIES' REPORT

ENCAMPED in the wilderness of Paran, 12. 16; cf. 10. 12, relatively near the border of Canaan, the Israelites had reached a decisive stage in their wilderness journeyings. It might appear the Lord commanded them to "search the land", 13. 1, 2, but they had already said, *"We* will send men before us . . . (to) search us out the land", Deut. 1. 22. The Lord Himself already "had espied (it) for them", Ezek. 20. 6. This search was not of God but of the will of man, and human determination ends in disaster.

Twelve tribal heads were commissioned to spy out the land, and they spied "the south . . . unto Hebron", v. 22.

From the valley of Eshcol in the vicinity of Hebron, the spies carried back one cluster of luscious grapes on a pole, borne by two, besides pomegranates and figs, v. 23. These three different fruits, evidence of Canaan's fertility, were emblematic of Christ. Grapes, fruit of the vine, mentioned first, direct our thoughts to "the true vine", John 15. 1, *Christ Himself,* and particularly His pre-eminence, Col. 1. 18. Pomegranates, associated with both the tabernacle and the temple, Exod. 28. 33; 2 Chron. 4. 12, 13, are connected with *worship*. Figs, and their sweetness, remind us of Christ as our sweet *sustenance*, cf. Song 2.2, as we search the Scriptures. These fruits were found in the locality of "Hebron", meaning "communion", and fellowship with the Lord is essential for partaking of Eshcol's Divine fruit.

Upon their return to the camp after forty days, v. 25, the spies reported that the land was good, but the people and their cities were strong, vv. 27, 28. This caused disquiet but the spy Caleb ("wholehearted") stilled the people saying, "Let us go up . . . and possess it; for we are *well able"*, v. 30. He displayed the *confidence of faith* in God.

The other spies said, "We be *not able* . . .", expressing their lack of faith, "for they are stronger than we", v. 31,—the *contention of unbelief,* which leaves out God.

These unbelieving spies then spoke among the people, saying, " we *saw* the giants . . . and we were . . . as grasshoppers . . .", v. 33,—the *conclusion of sight*. Let us beware, and "walk by faith, not by sight", 2 Cor. 5. 7.

Mar. 14th

READING : **Numbers 14. 1-45**

THE PEOPLE'S REBELLION

UPON HEARING the spies' report of unbelief, it is evident that the people were governed, not by faith, but by dark and depressing unbelief. They broke out into irrepressible lamentation, "Would God that we died in . . . Egypt! or . . . in this wilderness!", v. 2. They clamoured against the Lord Himself, v. 3, and determined amongst themselves to "make a captain, and . . . return into Egypt", v. 4. Tragically, they first despised their redemption from Egypt, and then displayed their wilful unbelief. To no avail, Joshua and Caleb interposed, vv. 6-9. As unbelief is unable to see reason, the people bade stone the two faithful spies, but the Lord in His glory broke forth.

The Lord was provoked to the point of smiting and disinheriting this rebellious people, vv. 11, 12, and Moses mediated for the people, prefiguring our great Mediator, vv. 13-19. In his plea, Moses was zealous for the Lord's honour, saying that if all these people were killed, "then the nations . . . will speak, saying, . . . the Lord was *not able* . . .", vv. 15, 16; ct. 13. 30, 31.

Having been tempted beyond the limit of His forbearance, the Lord told Moses that this rebellious generation would perish in the wilderness, 14. 20-25, except Caleb who "hath followed fully", v. 24. This rebellion foreshadows that one after the Lord's return for the Church, when the rebellious and apostate among the Jews will perish, but the godly remnant, having followed the Lord fully, as the two faithful spies did, will enter into millennial bliss; cf. Isa. 62. 4-5.

This apostate generation, aged 20 years and over at the first census, 1. 45, 46, were to die. Their children, too, would be not pilgrims, but wanderers in the wilderness for forty years—a year of wandering for each day of a fruitless search, vv. 26-35. Those ten faithless spies perished in a plague.

Incensed by the severe sentence from the Lord, and against Moses' warning, the people ascended presumptuously a hill to enter the promised land, but many fell by the sword of the Amalekites and Canaanites, vv. 39-45.

The inspired comment is, "they could not enter in because of unbelief", Heb. 3. 19. Yes, unbelief can prevent us from entering in and possessing now our heavenly portion.

Mar. 15th

READING : **Numbers 16. 1-40**

KORAH'S REBELLION

KORAH, the leader of a great conspiracy, was a Levite, and of the family of Kohath, who were responsible for the most holy things of the tabernacle, v. 1; 4. 4-15. He took three Reubenites, together with 250 princes, to start a revolt, vv. 1, 2. Significantly, "Kohath", to whose family Korah belonged, means "assembly", and "Korah" seemed to be dead in spirit, whilst his three Reubenite associates, descendants of the rejected firstborn, were malcontents. Sadly, sometimes in assembly life today, some carnally-minded members are disloyal, as Korah was, and others are discontented as the Reubenites were, both of whom are disruptive.

Having gathered themselves together "against Moses and against Aaron", these rebels said, "Ye take too much upon you", v. 3, although the Lord had called and fitted these two leaders, both of whom pre-figure Christ as Lord and Priest respectively. Pertinently, Moses asked them, as Levites, "seemeth it but a small thing unto you . . . to do the service of the tabernacle . . .?" Moses continued, "and seek ye the priesthood also?", vv. 8-10. The aim of Korah and his colleagues was not to serve in the tabernacle, as the Lord had appointed, but they sought the priestly position.

Acting upon Moses' instructions, these rebels stood before their tents, and "the earth opened her mouth" and these rebellious men "went down alive into the pit (*sheol*, R.V. marg.)", vv. 31-34. The children of Korah were excluded, 26. 11. The tragedy of Korah and the chief transgressors, who, without experiencing corporeal death, went down alive into *sheol*, has a prophetic significance. When Christ comes again in regal power, "the beast and the false prophet" will be "cast alive into a lake of fire", Rev. 19. 20.

Although we may tend to pay little attention to Korah and his conspiracy, Jude includes him with two other sinful characters, v. 11, not in chronological order, to illustrate and warn against spiritual declension at the end of the age: Cain acted in *self-will*, Balaam sought *self-enrichment*, and Korah aimed at *self-exaltation*. Besides the prophetic warning, there is also a practical one from Korah for us: do not aspire to do work that the Lord has not allocated to you!

Mar. 16th

READING : **Numbers 16. 41 to 17. 13**

AARON'S ROD THAT BUDDED

ALTHOUGH the Israelites had witnessed the calamitous loss of Korah and his company, they murmured against Moses and Aaron, saying falsely "Ye have killed the people of the Lord".

The people were gathered "against Moses and Aaron", v. 42, as Korah and his conspirators were, v. 3. In His wrath, the Lord was ready to "consume them as in a moment", v. 45, even as He was in the case of Korah and his company, v. 21, but this time pestilence broke out among the people. Therefore, Moses told Aaron to take a censer filled with fire from off the altar and to put incense upon it for making "an atonement for the people", and so "the plague was stayed", but 14,700 died, vv. 46-49. Allegiance to the priesthood was being cast off in the rebellion of Korah and his company, as it was likewise in the uprising of the people, only two days later. The authority and position of the priesthood had to be established again.

To vindicate the priesthood, 17. 1-7, the Lord told Moses to take twelve rods from the tribal heads, who wrote their names upon them; Aaron's name was upon the rod of Levi. The rods were to be laid in the tabernacle before the ark of the testimony. Then the rod of the man whom the Lord chose would blossom.

The next day, which was the fourth day after Korah's conspiracy, Moses went into the tabernacle, and he found that the rod of Aaron had budded, blossomed, and yielded almonds, 17. 8. There was not a single bud or blossom on the other rods! Only Aaron's rod blossomed, and bore fruit, indicating that Aaron's appointment to priesthood was not by man or of himself, but it was of God. His appointment to priesthood was vindicated clearly by the Lord, Heb. 5. 4.

The almond, said to be the first tree of the year to bud and blossom, is the herald of new life. Therefore, it is emblematic of resurrection, and particularly, in this instance, of the resurrection of Christ. Not in the wilderness was Aaron's rod placed to blossom but it was in the tabernacle that it blossomed. Not in the wilderness of this world does the Risen Lord exercise His priestly ministry but in "the true tabernacle, which the Lord pitched, and not man", even in "heaven itself " where He is our great High Priest, Heb. 8. 2; 9. 24.

Mar. 17th

READING : Numbers 20. 1-22

OPPOSITION FROM THE EDOMITES

WITH "the first month", the fortieth year since the Exodus dawned, v. 1, and the years of wanderings had come to an end.

From Kadesh a shorter route via Edom would have brought the new generation of Israelites into Canaan. To go round Edom, which extended from near the Gulf of Aqabah to the Dead Sea, meant a very much longer journey. Aware of the shorter route, Moses sent messengers from Kadesh to the king of Edom, requesting royal permission for his "brother Israel" to pass through his country. In spite of an assurance that the people would keep to the king's highway, vv. 14-17, the king replied "Thou shalt not pass through me", v. 18 R.V. In answer to a further plea from Moses, this churlish king still refused, v. 20. The inspired writer then adds, "Thus *Edom refused* to give Israel passage through his border: wherefore *Israel turned away* from him", v. 21. There is a two-fold spiritual significance for us.

Edom's refusal. As the Edomites were descendants from Esau, and the Israelites from his brother Jacob, there was the tie of nature between them. Co-operation on a brotherly basis was expected, but it was rejected. As the Hebrew word for "Edom" is akin to that for "Adam", Israel's brother according to the flesh symbolizes our unregenerate nature within us, termed "our old man", Rom. 6. 6. "Israel", meaning "God rules", is figurative of our regenerate nature, said to be "the new man", Col. 3. 10; Eph. 4. 24. *"Edom refused* to give Israel passage through his border", Num. 20. 21, displaying enmity toward his "brother Israel", v. 14. Enmity cannot be changed into friendship, as Moses had hoped. The same principle applies spiritually: our two natures, the old and the new, are incompatible, as Edom and Israel were. So "the flesh lusteth against the Spirit", Gal. 5. 17.

Israel's reaction: Faced with this opposition, Israel did not resort to arms to force a passage through Edom, but *"Israel turned away* from him", v. 21. With us, the flesh is not fought, because "our old man", having been crucified with Christ, is reckoned dead, Rom. 6. 6, 11, and "Christ liveth in me", Gal. 2. 20. So we should "Flee also youthful lusts", and "walk in the Spirit", 2 Tim. 2. 22; Gal. 5. 16.

Mar. 18th

READING : **Numbers 22. 41 to 24. 25**

BALAAM'S PROPHETIC "PARABLES"

HAVING reached their journey's end, Israel "pitched in the plains of Moab", 22. 1. Fearful of this triumphant people encamped near his country's boundary, Balak, the king of the Moabites, sent for Balaam of Midian to curse them, 22. 2-11. For the purpose, Balak took Balaam to three viewpoints.

Taken "up into the high places of Baal", 22. 41, Balaam gave his *first "parable"*, 23. 7-10. Refusing to "curse, whom God hath not cursed", he said "the people shall dwell alone, and shall not be reckoned among the nations". Separation marks out Israel, as it does the church, John 17. 14.

Complaining that he saw only "the fourth part" of the camp, Balak took him to "the top of Pisgah", 23. 14, for a broader view, and demanded a curse to be uttered. In his *second "parable"*, 23. 18-24, Balaam said, "He (i.e., God) hath not beheld iniquity in Jacob". With transgression forgiven, and sin covered, Israel is seen justified; cf. Psa. 32. 1; Rom. 4. 6-8.

The enraged Balak took the unwilling prophet "unto the top of Peor", 23. 28, to deliver his *third "parable"*, 24. 3-9. Balaam said, "How goodly are thy tents, O Jacob", as he saw the orderly arrangement of the twelve tribes encamped. He predicted Israel's "king" to be higher than the highest, "and his kingdom shall be exalted". With all enemies subdued, Israel will be secure "as a great lion: who shall stir him up?".

Hearing this third "parable", Balak was filled with fury, and bid Balaam to flee for his life, 24. 10, 11. Before departing, Balaam gave his *fourth "parable"*, 24. 15-24, which related to "the latter days", v. 14. He prophesied, "there shall come a Star out of Jacob, and a Sceptre shall rise out of Israel". As a "Star", Christ will come humbly from out of an unbelieving people, "Jacob". In contrast, not identified as a mighty monarch, but personified as "a Sceptre", symbolizing imperial authority, He will yet rise out of a regenerate "Israel", whose enemies He will subdue, and He will reign supreme.

Supernaturally, Balaam was restrained from cursing Israel. Wonderfully, he was constrained to bless Israel, whom the Lord has set apart from among the nations to be justified in a coming day. They are destined for the pinnacle of power in association with their Messiah-King.

Introducing Deuteronomy

THE BOOK of Deuteronomy, the fifth book of Moses, completes the TORAH, the first section of the Jewish Scriptures. It is a vital re-statement and amplification of the statutes and ordinances given to Moses. The laws presented are not only factual injunctions; they are also an appeal to the conscience of the hearer. Moses, as he utters his last message, longs to gain his nation's heart.

We notice five main features of the book:

1. The declaration of the *supremacy of God*, 4. 39; 5. 6; 6. 4-5. These and other references show that He is not one God among the many, but the Only God. Monotheism is stamped upon all the laws, giving them unique authority.

2. The affirmation of the *love of God* for His people, 7. 7-8; 10. 15; 23. 5. God's sovereign choice of the nation arises out of unmerited, often unrequited love. He loved the fathers, and His stedfast love bore with the folly and failure of His people.

3. The terms of the *covenant of Sinai* are re-affirmed, and are the backcloth against which Moses addresses the nation on the threshold of Canaan, 4. 9-13; 5. 1-27; 29. 1-4. They were a people who had broken the covenant!

4. Israel were a *holy people* — separated unto the Lord their God, 7. 6; 14. 21; 26. 19; 28. 9. He desired them for His own possession. Holy laws were designed to build a holy nation.

5. Well-being and prosperity lay in *obedience* 11. 8-9; 28. 1-14. Disobedience would bring down the curses, 28. 15-68.

Outline.
1. Proclaiming the *design* of the Law, 1. 1 to 11. 32.
    (i) First Address of Moses, 1. 1 to 4. 49.
    (ii) Second Address of Moses, 5. 1 to 11. 32.
2. Proclaiming the *demands* of the Law, 12. 1 to 26. 19.
    (i) Religious Institutions, 12. 1 to 17. 7.
    (ii) Representatives, 17. 8 to 18. 22.
    (iii) Regulations, 19. 1 to 25. 19.
    (iv) Responses, 26. 1-19.
3. The Blessings and the Curses, 27. 1 to 30. 20.
4. Last Words and Death of Moses, 31. 1 to 34. 12.

Jesus gave His affirmation to the authority of this book when He answered the devil, "It is written". Satan had no answer!

Mar. 19th

READING : **Deuteronomy 1. 1-8, 19-46**

WILDERNESS WANDERINGS

DEUTERONOMY is the proclamation or preaching of the law. The book begins "These be the *words* which Moses spake unto all Israel", v. 1. This opening stamps the book with its special character as it takes its place in the Pentateuch. Moses recounts the precepts and commands which God gave to the people; cf. 31. 24. The words were not only spoken, but written in a book which was put in the side of the ark of the covenant. We are impressed at the outset, with the realization that, when God speaks, *what* He has to say is vitally important to the well-being of His people. This fact is stressed throughout the book.

Notice *where* the book begins, and *when* Moses spoke to the people, "on this side Jordan in the wilderness," v. 1. It was on the threshold of the promised land, as they were about to possess their inheritance, that they were reminded of those Divine commands. And it was in the fortieth year — after the long wanderings in the wilderness — that Moses faced the nation with the Word of God. Often in life, the place and the time that God chooses to speak to us have a vital bearing on the course of our spiritual experience. It did with Israel.

Moses was speaking to a *wayward* and *wandering* people. Note verses 2-3. Horeb to Kadesh-barnea was eleven days journey; yet it took forty years from the time Israel left Egypt to the point where they were commanded to go into Canaan, vv. 5-8. Because of unbelief and hardened hearts, they had wasted valuable years in unintentional wanderings. Instead of *walking* in God's ways they had *wandered* and a whole generation perished in the wilderness. We either walk with God, loving His ways, or we wander aimlessly without Him; see Eph. 5. 15-16.

Moses reminds the people of their *wickedness*, Deut. 1. 19-46. They murmured when the spies returned with a good report of the land, vv. 26-28. They refused to believe that the mighty God could take them through, vv. 32-33. Their behaviour was an insult to the mighty power and the deep love of Jehovah. Only Caleb and Joshua, men of faith and courage, lived to enter the land, vv. 34-38. Yet God said, "go in and possess", vv. 8-21. To hold back was sin. Learn today that *what the Lord promises we must possess.*

Mar. 20th

READING : **Deuteronomy 2. 1-7, 24-31; 3. 21-29**

GOD THE PROTECTOR

MOSES STRESSES in his proclamation the fact of the unfailing care of God for His failing people. He did not bless them because they were righteous — their history was dark with sin. Yet He blessed them in spite of their waywardness. They are told often to remember the way that the Lord their God had led them. God was the mighty *Protector* of His people.

Our readings lead us to consider the way in which the Lord *planned* the pathway of Israel. Notice how He dealt with nations such as Edom and Moab, to make sure that His chosen ones were preserved; e.g. 2. 7. All their works had been favoured with His blessing. Overshadowing their ways was His perfect knowledge — the understanding of all that the wilderness meant. During forty years of wandering, Jehovah had not abandoned them — He had been with them. They had wanted for nothing. Here was *planning* that resulted in their *preservation* and blessing. So it is that Israel is told to remember all the way that He had led them, 8. 2-4. God knew what He was doing. Think of the implications of this for us. We can rest in His knowledge of all our ways.

We need to understand the meaning of God's *power* in His ways with His people. When the time drew near for the conquest of Canaan, He makes sure that news of the doings of His people shall go before them. His intention is to put the fear and dread of them upon the godless nations. Notice the details of the victory over Sihon of the Amorites and Og, king of Bashan. Giants meant nothing to God; He is for His people. "If God be for us, who can be against us?"; see Rom. 8. 31-39. Let us search out and rejoice in the *possibilities* of His *power*!

One final thought for today concerns God's *purpose* in the leadership of His people. Moses was excluded from the promised land, 3. 23-28. He asked to go over to the good land, yet how sad the words are, "the Lord was wroth with me for your sakes", v. 26. So it was that he was allowed to see but not to enter in. What a reflection on the nation's behaviour — "for your sakes!" Joshua — Jehovah the Saviour — will take them in, and Moses charges him to courage and faithfulness. The *lawgiver* could bring Israel to the threshold of the land. The one whose name meant *Saviour* took them in!

Mar. 21st
READING : **Deuteronomy 4.1-13, 32-40**

LISTEN CAREFULLY—GOD HAS SPOKEN!

LISTENING IS not always as easy as it seems to be! This chapter begins by calling for attentive hearing when God's statutes and judgments are being taught, v. 1. Only in this way would the nation live, and eventually possess the land. The Lord looks for open ears so that His Word can be appreciated. It is vital that the Word in its *entirety* should be valued and obeyed. Inspired truth must not be tampered with — this is relevant in every age.

The fruit of a right attitude to the Word of God is *exemplified* by the well-being it produces, vv. 4-8. Personal preservation is said to be the reward of obedience, v. 4. This obedience must be carried over into the promised land, v. 5. The implications of verses 6-8 are tremendous when the purposes of God are linked with the future of the nation. Israel's God was near at hand. Obedience to His statutes only could bring the height of wisdom and the depth of understanding of His character. Note the emphasis on the uniqueness of Israel in the wonder of its God, and the righteous quality of its laws. Our times, and the relationship we have with the Lord, may be different; the underlying principles here can teach us much; cf. Rom. 15.4.

Careful *exercise* is needed in responding to God's commands, vv. 9-13. "Only take heed . . . keep thy soul diligently"; these are words of intensity. The awe-inspiring atmosphere of Sinai is remembered. It was amidst the fire and the darkening clouds that the law was given. They were never to forget it. No superficial approach to the Word can meet our need, or honour the God who is its Author; cf. 2 Tim. 2. 15.

Notice in our meditation how God *explains* His reasons for the unique revelation given to the nation, vv. 32-40. Moses was set to proclaim in detail the terms of the covenant, and the outlines of the commandments. What a privilege to hear the voice of Jehovah out of the fire, v. 33. His choice of the people and His companionship in their wanderings, were designed to express His love, v. 37. Wonderful sovereignty! Through Divine power, salvation and victory were assured, v. 38. So it is that *experience* alone will prove the value of obedience, vv. 39-40. Let this be a challenge to us today, as we apply the precious truths of His Word.

Mar. 22nd

READING : **Deuteronomy 5. 1-21; 6. 1-15**

NO OTHER GOD!

THESE TWO chapters unfold the unique character of Israel's God. The surrounding nations had gods in abundance. Their idol images were tangible yet lifeless. No certainty or peace attached to their worship. But for God's chosen people, although the Lord God was unseen, they knew Him and there was reality. The glory and greatness of God was shown as He gave to them His laws, 5. 24 — this was miracle indeed!

"Hear O Israel: The Lord our God is one Lord", 6. 4. The Shema, so described after the Hebrew word with which it opens (= hear), confesses the *character* of God. Israel had One God — the only God. The grandeur of this truth was, and still is, confessed morning and evening by every faithful Jew. It is still central to Jewish orthodoxy. The literal Hebrew meaning states that God is the "ever existing One"; "our Elohim (the plural hinting at Triunity) is One Jehovah". Every act of God had behind it the fulness of His character. There was no other God like Him; in fact there *was* no other God. Israel needed to know their God. So do we, Col. 1. 9-10.

Moses without hesitation, presented the *claims* of Jehovah to the nation. Every part of man's being, every power he possessed, were His. They should love Him with heart and soul and might, Deut. 6. 4. His claims were legitimate, and they should fear Him and serve Him and swear by His Name, v. 13. He is a jealous God!, vv. 14-15, yet not with selfish possessiveness. Not at all! His jealousy is based on His holiness and His love. He redeemed them from Egypt's bondage, v. 12. Their allegiance and love were a reasonable response. Divided loyalties can never satisfy or honour our God!, Rom. 12. 1-2.

Notice how Moses restated the commandments, 5. 1-21. This is not a second law; it is a re-preaching of Sinai's covenant. These "words" were the foundation of the nation's relationship with its God. There is personal force in Moses' application of the commands. "The Lord talked with *you* face to face", v. 4. Every succeeding generation was personally accountable to obey the terms of the covenant. Solemn thought! Commands once given by God demand constant *commitment*. How challenging for us to hear again the Saviour's words; "If ye love me, keep my commandments".

Mar. 23rd

READING : **Deuteronomy 7. 1-26**

A SPECIAL PEOPLE

THIS CHAPTER has deep significance in connection with the nation of Israel as God's chosen people. History and circumstances would make us ask many times, "Why ever did God bother so much with them or us?" To read these verses leads us to one conclusion; the answer is in Himself, in His own heart, in His unquestionable sovereignty. The chapter moves us to worship and to wonder.

First we have instruction that there was to be *no compromise with the surrounding nations*, vv. 1-5. In battle they must be utterly destroyed, v. 2. None was to be spared, and nothing was to be left. God's reasons were clear: there was to be no unholy intrusion into the sanctity of Israel's worship, nor any association with the profane values of idol shrines. The gods once destroyed would not be a danger to Israel.

Israel was a chosen nation, vv. 6-11. Note the beauty of expression in these words. They come from God's heart. A special people, chosen for Himself, they were set apart for the Lord. Numerical greatness had no part in this: "Because the Lord loved you", here is the only explanation for such a choice. It is wonderful and enough! Thus we can appreciate that His promise, power and purpose were bound up in His choice. How much is ours because we are chosen in Christ, and accepted in the beloved!, Eph. 1. 3-14.

We can consider the *course that is open to those whom God has chosen*, Deut. 7. 12-16. "Wherefore . . . if ye hearken", v. 12. This oft-repeated injunction was essential if the blessing of the Lord was to be experienced. Notice, here, the earthly character of Israel's blessing. It consisted in material prosperity. God desired a spiritual relationship with them. But the favour of God meant possession of the land, and the prolongation of life.

These next verses inspire *courage in the possibility of conquest*, Deut. 7. 17-24. Thou "shalt not be afraid", v. 18. To remember past victories would inspire future confidence, for the Lord their God was amongst them, v. 21. Every enemy would be destroyed; victory was assured. So *the solemn charge* is given, vv. 25-26. Every graven image was to be destroyed. His might and power proved Him to be the Only God. To Him "be honour and glory for ever and ever. Amen", 1 Tim. 1. 17.

Mar. 24th

READING : **Deuteronomy 8. 1-20**

A GOOD MEMORY

ONE OF the key words of Deuteronomy is *remember*. It occurs 14 times in English, and is the main theme of our reading today. Moses insisted on a place of priority for God's Word in the lives of His chosen people. What need there was to observe the commandments for their life and prosperity, v. 1. As the chapter ends, the reason for judgment is unmistakably stated, "because ye would not be obedient unto the voice of the Lord your God", v. 20.

Consider some of the things that Israel were to remember. They help to highlight God's deep involvement in the lives of His people. *He tells them to remember the pathway*, v. 2. It was a way that took them through the wilderness. Yet notice that God led them "all the way" — wonderful companionship! It could be that those who had lived through those dreadful days just wanted to forget them. They were not to!

In their history *God revealed His purpose*. We may wonder why it was that all the adversities of the wilderness were allowed. God was determined to humble them, exposing what really lay in their hearts towards Him. He was also seeking to show them that material things were secondary — they must live by His Word, vv. 3-6. None of God's ways with His people are wasted or unnecessary. He chastens that He might prove His love and purify His children, v. 5. Goodness and grace are in His ways, even when the clouds are dark and the path is hard; cf. Heb. 12. 4-13.

Israel were never to forget God's provision, especially when they had eaten and were full, Deut. 8. 10. Contentment could lead to complacency, and abundance to a sense of apathy in obeying God's commands, vv. 9-11. In promising them the fulness of Canaan, He would remind them of the deliverance from Egypt, v. 14. How subtle is human pride. How easy to attribute our well-being in times of prosperity to our own goodness. They needed to remember, because only in trust in God could security and strength be experienced.

Finally, *they were always to remember God's power*, Deut. 8. 14-18. The power that made them a nation was His, not their own. All their resources to do and to get and to be were in Him. Self-confidence means self-destruction!

Mar. 25th
READING : **Deuteronomy 9. 1-29; 10. 12-22**
GOING OVER JORDAN

DEUTERONOMY COULD be described as the "ante-room" to the Book of Joshua. Moses states the certainty of Israel's possession of the land of promise. In saying "this day", we have the impression of imminence as well as the certainty of conquest. Giants they would be sure to meet, but the might of God would go before them and destroy their enemies. They were on the victory side!, 9. 1-3. They are assured of their inheritance.

It is at this point that *the behaviour patterns of the nation are reviewed*. Why is it that they are to enter into such a good inheritance? "Not for thy righteousness, or for the uprightness of thine heart". It would be easy for them, in the first flush of triumph, to let pride prevail and say, *"my righteousness"*, vv. 4-5. The Lord halts any thought of this. Possession means the fulfilment of His promise, the oath of the Lord to the patriarchs. We are impressed again with the unswerving faithfulness of Jehovah to His faithless people.

Moses gives *a sad record of sins they committed*. How deeply they provoked the Lord to anger in the wilderness!, vv. 6-7. There is deep emotion in the words of this great man of God as he spells out their evils. It was during the actual receiving of the commandments that Aaron and the people worshipped the golden calf. All through the journey this "stiffnecked people" murmured and rebelled. Humanly speaking, everything was going for them. By their very perversity they threw blessing away. Are we not often like this?

Against this dark backcloth, the beauty of *Moses' relationship with the people* is shown, vv. 25-29. He became their great intercessor, and how much they owed to this. "I prayed". He pleaded their cause and stood by them in their sin. His great pleading before Jehovah was for the honour of His Name. The Lord's people in every age have owed much to a leadership that is given to prayer. Israel went into Canaan with the power of this intercession behind them.

Finally we note *the requirements of God*, 10. 12-22. The demands of Deuteronomy are epitomized here. God's desire is that holiness should lead to spiritual health, and that His people should be absolutely His. Consider the beauty of superabundant mercy in the face of abundant sin, vv. 21-22.

Mar. 26th

READING : **Deuteronomy 12. 1-32**

THE CHOSEN PLACE

THE OLD TESTAMENT makes it clear that the place where people offered their sacrifices and worshipped was very important. In the life of Abraham, the places where he built his altars are marked out as special, e.g. Gen. 12. 8; 13. 18. As the people of Israel increased, and as the national life developed in the land, it was more and more vital that the people should know where the centre of spiritual life and worship was set.

The people were told that pagan shrines and idol images must be utterly destroyed, Deut. 12. 1-3. The temptation to go after other gods would be very real when they entered Canaan. It was because of the wickedness of the Canaanites and inhabitants of the land that Israel were commanded to conquer and destroy the cities they came to, 9. 5. The high places and idol groves were a menace to God's people. In times of national revival, such as those under Hezekiah and Josiah, they were ruthless in destroying these centres of sacrifice and worship. Repentance meant a returning to the Lord God.

But there was one place to be marked out where the presence of Israel's God could be found. It was "the place which the Lord your God shall choose out of all your tribes to put his name there", 12. 5-7. This expression, and ones similar, occur over twenty times in the Book. Look at them. What was the significance of this regarding the worship of Israel?

There was to be no confusion regarding the location of worship. *They must seek the dwelling place* of the Lord, v. 5. Holy sacrifices could not be offered in every place they saw, v. 13. For the surrounding nations, their *many* gods meant *many* shrines to contain them. Not so Jehovah, for He was Israel's *one* God, 6. 4. There was to be *one* place, chosen by Him, bearing His Name, and this must be sought out. *They were to come to this place*, v. 5. It became the place where they met with their Lord. And *they were to bring to it their sacrifices*, and *eat and rejoice before the Lord*, vv. 6-12. Here He deigned to dwell among them. How much more blessed we are today. Whenever we gather to His Name, Jesus has promised to be with us, Matt. 18. 20. No place can contain the greatness of God. Yet how often we feel the warmth of His presence as we gather. What a privilege!

Mar. 27th

READING : **Deuteronomy 15. 1-23**

THE WILLING SLAVE

THERE IS a unique humanitarianism about the laws proclaimed in Deuteronomy. A study of these will provide ample proof of this. This chapter prescribes obvious safeguards against oppression. In Amos' times of national decline, these were the laws that were broken. Unrighteousness and oppression were the burden of his condemnation, Amos 1. 6-7; 5. 12; 8. 4-6.

The law concerning the release of slaves indicates two vital intentions that God had for His people. The first was *freedom*, Deut. 15. 15. They were to remember Egypt's bondage, and the dramatic deliverance by God's power. They were the Lord's free people! The second intention was *fulness*, v. 6, the great potentials of wealth contained in the blessing of the Lord. It can be said that if Israel were right with God, then there would be no poor in the land, vv. 5-6.

The law of the year of release, the seventh year, was vitally important as a means of balancing relationships among the people. It was *a year of adjustment*. It was called the Lord's release. He was watching over the interests of all the people, not just a favoured few. Contrast "there shall be no poor", v. 4, with "If there be among you a poor man", v. 7. Intentions and actual conditions were not tallying up. Thus the year of release filled a deep need in the nation's life. It was a reminder that God was an open-handed Giver, whose heart was generous and whose ears readily caught the cry of the oppressed. God is presented in the same generous light as a Giver in 2 Corinthians 8-9, and He loves a cheerful giver. There should be equality in His people's response so that there should be no inequalities among those who live for Him.

The actions of the willing slave are significant, Deut. 15. 12-18. He was free to leave his master, and every provision was to be made for his well-being. Yet love for his master meant more than the prospect of liberty, v. 16. So the sign of unending service was put in his ear — he was his master's forever!, v. 17. Duty was lost in devotion. Paul described himself as the "bondslave of Jesus Christ". He truly loved his Master, and found in such bondservice the highest possible freedom. For "love's sake" is the truest motive for service, Philem. 9.

Mar. 28th

READING : **Deuteronomy 16. 1-22**

THREE TIMES A YEAR

THE IMPRESSION has often been given that Judaism was a faith without joy regulated by cold legalism and demanding ritualism. This is totally wrong. Our chapter speaks not only of causes for celebration, but of regulations given to make sure that times of jubilation and thanksgiving were regularly to take place. Each year at set times Israel celebrated the goodness of God in the place where He had put His Name. "Observe the month of Abib", v. 1. The word, observe, is often repeated; e.g. 5. 1 R.V.; 6. 3; 11. 32, etc. Study them! But here it had to do with happenings and rejoicing.

Israel had much to remember concerning the good ways of God and His gracious dealings with them. The calendar of Judaism was filled with set times of festival, so that His activities among them should not be forgotten, Lev. 23. Deuteronomy 16 is not only retrospective but prophetic as well, telling of times when the joy of Israel will be full. Three times in the year were set aside for special celebration, and all the males in the nation were to appear "before the Lord", v. 16. This verse is the "heart" of the chapter. It speaks of a positive response to the blessings given to them by the Lord.

In the Passover and Feast of Unleavened Bread, Israel celebrated its *salvation from Egypt*: "that thou mayest remember the day when thou camest forth out of . . . Egypt", v. 3. Their history as a nation began when they were sheltered by blood and delivered by power from Egypt's cruel bondage. Could they ever forget? They did but the annual Passover provided a reminder. They kept festival and rejoiced in the Lord who had saved them. Surely for us too, it is good to keep festival; we remember Christ our Passover, 1 Cor. 5. 7-8.

Pentecost, 50 days afterwards, was a feast linked with harvest joy. *Their blessedness* as His people was evident as they brought their gifts to Him. It is significant that the giving of the Holy Spirit is connected with Pentecost; the Church came into being, Acts 2.

Finally, the Feast of Tabernacles celebrates the *satisfaction of Israel*, in the joy of full harvest and vintage, dwelling in peace before the Lord. So too, even now "we also joy in God through our Lord Jesus Christ", Rom. 5. 11.

Mar. 29th

READING : Deuteronomy 17. 14 to 18. 22

KING, PRIEST AND PROPHET

IT WAS important that the people should be ruled and represented in a worthy manner before God. Regulations touching the offices of king, priest and prophet are given. Moses outlined something of the responsibility which attached to these offices. In Israel, each was exercised separately.

Notice *the requirements of kingship*, 17. 14-20. 1 Samuel 8 describes how the desire for a king was born out of the desire to be like other nations. This displeased the Lord and Samuel, but their request was granted. Our reading provides God's pattern for the reign of a king and for his character. He must be taken from his brethren, v. 15. His disposition must be godly and pure. He must be absolutely committed to the terms of the law, vv. 18-20. History reveals that the kings who contributed most to the nation's prosperity were those who "did that which was right in the sight of the Lord", e.g. 2 Kings 22. 1-2.

The place that the priest held among the people is emphasized, Deut. 18. 1-8. He also must be taken from among his brethren, and be chosen by God. He stood to minister in the name of the Lord, v. 5. He was separated unto the Lord, and was set to represent the people in the Lord's presence. The Lord was His portion, yet he was the subject of the people's care, v. 3.

The prophetic office has great importance in Israel. Men of God were the voice of God to the people, especially in times of departure. False prophets would arise in abundance, vv. 9-14, but the proof of truthfulness would be demonstrated by the fulfilment of the word of the Lord, vv. 21-22. To speak when the Lord had not spoken was presumption, and judgment would be meted out, v. 20.

Let us look at the person of Christ in relation to these three great offices. He is *God's King*, Psa. 2. 6. All ideals of true sovereignty will be fulfilled when He reigns as King of kings and Lord of lords, Rev. 19. 11-16. He is *our Great High Priest*. The Levitical priesthood failed because of human weakness and sin. Robbed of its best, it pointed on to Christ, who "ever liveth to make intercession" for us, Heb. 7. 25. Also, the Word of God, who came forth from God, fulfilled and developed all that was demanded in *the prophetic office*, Acts. 7. 37. Praise God for the official glories of our Lord Jesus Christ.

Mar. 30th

READING : **Deuteronomy 19. 1-21**

FLEEING FOR REFUGE

THE STANDARDS of justice contained within the framework of Israel's laws were of the very highest. They reflected the righteous character of the God who gave them. The demands for retribution were severe indeed. "And thine eye shall not pity; but life shall go for life, eye for eye, tooth for tooth, hand for hand, foot for foot", v. 21. The punishment must fit the crime! Note the punishment of a rebellious son!, 21. 18-21.

Yet the severity of justice was tempered with the quality of mercy. We have an example of this in the cities of refuge. Take time to read Numbers 35. 9-28 and Joshua 20. These provisions mark the difference between manslaughter and murder, between a premeditated act of violence and that which was accidental. Notice that strangers and foreigners were accorded the same provision, Num. 35. 15.

The reason behind these regulations is "that innocent blood be not shed in thy land . . . and so blood be upon thee", Deut. 19. 10. The sacredness of human life was paramount in all the laws given by Jehovah. Because God is man's Creator, life taken unjustly not merely stained the murderer but stained the land, the sacred heritage of Israel; see 21. 1-9.

Blood shed unlawfully cried for revenge; see Gen. 4. 10. The nearest kinsman, the "avenger of the blood", had the right to seek vengeance to satisfy family honour, Deut. 19. 6. This right is not questioned, but because the unwitting slayer was not worthy of death the refuge cities were provided. To shelter within their gates meant life and preservation. To move out again meant death.

God's provision of a place of refuge for His people reveals Him as a just God and a Saviour, Isa. 45. 21-22. The same law that demanded death of the murderer provided a way to life for the manslayer — the unintentioned killer. "I have sinned in that I have betrayed the innocent blood", Judas cried, Matt. 26. 3-5; Israel's land was stained with the blood of the sinless Saviour. Yet who can number the sinful souls who have found refuge in that same precious blood?, 1 Pet. 1. 19. Thus, breaking through the black clouds of judgment demanded by the law, we have seen a bright shaft of the sunlight of Divine mercy — the city of refuge, Heb. 6. 18-20.

Mar. 31st

READING : Deut. 22. 1-8; 24. 10-22; 25. 1-3; 26. 16-19

LAWS FOR A HOLY PEOPLE

DEUTERONOMY IS a proclamation of Israel's laws. Moses spelt out the statutes and ordinances, and amplified them, that as the nation entered the new sphere of the promised land, they would have no doubts as to the Lord's requirements. Some of the details now may seem trivial and irrelevant, yet they speak one message, "Holy laws for a holy people!" Well-being for them and satisfaction for a holy God would be the result of their obedience.

We notice *the consideration given for the needs of all* who were under these laws, 22. 1-8. The beasts were to be the subject of care. If a beast strayed, or possessions were lost, help was to be given. It was the same with their houses; care that no accident should threaten visitors' safety was taken, v. 8. Even the treatment of birds was included, v. 6. The Israelites were true conservationists, and we can remember that their God was the one who cared for the falling sparrow. His kindness is seen in His laws.

The laws also displayed respect for *the claims of the people upon each other*. Lending to one another was to be a matter of honour, 24. 10. It was not to be used as a means of increasing possessions. Whatever token was given by the poor was to be returned by sunset: "it shall be righteousness unto thee before the Lord thy God", v. 13. So there was to be no oppression among them. The poor and the destitute, the fatherless and the widow, each had a claim on the other and must be graciously provided for. The Lord said, "thou shalt love thy neighbour as thyself ". Even in punishment there had to be restraint, 25. 1-3. In our dealings we are to "Owe no man anything, but to love one another", for "Love is the fulfilling of the law".

We conclude with *the commitment involved* both for Israel and the Lord, Deut. 26. 16-19. There was an avowal of allegiance. The people "avouched" God to be theirs, and to walk in His ways. He "avouched" them to be His own possession, a holy people for Himself. Thus behind all these *laws* of God we see His *love*. He desired a response from His redeemed ones, an obedience motivated by love to Himself. How often was His heart broken by their infidelity! What a challenge to us who are "under grace". "If ye love me, keep my commandments".

April 1st

READING : **Deuteronomy 27. 1-13; 28. 1-19**

EBAL AND GERIZIM

THE ENJOYMENT of the blessing was vital to the nation of Israel. In it lay their only hope for growth and prosperity. In the early promises to Abraham when God called him out of Ur, Gen. 12. 1-3, blessing and cursing were linked together. "I will bless them that bless thee, and curse him that curseth thee". The right to bless and to curse belonged to God, and Israel's well-being was measured by their experience of God's blessing.

Chapter 27. 1-10 lies at the heart of the ideas of blessing and cursing. Here *the claims of the Lord are restated*. Their position would not change as they passed over Jordan. In the heap of stones with the written law upon them, lay their affirmation of this fact and their acceptance of them. The altar and the sacrifices sealed the relationship that was theirs. Vital transaction on the threshold of Canaan!

Mounts Gerizim and Ebal are set over against each other physically, and also spiritually as places of blessing and cursing. With six of the tribes on the one and six on the other, the tension is heightened. The scope of both blessing and cursing is limited to material things, the city and the field, the fruit of the body and of the ground, etc. As God's "earthly" people, entering in to the land of their inheritance, here lay the sphere of their possessions. Yet it is obvious that God's intentions for His people went deeper than this, as verse 9 reveals. They were His holy people.

The people gave their affirmation, 27. 14-26, as they said Amen to the curses pronounced by the Levites. Sad it was that these found their *confirmation* in their future history. Those things which were meant for their highest blessing, were turned into the bitterness of the curse through their disobedience. Yet when Balaam was commanded to curse Israel, in His love God turned the curse into a blessing, 23. 3-6. Balaam had to say, "I have received a commandment to bless: and he hath blessed; and I cannot reverse it", Num. 23. 20. Let the heathen touch God's people, and He would show where His love and blessing lie. They were the apple of His eye. His delight was to bless them. God's grace provided the basis, for Christ was "made a curse for us . . . that the blessing of Abraham might come".

April 2nd

READING : **Deut. 31. 1-6; 32. 1-6; 33. 1-5; 34. 1-12**

THE PASSING OF A LEADER

THERE IS an unmistakable pathos about the closing chapters of Deuteronomy. Moses is taking his leave of Israel, his beloved people. Like a shepherd who has guided and cared for his flock, he recognizes potential dangers ahead and seeks to shield them from trouble. He is to die unseen, buried by the Lord on Nebo, 32. 48-49; 34. 5. So we have his last words, ch. 31, his great song, ch. 32, and his final blessing, ch. 33. The final commendation of Moses leaves no doubt as to his stature, both as a leader and as a prophet of the Lord, 34. 7-12.

Consider four final thoughts concerning Moses.

1. *His final declaration* of the terms under which the people moved with their God into the promised land. First to the people, then to Joshua on whom the mantle of leadership would fall, Moses gave the command to be strong and of good courage because the Lord would be with them and would not fail, 31. 6-8. He also wrote the law in a book and gave it to the priests to handle aright and read to the people, 31. 9-13.

2. *In the song Moses reveals a deep desire for the well-being of his beloved nation.* He describes the nature of the chosen people. Undeniable waywardness and perversity are evident. In their greatest prosperity and blessing lay their greatest sin, 32. 7-15. Yet God is their Rock, unique and mighty to save. Observe "to do, all the words" is his advice, 32. 45-47.

3. *The blessing of Moses reveals the destiny of the tribes* — the furthest reaches of Divine blessing. Each has its own setting, and linked with the blessing of Jacob, Gen. 49, provides a panorama of prophetic ideas associated with the nation. Hence the triumphant refrain, "Happy art thou, O Israel", Deut. 33. 29. Taste the comfort and assurance of this chapter.

4. *The death of Moses.* Who would not want to be described as he was, a man "whom the Lord knew face to face"? As he ascended Nebo, the words of the oath to Abraham, Isaac and Jacob are repeated, 34. 4. He saw the fulfilment with his eyes, but could not enter in then; ct. Matt. 17. 3-4. The tender hands of the God he had served buried him in the mount. Perhaps his epitaph could be "those things which are revealed belong unto us and to our children for ever", Deut. 29. 29. Give attention to reading!

Introducing Joshua

It is a mistake to commence the study of the book of Joshua before paying attention to the progressive steps of Joshua's preparation outlined in earlier Scripture. The following passages indicate the several phases by which this man of God became the fitted successor of his honoured master, and should be considered carefully: Exod. 17. 8-16; 24. 13; 32. 17-18; 33. 11; Num. 11. 24-29; 13. 3, 8, 16; 14. 6-10; seven in all.

The Book outlines the "ascent" of God's people to "higher ground". Having gone "down" in Genesis, "out" in Exodus, then "in" in Leviticus, and "through" in Numbers, Israel is now to go "up" in Joshua, Deut. 1. 21. The Book of Joshua is the Old Testament anticipation of Ephesians. Israel's entering into their promised inheritance illustrates our entrance into all the spiritual blessings in "the heavenlies in Christ Jesus", from wilderness wanderings to inheritance wealth, seven "cairns" in all; 4. 9; 4. 3; 7. 25-26; 8. 29; 8. 30-32; 10. 27; 24. 24-28.

The Book, viewed from Joshua's point of view, divides in two at chapter 13. 1. Here he becomes the man with a second ministry. He who has been the leader of the people in warfare, becoming old, is not considered redundant by his God. He now becomes the administrator in the midst of the nation. Martial days being over, the old warrior becomes the trusted veteran to advise. Age never ends service, it only changes its nature.

With our eye on Joshua let us ever have in mind our greater Joshua (Jesus, Heb. 4. 8-11 R.V.), who in resurrection leads us, His heavenly people, into rest. Moses, the representative of the law, could never conduct a redeemed people into their "Canaan". One who was greater than Joshua — Jehovah the Saviour (Jesus) — was needed for the task, our risen Saviour who is alone the Rest-Giver. We see in Moses' disobedience and consequent death, Num. 20. 12; Deut. 3. 23-28, both the responsibility of man and the sovereignty of God in evidence, and strangely blending to fulfil the divine requirements.

For God's glory — Israel successfully conquered the Land, chs. 1-12: 1. 9; 3. 10; 4. 23f; 6. 16; 8. 1; 10. 14; 11. 6ff; 23. 3.

By God's grace — Israel was granted possession of the Land, chs. 13-22: observe the 12 tribal allotments and Map 2, p. 118. Therefore they were to *love* and *serve* Him, chs. 23-24.

April 3rd

READING : Joshua 1. 1-18

JOSHUA TAKES OVER

THE GREATEST of men die, and successors are needed, v. 2. Thus Moses expressed his concern that the congregation "be not as sheep which have no shepherd", Num. 27. 15-17. In our day we need men with Joshua's ready response, and who are willing to follow the way that the Master went, Josh. 1. 7a.

In our chapter three things call for attention today.

1. *The Divine Call*, vv. 1-5a. A reminder arrests, v. 2a, and a directive alerts Joshua, v. 2b. God's call for action is based, as always, on a divine promise of (*a*) Extensive Possession, vv. 2-4, and (*b*) Extended Protection, v. 5b. How sad that God's people never fully appropriate all that He abundantly gives.

2. *The Human Committal*, vv. 10-12. Note the "Then" of verse 10 following the "now" of verse 2, and let us learn that unhesitating obedience is the only fitting response to every call of God. However, between the Call and the Committal there comes

3. *The Divine Charge*, vv. 5b-9. Here are conditions to be fulfilled, and these must be the point of emphasis for today's reading. This focal paragraph is a literary gem, and demands attention and obedience. It has a centre of vital importance with concentric rings of promise and challenge. The outer ring is the promise of the Lord's unfailing *Embrace* for the task to which Joshua is committed, vv. 5b, 9b. Assured victory depends upon it, v. 5a. It is measured positively, "*as* I was with Moses, *so* I will be with thee", and negatively "I will not fail thee, nor forsake thee". It is then fully endorsed, v. 9b, guaranteeing to Joshua faithfulness and might (Jehovah thy God) to be with him not only always, v. 5b, but everywhere. In this embrace Joshua must develop his soul *Exercise*. The challenge is "Be strong (the inner secret) and of a good courage (the outward sign)", v. 6a, and God supplies encouragement for it, v. 6b. This challenge is also repeated in verse 9a. This is the inner ring. Now comes the spiritual *Essential*, the vital centre, the divine command, vv. 7b-9a. My soul's attitude to Scripture determines all. For "be strong . . . to do" ensures "good success", vv. 7, 8. I must not *detract*, v. 7a, *deflect*, v. 7b, *depart*, v. 8a, from the Word, nor *disobey*, *v. 8b*.

Lesson. The Word must be the centre of my life's orbit.

April 4th
READING : Joshua 2. 1-24
OPERATIONS BEGIN

THE SUBSTANCE of the chapter gathers around three factors; a city, a confession, and a cord.

1. *The City*, v. 2. "Go view the land, even *Jericho*". It may have been beautiful, Deut. 34. 3, but it was the very bastion of wickedness, idolatry and devilry. God said everything must be "devoted" to judgment. Joshua was to move straight for the bulwarks, the major obstacles not the minor, the strongholds of Satan; cf. 2 Cor. 10. 3-6. What is the Jericho that is barring the way to my inheritance?

2. *The Confession*, vv. 3-13. The harlot was kind to the spies and protected them by means of falsehood, vv. 4-7. No doubt she reverted to this because she was afraid of the news she possessed, vv. 9-11a, and feared for her own life while hoping for mercy. Her confession is stirring: "the Lord (Jehovah) your God, he is God in heaven above, and in earth beneath", v. 11b. She pleaded for mercy for herself and her family, to be delivered from "the wrath to come", 1 Thess. 1. 9f.

3. *A Cord*, vv. 14-24. Four things are said about it. (i) It was *scarlet*, v. 18. Their safety was to depend upon it. How suggestive. Scarlet reminds of sin, Isa. 1. 18, and she was a sinner! Was the cord a symbol of her trade? It also speaks of atoning blood. What a foreshadowing of a greater means of escape, the precious blood of the One made sin for us. (ii) It is called a *thread*, v. 18. Binding it in her window she may have thought, what a slender hope it was upon which to lay hold; cf. Jud. 16. 12. How many since have refused the scarlet thread of the blood of Christ as totally insufficient to deliver from judgment. Yet it was (iii) a *cord*, v. 15. She had witnessed its strength to provide escape for others, v. 18, cf. Jer. 38. 6, 11ff, and she was only asked to trust that in which they had trusted. It was also called (iv) *a line*, vv. 18, 21. Here was a life-line indeed, 6. 22-23. Christ's sacrificial death is *the* lifeline.

The spies return with a report of confident victory saying "the Lord hath delivered into our hands all the land", for dread had fallen on all the inhabitants of the country.

Lesson. Binding the cord in the window she confessed her sin and exposure to judgment, while trusting in the God-appointed token, vv. 18-19.

April 5th

READING : **Joshua 3. 1 to 4. 9**

THE ONLY WAY IN

JORDAN CANNOT be circumvented! Israel cannot pass round it, but must pass through it. There is no inheritance to possess or enjoy any other way. How Old Testament picture anticipates New Testament precept. The believer's inheritance in the heavenlies, Eph. 1. 3, is only reached via Ephesians 2. 4-6.

1. *The Way through was forged for them.* They did not know the way, 3. 4, nor could they have stemmed the flood, v. 15b. "Another" goes before them, vv. 6, 11, 14, the Ark of the Presence. The Ark, as borne by the priests, enters the flood alone, v. 4. In the flood it "stands still", v. 8, is at "rest", v. 13, and "stood firm" v. 17. Thank God for One who breasted something more terrible than Jordan's waves for us; cf. Psa. 69. 1-2, 14-15; Jonah 2. 3; Luke 12. 50. The priests' feet, however, only "dipped in the brink" (R.V.) when the waters stood and rose in one heap, vv. 15-16; ct. Psa. 69. 2. Christ, like the Ark, went "over before you into Jordan", Josh. 3. 11, yet what a distance between, v. 4!

2. *The Way through was by identification with the Ark.* Having had the "going before" significantly emphasized four times, now the command is "go after it", v. 3. Pause now to read prayerfully Romans 6. 1-11, for this is *our* "going after it". Have we really followed? The fact that Israel did is permanently demonstrated by twelve stones in the bed of the river, Josh. 4. 9. Romans 6. 11 is my representative stone.

3. *The Way through was guaranteed to them.* The people "passed over", 3. 16, yea "clean over", v. 17, on dry ground. As their crossing was permanently marked, v. 9, so was their arrival at the other side, 4. 2-8, a memorial for ever, v. 7. The incident illustrates our identification with Christ in death, burial, and resurrection, which, whilst a once for all act, is to be endorsed by us continuously. However, it is the passing over that immediately confronted them with the enemy. It was their crossing which brought the people "right against Jericho", 3. 16. Spiritual conflict in my life is the sign that I stand on inheritance ground, Eph. 6. 12.

Lesson. On which side of the "Jordan" am I standing? Am I satisfied with wilderness conditions, or enjoying every spiritual blessing in the heavenlies?, Eph. 1. 3.

April 6th

READING : Joshua 5. 13 to 6. 27

THE INITIAL VICTORY

JORDAN CROSSED, reproach rolled away (see Col. 3. 5), the passover kept after 38 years (significant sequence), and now a new fare for Israel, the old corn of the land. This points to Christ in resurrection! Jericho now confronts Israel, a conflict not so much of Canaanite and Israelite, but Satan and God!

1. *The Inspiring Fact of the Matter*, 5. 13-15. Joshua facing the first bastion of evil, sees not the walls but a Man! The issue is not between him and the city, but between the Lord and the foe, v. 14a. As His is the Captaincy, so His is the strategy. The secret of Joshua's victory is his posture, v. 14b, and his obedience guarantees his enabling, v. 15; cf. Eph. 6. 10.

2. *The Informed Fashion of the Manoeuvre*, 6. 1-5. "The Lord said"! So Joshua's Captain *was* Joshua's Lord! What grace! The Lord knows our weakness, and our potential to boast in victory. "I have given," v. 2; victory was already assured! Then the "ye shall" of verse 3 imposed conditions while introducing the plan. In true military fashion the orders were short, sharp, and concise. Did Joshua consider the scheme preposterous? His was not to reason why!, Isa. 55. 8f. Note the imprint of Divine perfection suggested by the repeated "sevens", Josh. 6. 4.

3. *The Implicit Fulfilment of the Method*, 6. 6-20a. Mocking crowds on the battlements enjoyed a week of increasing entertainment. But the Lord taking control, and now precedence (the ark), the procession became the symbol of His might and faithful presence. The seventh day arrived, and the last circuit began. Final orders were given and mute silence reigned, for the work was the Lord's. The victory shout was prepared, and the citizens were "devoted" to judgment, and the valuables "devoted" to the Lord.

4. *The Instant Fulness of the Mastery*, 6. 20b-27. One last trump, and one sustained shout, and it was as good as over. The walls fell, not simply "down" but "down flat" or "under it", v. 20, and marg. They sank into the earth and offered no obstacle, v. 20. Note the final stroke of victory, not by weapon but prophetic word, v. 26; 1 Kings 16. 34.

Lesson. The way to victory in every spiritual conflict is first to cast oneself at the feet of the Captain of the Lord's host.

April 7th
READING : Joshua 7. 1-26
DEFEAT! SO SOON?

LET NOT success make us careless or self-confident, for our Jericho victory may be followed by an Ai defeat. Little obstacles can gender greater disasters. Note three things:-

1. *An Ignominious Defeat*, vv. 2-5. The Lord, and not Israel's strength of arms, wrought the victory over Jericho. Then why assess the need in terms of mathematics when facing Ai? Was it needful for Joshua to "spy out the land"?, v. 2 R.V. Their eyes would have been better focused on their Captain! Why is Joshua not seeking directions? How verse 3 savours of self-sufficiency and pride. They must learn, and we too, that the conquest of Canaan is not a battle but a campaign. So in trusted self-strength there "went up . . . about 3000 men", and — note — "fled", "smote", "chased", "smote", "melted". What shame! This is the price of presumption. Never underestimate your enemy.

2. *The Interrupted Intercession*, vv. 6-10. What a contrast to 5. 14! Note the long wrestling of verse 6 compared with the short but decided submission of the former. The "what shall I say" of verse 8 would better have been "What dost Thou say?" There are times when God desires not prayer but action; not intercession but introspection, v. 10.

3. *The Indicated Cause*, vv. 1, 11-26. The reader is put wise to this as the chapter begins, but it must have been a shock to Joshua when God said "Israel hath sinned". Note the Divine exasperation — God repeats "yea, they have *even* . . . yea, they have *even*" v. 11 R.V. They have "transgressed", "taken", "stolen", "dissembled", "become accursed". What a charge, and what a consequence! The moral elements are:

1. You cannot hide, however carefully, from God, v. 21.
2. The Lord adopts the method of progressive detection.
3. Can confession come too late? God had given time.
4. Beware of the lust of the flesh, the lust of the eyes, and the pride of life, v. 21; cf. Gen. 3. 6.
5. The individual can endanger the community.
6. Note "except", v. 12, and "until", v. 13.
7. Make every defeat a monument to remind, v. 26.

Lesson. There *is* a gospel of recovery, ch. 8. Note it and be encouraged.

April 8th

READING : **Joshua 9. 1-27**

BEWARE! GIBEONITES

BEING INHABITANTS of the land, v. 16, the Gibeonites represent those who are already inhabitants of the sphere of the believer's inheritance in the heavenlies, Eph. 6. 12. Their leader is the devil, v. 11, and he too is a deceiver able to "change his coat", 2 Cor. 11. 14; 1 Pet. 5. 8. Israel's advance is steadily reaching finality (see Josh. 10 and 11; especially 11. 23), and their initial victories are still causing consternation, 9. 3; 10. 1. The Gibeonites see the inevitable, and prepare accordingly. Like the devil, theirs is not surrender but subterfuge, for they "work wilily", 9. 4. Their disguise was perfect, their address plausible, but the consequence was perilous to Israel, vv. 14-27. Note specially verses 17-20. Beware, Joshua! Have you forgotten your error at Ai? Once again, though somewhat suspicious, v. 7, they "asked not counsel at the mouth of the Lord", v. 14. Joshua made peace with them, and a covenant. You cannot, and must not, do this with the enemy — it is to be relentless warfare. Read carefully Deuteronomy 7. 2. Joshua, have you so soon forgotten the basic secret of your promised success?, Josh. 1. 8.

We must not judge according to the sight of our eyes, or the hearing of our ears, but seek the One who does not need so to do, Isa. 11. 3. Could Joshua not wait on the Lord? In but three days he knew the truth, but it was too late, and he must now honour his word. The breaking of this covenant later led to trouble in Israel, 2 Sam. 21. 1-10. If we make promises like this without seeking and heeding the Lord's mind, He may keep us to them, 2 Sam. 21. 1-2.

How the enemy, like the Gibeonites, can often work successfully on the gullibility of so many of the Lord's people. They appeared so knowledgeable as to the ways of the Lord, v. 10, and could seemingly quote Scripture so adroitly, v. 24, and feign a sincere attraction to Israel's God, v. 9. But let us remember that, like them, our enemy "is a liar and the father of it", John 8. 44. Be on your guard regarding his manoeuvres.

John warns us that "many deceivers are entered into the world", 2 John 7. Such would "deceive the very elect", Matt. 24. 24. "Little children, let no man deceive you", 1 John 3. 7.

Lesson. Be sure to "try the spirits whether they are of God".

April 9th

READING : **Joshua 20. 1-9**

FINAL MINISTRIES FOR ISRAEL

JOSHUA'S YEARS are quickly ebbing. He was "old and well stricken in years", 13. 1 R.V. He confesses it, 23. 1-2, aware he was "going the way of all the earth", 23. 14. He was old, but not too old for God. Are we too ready to seek retirement from Divine service? There are no redundancy lists in the Lord's employ! War had ceased, 11. 23, although much land remained unpossessed, 13. 1. However, Joshua's military days were over. God has another ministry for the old warrior. He will no longer lead in battle, but he will be central to the administration. What an example to aging saints!

The remaining chapters give facets of his new ministry.

1. His was to distribute the inheritance, 13. 7; Map 2, p. 118.
2. His is concern for those otherwise defenceless, 17. 3-4.
3. He wisely admonishes the self-assertive, 17. 14-18.
4. He inspires the indolent, directing operations, 18. 1-6.
5. He attends to those without tribal inheritance, ch. 21.
6. He encourages and advises the faithful, ch. 22.
7. He instructs by that from which he had benefitted, ch. 23.
8. Note his patience for individuals and groups, 14. 6-14.
9. He provides for those exposed to danger, ch. 20.

Reverting to our chapter for the day, are we sufficiently exercised about those under our care, who by force of circumstances are open to adversity?, cf. Acts 20. 28-31. This record of the God-given care administered under the superintendency of the aged Joshua is suggestive. The cities of refuge, normally used as a gospel illustration, provide lessons for us in our care for others. Note how this provision ministered sympathy, Josh. 20. 4, salvation, v. 5, and shelter, v. 6.

The provision ensured geographic availability, for there were three cities on each side of Jordan; topographical appropriateness, in the hill country, v. 7, and wilderness table land, v. 8, meeting various handicaps; and they were at the disposal of all alike, v. 9; see Map 2, p. 118. How do *we* meet those in desperate need? Let us remember, no man liveth unto himself. Each man *is* his brother's keeper!

Lesson. Even "Paul the aged" finished his course in harness, 2 Tim. 4. 6-7. Are we rusting out or burning out?

April 10th

READING : Joshua 24. 1-33

THE LAST CHAPTER OF A GREAT MINISTRY

SHECHEM! The old oak; a lone patriarch; a pitched tent; a raised altar — and a promise, Gen. 12. 6-7.

Shechem! Years of pilgrimage; years of bondage; years of wandering; years of possessing, and now, an older oak; a mighty host; an upraised stone — and the inheritance, Josh. 24. 25-28. Truly, the promises of God are "yea and amen". The cycle is complete, and the wanderers are home. In the early part of the chapter observe:-

1. *The Collected Tribes.* The past of God's unfailing goodness is reviewed by Joshua, vv. 1-10. The present of God's unstinted giving is rehearsed by him, vv. 11-13.

2. *The Challenged Tribes,* vv. 14-24. "Now therefore", vv. 14, 23. Blessing and privilege beget responsibility. Joshua bases the challenge on his own re-stated commitment, v. 15. His courage, demanded at the start, 1. 6-7, is now freshly evidenced at the end. How needful to finish well, as also to begin well. Only such men can lead others to faithfulness. Reminded of the cost of faithfulness, vv. 19-20, four times Israel state their vow. In answer to the challenge "fear" Him, "serve him", v. 14, they respond that they would serve the Lord, vv. 16, 18, 21, 24.

3. *The Covenanted Tribes,* vv. 25-28. Abraham raised the altar to worship, because of the promise. Joshua raises a stone to witness the vow at the fulfilment of the promise. God has done great things for *us!* Where is our altar (Rom. 12. 1) and our stone? The altar is necessary to fix the heart, and the stone to hold the will. Now in the latter part of the chapter we have the closing obituary. Here is revealed:

i) *A Service Recognized* — Joshua, vv. 29-31. He was laid to rest in his high place of inheritance, v. 30, and was remembered and followed by his people, v. 31.

ii) *A Hope Realized* — Joseph, v. 32. Long before, he had left Shechem to search for his brethren, Gen. 37. 14, never to see it again, yet his eye and heart were ever set upon it, Gen. 50. 24-26. In burial his hope and lot were realized!

iii) *A Ministry Ratified* — Eleazer, v. 33.

Lesson. What will be our obituary? Fought well (Joshua); Finished well (Joseph); Kept well (Eleazer = God has helped)?

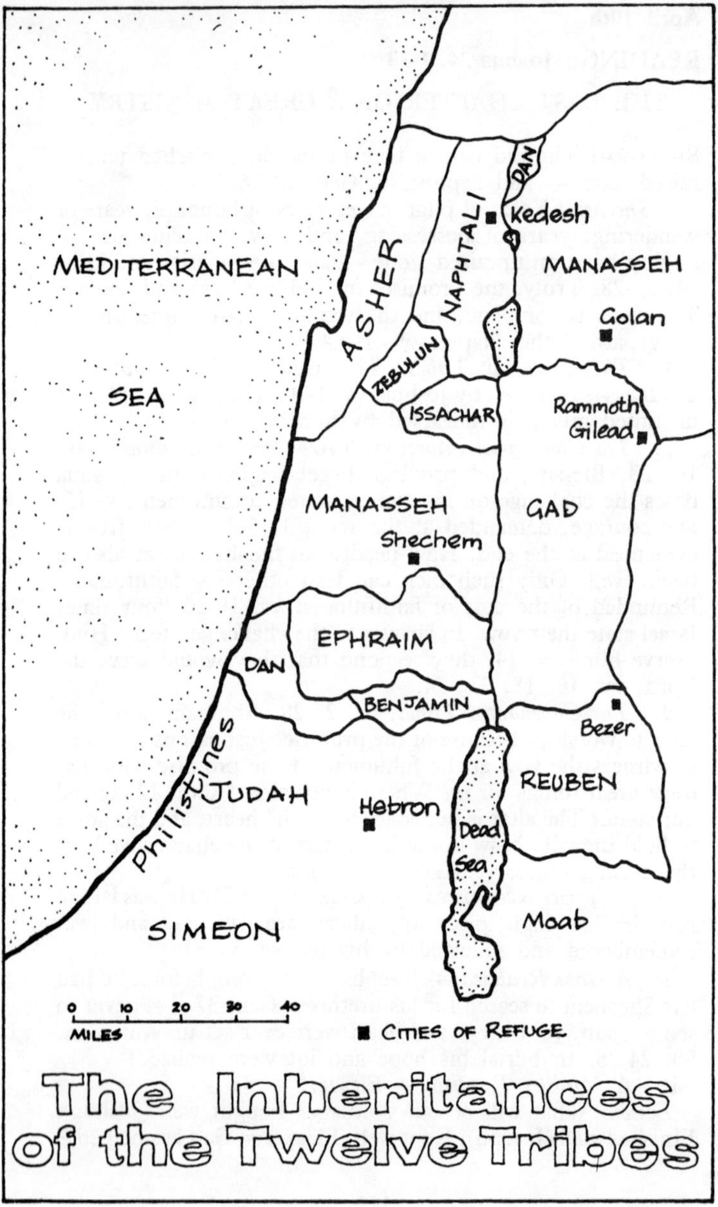

The Inheritances of the Twelve Tribes

April 12th

READING : **Judges 3. 7-31**

OTHNIEL AND EHUD

THE NATION'S departures are met with Divine *discipline*, bringing them into great *distress*, each tragic cycle being climaxed by *deliverance* when there had been repentance.

1. *Othniel and Chushan-rishathaim*, vv. 7-11. Departure from God, morally, v. 7a, and idolatrously, v. 7b, inevitably leads to being engulfed by the world. This may be allowed by the providential hand of God in discipline, v. 8a. Mesopotamia, the place whence Abraham came, represents the world in its glory, requiring the vision of a greater glory to lead one out of it, Acts 7. 2. Its ruler is Chushan-rishathaim (prince of double wickedness), viz., the prince of this world. Instead of years of "risen life" (eight, Josh. 3. 8), they experienced years of worldly, earthly subjugation. Who can, under God, deliver from such captivity? Those who, like Othniel, the lion-hearted, know what it is to win the victory in the power of a first love; cf. 1. 12-13. As this first judge overcame in the energy of a first love, the first church in Revelation 2-3, failed through lack of it, 2.4. Remember 1 John 2. 15. Love for God, moving in the power of the Spirit, Jud. 3. 10, overcomes the world.

2. *Ehud and Eglon*, vv. 12-30. If the foe to be faced was the world with Othniel, it is now the flesh. Moab, the *product* of the flesh, Gen. 19. 30-38, with his equally fleshly brother, Ammon, linked with Amalek, the *power* of the flesh, cf. Exod. 17. 8-13, attack Israel and subjugate it. They do this as led by Eglon, the true epitome of all three. He was a fat man, v. 17, who loved his ease, v. 20. Who can now deliver from such? A man of "the right hand", a Benjamite, Gen. 35. 18, who incidentally was a man of the left hand, Jud. 3. 15. Is this being spiritually ambidextrous? If I am at God's *right* hand, my *left* hand of weakness will be in touch with omnipotence! Such are likely experts in the use of the double-edged sword, Heb. 4. 12, making it their own, Josh. 3. 16. This alone is effective in slaying the flesh, vv. 21-22; cf. Gal. 5. 24. How the "message from God", Josh. 3. 20, appropriately associates in thought with the sword, double-edged, v. 16.

Lesson. With first love for God in our hearts (Othniel), let us ever turn from the "graven images", v. 19 marg., and use the sword for the destruction of the flesh (Ehud).

April 13th

READING : **Judges 4. 1-24**

DEBORAH, A MOTHER IN ISRAEL

MESOPOTAMIA was the enemy from afar; Moab, (the flesh) a relative, next door; now, Israel had to face the Canaanites within the land! Surely spiritual wickedness in high places now confronts us. Typically, we have met the world and the flesh; now the devil is rampant. The devil's first victory was over and through the woman, Eve. His overthrow here is to be through a woman. Deborah is the great encourager of women of God.

1. *She knew her God.* She was a prophetess, v. 4, in touch with God. She became a judge, v.4, in touch with men. What a need there is today for godly older sisters who can give counsel to the younger; see Titus 2. 3-5.

2. *She knew her place.* The question may arise, "Why a woman judge?". The answer may be supplied in Deborah's song. "The *rulers ceased,* in Israel, they ceased, *until* that I Deborah arose", Jud. 5. 7 R.V. She confesses she arose "a *mother* in Israel". The omission of "the Lord raised up", as seen for example in 3. 9, 15, is suggestive, and the Divine movements calling Gideon and preparing Samson have no parallel here. Was there no man God could use? How the imbalance of sisters over brethren in our missionary prayer lists challenges us! Deborah's stance is significant. Her service is beautifully expressed; "she dwelt under the palm tree of Deborah . . . and the children of Israel *came up unto her* for judgment (advice, counsel)", 4. 5. Here was no taking the lead!

3. *She knew her man.* She was in touch with what was of worth in the land, and could put her hand on Barak, though even he was far from strong, Jud. 4. 8. Nevertheless, encouraged by her presence, complying with God's command, v. 6, obeying the Lord's instructions, v. 6, inspired by God's promise, v. 7, and profiting from Deborah's guidance, v. 14, the enemy is engaged and the battle fought. It is good for young men not to despise the help of godly sisters, and to remember that an undue hesitancy in consecrated manhood may sacrifice the honour of the day, v. 9. True to Deborah's word, Sisera escapes the sword of Barak, and falls to the hammer and tent-pin of another female. How the hand of the Lord in sovereignty, moves for us in our conflicts, vv. 11, 12.

Lesson. Do not de-value your womanhood, consecrate it!

April 14th

READING : **Judges 6. 11-32**

GIDEON: THE WAY TO VICTORY

MIDIAN is the enemy representing the mercenary spirit so often plundering and paralysing the people of God. Midian was Abraham's offspring, Gen. 25. 2, thus related to Israel, but they appear on the Biblical scene as "merchantmen", Gen. 37. 28. Heed the principle of Proverbs 11. 24; cf. Jud. 6. 1-6. Now there was a young man in Israel who

1. *Valued basic things*, v. 11. He is seen engaged in essential activity, in unusual environs, to counter the plundering enemy of his people. He thus engages the attention of Deity, vv. 11-12. He is

2. *Vexed with prevailing conditions*, v. 13. They are obviously of concern to him, and "the Lord looked upon him", showing further interest, v. 14. He

3. *De-values his worth*, v. 15, but asks for a sign, v. 17. The sign will be based on a demonstration of his willingness to sacrifice the scarce and essential things of his life to his God, vv. 17-19. In principle, the Midianite spirit is thus defeated in his own life. The Lord thus speaks peace to him, v. 23, and he fittingly celebrates the Lord of Peace — Jehovah - Shalom, v. 24, the altar remaining confirmatively. He is now called to

4. *Verify his expressed conviction*, v. 25, "the same night". He must make known in a wider sphere what is in his own heart, first in his family. Private conviction expresses itself in public action. He must take the *second* bullock (significant principle!) which had been safely guarded during the whole period of Midianitish oppression, cf. 6. 1 and 25. Then, breaking down the family altar to Baal, Israel's basic sin, he is to erect an altar above it to Jehovah, and offer upon it the expression of the nation's true sacrificial conviction. With deep apprehension, he employs the cover of night — but he does it! They who will go forward in the fear of the Lord, prepared to give Him that which at times they can ill afford, but thus recognizing the Divine rights, are on their way to defeating Midian, and restoring the true riches of the people of God. By our withholding from God because of some "Baal" in the life, God may remove through "Midian" what we have.

Lesson. Victory over Midian in the realm of my soul prepares for his overthrow in the arena.

April 15th

READING : **Judges 6. 33 to 7. 25**

GIDEON: THE WAY OF VICTORY

THE MIDIANITES, we have learned, speak of the spirit which takes and retains all for self. In discipline, they have been used of God to strip Israel of that which they have been retaining for self and not giving to God. They were too busy with Baal. Yet, God answers the ascending cry, 6. 6, and yesterday we saw Him selecting and preparing His man for deliverance. The principle of this deliverance must be in that which is the opposite to the cause of the captivity.

1. Gideon, the man of true values, is seen as a *Worshipper*, that is, he gives God his sacrificed best. Note his costly present, 6. 18-19, his altar, v. 24, his further most costly offering, v. 26, and his worship, 7.15. The first step to victory in this instance is total consecration, a retaining of nothing, the giving all to God. Thus will Midian be defeated!

2. Gideon is consequently seen as a *Warrior*, but in a strange guise. Having given God what he had, he faces the battle with nothing! Nailing his colours to the mast in chapter 6, he immediately draws out the enemy's response; note "Then", v. 33. His proclaimed conviction is bound to stir the spirit of any trafficking Midianite, but the Spirit of the Lord is match for any such, v. 34. A man emptied of self is a fitted vehicle for God's Spirit. Note the denuded warrior, with but 300 men, 7. 7. He is seen by others as a "cake of *barley* bread", v. 13, a fitting symbol of poverty. He has only trumpets, *empty* pitchers, and firebrands! But with these he has *God!* Hence, his is victory without a stroke, vv. 21-22. Their hands were otherwise occupied, and others move in to the kill, vv. 20-25.

In seeking encouragement in all this, let us not forget Gideon was, at best, just a man of like passions with ourselves. Note his confessed insufficiency, 6. 15, the doubt hidden away in his pessimism, v. 13, his request for a sign, v. 17, his fear of men, v. 27, the request for a double sign giving confirmed assurance, vv. 36-40, and his nervousness of the enemy, 7. 10. Remember God can still use tumbling cakes of barley bread!

In these days of increasing affluence, despite constantly rising costs of living, the Laodicean spirit of getting and possessing still tends to cool the fervour of the Lord's own.

Lesson. When God has all, I have everything.

April 16th

READING : **Judges 9. 1-22**

ABIMELECH

THE TRAGEDY in this chapter is that Israel are not fighting their enemies, but massacring one another. We see that ability for God is not communicated through the family bloodstream, 8. 30-31. Taking a second look at Abimelech, we are reminded that self-opinionated and self-elected men are dangerous. Israel had once again turned to Baal after Gideon was dead. Is God allowing a lash of different character to fall on His wayward people? A man prepared to kill his own kin to achieve kingship, can he truly rule a people? There have been Diotrephes in every age, 3 John 9-11! Abimelech's name means "My father was king", but his father had refused kingship, Jud. 8. 22-23, and had refused it to his son. How hateful is canvassing for position in spiritual matters, receiving the hire of men (and demons, 9. 4), and going to the lengths of force to achieve ambition. Crowning a man king, even at the famous oak of the pillar of Shechem, does not confer royalty! How blessed that Jotham escaped, for he has much to teach us. In his parable, the call of the trees for a king,

1. The olive refuses the crown on the ground of a superior service of bringing honour to God and man.
2. The fig refuses the crown on the ground of the desired ministry of fruitbearing.
3. The vine refuses the crown, preferring to bring joy to the heart of God and man. We learn, therefore, that there is more in spiritual fatness, fruitbearing, and fragrance, than in wielding the sceptre. Note, all these trees are Bible figures of Israel. They were not to rule, but to be ruled. See Gideon's word "the Lord shall rule over you", 8. 23. The bramble (or thornbush) accepts! What a travesty! How did Abimelech react to this? From 9. 15 observe how the incompatible can make his demands. Either submit to absolute authority, or else be suppressed. He would destroy even the noblest, "the cedars". The parable and pronouncement of Jotham receives exact fulfilment, v. 20. How fire came out of Abimelech, vv. 45-49, but men like him sign their own death warrant, v. 53. Thus God requited the wickedness of Abimelech, v. 56.

How the word of James needs to be heeded, 3. 1.

Lesson. Be content *to be* something for God and man!

April 17th

READING : **Judges 11. 1-40**

JEPHTHAH

Now the enemy is Ammon, another relative of Israel. He would rob Israel of *territory* (his inheritance), whereas Moab, his brother, would rob her of *victory*, 3. 13. Guard your inheritance in Christ! Jephthah began with a double handicap for which he was not responsible, 11. 1-2, but God can use handicapped men! Note Israel's extremity, 10. 6-10, the divine exasperation, vv. 11-14, Israel's repentance, vv. 15-16a, and God's grief, v. 16b. The elders' call for help becomes the call of God, 11. 5-6, for God has a work for Jephthah, 12. 7. Jephthah knew what it was to be chased out of an inheritance, 11. 2. He will fight for Israel's inheritance. He was a man who could sink revenge, and master his spirit, vv. 6-11. He will confront the enemy with the *word* before the *sword*, and he does it graciously, v. 27, reasoningly, vv. 23-26, spiritually, v. 27b, and accurately, vv. 14-28. He knew his history, and therefore values the inheritance. Is the church despising her inheritance because she is unmindful of her history? Ammon's rebuff drives Jephthah to the sword and, by the Spirit of God, v. 29, the battle is joined and the territory held.

Jephthah's determination is expressed by his vow, vv. 30-31. Now vows can be dangerous. Samson broke his, but Jephthah keeps his. Guarding the inheritance meant more to him than all. What was the nature of the vow? Did it mean death? The believer's ascending offering is *living*, Rom. 12. 1! Reviewing the occasion, let us remember Jephthah *is* celebrated in Hebrews 11! Would God encourage a crime by granting victory? Jephthah appears a true Israelite who knew his book. Burnt offerings for the altar were male, Lev. 1. 3. If death had been two months away, would the girl have left her sorrowing father? She goes to bewail not her *life*, but her *virginity*, Jud. 11. 37. Was not this a matter worse than death to a Hebrew maid? Being his only child, v. 34, and now never to be given in marriage, v. 39, hers was to be a life dedicated to God, and, incidentally, Jephthah's name was never to be perpetuated in Israel. Ammon's birth was due to a daughter's unfaithfulness; Jephthah's daughter will mark the victory by faithfulness.

Lesson. How fickle is the flesh, 12. 1-6. Let *us* pay our vows, and maintain their spirit *afterwards*.

April 18th

READING : **Judges 13. 1-25**

SAMSON IS RAISED UP

IT IS SINGULAR that the last enemy of Israel in the Book is the Philistines, termed regularly "the uncircumcised Philistines", representing religion without mark of covenant or separation. Following their migratory course (also from Egypt), their route has no equivalent to redemption by blood or power (Red Sea), and no Jordan crossing! Compare, too, the last church mentioned in the New Testament, Laodicea. There was much form, but little reality!

Before God provided His deliverer, He selected the channel. Note the Hannah's and Mary's of Scripture! This woman remains nameless (note the repeated "the woman"), but with God anonymity does not signify insignificance. Does this encourage the reader? This mother-to-be was one in whom

1. God's principle of life would operate, for her body was dead, Jud. 13. 2. Only such are usable by God.

2. She was open to receive the Divine communication ordering her life, that she may become fitted to prepare for another, vv. 4-5. She thus was moved to action, vv. 6-7, and then desired further direction, vv. 8-14.

3. All this led on to worship and consecration to the Lord's will, and issued in a deep realization of the grace and faithfulness of God, v. 12a, 15-23. How this simple yet believing woman grew! Then "the woman bare a son", v. 24. What an example to all believing mothers who would be used of God these days. The coming deliverer had

a) A good *beginning*, for he had a good mother who quitted herself faithfully, that her way of life might be communicated to her son, vv. 4-5. What a ministry a godly mother has. Such can bare men for God, v. 24.

b) A God-impelled *beginning*, v. 25. He did not move; he *was* moved, by the Spirit of the Lord. God needs Spirit-impelled men, those who will respond instantly to Divine prompting, their work being not of the flesh, but of the Spirit.

c) A call to a work of *beginning*, v. 5. The Philistines continued to be thorns in Israel's side on into the days of David, but Samson was chosen as the "Beginner".

Lesson. Have you had a privileged beginning? Will you be a beginner for God, just where you are?

April 19th

READING : Judges 16. 1-31

SAMSON HAS FALLEN

WAS THERE something particular about Gideon, Samson and Samuel, seeing, unlike the rest of the judges, they were called by Divine visitation? Yet, however we look at Samson, despite his special preparation, he appears a relative failure. Reviewing his activities, we never see him engaged in a campaign, but only in a few unrelated sorties. On five occasions it is recorded "he went down". He constantly broke the laws of his Nazariteship, see Num. 6, and in both his love affairs he broke the Mosaic law regarding marriage, Deut. 7. 3. Breaking his Nazarite vow, he made no confession thereof, 14. 6, 9. He fulfils his calling in such unorthodox ways, and it is only the gracious sovereignty of God which adds the success. Note the following passages, 14. 4, 6, 19; 15. 14; 16. 28. Nevertheless, let us learn, as Samson did too late, that there comes a time when God will refuse His presence and aid, 16. 20. How much more would God have used him had he been faithful. If we have seen the Philistine character as representative of Laodicean church conditions, we also see Samson reflecting the same. See him at last blind, denuded, wretched and miserable; cf. Rev. 3. 17. It is also significant that we see him ending his course exactly where he started it, Jud. 13. 25; 16. 31. Is our spiritual service a mere "vicious circle", or one of progressive achievement? Samson's attacks on the enemy were always because he, personally, had been affronted, and not because his people had been down-trodden.

Such was the darkness of Israel's hour that, truly, the demand was for a fitting and competent deliverer. God, in His mercy, did all necessary to supply such a one, dedicated to God by his vow, and thus separated from all else; see again ch. 13. Yet there is relative failure. The blame rests squarely on the faithlessness of the instrument. Let us learn herefrom that these last days are our "dark days", and that we, like Samson (and Esther), "have been brought to the kingdom for such a time as this". Are we fulfilling our calling or failing in it?

Lesson. Greater space is given to the record of Samson's overthrow than to his exploits! What will be the ratio of success and failure in our biography? Each one of us is to "receive the things done in his body . . . good or bad", 2 Cor. 5. 10.

April 20th
READING : Judges 17. 1-13
MORAL CONDITIONS DURING THE JUDGES

ONE READING must suffice for the closing section of this book, viz., chapters 17-21, and we begin by reminding ourselves that their substance runs parallel with chapters 1-16. Thus they could be considered first before attending to the earlier chapters, seeing they present the moral conditions prevailing throughout the period. Our chapters portray the inner condition of the nation, the root matter; the earlier chapters supply the outer manifestations, the fruits of the root. Note the repeated phrase "in those days there was no king in Israel: every man did that which was right in his own eyes", 17. 6 R.V.; 21. 25; cf. 18. 1; 19. 1, a constant reminder that where rule and authority are absent, self-pleasing and anarchy dominate. In this kind of soil, corruption of all kinds rapidly breeds. God reveals the dominant conditions in a moral order. He teaches that where there is idolatry and departure from God, chs. 17-18, there will inevitably follow corruption, ch. 19, strife and violence, chs. 20-21. Wrong relationships Godward issue in distorted relationships manward.

What confusion our chapter presents. We find the beginnings of idolatry in God's nation — not that belonging to the nations around, but their own hybrid brand! Note its *basic elements;* silver, theft, a curse, blessing, and dedication unto Jehovah, and out of this a graven image. The *instigator* is a woman, cf. Matt. 13. 33; Rev. 17, and a *mother!* What irresponsible motherhood. Note how idolatry starts, v. 5a, and develops, v. 5b, divine ideas being added thereto; cf. vv. 12-13. Watch what is "taking shape" in your house! This situation is further aggravated when men of God wander out of orbit, and depart from Bethlehem-judah, vv. 7-8.

Such conditions can never be contained within their initial limits. Leaven spreads. The Danites are reconnoitering! "Dan shall judge his people", said Jacob, Gen. 49. 16; yes, but also he was to be "a serpent in the way", so that "his rider falleth *backward*". Read carefully chapter 18. 30. The whole tribe is infected, v. 19. This was a festering sore in the land, v. 31, and therefore nothing in chapters 19-21 surprises us.

Lesson. Fellowships are marred through departure from God in the household.

April 21st

READING : **Ruth 1. 1-22**

CLOUDS WITH A SILVER LINING

THE CHAPTER before us falls into three distinct sections.

1. *The Departure and Why*, vv. 1-2. In view of the times, this famine must have been one of divine discipline, God using natural causes or enemy oppression to bring it about; cf. Deut. 8. 8-9. Elimelech (= my God is King), whose name belies his actions, decides to leave Bethlehem, the "house of bread". Himself an Ephrathite, or Ephraimite, "fruitful", he appears to be seeking the physical salvation of two ailing sons — Mahlon, "sick" or "sickly", and Chilion, "pining" or "weak". It would seem Naomi had no choice but to comply. Her name (= pleasant) might imply she was spiritually fragrant. Of all places, he goes to Moab; see Num. 22-25; Deut. 23. 3-6. Why turn from a God who controls to a people who curse?

2. *The Sojourn and What*, vv. 3-5. A stay of about *ten* years suggests divine testing. The result is a threefold tragedy, not salvation. Elimelech, the would-be deliverer, himself dies, v. 3; his sons add spiritual disaster to physical distress, v. 4, and then they succumb! The innocent party is spared, but how denuded, "left", v. 5. Our faithlessnesses endanger others.

3. *The Return and Who*, vv. 6-22. Five verses are enough to record the departure and its cost, whereas seventeen are used to describe the return! It is easy to backslide; restoration can be a difficult process. But Naomi's heart is right, for she responds immediately; note the "Then" in verse 6. Had her heart ever left Bethlehem? Do verses 8-13 suggest Naomi remembered Deuteronomy 23. 3-6? Orpah turns back — and forever vanishes, vv. 14f. Ruth cleaves! Her heart was true, undoubtedly stirred by Naomi's example, and her lips confessed it in the sublimest of words, vv. 16-17. Confession confirms conversion, Rom. 10. 10. Ruth's mind is made up, v. 16a, her determination is expressed, v. 16b, her identification with the people and God of Naomi is deeply registered, v. 16c, and its duration measured, v. 17a. With solemn vow she endorses it, v. 17b. So Naomi returns with a precious reward, though departure always leaves its mark, vv. 20-21. In returning, it must always be to the point from which we departed, v. 22.

Lesson. When the soul returns home, the harvest of plenty always immediately begins, v. 22.

April 22nd

READING : **Ruth 2. 1-23**

A NEW LIFE AND A NEW PURPOSE

IF SOVEREIGNTY is despised in chapter 1, it is demonstrated here. Verse 1 is a fact apparently unknown to Ruth at the time. Compare "Let me now go", v. 2, "her hap", v. 3, and "behold, Boaz came", v. 4. How God's hand begins to move purposefully for us when we come to Him. Elimelech might have known such had he waited! This chapter plots the progress of a soul who has "turned to God". We saw Ruth's *Expresed Devotion,* ch. 1, now we see her.

1. *Exercised Desire,* v. 2. Ruth unfolded her proposal for approval by the elder Naomi; always a wise step. She desired to work, however humbly, reminding us again of those who "turned . . .to serve", 1 Thess. 1. 9. She wanted to glean "after him in whose sight I shall find grace". How suggestive!

2. *Earnest Dutifulness.* Ruth was concerned to provide for her mother-in-law, whom she knew had returned "empty", and was "too old", 1. 12. She truly was an imitator of God, Deut. 10. 18, and anticipates the as yet unwritten maxim of James 1. 27! With what satisfaction Naomi and Ruth enjoy the result of her labours, vv. 18, 19, the prepared parched corn, which remained of Boaz' liberal provision for Ruth's meal; cf. vv. 14 and 18c R.V.

3. *Engaging Diligence.* She becomes a model for all who would serve the Lord and others. Her labour was *strenuous.* You bend to glean! It was *steadfast,* v. 7b. It was with *sedulity,* even "until even", and it was *sufficient,* for she "beat (it) out". Are our tasks always so completed?

As newborn souls, what do we know about gleaning in the field of our greater than Boaz, and not in any other?, v. 8. Truth is not reaped, but gleaned grain by grain, which yet mounts up to a goodly supply, v. 17. Such diligent and patient gleaning in the field of God's Word will conduct us, like Ruth, into an increasing knowledge of our Boaz, vv. 11-13, into a deepening fellowship with Him at His table, v. 14, assure us of His protection and further provision, vv. 15-16, and give us His needed directive for our pathway, vv. 21, 23. God's provisions are to be discovered through the Word of God.

Lesson. How often am I diligently gleaning, and beating out the barley and wheat of God's Word?

April 23rd

READING : **Ruth 3. 1-18; 4. 10-13, 17**

ANOTHER LINK IN MESSIAH'S CHAIN

THE DELICACY and modesty of Ruth must be patent to all, and not least to the watchful Naomi and the benevolent Boaz. She takes nothing for granted, yet everything with gratitude, e.g., 2. 13. Are her spirit, conduct, 2. 11; 3. 10, and need winning Boaz' heart? Time is passing, and Naomi, concerned for her, determines to seek her "rest". There was a law of redemption concerning property in Israel, Lev. 25. 25, and also a law designed to preserve the name of such as Ruth's deceased husband, Deut. 25. 5. Strictly, this would be the responsibility of the deceased's brother, but he, too, was dead. Naomi knows that kind and wealthy Boaz is a kinsman, 2. 1, 20, and he has already shown interest. Has this not been observed by Ruth through his many advances? So Naomi, as now the responsible "parent" of Ruth, proposes, 3. 1-4.

1. *The Scene*, vv. 3-7. Read this again, carefully and prayerfully. Naomi is not pressing this innocent girl into indecency, nor is Ruth acting immodestly. Do not bring a modern, and western mind to bear on this. The spirit of the Levitical and Deuteronomic laws were undoubtedly influencing all parties. For once, the glorious end of this "rest-seeking" is to justify the means, 4. 17; Matt. 1. 5-6. With suited preparation and means, Ruth 3. 3, others obviously being present, she does what was custom in Israel, for one claiming protection and redemption. What modest submission, v. 7.

2. *The Success*, vv. 8-18. Observe the divine hand in the awaking, v. 8; cf. Esth. 6. 1-9, the sense of tremor in her request, v. 9, the ready acquiescence, vv. 10-13, inferring an already prepared heart, the modest leave taking, v. 14, and the gift at departure, almost an "earnest", v. 15.

3. *The Seed*, 4. 10-13, 17. Boaz acts expeditiously, indicating both hearts are one, cf. 3. 18, yet wisely, regarding the nearer kinsman, and acting before witnesses that the union might become ratified in law. Later, Obed is born, Naomi is blessed, 4. 14-16, and lo! the way for David, and thence the Christ, is established. What a message for the heart today. His *blessings* are great, but the Redeemer *Himself* is greater. —

Lesson. Do I know *real* union with Christ, and am I bringing Him nearer to others?

Introducing the Books of Samuel

THE BOOKS OF SAMUEL and Kings make up the greater **part of the Former Prophets** (Joshua - 2 Kings). This description indicates something of the character of these books. Here we are not to expect history written from man's point of view. Rather, using as a touchstone that "righteousness exalteth a nation", our books probe the past for the meaning of history, putting its significance to work for the guidance of posterity. The lessons of history can be appreciated rightly only if our vantage point is God's watchtower, and if all is seen in relation to Him. If He is not our centre, then all is eccentric. Throughout history God is *forthtelling*, expressing His ways and His will, teaching us and warning us.

Many would accept that history has a strange way of repeating itself. Westcott said that the O.T. does not merely contain prophecies of the Christ, but that it is from first to last one vast prophecy of Him. Hence the element of *foretelling* is latent in these Former Prophets. David, the anointed, the caring shepherd, the courageous warrior, the rejected prince, and finally the crowned king, is a faint and poor projection of the greater than David, his Son who is his Lord, Psa. 110. 1.

The essential link between the Books of Samuel and Kings is further suggested by the title **The Books of Kingdoms** given to all four in the LXX (Greek) and Vulgate (Latin) translations of the O.T. The contrast seems to be between the failing rulers and their methods of rule, and the overruling of God. Whilst the history covered here does record the transition from Theocracy to that of the Monarchy, it must be stressed that God did not thereby cease to rule.

Much more could have been said, as reference to the many sources drawn upon indicates, cf. 1 Sam. 10. 25; 2 Sam. 1. 18; 1 Kings 14. 29; 2 Kings 15. 31, etc. Everything included brings out **the factors involved with rule,** both what is of God, and that which is contrary to Him, so that we may learn the importance which God sets upon the godly leading of His people. Properly led, His people will learn to behave themselves in His house, cf. 1 Tim. 3.

The monarchy formed an essential part of the purpose of God. It had been promised to Abraham, Gen. 17. 6, and the sceptre was assigned to Judah, 49. 10; cf. Num. 24. 7; Deut. 17. 14-20. The disorders of the times of the Judges were traced to there being no king then in Israel, Jud. 17. 6; 18. 1, etc. The monarchy was a necessary preparation for the coming Messiah, 1 Sam. 2. 9f, who would be anointed with the oil of gladness above His fellows, Psa. 45. 6ff; Heb. 1. 8f. Monarchy was right, but, initially, the timing was wrong. The man the people chose, Saul, failed: God gave him to them in His anger, Hos. 13. 9-11. But the man after God's own heart, David, was in the wings, waiting God's time to be called on stage. He was God's choice for them, Acts 13. 21-23.

In the Books of Samuel we are shown:-
1. *The Need for Rule,* 1 Sam. 1-8 (cf. Jud. 17-21). Eli, the priest-judge is the foil for Samuel, the prophet-judge. Failure here leads to a section depicting
2. *The Man for Rule,* 1 Sam. 9 to 2 Sam. 8.
   (*a*). Saul the people's choice, independent, disobedient
   (*b*). David, God's choice, dependant, obedient.
   In both sections God takes away the first that He might establish the second. The question of the succession after David is then resolved. So
   (*c*). Solomon rules, not Amnon, Absalom, Adonijah, all of whom were David's sons, 2 Sam. 9 to 1 Kings 2.

Throughout it is **the man qualified to rule** that is being sought. There is a disproportionately large number of references to man/men in Samuel (cf. also Judges). Certain of these appear in what are turning points in the history, 1 Sam. 1. 1; 9. 1; 17. 4 (champion=middle-man); 25.2, and to these may be added others who appear in far from favourable light, e.g. the sons of Eli, the sons of Samuel, etc. Conversely, consider the fine examples of God's men in Samuel and David.

But man in authority needs a help suited to him, and in 1 Samuel the godliness, discernment, humility, and dependence of women further God's cause, e.g. Hannah, the wife of Phinehas, the women of Israel, 18. 6f, Michal, and Abigail. Failure among them is of a different kind, but no less catastrophic in result, e.g. the witch, 28. 7ff, Michal and Bathsheba in 2 Samuel.

April 24th

READING : **1 Samuel 1. 1 to 2. 11**

TUNE MY HEART TO SING THY PRAISE

THE OPENING CLAUSE "Now there was a certain man" introduces us to the first of a number of men in the book who are not after God's heart. True there were evidences of consistent piety, vv. 3, 4, 7, 19, 21-23, but Elkanah's heart was divided, v. 2, with all the problems that this produced, vv. 6, 8, 10. He was self-satisfied, v. 8, despite the patent barrenness which was a token of the Lord's withholding, v. 5.

The failures of the man are set against the spiritual qualities of his wife, Hannah="grace". She teaches us to yearn after fruitfulness. She took her burden to the Lord in prayer, fasting and weeping, vv. 8, 10. Her appeal was addressed to the Lord of hosts, v. 11, with whom all things are possible. She poured out her soul, v. 15, and He heard the words in her heart, v. 13. Assured that her petition would be answered, and she would "find grace", v. 18, her sadness vanished, and *they* worshipped before the Lord, v. 19.

In course of time her son was born, and was named Samuel. He was an embodiment of God's response to her asking, vv. 17, 20, 27, 28; 2. 20. His education began at his mother's knee, cf. 2 Tim. 1. 5; 3. 15, but already Hannah had determined that as he had been granted to her, she would grant him to the Lord, v. 28.

The Hannah who prayed and wept, 1. 10, now prays with rejoicing, 2. 1. She read in her own experiences certain general principles which we, too, should take to heart today. The salvation of God is to be *experienced*, and become a source of joy to us. Only then will our hearts exult in the Lord Himself, and our voices be heard to His praise, 2. 1. Ponder His Person, vv. 2-3, and His providence, vv. 4-8. His ways are quite different from those of men, praise His name, vv. 5b, 21. But excelling all is that note of confidence with which her song ends. The same Lord who keeps His people, and will yet silence and break all opposition, has decreed that "by strength shall no man prevail", v. 9. Further, "he shall give strength unto his king, and exalt the horn of his anointed", v. 10. Universal administration in righteousness is to be established.

Teach me, Lord, to rise from sorrow, to supplication, and thence to song.

April 25th

READING : **1 Samuel 3. 1 to 4. 1a**

SPEAK; FOR THY SERVANT HEARETH

SAMUEL'S MOTHER had sung "He (the Lord) will keep the feet of his saints", 2. 9. To sing truth is not enough. Her son, Samuel, was now to prove this, and that in a sanctuary desecrated by Eli's sons. For even there he made spiritual progress, from the child ministering to the Lord, 3. 1, to the mature prophet of the Lord, v. 19f. "Preserve me, O God", Psa. 16. 1!

There is, perhaps, no clearer proof of the bankruptcy of the flesh than where, despite the highest privilege, human decline is seen in God's things, 3. 1-3. "And the word of the Lord was precious in those days". In one sense, of course, it should be highly valued, prized, esteemed by us. But the chilling fact expressed here is rather that the word was rare, as the parallel shows, for there was no openly published vision either, cf. Isa. 13. 12. There was *no voice;* there was *no vision*. Notice too that the high priest "was laid down", *no priestly energy;* and "his eyes began to wax dim", virtually *no spiritual discernment*, 1 Sam. 3. 2.

Out of this darkening scene a new day was about to dawn, for "the Lord called Samuel", vv. 4. 10. Here there was both *vision,* for "the Lord . . . stood" and presented Himself, and there was a *voice*, v. 10, cf. 21. The Lord is longing to make Himself known, and to make His word a living oracle to you now. Ask Him to "Speak". Tell him you are ready to hear, and will be quick to obey, v. 10.

The revelation given, vv. 11-14, was faithfully communicated by Samuel to Eli, vv. 15-18, and the judgment reserved for his house, v. 13, came to pass, v. 19 and ch. 4. Yet in wrath, as ever, the Lord remembered mercy. In Shiloh, once again, the Lord revealed Himself to Samuel "by the word of the Lord", v. 21. The Lord *spoke* to His servant. Not that this was an end in itself, for, as the Lord intended, "the word of Samuel came to all Israel", 4. 1a. It was not handed on as unfelt truth. God's word was channelled through such a committed servant, altogether in harmony with the ministry committed to him, that "the word of the Lord" to him, became "the word of Samuel" to them. May it be so through you today!

April 26th

READING : 1 Samuel 7. 1-17

FROM ICHABOD TO EBENEZER

CHAPTER 4 dealt with the victory of the Philistines over Israel at Ebenezer, named there *anticipatively*. Over that "no glory", Ichabod, could be written, for the glory of the Lord had departed indeed from Israel, 4. 21f. Chapter 7 deals with the defeat of the Philistines by Israel at Ebenezer, "the stone of help", now so described *experientially*. Truly, "Hitherto hath the Lord helped us", 7. 12. Our reading provides us with some of the secrets of such reversals in the lives of God's people, so that they rise from shameful defeat to storming triumph at the very same spot. Note that repentance, vv. 2-6, led to the rout of the foe, vv. 7-12, and brought Israel into rest under Samuel's judgeship, vv. 13-17.

Throughout some twenty years Samuel sought to bring the Word of God to the people. Consequently, "all the house of Israel lamented after the Lord", v. 2. The prophet consolidated this by spelling out the features of a return to the Lord "with all your hearts", v. 3. Let us heed these challenges today. First, *put away* — what place is there for strange gods? Then, *prepare your hearts* — let there be that determination of mind and will toward the Lord. Again, *serve Him only* — Him alone are we to worship, for Him alone are we to work, Matt. 4. 10. Further, the Lord had impressed Israel with a sense of *their own insufficiency*, the need for self-imposed *restraint upon their appetites*, and they were brought to a *full confession of their sins*. Their lives were adjusted to the will of God, 1 Sam. 7. 5f.

The people that responded to Samuel's preaching felt their need of his prayers too, v. 8. Their traditionalizing, which proved so fatal to them against the Philistines in chapter 4, is now past. There is no *it* that can save them, or us, though that *it* be the ark itself, 4. 3. They had now discovered, and so must we, that "the Lord our God . . . *he* will save us out of the hand of the Philistines", 7. 8. What the people's shouting with a great shout could not do, 4. 5, the Lord's thundering with a great thunder did do, 7. 10. Let us raise our Ebenezer. The Lord has *helped us hitherto*. We are also to trust Him as a *very present help* in time of trouble, Psa. 46. 1. Here we build our altar!

April 27th

READING : **1 Samuel 8. 1-22**

MAKE US A KING!

WE COME TO A WATERSHED in God's ways with Israel. The nation had been a *theocracy*. They are now to enter the period of the *monarchy*. Note the immediate circumstances prompting the change, vv. 1-3, leading to the people's desire for a king, vv. 4-9, whereupon the prophet made known the insatiable demands of a king, vv. 10-18, despite which the nation was determined to have a king, vv. 19-22.

The purpose of the Most High God involves the visible control of the whole earth, yea the universe, through His Messiah, 2. 9f; Eph. 1. 10. Here they would impatiently precipitate this. It was failure among the priests, 2. 12-17, 22, and of the prophet Samuel and his sons, 8. 1-3, that provided restless and faithless flesh its opportunity, prematurely, to seek change, though the seed of discontent had long since been sown, v. 7f. Samuel, wrongly, had "*made* his sons judges", v. 1: the people felt sure he could "*make* us a king", vv. 5, 6, 10, etc. Faith alone is blissfully aware of the direction and benevolent control of heaven's throne, and the privilege of touching things unseen, Heb. 11. 1. It was not Samuel, but this, which Israel rejected, preferring to walk by sight, vv. 5, 7, 22. God's direct rule was exchanged for man's, 10. 17-19, the spiritual for the carnal. Yet "It is better to trust in the Lord than to put confidence in princes", Psa. 118. 9. Count on this now! Men may deny God His rightful place, but they cannot dethrone Him, nor defeat His sovereign purpose. God is still on the throne!

God's people wished to be "like all the nations", vv. 5, 20, though chosen that they might not be reckoned among them, Num. 23. 9. Do not lose the desire to be different, Rom. 12. 2.

Insistence on our own way is a costly business; note the burdensome refrain "he will take", 1 Sam. 8. 11, 13, 14, 15, 16, 17; cf. 14. 52, tolling out the heavy demands of the king, esp. 22. 2. In the Lord's kingdom, happily, He will "satisfy her poor with bread", Psa. 132. 15. His present kingdom is not one of "meat and drink; but righteousness, and peace, and joy" in the Holy Spirit, Rom. 14. 17. Now is not the time for reigning. We are to "have grace, whereby we may serve God acceptably with reverence and godly fear", Heb. 12. 28.

April 28th

READING : 1 Samuel 12. 1-25

CONSIDER HOW GREAT THINGS HE HATH DONE

OUR READING COMPLETES the drama commenced at chapter 9, see esp. 10. 1, 24; 11. 15. *Wilfulness* insisted on having a king, 8. 19f; now it is owned as *wickedness*, 12. 19f; cf. Hos. 13. 9-11.

Samuel here addressed king and people alike; see the repeated "And Samuel said", vv. 1, 6, 20. Firstly, he asserted his own personal/official integrity, vv. 1-5; then he pleaded all the delivering acts of the Lord, in the face of which they sought their own king to rescue them, vv. 6-19; finally, Samuel encouraged them in the light both of the Lord's and his own ongoing commitment to them, vv. 20-25.

Samuel could speak of *his integrity*, v. 2f. They freely acknowledged his blamelessness, v. 4. Transparent honesty is demanded of us as we seek to represent a glorified Christ, 2 Cor. 2. 17; 4. 2. Walk worthy! Then he referred to *his instruction* of them, cf. 1 Sam. 12. 23. His message demanded that they "stand still", v. 7, and ponder. They were also to "stand still" in the presence of divine miracle, as God demonstrated His anger against their sin, v. 16. R.V. The government of God continues to bring clouds into our summer skies. His still small voice has sometimes to be replaced by thunder and rain. Note, specially, Samuel's loving concern in *his intercession* for the people. It is one thing to cry out to the Lord when we are in dire straits, vv. 8, 10. It is quite another to be known as men and women of prayer. Here, the prophet not only calls to the Lord to demonstrate His disapproval, v. 18, but he vows an unceasing prayer ministry on their behalf, v. 23. How often we sin just here against those with whom we enjoy the happiest relationships. Samuel, however, was committed to a people that had grieved him, and rejected the Lord, cf. 2 Cor. 12. 15. Here, surely, is the very spirit of Christ, Luke 23. 34 — make me more like Thee, Lord, cf. Acts 7. 59f.

The people knew that to Samuel He was "the Lord *thy* God", 1 Sam. 12. 19, and Samuel saw their hope in the fact that He was "their (your) God", vv. 9, 12, 14. This God would never forsake His people, v. 22, a promise even more preciously true to us, Heb. 13. 5. His own reputation was bound up with this, because they were His elect, v. 22.

April 29th

READING : **1 Samuel 15. 1-35**

TO OBEY IS BETTER THAN SACRIFICE

SAUL'S ELECTION to office is followed by his rejection, chs. 13-15. In our portion, Saul was commissioned to destroy Amalek, 15. 1-4, and his campaign was successful, though spoiled by partial obedience, vv. 5-9. Samuel, being made aware of this, faced Saul, condemning his disobedience, vv. 10-19. Saul first sought to cover up, vv. 20-23, but at last owned up, vv. 24-25. Samuel turned from Saul, who tore the prophet's garment in attempting to prevent his departure. Samuel proposed that this symbolized that the kingdom had been rent from Saul, and was to be given to another, vv. 26-31. The prophet then executed Agag, vv. 32f, and parted from Saul, vv. 34f. The Lord's *grace* toward us is *utterly free*, but we need reminding that His *demands* upon us are *totally binding*.

Amalek is a telling representative of the flesh, one of the great enemies of God's people. Its inroads are many and varied, Gal. 5. 19-21, and so often clearly contrary to the Spirit that we are ready to war against it, 1 Sam. 15. 9b. Hence the description "the sinners the Amalekites", v. 18. Too many believe, however, that the best of the flesh may adorn the service of God, v. 9a. The error of this is exposed here. Sparing the best is not acceptable to Him, v. 15, it is to do "evil in the sight of the Lord", v. 19. For awareness of the best, of any good in me, promotes pride, which will raise its monument to its own achievements, v. 12, and want an Agag (=high) to grace its victories. There is safety only when one is little in one's own sight, v. 17. We must own, not only that "they that are in the flesh cannot please God", but that *"in me* (that is, *in my flesh,)* dwelleth no good thing", Rom. 8. 8; 7. 18.

Weigh the consequences of partial obedience. Sacrifices cannot cover up stubbornness. It is not enough for Saul to attempt to rid the land of witches, 28. 3, while forgetting that "rebellion is as the sin of witchcraft", 15. 23. Eventually, he is reduced to consulting a witch because the "Lord answered him not", 28. 6ff. If Saul spares Amalek here, an Amalekite will be there at his death, 2 Sam. 1. 2-10. Inevitably, rejection of God's Word, vv. 19, 23, 26, leads to rejection by the Lord, vv. 11, 23, 26, 28, 35. "Behold, to obey is better than sacrifice, and to hearken than the fat of rams", v. 22.

April 30th

READING : **1 Samuel 16. 1-23**

THE LORD LOOKETH ON THE HEART

DAVID'S NAME, meaning "beloved", fairly describes what he was to God, "a man after his own heart", 13. 14; Acts 13. 22, "a neighbour of thine (Saul), that is better than thou", 1 Sam. 15. 28. In this reading he is first anointed by Samuel, as the successor of Saul, vv. 1-13, and then introduced to the court as the soother of Saul, vv. 14-23.

Samuel still mourned for Saul whom the Lord had rejected, v. 1, and was fearful of him, v. 2. The prophet was even convinced by the external attractiveness of Eliab, Jesse's firstborn, that "Surely the Lord's anointed is before him", v. 6. Jesse, too, called in six more of his sons, only to hear that "The Lord hath not chosen these", v. 10. He had not even considered the youngest as a likely candidate, v. 11. Yet, by now, Samuel knew that they could not sit down (lit. around) without him; he must be in their midst if their sacrificial feast was to be enjoyed, cf. v. 11b. So it is ordained for us, and for Israel, and even for heaven. The Lord's Christ (anointed) must be in the midst, Heb. 2. 12; Psa. 22. 22; Rev. 5. 6.

"Arise, anoint him: for this is he", the Lord said, as David was brought in, v. 12. He was anointed "in the midst of his brethren", while our Beloved was anointed with "the oil of gladness" above His fellows, Psa. 45. 7; Heb. 1. 9. From that time, David was specially equipped for his God-given work as "the Spirit of the Lord came upon" him mightily, 1 Sam. 16. 13. It was not what he was in himself that made him sufficient, though this was noticed, vv. 11f, 18; 17. 42. His sufficiency, as ours, was of God, 2 Cor. 3. 5. We are never called to a work without the divine gift, and the Spirit's power, to do it.

It may be surprising to some that Saul's melancholy is traced to the Lord, but thus was his disobedience governmentally dealt with, v. 14. The very plight of Saul occasioned the first introduction of David to the court, v. 21. Amid the demands of his daily occupation David so proved his God, v. 18, seeing Him in every scene and circumstance, that He became the substance of his song. Only such a saint, experienced and spiritual, can help a troubled soul, and make it well, vv. 16ff, 23, for "the Lord is with him", v. 18. What song of praise can your soul create "touching the king" today?

May 1st

READING : 1 Samuel 17. 1-54

THE LORD SAVETH NOT WITH SWORD AND SPEAR

DAVID NEEDED grace indeed to rise above the scorn of his brother, v. 28, the incredulity and interference of Saul, vv. 33, 38f, and the contempt and the curses of Goliath, vv. 42ff. He, too, was aware of the size and strength of the foe, v. 45. Goliath was indeed a man of war from his youth, vv. 4-7. What good David's staff now, those five smooth stones, a shepherd's bag, and a sling? Yet, one stone drawn from the bag, and hurled from the sling, felled that massif of flesh that dared to set itself up against God's people, and curse God's anointed. For us, there is safety in "the whole armour of God" alone, Eph. 6. 13-18.

Wherein did all but David err that day? Surely, it was in a wrong assessment of the greatness of the foe's wickedness. Because Goliath construed his action as a defying of "the armies of Israel", v. 10, the people responded "surely to defy Israel is he come up", v. 25. David's assessment was far more penetrating. Who, indeed, was "this uncircumcised Philistine, that he should defy the armies of the living God?", v. 26.

Lay tremendous value on proving your God in the everyday demands of life. David was a shepherd by occupation, vv. 15, 34; cf. 16. 11, 19, counting this as a charge from God. In his work-a-day life, David the faithful, became David the fearless. His Lord *delivered* him "out of the paw of the lion, and out of the paw of the bear", v. 37, as he, in turn, *"delivered"* a lamb, vv. 34-36. How this strengthened him now. He could count on God in this emergency situation too, for "he will *deliver* me out of the hand of this Philistine", v. 37; cf. v. 45f. He confessed, in unshakeable faith, "the battle is the Lord's, and he will give you into our hands", v. 47. Count on God at every turn.

In the wisdom of God the battle was initiated by a stripling "that *all the earth* may know that there is a God in Israel", v. 46. The world looks on at our responses under pressure also, and we need grace that His might be the glory. But equally, if not more important, was it that *"all this assembly* shall know that the Lord saveth not with sword and spear", v. 47. Have we been slow to learn that "though we walk in the flesh, we do not war after the flesh . . ."?, 2 Cor. 10. 3-5.

May 2nd

READING : **1 Samuel 17. 55 to 18. 30**

LOVE FOR DAVID — A DIVINE TOUCHSTONE

THE VICTORY over Goliath is a great turning point in our book, and in the life of David. *For Jonathan* David became the object of his affection, 18. 1-5. The evidences of his quenchless love in the ensuing story become as so many stepping stones through the floods of opposition to his beloved, 19. 1-7; 20. 1-42; 23. 15-18. *For the women* David's prowess far outstripped that of Saul, the subject of their song, striking discords in Israel and Philistia alike, 18. 6-11; 21. 11; 29. 5. *For Saul* David now became the subject of bitter jealousy and hatred, vv. 8f, 10-30, a theme to be pursued further in alternation with the unfolding of Jonathan's love. This radical worsening of Saul/David relations is demonstrably a part of divine purpose, both in the frustration of Saul, cf. vv. 11b, 12, 13, 15b, who senses how things might work out, v. 8, and in the successes of David. Let your heart be encouraged by the record — "all things work together for good to them that love God".

No doubt, what the women expressed in song was true. It was hardly wise! How wisely David behaved himself, vv. 5, 14f, 30. "Walk in wisdom", and "ask of God" should you lack it.

Many loved David from this time, vv. 16, 20, 28; ct. v. 22; specially Jonathan "loved him as his own soul", v. 1. How closely he identified, his very life being bound up with David's, cf. Gen. 44. 30. Jonathan and David made a covenant in the light of Jonathan's love. Already, he was happy to acknowledge David as his replacement, stripping himself of that which was the mark of his dignity, vv. 3f. The future heir to the throne, as it were bows out, and hands it on to one greater and better than himself. This is portrayed not only negatively, as he "stripped himself of the robe", but positively as he "gave it to David", together with his garments, sword, bow, and girdle, v. 4. What things were gain to him, he counted loss for David: is it so with you?, Phil. 3. 3, 5, 7f. David accepted this true expression of love's acquiescence to the place given him of God, ct. 1 Sam. 17. 38f. Has not great David's greater Son delivered us from the authority of darkness, translated us into His kingdom, and won our hearts for Himself? Does He have the first place, the pre-eminence, in your life?, Col. 1. 13, 18.

May 3rd

READING : **1 Samuel 20. 1-42**

THERE IS BUT A STEP BETWEEN ME AND DEATH

IN THE MATCHING UNIT, 19. 1-7, Saul spoke to Jonathan, who told David and then spoke good of David to Saul. Saul relented, and restored David to his presence. In our chapter, David flees to Jonathan, appealing to their covenant, and in the ensuing dialogue, the two reaffirm their commitment to each other, vv. 1-2a. Saul, noting David's absence at the feast, questioned Jonathan, was angry with him for siding with his rival for the throne, and cast his spear at him; Jonathan left in fierce anger, and grieved for David, vv. 24b-34; cf. 15. 35; 16. 1. Jonathan conveyed the facts to David as pre-arranged: they then kissed and wept, restating their common oath, and parted, vv. 35-42. There was no reconciliation to Saul here; David was now to become the fugitive.

Jonathan is as one with Saul, v. 2. Saul even refers, and only here, to Jonathan's future kingdom, v. 31. Yet it is here, when he is all but king, that Jonathan identifies with David and his cause, vv. 2, 9, cf. vv. 12f. Saul saw Jonathan's commitment to David ending in his own earthly loss, vv. 30f. It nearly ended in his death by means of his father's spear, v. 33; cf. 18. 11; 19. 10. Could there be greater proof of his oneness with David at this stage? Contrast the Corinthian spirit of many of us, for whom to reign as kings now is more attractive than to become a spectacle to the world, to identify with a rejected Christ, and experience persecution, 1 Cor. 4. 8-13. Weigh again the cost of discipleship!

David's assessment of Saul's determination to kill him was correct, vv. 31, 33. His morbid obsession with this was wrong. Was there "but a step between me and death", especially as "the Lord liveth"?, v. 3; ct. 19. 23f. Why, then, all this pressure upon Jonathan, the claim based on his covenant, the placing of him on oath? Jonathan felt David's future to be more secure than his own, v. 14f! At most, "the Lord hath sent thee away", v. 22. However Jonathan could only rise to ask "the Lord be with thee, as he hath been with my father", v. 13. The Lord had so much more for David than this. So be anxious for nothing: let your requests be made known to God. Thus you shall have the peace of God garrisoning heart and mind, grander by far than even a Jonathan's "Go in peace", v. 42.

May 4th

READING : **1 Samuel 21. 1 to 22. 5**

THERE IS NONE LIKE THAT; GIVE IT ME

THERE WERE LESSONS for David to learn as *a courtier*. The syllabus became more demanding for him as *a fugitive*. Our reading presents David's visit to the priests, 21. 1-9, his flight to the Philistines, vv. 10-15, and a temporary respite, sanctuary in a cave, 22. 1-5.

What can sustain David when rejected? The showbread is the only answer, vv. 4, 6. Were all in order, this was not lawful. But the priesthood had hopelessly failed, the lamp of God had all but gone out, 3. 3, the ark of God was no longer in the tabernacle, 7. 1, and God's anointed was rejected by the nation generally. While God had far from done with these institutions as yet, all was "in a manner" profaned, rendered common. David may have it rightfully, as the man after God's heart, and with whom His future purposes rest. Without the Lord of the sabbath, there can be no rest in ordinances, Mark 2. 25-28. So it is with us. Without Jesus Christ, our advocate upholding us before the Father, as suggested by the table, and without our feeding upon that which God sees us to be in Him, as suggested by the showbread, what is there for a fearful, failing saint?

David not only sought food. He felt the need of weapons, ct. 17. 47. The priest's offer of "The sword of Goliath the Philistine" took him back to that memorable God-given victory. But now his conscience was overridden by fear, v. 8f.

Fear of Saul drove him yet further. He went over to the Philistines at Gath, Goliath's home town of all places. However slow many in Israel were to recognize him, these Philistines said "Is not this David the king of the land?"; here was the slayer of ten thousands, v. 11. David was now *"sore afraid of Achish"*, ct. Psa. 56. 4. His self-chosen path brought him lower still as he pretended to be mad. God could have no direct part with him, though He overruled in the matter so that "David therefore departed thence", 22. 1. *Fear God alone*.

Fear through looking at the things that are seen, confidence in the help of good friends, speaking one untruth following hard upon another, even seeking shelter with known enemies, is a slippery slope not a few of us have embarked upon. Be warned, for that is the very purpose of this record.

May 5th

READING : 1 Samuel 25. 2-44

THE LORD THAT HATH PLEADED MY CAUSE

NABAL'S PROVOCATION of David, vv. 2-13, called for Abigail's prompt action, vv. 14-22, and timely prudence, vv. 23-35, the dramatic outcome being God's handiwork, vv. 35-44.

Heed the warning in Nabal. He had neither eyes nor ears for David, v. 10. He lived at ease, ruined by the corroding influence of wealth, v. 2. He spoke of his food and water, v. 11, heedless of his indebtedness to God, who daily loaded him with benefits, and to the ceaseless vigilance of David and his men, vv. 7, 15f. He was rough, harsh, ill-behaved, with neither his bodily appetites, nor his tongue, under control, vv. 14, 36; cf. James 3, a worthless good-for-nothing, having an ungovernable temper, vv. 17, 19, 25, 36f. Here was a sheep *shearer*, who repaid good with evil, v. 21. David's God called him to account unexpectedly, vv. 29, 37f; cf. Matt. 24. 48-51. Do not miss the opportunity to share with a rejected Christ. Remember "Inasmuch as . . .", Matt. 25. 40.

Follow the example of Abigail, who found her resource in God, though living in unbearable company. She had eyes to see that David fought the Lord's battles, v. 28, and ears to hear the good his Lord had spoken of him, v. 30. To her, David was the chiefest among ten thousand.

But then, what she knew of him spurred her into action. She collected a sixfold abundance, v. 18, exceeding both the paltry bread and water refused by Nabal to David, and the modest request of David himself, v. 8; cf. Philem. 21. She became a lowly suppliant before David, 1 Sam. 25. 24 (+14 refs. to "my lord"), winning him by the terms of his divine calling.

The lavish provisions she had brought met the practical need of the hour. Tomorrow could be safely left for the Lord to work out, vv. 28, 30f. David would enter into his glory then without any regrets resulting from maintaining his own cause. His divine calling demanded that he fight the Lord's battles, v. 28, not his own. Vengeance belongs to the Lord, v. 29ff.

Abigail is a shining example, highly intelligent, beautiful, v. 3, approachable, v. 14, liberal, v. 18, humble, submissive, v. 23f, penetratingly logical, vv. 24ff, spiritually discerning, winsomely wise, v. 33. Are you open for the Spirit of God to develop increasingly these graces in you?

May 6th

READING : **1 Samuel 26. 1-25**

BEHOLD, I HAVE PLAYED THE FOOL

It is difficult to understand the Ziphites treachery, cf. 23. 19 to 24. 11; Psa. 54. Saul quickly grasped this fresh opportunity to destroy David (note the presence of Abner), vv. 1-5. David determined "to take the battle to Saul" by demonstrably saving his life, vv. 6-12! By this means David established his innocence, and the senselessness, not to speak of the wickedness of Saul's course (note the chiding of Abner), vv. 13-20. Finally, Saul confessed his sin and folly, acknowledged that the Lord's blessing was with David, and promised to David no harm should he return. David preferred to rely on the Lord, both to reward his righteousness and faithfulness, and to continue to rescue him from all tribulation, vv. 21-25. So "let him deliver me" — make this your prayer; "thou shalt . . . surely prevail" — this is your hope, for God's honour is bound up with it.

As Saul lay in a deep sleep, v. 12, Abishai construed this as God delivering David's enemy into his hand, so Saul should be despatched into eternity. Abishai, expert in war, would not need to "smite him the second time", v. 8. This was not the Lord's mind, and such action would bring judgment inevitably, v. 9. David would not allow him to smite Saul the first time! He spoke of him as "the Lord's anointed", v. 9. That Saul must yield place to him he knew to be the Lord's purpose. David left the working out of the details to the Lord, whether by this means or that, v. 10. Put away from you all that would wrongly precipitate the fruition of His loving plans for you. It is to be by the meekness and gentleness of Christ that the Lord's work is to be prosecuted, 2 Cor. 10. 1-3. Learn what manner of spirit ye are of, Luke 9. 55.

Saul acted foolishly. First, by that disobedience that cost him his kingdom. Then, by that ill-natured, wilful ignorance which would not submit to God's part-revealed purpose to replace him, and his house, by another better than himself, 13. 13f; 15. 28. Because he refused to give place to that one who would not forcefully take the place assigned him by the Lord, his whole life became unprofitable, and self-defeating, cf. v. 20. The Lord alone can keep us from acting foolishly, and teach us to walk humbly with Him.

May 7th
READING : 1 Samuel 30. 1-31
THEY SHALL SHARE ALIKE

CONSIDER AGAIN the reactions of David and his band on their return to plundered Ziklag, vv. 1-6, divine guidance sought and given, leading to the raiders' pursuit, vv. 7-15, the overthrow of the Amalekites, the rescue of their own, vv. 16-20, the spoils shared among the band, vv. 21-25, and friends in the south of Judah, vv. 26-31.

Mistakes bring their inevitable consequences. The charred city, and their captured loved ones, brought this home to them all, v. 4. David tapped, immediately, the only resource left to him when his nearest friends rounded upon him. Crises prove what we are made of. David in his weakness drew his strength from the Lord *his* God, v. 6b. This is just one of the peaceable fruits of righteousness to those responsive to the chastening of the Lord, Heb. 12. 11.

What is there for a *sinner*, like this poor Egyptian (a child of wrath by nature), who had been the servant of an Amalekite (a slave to the flesh by practice), but death, v. 13. Yet, for such an one, brought to David, there is the bread of life, water to slake the thirst, a cake of figs for healing, and a fresh lease of life, 2 Kings 20. 7, and a double portion of bunches of raisins for the sweet sustenance of joy unspoiled by excess, 1 Sam. 30. 11f; cf. 25. 18. Little wonder one so blessed had no wish to be delivered into the hands of his old master again, v. 15!

There was even more for those who were *saints*, but who were so faint that they could not go to the battle. They had tarried by the baggage, so lightening the load of those who were able to pursue, vv. 9b, 21, 24. While some would condemn these as loiterers, not worthy of a share in the spoils, v. 22, David estimated their part altogether differently. David attributed the overwhelming success of those that pursued to the Lord, v. 23. When the Lord is given the glory, we rightly assess the value of the contribution of each of His people. How dependent upon Him we are, and how interdependent too, for no member truly can say "I have no need of thee". Seek for all God's people His peace, v. 21b lit. Veto that rising thought against freely giving as you have freely received, v. 22ff, for "*as his share . . . so* shall his share be", v. 24 R.V.; cf. Psa. 68. 12ff.

May 8th

READING : **1 Samuel 31. 1 to 2 Samuel 1. 27**

HOW ARE THE MIGHTY FALLEN!

THE OUTCOME of the battle on Gilboa was humiliating. The Philistines took possession of many cities, gathered the spoils of victory, decapitated Saul's corpse, and fastened the bodies of Saul and his sons to the walls of Beth-shan, 31. 7-10. Yet for David, humanly, this could have been a moment of relief, rather than regret. For he had more just cause to castigate Saul than most. Were he to have expressed the words of our title in the form of a question, he could have rehearsed ample reasons for Saul's disastrous end. Saul's sowing inevitably ripened into judgment's harvest.

But the words of our title are not questioning the reason for, nor even the means by which, the nation had been so humbled in battle. The thrice repeated exclamation breaks up the stanzas of this national elegy, composed by a selfless David as a suiting tribute to their national heroes, 2 Sam. 1. 19, 25, 27. How ignominiously those who had been Israel's glory had been slain at the hands of the profane, the uncircumcised. David would suppress the enemy's triumphant refrain, vv. 19f. He even wishes a material desolation upon Gilboa, the scene of this tragedy, so that it might physically reflect the immense indignity suffered by the nation then, vv. 21f. The daughters of Israel, who were quick to celebrate victories, 1 Sam. 18. 6f, were urged to lament the great material loss sustained, v. 24. Aye, it was facing the foe, the mighty had fallen, vv. 23, 25, and with their death the military strength of the nation perished, v. 27.

Is there anything to surpass this song's generosity of spirit? David looked back over Saul's life without personal bitterness. He recognized all that was noble in the fallen king. Here is an instance of love covering a multitude of sins, Prov. 10. 12; 17. 9; 1 Pet. 4. 8. Emulate David's example!

Though certain sins in David's life have lingered in the memories of men, we may be sure that, in addition to his own brokenness and confession regarding these, see Psa. 51, his merciful and magnanimous spirit will contribute to his joy in the day of review. "So speak ye, and so do, as they that shall be judged by the law of liberty. For he shall have judgment without mercy, that hath shown no mercy", James. 2. 12f.

May 9th

READING : 2 Samuel 1. 17-27

SURPASSING LOVE

IN THEIR *mutual human relations*, Saul and Jonathan were "pleasant in their lives", v. 23a. It is both good and pleasant when brethren, by way of *spiritual relationship*, dwell together in unity, Psa. 133. 1; cf. N. T. brotherly love. But to David, Jonathan was "very pleasant . . . unto me", his "love to me was wonderful", that is, quite extraordinary, v. 26; cf. 1 Cor. 13. 4-7. It simply could not be compared with the love of a woman, whether character and conduct had led to the union, as in Abigail's case, 1 Sam. 25, or that external attractiveness of the "prince's daughter" which led Solomon to exclaim "How fair and how pleasant art thou", Song 7. 6.

The woman was made for the man. Headship and subjection find their complementary expressions in their relationships, their spheres being different, while their union is perfect, cf. Eph. 5. 22, 33. The two are knit together, *they become one flesh*, even in intimate physical terms, though this demands a certain privacy, and shielding from shame. The man also loyally cleaves to his wife, Gen. 2. 23f; Eph. 5. 30-32.

But here was a relationship on a higher plane still. It was between two whose creation place was the same. Love was not prompted by the physical, but rather Jonathan loved David as his own soul, 1 Sam. 18. 1, 3; 20. 17; cf. Deut. 13. 6; Col. 2. 2, and *their souls were knit together*, 18. 1, with uninhibited purity, and unswerving loyalty, Prov. 17. 17. It would doubly guarantee itself in terms of a sacred covenant, reflecting the very loyalty of the Lord Himself, 1 Sam. 20. 8, 14. We may compare here a similar instance of inseparable love and union between two women, for Ruth clave to Naomi, Ruth 1. 14; cf. 4. 15. Jonathan, after the flesh, held a higher station as king's son and heir, but he intuitively appreciated David as God did, which drew out his love, so that he stripped himself, and gave all to him, 1 Sam. 18. 4. Little wonder, then, that while David encouraged a nation to sing of their tragic loss, he mournfully expressed his own deep personal distress at losing one uniquely his brother, v. 26, by ties of soul not flesh. Here was a friend (lit. "lover") that clave closer than any brother, Prov. 18. 24. Treasure, and enrich, those human ties with which God has favoured you.

May 10th

READING : **2 Samuel 2. 1-7; 5. 1-16**

ALL THINGS WORK TOGETHER FOR GOOD

IT WAS OVER seven years after his anointing as king over Judah, 2. 1-4, that David was anointed king over Israel also, 5. 1-3. Throughout the intervening chapters, we are conducted through the various bloody stages of civil war that removed the last serious rival to the throne from Saul's line. David waxed stronger and stronger, greater and greater, perceiving that "the Lord had established him" and "exalted his kingdom", 3. 1; 5. 10, 12. Many details in life raise questions in our minds, as delays and disturbances are strewn along our path. But if we are in the Lord's will, when the whole tale is told, He will bring us to glory both stronger and greater, and the seemingly circuitous and dangerous route will prove to be the most direct and blessed way after all.

For David, knowing the mind of God was essential at every new turn, 2. 1; 5. 19, 23; 1 Sam. 22. 10, 13, 15. Let us not follow our own inclinations, nor even the wisdom of the wise, 2 Sam. 16. 23. Rather, let us inquire of the Lord carefully (cf. 20. 18, lit.=ask with asking), even insisting on being doubly assured, 1 Sam. 23. 2, 4, 9-12. Know the specific purpose of God: not only "Shall I go up", but "Whither shall I go up?".

It was to Hebron (=union, communion, association) that this dependent man was directed. Abraham built his altar here, Gen. 13. 18, and David also found himself "before the Lord", 5. 3. This city of refuge, Josh. 21. 13, became David's first royal city, 2. 1, 11. Here Judah (=praise) anointed him, obedient to God's known will. This was stage one in uniting God's people, resulting in a kingdom vibrant with praise.

Slow though they were to own it, all the tribes of Israel came to David in Hebron, confessed their close relationship to him as "thy bone and thy flesh", 5. 1, whereupon he made a covenant with them, v. 3. This anticipates that day when the nation will incline their ear, and come to their Anointed, and an everlasting covenant shall be made with them, "even the sure mercies of David", Isa. 55. 3f. Observe, Israel had known all along that David had conducted their campaigns, that the Lord had appointed him to feed His people, and to be prince over Israel, 5. 2. We need to be on our guard against any slowness to respond to the claims of the Lord upon us.

May 11th

READING : **2 Samuel 6. 12-23**

BRINGING UP THE ARK

AFTER TWO successful battles against the Philistines, 5. 17-25, David attempted to bring the ark of the Lord to Zion, 6. 1-23.

The second attempt at *bringing up the ark* was successful, prompted by *the Lord's evident blessing*, 6. 12-15; Psa. 24; 132. So it will be when the Lord's people not only do *what* the Lord wills, but also *how* He wills it. David was lost in joyous wonder, and the work was done in the spirit of worship "before the Lord", vv. 14, 16, 17, 21. Service is to be joyful, thankful, and done with all our might, with the shout of victory, v. 15; cntr. 1 Sam. 4. 5f, and with the certain sound of the trumpet.

When the ark was *brought in to the city*, David *blessed the people*, vv. 16-19. When the ark was set in its place, and David had offered burnt and peace offerings, he blessed the people in the name of the Lord of hosts (how reassuring), vv. 17f. Typically, their devoted service was set in the perfection of Christ's sweet savour offering, resulting in fellowship with the Father, His Son, and with one another. With regal liberality, David provided everyone present with bread, meat (of the peace offering), and raisins, and in the spiritual strength of that food they went home, v. 19.

"Then *David returned to bless his household*", vv. 20-23. Michal had observed his behaviour from the palace window, detached and at ease, v. 16. In describing her as "the daughter of Saul", vv. 16, 20, 23; cf. v. 21, the Spirit exposed her true nature, and lack of sympathy with her husband's uninhibited joy in God. In her judgment, divesting himself of his royal robes, and appearing before the people in a linen ephod, was degrading to "the king of Israel". Her pride led to her humbling, while David's willingness to abase himself issued in his exaltation, cf. Matt. 20. 25-28; Phil. 2. 5-11. If Michal sarcastically asks "How glorious was (lit. what *honour* had) the king of Israel today?", David knew he would "be had in *honour*", vv. 20, 22. Michal suffered the stroke of barrenness, as well as estrangement from David. But David, chosen and appointed of the Lord, v. 21, and in the good of God's blessing, was made a blessing to his people generally, and also to his household, vv. 12, 18, 20. Lord, bless me, and make me a channel of blessing today!

May 12th

READING : 2 Samuel 7. 1-17

WHEN THE KING DWELT IN HIS HOUSE

"Go, do all that is in thine heart", vv. 1-3. David had been exalted to kingship, vv. 1, 2, 3, prospered, and been given rest, v. 1. He unfolded to Nathan the contrast between his own house of cedar, and the curtain covering under which the ark of God dwelt, v. 2. Whereupon Nathan endorsed the king's desire, v. 3. "My soul, wait thou only upon God"!

"Go and tell my servant David", vv. 4-17. Our very best proposals which go beyond God's Word will be met with "spake I a word?", v. 7. Note the subtle switch from "the king", vv. 1-3, to "my servant David", vv. 5, 8. Our only safety lies in dependence upon the One whom we serve.

The Lord of hosts was mighty and munificent. "I took thee", v. 8, "I have been with thee", "I will make thee a great name", v. 9 R.V., and "an house", v. 11. If David would "build me (the Lord) an house", then "the Lord will make thee (David) an house" vv. 5, 11 R.V. The Lord's ways with the prince were matched by His promises for "my people Israel", vv. 7, 8, for whom He would appoint a place, then plant them, and cause them to rest, vv. 10-11.

The Lord also would set up David's seed after him, establishing his kingdom, and his seed would build the very "house for my name" after which David had longed, vv. 12-13, yea "I will be his father, and he shall be my son", v. 14. In a chapter richly strewn with divine titles along the trail of self-revelation, this unfolding flower must be the most breathtaking of all. Solomon was the divinely appointed heir, who would know the watchful care of God as Father, and who was to respond in loyal trust, and filial obedience. But there was tragic breakdown in Solomon, and those that followed in David's dynasty, and God had in view a Son of another kind. The common Rabbinic teaching here points to the Messiah, for whom the title "son of David" became a synonym. David, in another place, called this Messiah "my Lord", Psa. 110. 1; Matt. 22. 42-45. The Lord Jesus Christ is the root and the offspring of David, Rev. 5. 5; 22. 16. He is the eternal Son of God, to whom God is uniquely Father, Psa. 2. 7; Acts 13. 33; Heb. 1. 5; 5. 5. He it is that shall build the temple, and He shall bear the glory. Oh! come let us adore Him!

May 13th

READING : **2 Samuel 7. 18-29**

DAVID SAT BEFORE THE LORD

WHAT THANKS could David, or we, give to the Lord for all that He has been, and done? For the Lord God not only knew His servant, v. 20, but He would make His servant know His purpose too, v. 21; cf. vv. 11, 22, 25. Those who know they are numbered among "thy people", vv. 23, 24, and that they are "thy servants", vv. 19-21, 25-29, find it in their heart to "pray this prayer", v. 27. The prayer is not prompted by a sense of need. But with affections quickened, and intelligence illuminated by the revelation of the Lord and His purposes, David pants after the Lord, and the glorious vista opened before him. Note the several phases of his response.

"Who am I, O Lord God, and what is my house?", vv. 18-19. To have been brought thus far is marvellous, v. 18, but there is so much more ahead "for a great while to come", v. 19!

"And what can David say more unto thee?", vv. 20-22. His causeless grace leaves us all speechless, v. 20. All the great things God had done convey the unchanging character of His promises and faithfulness, and the measurelessness of His love, v. 21. The great things lead us to confess "thou art great . . . there is none like thee", v. 22.

"And what one nation . . . is like thy people?", vv. 23-24. God Himself redeemed them, both *out of* Egypt, and *unto* Himself, for a people, earning Himself a unique reputation in the process, v. 23. Israel had been established "a people unto thee for ever", and the incomparable, covenant keeping Lord had become "their God", v. 24. And this is our God for ever!

"And now, O Lord God . . . do as thou hast said", vv. 25-27. It is one thing to be bold in our God when persecution is our lot, 1 Thess. 2. 1-2. It is quite another to be bold in our heart to pray intelligently and fervently along the line of God's revealed promises, v. 27 R.V. marg. Urge the Lord to do as He has said, and to magnify His own name in the process, vv. 25f.

"And now, O Lord God . . . let it please thee to bless", vv. 28-29. Who He is, what He is, and what He has promised to do, v. 28, combine to encourage us to cast ourselves upon the Divine good-pleasure: "with thy blessing let the house of thy servant be blessed for ever", v. 29. And how He has blessed us "with every spiritual blessing in the heavenly places in Christ".

May 14th

READING : 2 Samuel 4. 4; 9. 1-13

SHOWING THE KINDNESS OF GOD

AT FIVE YEARS of age, Mephibosheth suffered an accident. He was a cripple all his life, a condition demanding daily attention. What care has to be taken of the young. When summoned to David, 9. 4f, he had a young son of his own, 9. 12.

The Preliminaries, 9. 1-5. David's initial question finely expresses his steadfast love "for Jonathan's (=gift of the Lord) sake", v. 1; cf. Rom. 11. 29. The remaining questions are all prefaced by reference to "the king", vv. 2, 3, 4, as are Ziba's answers, vv. 3b, 4b. With authority "king David" sent for Mephibosheth to Lo-debar (=place of no pasture), vv. 4f.

The Amazing Proportions of Steadfast Love, vv. 6-8. The word king is not used here. Note Mephibosheth's responses, initially, v. 6a, and finally on being overwhelmed by David's determined love to him. Only when we rightly estimate our own nothingness as but "dead dogs", does the causeless and measureless character of divine love bring us to love much, v. 8. That which "David said" is central. First, as the good shepherd he calls his own sheep by name, v. 6b; cf. John 10. 3. Then the fourfold expression of his love falls upon Mephibosheth's ears: "Fear not" — assurance; "I will surely show thee kindness" — guaranteed covenant love; "I will restore thee all the land" — a complete inheritance regained, and "thou shalt eat bread at my table continually" — loftiest grace and privilege. Sadly, Mephibosheth still only saw himself as "thy servant" rather than as "one of the king's sons". The servile spirit ill-befits one in whom "grace reigns".

"*Royal Authority and Royal Grace Establish All*, vv. 9-13. Whenever Ziba is involved it is with "the king", vv. 9, 11; there is authority but no nearness. Contrast the tone following "As for Mephibosheth", v. 11b. The use of "king" here stresses the regal character of David's love, for Mephibosheth was to be "as one of the king's sons", v. 11, eating "at the king's table", v. 13 (omit italicized ref. in v. 11), in Jerusalem. What a contrast to the "place of no pasture"! True, he was still lame, v. 13b, but the grace that had brought him to the table, had provided by that very means a hiding of all his infirmities. Rejoice, my heart, for the Lord has "brought me to the banqueting house, and his banner over me was love".

May 15th
READING : 2 Samuel 12. 1-25
THOU ART THE MAN

THERE ARE five scenes in the whole drama. First, the *conflict* between Israel and Ammon, and the siege of Rabbah, 10. 1 to 11 (A). Then follows the *carnality* of David even as the battle ensued, 11. 2-27 (B). Central to the whole is David's *conviction and confession*, 12. 1-15a (C). Through his carnality (B), *chastisement and comfort* are called for, 12. 15b-25 (B-). The curtain falls with the *capture* of Rabbah, 12. 26-31 (A-).

Conviction and Confession, 12. 1-15a; cf. 11. 27b. The prophet's *illustration*, vv. 1-6, led to a telling *application*, vv. 7-12, and on to David's *confession and forgiveness*, vv. 13-15a.

The story to stir a shepherd has to do with a lamb! David responded as an angry judge. The culprit had no pity, was worthy of death, and should restore the lamb fourfold, vv. 5f. It is relatively simple to detect the merest splinter in another's eye. Judge not, that ye be not judged, Matt. 7. 1.

Suddenly, the judge had become the criminal, v. 7. Divine favour made him the more guilty, vv. 7f. In adultery and murder, he had "despised the commandment of the Lord", and had "despised" the Lord Himself, vv. 9f. "Now therefore": God was to apply David's fourfold yardstick in chastising His erring servant, vv. 10-15. Beware! God is not mocked. We shall reap what we sow.

David confessed that he had sinned against the Lord, v. 13a; cf. Psa. 51. How speedily the Lord put it away, and spared his own life, v. 13; cf. Psa. 32. Blessed is the man whose transgression is forgiven; cf. 1 John 1. 9.

Chastisement and Comfort, vv. 15b-25. Inevitably, there was *chastisement*, vv. 15-23. While David cast himself upon the Lord for the child's deliverance, vv. 15b-18, he equally wholeheartedly submitted to the Lord's sentence once executed, vv. 20-23. His worship, and specific hope, vv. 20, 23b, were surely two of those peaceable fruits accruing to those who respond to the hand of the Lord upon them. Now, there is *comfort*, for if the "child" died, Bathsheba now bares "a son", vv. 24-25. For David, the son was a monument of his reconciliation, and he appropriately named him Solomon (= peace). The prophet named him Jedidiah. He was "beloved of the Lord" personally, and the king of peace officially.

May 16th

READING : 2 Samuel 15. 1-37

THE THOUGHTS OF MANY HEARTS REVEALED

A DESCRIPTIVE MASTERPIECE, full of penetrating psychological insight, opens here. Absalom "stood beside the way of the gate", v. 2, stealing the people's hearts, v. 6. At the close, David "sat in the gate", 19. 8, among his loyal supporters. David's response in crisis, both in his flight from Jerusalem, 15. 13 to 16. 14, and on his return, 19. 16-40, is instructive.

Ambitiously, pompously, Absalom presented himself as the heir apparent, 15. 1, while being unfittingly familiar with the people, v. 5. He undermined their confidence in the existing administration, vv. 2ff. Subtly he stole their hearts, v. 6. It needed little discernment to see that Absalom offered no viable spiritual alternative. Beware of the plausible talker, with his promises of overnight improvement were he to hold the reins! The coup was strangely successful, vv. 10, 12.

Some "knew not anything", their integrity was not in question, v. 11. The "simple" believe every word, not foreseeing the ramifications of things, Prov. 14. 15; 22. 3; 27. 12. Be "not children in mind . . . in mind be of full age".

With *Ahithophel, the counsellor*, vv. 12, 31; 16. 15 to 17. 4, 23, it was quite different. He treacherously sponsored the rebellion. The grandfather of the wronged Bathsheba, he was motivated by personal animosity; he sought to get even with David alone, 17. 1f. But vengeance is the Lord's prerogative.

Discouraging though it was that Israel were "after Absalom", 15. 13, the Lord cheered David with the loyalty of *Ittai, the warrior*, v. 21. A stranger to the covenants of promise, yet he had given his heart to David. He was a newcomer, yet he was to do veteran service for the king, v. 20; 18. 2, 5, 7. All are called to "endure hardness, as a good soldier of Jesus Christ".

Zadok and Abiathar, the priests, along with their sons, were one with David. But their place was Jerusalem and the sanctuary. A spiritual cause is recognized and maintained by those at home in the presence of God. How David needed men in touch with God, and who would keep in touch with him.

Lastly, *Hushai, David's friend*, was encouraged to return to undermine the influence of Ahithophel, vv. 32-37. Having sought the Lord's help previously David turned to his own devices. Never adopt dubious means to achieve a good end.

May 17th

READING : 2 Samuel 16. 1-4; 19. 24-30

WHEREFORE WENTEST NOT THOU WITH ME?

THESE TWO INCIDENTS highlight the wickedness of Ziba, the hastiness of David, and the devotedness of Mephibosheth.

"What meanest thou by these?", 16. 1-2. As David fled from Absalom, ill-provided for a long journey, he was met by Ziba bearing *a most welcome gift*. Ziba's answer disarmed David, who was encouraged by his helpfulness, cf. Prov. 18. 16.

"And where is thy master's son?", vv. 3-4. Ziba's *covetous spirit* now activated a *crooked tongue*. He estranged David's heart from Mephibosheth, not expecting to see his master again. David, bewildered and grieved, hastily transferred Saul's estate in its entirety to Ziba. Never pronounce on a matter without first obtaining all the facts, and hearing both sides of the case.

"Wherefore wentest not thou with me, Mephibosheth?", 19. 24-28. On David's return, the truth was out at last. What a shock awaited Ziba! David searchingly questioned Mephibosheth's loyalty. But how deeply he had mourned for his absent master, his unkempt appearance betraying his inward grief, v. 24. Ziba had been commanded to prepare an ass for him, and the wickedness of the servant was aggravated by the heartlessness which would leave his master helpless. He deceived not only Mephibosheth, v. 26, but also David. To achieve his nefarious end he also slandered his master before David, v. 27a; 16. 3. Mephibosheth left all to David's penetrating assessment, v. 27b, also casting himself upon David's continued kindness, v. 28.

"Why speakest thou any more of thy matters", vv. 29-30. Speaking abruptly, and compromisingly, David seeks to quieten his conscience with a half-hearted decision. Mephibosheth spelled out his total disinterest in the material, having all that his heart desired now that the king he loved had safely returned. He truly was a son of Jonathan! What is more, to have received any part of the inheritance under these terms would have involved a certain incrimination.

Judge nothing in the field of motive before the time, then, *as David did,* for, after the Lord's return, He will expose the hidden things of darkness, *as in Ziba's case,* and will reveal the counsels of the heart, *as with Mephibosheth,* "and then shall every man have (his due) praise of God", 1 Cor. 4. 5.

May 18th
READING : 2 Samuel 22. 1-51
I LOVE THEE, O LORD MY STRENGTH

THE WORDS of our title form the opening verse of Psalm 18 which, with slight variations, is a duplicate of our chapter. Menacing though his circumstances had been, 2 Sam. 22. 1, they had ministered to David's apprehension of his God. "The Lord is *my* rock, and *my* fortress, and *my* deliverer, even *mine*", v. 2 R.V. The last two words do not appear in the parallel, Psa. 18. 2, and peculiarly emphasize his bold appropriation of that which his God was to him, as does the personal pronoun "my" prefacing so many of the titles and descriptive similes of God.

The Lord is "*my* rock", and a cleft rock at that, cf. 1 Sam. 23. 28 marg. What sheltering, protecting care there is in our God: the shadow of a great rock in a weary land, Isa. 32. 2. We may apply the words "let the inhabitants of the rock sing".

But He was for David "*my* (strong) fortress" too, vv. 2, 33 R.V.; cf. Psa. 31. 3; 71. 3; 91. 2; 144. 2. Visitors to Israel are almost invariably taken to see Masada, an isolated mountain-top fortress perched about 400 metres above the Dead Sea. It is most appropriately named, a form of the same word used here, and found often in connection with David's outlaw life, vv. 5, 17; 23. 14; 1 Sam. 22. 4, 5, sometimes in the context of "the cave of Adullam", 22. 1. But these, and other strongholds of Judea, impregnable fastnesses though they seemed to be, were not to be compared with the personal fortress the Lord had proved Himself to be. David had walked righteously, vv. 21-24, his eyes meanwhile beholding the king in all his beauty.

The Lord was also "*my* deliverer" to David, cf. Psa. 40. 17; 70. 5; 144. 2. The Lord not only keeps His people safe, but He provides a way of escape, and delivers them. Thanks be to God, who has delivered us, who does deliver us, and who will also yet deliver us, 2 Cor. 1. 10. In Jesus, the Christ, He has provided the believer with a Deliverer from the coming wrath.

He is also "The God of *my* rock", v. 3; cf. vv. 47, 32, a different word indicating support, "*my* shield", v. 3; cf. vv. 31, 36, "the horn of *my* salvation", v. 3, "*my* high tower", v. 3, "*my* refuge", v. 3, "*my* stay" (=staff, Psa. 23. 4), v. 19, "*my* lamp", v. 29, "*my* God", vv. 7, 22, 30, and "*my* saviour", v. 3. Think on these things, let the heart respond "*even mine*", and exalt "the God of the rock of my salvation".

May 19th

READING : **2 Samuel 23. 1-7**

THE SWEET PSALMIST'S SWANSONG

WE HAVE MANY of David's words on record, but none are more pregnant than these, "the last words of David", v. 1. Earlier, David could hardly grasp the favour proposed in his becoming the king's son-in-law, 1 Sam. 18. 23. Here, too, he humbly owns his lowly origin in order to magnify God's grace that had indeed raised him on high, v. 1; 7. 8; Psa. 78. 70f. Consider the heights to which God's grace has elevated you.

It is "the God of Jacob", a title emphasizing His faithfulness despite the people's continuing failures, cf. Mal. 3. 6, that had called for David's anointing, v. 1. This gave him ample cause for singing. The complementary expressions "the last words of David", and "the Spirit of the Lord spake by me" enshrine the inexplicable miracle which makes this Book not only transcendent literature, but living oracles to the believer, vv. 1-2.

What David wrote by inspiration had been communicated to him by divine revelation first. "The Rock of Israel *spake* to me", and that Rock of ages was the One that *supported* him too. If there is no unrighteousness in Him, Psa. 92. 15, there can be none in the One whom He sets up to rule over men, "a righteous one", 2 Sam. 23. 3 R.V. marg; cf. Jer. 33. 15; 23. 5; Zech. 9. 9; Psa. 72. 1ff. Righteousness manward has its springs in reverence Godward, two essential and distinguishing features of the Messianic ruler, v. 3; Isa. 11. 2ff. When He comes, all will be replete with the blessings of the sunrise in a cloudless sky, v. 4; Mal. 4. 2. "He shall come down like rain".

As David gladly described the character of the future ruler, he confessed that his own house was not so, v. 5. It is of pure grace that, knowing David, God nonetheless made with him "an everlasting covenant", v. 5. The Davidic covenant has the Messiah in view, 7. 11-16; Psa. 89; Jer. 33. 17, 20f, 25f. We also join with prophet and apostle in looking for the sure mercies of David, Isa. 55. 3; Acts 13. 34. Yet for our failing hearts the divine assurances are more intimate by far.

The promises of God to David were not being made to grow just then, v. 5, but he confessed them and awaited their fulfilment. So it is to be with us, for "if we hope for that we see not, then do we with patience wait for it", Rom. 8. 25. There is no such hope for the ungodly, 2 Sam. 23. 6f.

May 20th

READING : 2 Samuel 24. 1-25

DAVID BUILT THERE AN ALTAR UNTO THE LORD

THE NUMBERING of the people was proposed and prosecuted, vv. 1-9, whereupon David's conscience was pricked, and he was offered a choice of punishments through Gad, vv. 10-14. Then the judgment proceeded, the angel's hand was stayed, David cried to the Lord, Gad came, Araunah's threshing floor was purchased, the altar was set up, the animals were sacrificed, and the plague ceased, vv. 15-25.

Who can stand among the numbered before God apart from their name being in the roll of the redeemed?, Exod. 30. 12; Num. 1. 2; 26. 2. But it was not until the census was largely completed, v. 8; 1 Chron. 21. 6; 27. 24, and the information given to David, that his conscience troubled him, v. 10.

The plague came, yet when the angel stretched out his hand toward Jerusalem the Lord said "stay now thine hand", v. 16. David's further confession and his cry to the Lord, resulted in his being pointed to the place and the propitiatory sacrifices which alone could cause the plague to be stayed, vv. 21, 25. David insisted on purchasing both the threshing-floor (50 shekels of silver=redemption accomplished), v. 24, and the whole surrounding area, the place (600 shekels of gold for the temple site=the glories to follow), 1 Chron. 21. 25. David could not accept it as a gift. Costly sacrifice is the very essence of that which is acceptable to God.

This site was soon to become incorporated within the city. King and people alike at last symbolically embraced Moriah. There an obedient Abraham had rejoiced to see Christ's day, John 8. 56, when God would "provide (for) himself a lamb for a burnt offering", Gen. 22. 8. What a contrast here as David, through self-willed disobedience, exposed the nation to judgment. The burnt offering, referring us to the perfect devotion and obedience of God's Son, was appropriate for Abraham to offer. David needed additionally the peace offering benefits of Moriah's sweet savour work in order that reconciliation might be made and enjoyed. Thus alone was the Lord "intreated for the land, and the plague was stayed from Israel", v. 25. God's judgment for the saint ends at the threshingfloor: it is a matter of corrective discipline, perfect control and great mercies guaranteeing the removal of chaff, Luke 22. 31f.

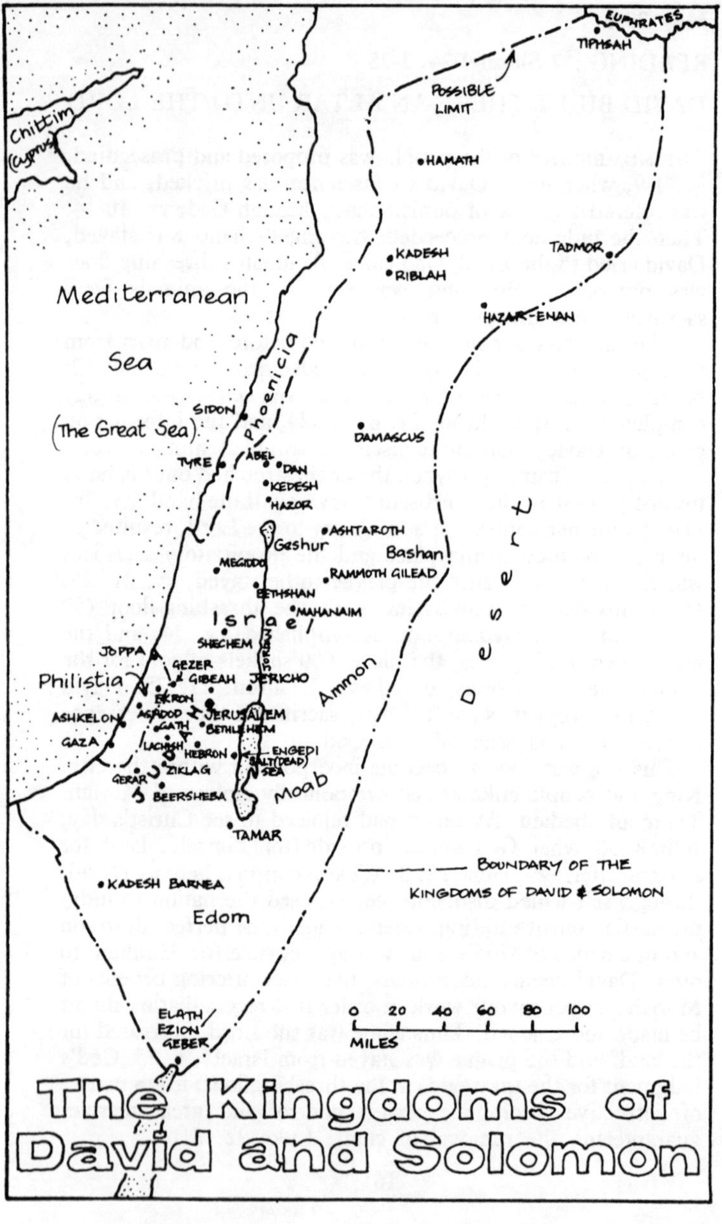

The Kingdoms of David and Solomon

Introducing the Books of Kings

WE HAVE SEEN that the Books of Samuel and Kings are inextricably bound together, p. 133 f. If in Samuel, the *need* for rule and the *man* for rule are the foci of attention, then in Kings the emphases are rather upon the *mainstay* of rule, and the several *methods* of rule. This shift from interest in the more personal to the more official is everywhere apparent. For example, observe that the kings are frequently designated officially and formally, king David, 1. 1, king Solomon, 1. 39.

Here, over 400 years are selectively reviewed, throughout the several phases of the *United*, 1 Kings 1-11, the *Divided* (Judah and Israel), 1 Kings 12 to 2 Kings 17, and the *Single* Kingdoms, 2 Kings 18-25. In Judah the Davidic dynasty continued throughout its 21 reigns, whereas 9 distinct dynasties supplied the 19 kings of Israel, the Northern Kingdom, over a considerably shorter timespan (approx. 170 years).

The Books of Kings begin with King Solomon and Jerusalem, but end with Nebuchadnezzar, King of Babylon. The curtain opens with God's house built, beautified, dedicated, and sanctified, whilst the curtain falls with the same house broken up, burned, despoiled and desecrated. That house of God is the touchstone by which all the kings, and their differing houses (dynasties) are tested. Kings, and their houses, are all set up under responsibility to God. His house, and the righteous and fruitful government it reveals and promotes, is His answer to all the problems and failures arising in the day to day administration of that mediatorial rule committed to kings; see especially 1 Kings 8. 31-53. Of course, the failure of the several kings, and their houses, under this divine test was to be expected, for kings, as do all others, sin. But whereas their sins, through their lack of dependence and obedience, brought the period of the monarchy to a close, all was not lost. What man in responsibility is unable to achieve, the sovereignty of God will establish according to promise.

The principle of the king's accountability is stressed, then: "If he commit iniquity, I will chasten him with the rod of men", 2 Sam. 7. 14. Compare David faithfully stressing this to Solomon, 1 Kings 2. 4. Obedience to the Word of God, insisted on in Deuteronomy, is the guarantee of dynastic continuance and the blessing of God; cf. 3. 14; 9. 4-9. The king must keep the charge of the Lord, walk in His ways, keep His commandments, do what is right, and cleave to the Lord. That is, he must be responsive himself to God's rule, be submissive to God's government, learning how to behave himself in God's house, and how to rule his own house well, in order that he may properly lead, and take care of God's people, 1 Tim. 3. 1-7, 14f. Those kings who, by their dependence upon, and devotion to God, are obedient to His direction, earn a resounding "well done", whilst those who provoke the Lord to anger, doing that which is evil in His eyes, and who consequently cause Israel to sin, bring down upon themselves and their house, aye, and upon God's people, the just displeasure and discipline of God; see especially 2 Kings 17; 23. 26f; 24. 3f. The king's rule (house) was always intended to be seen as bound up with, and an expression of God's rule (house), and his delight in, concern for, and response to God's house as the secret of all success. It is failure just here that makes the history frequently such sad reading, and the end of it so catastrophic.

An Outline. Note: (1) the detailed description and dedication of God's house, 1 Kings 6-8, together with the recurring references to this temple throughout, and (2) those instances where God's house and the king's house are brought together in the text, as they are in physical terms in 1 Kings 6-7: see 10. 4f, 12 and 14. 26; 15. 18f; 2 Kings 12. 18 and 14. 14; 16. 8, 18; 18. 15f (ct. 19. 36-37); 20. 13-17 and 24. 13; 25. 9.

The Problem of Succession Resolved, 1 Kings 1. 1 to 2. 46.
God's House, the Touchstone of All, 3. 1 to 9. 25.
The Several Kings' Houses, 9. 26 to 2 Kings 25. 26.
    First Round of Tests—Egypt Removes Treasures, 9. 26 to 14. 31.
    Second Round of Tests—Israel Removes Treasures, 15. 1 to 2 Kings 14. 22. Note Cycle, Israel-Syria-Syria-Israel.
    Third Round of Tests—Babylon Removes Treasures, 14. 23 to 25. 26. Complex Cycle Involving the Exile of Israel, then Judah, and the nations Assyria, Egypt, and Babylon.
A Glimmer of Hope, 25. 27-30; cf. Matt. 1. 1-16.

May 21st
READING : 1 Kings 1. 1-48
WHO IS THE KING OF GLORY?

THROUGHOUT the vicissitudes of David's latter years, God was in control so as to establish His man, in His time, upon David's throne. That throne was for that one only to whom it had been promised, yes, sworn, by his father, vv. 13, 17, 30, according to the Lord's word, 1 Chron. 22. 9. This is the more remarkable in the light of all the intrigue that it might be otherwise. Three types of aspirant were removed by death. It was not to be the fleshly, self-indulgent, passionate Amnon, 2 Sam. 13, nor the ambitious, self-vindicating, proud Absalom, 2 Sam. 15, nor yet Adonijah, whose self-interest and lust for power is highlighted in 1 Kings 1-2. His coup, carefully plotted and prosecuted, 1. 5-10, was more than matched by the counter-plan of Nathan, vv. 11-14, which was prosecuted successfully by Bathsheba, vv. 15-21, and Nathan, vv. 22-27. The Lord's candidate was at last identified privately, vv. 28-31, and publicly, vv. 32-40.

The court and the country alike supported Solomon's appointment, vv. 34, 39. And this despite the fact that, throughout all the intrigues, Solomon had not defended his claim, or personally furthered his own cause. Solomon's name is used only of him by others here, cf. 1. 10 and often. God's promise and his father's oath were sufficient for him. He waited the moment when he would appear as the vindicated king. How like the greater than Solomon: how unlike us! The Lord direct our hearts into the patience of Christ! And let the song go round the earth, "Jesus Christ is Lord".

Priest and prophet alike unite in anointing God's king, vv. 34, 39. Along with the appointing, vv. 35-37, 43, there must be the anointing. For apart from the oil (emblem of the ministry of God's Spirit) poured out upon the king from the horn (representing power, yet made available through death) he will be found lacking officially, neither will he be declared king openly. It is the Messiah (anointed) that is to be King in David's stead, v. 35, and whose throne is to be greater than David's, v. 37, and who is to have a better name, v. 47.

God, out of His sufficiency, had given one to sit on the throne that day. His praise began then, v. 48. What will it be when "Thine eyes shall see the king in his beauty"?

May 22nd

READING : **1 Kings 3. 1-15**

WHO IS SUFFICIENT FOR THESE THINGS?

BY WHAT STEPS are we conducted from the altar to the ark?

1. *The Lord appeared,* v. 5, in grace, using a revelatory dream as the vehicle of communication. "Ask . . .", said He.

2. *Solomon apprehended God's ways,* vv. 6-7a. *"Thou hast shown (lit. done)"* great kindness to David in delivering him from all his troubles. Walk in truth as David did, vv. 3, 6, 14, and know this boon. Follow yesterday's faithful examples, Heb. 13. 7. But also *"thou hast kept* for him this great kindness", a son to sit on his throne, thus honouring His covenant commitment; cf. 2 Sam. 7. 15; 22. 51; Psa. 89. 29, 34. Further, *"thou hast made to reign (lit.)"* thy servant (Solomon), instead of David. When referring to his own personal experience of God's ways, Solomon says, "O Lord *my* God". Prove the Lord for yourself today, Heb. 13. 8.

3. *Solomon appreciated his own littleness,* vv. 7b-8. The one who is to be greatest in the kingdom has to learn this hard lesson; cf. Matt. 18. 4. Solomon knew not "how to go out or come in", sensing his own inadequacy in the light of all the demands and undertakings of leadership. A proper grasp of the greatness of a God-given task would prevent our entering upon work for Him lightly. Once having entered upon "a great work" as "thy servant", 1 Kings 3. 6, 7, 8, 9, we are to rebut any suggestion of giving it up; cf. Neh. 6. 3.

4. *Solomon asked for an understanding (lit. hearing) heart,* v. 9. A more thorough involvement, a more penetrating assessment, a more discriminating response issue from a hearing heart. How we all need to discern between good and evil, v. 11, 16-28; cf. Heb. 5. 14. Sensing our lack of wisdom we are to seek it of God, James 1. 5. It is not only Solomon that needed help, 1 Kings 3. 5, 10, 11 (5), 13. Could it be true that we are inadequate, we "have not", because we "ask not"?, James 4. 2.

5. *The Lord awarded more than Solomon asked,* 1 Kings 3. 10-14. The Lord is pleased when we seek a good thing, v. 10, and loves to do more than we ask or think. Solomon was unsurpassed, for the Lord gave him *a wise and* understanding heart, v. 12; cf. v. 9. To this was added riches and honour, v. 13. Our God is indeed a superabundant Giver, vv. 5, 9, 12, 13. Walk in God's ways, and enjoy more of His bounty, v. 14.

May 23rd

READING : **1 Kings 6. 1-14**

SO SOLOMON BUILT THE HOUSE, AND FINISHED IT

THE COMMENCEMENT of Solomon's building work is dated from the Exodus from Egypt, 6. 1. The redeemed alone can build for the Lord. The record presents, *firstly,* the basic structure, vv. 2-14, as "'finished", vv. 9, 14. *Secondly,* the interior was beautified, and the inner court was "finished", vv. 22, 38, the king's palace complex also being "finished", 7. 1, the details of which extend to 7. 12. *Finally,* the furnishing of the court (Hiram's work), vv. 22, 40, and of the house itself (Solomon's work), was all finished, v. 51. Each completed stage of our work for God brings us nearer that moment when we may say, "I have finished my course", 2 Tim. 4. 7.

Phase one, then, describes the fundamental structure of the Lord's house, 6. 2-14. It was 60 × 20 × 30 cubits (halve these for approx. size in metres), having a porch which extended the length by another 10 cubits, vv. 2f. This house was not only in touch with the earth via its porch, i.e. it was outgoing, but through its windows it was cognizant of all, v. 4. God's government, represented by the house, is real, relevant, and intelligent; cf. the oft-repeated assessment of things being good or evil "in the eyes (sight) of the Lord"; see also 2 Chron. 16. 9.

Chambers were clustered around this house in three tiers, vv. 5f, 10. Their support was provided for by the step-like projections around the walls of the house itself, v.6, and their timbers of cedar actually "rested on (these steps of) the house", v. 10. Dependence upon God as He would order all the affairs of His own kingdom will ensure, not only the support, but also the unity, of His people; cf. v. 8. Within these verses describing the chambers is the statement that the building progressed without noise, v. 7. When we trust upon Him, each "living stone", pre-prepared by God's Spirit, is "fitly framed together" with others, and grows "unto an holy temple in the Lord", Eph. 2. 21.

Insistence upon the king's responsibility to obey God in the context of the building of God's house is appropriate, v. 12f. God's government among His people cannot co-exist with their self-will. God demands obedience from the king and the people alike. Is ours a joyful and a fulfilling obedience from the heart?

May 24th

READING : **1 Kings 6. 15-38**

WITHIN THE ORACLE HE MADE TWO CHERUBIM

THE WORD ORACLE is a description of the holy of holies peculiar to the temple. It is used seven times in our reading, vv. 16, 19, 20, 21, 22, 23, 31, impressing us with its importance. Ponder over these passages. By means of the oracle, the living voice of God reverberated throughout God's house, and His kingdom. In the oracle God hears; from the oracle God speaks so that His people's character and case are clearly different from those around them; read Psa. 28. 1-2. Look to the oracle and listen today!

The two olive-wood cherubim here are quite different from those of pure gold upon the mercy seat, Exod. 25. 18-20; 1 Kings 6. 23-28. Wood prompts us to think of humanity, olive wood of a spiritual humanity, the gold overlay of a glorified humanity, vv. 23, 28; cf. 1 Cor. 15. 44. In the two, perfect correspondence and compatibility were seen to harmonize with distinctiveness of place and ministry. In fact, only by the sum total of their wingspan was the whole breadth of God's oracle embraced, vv. 24, 27. These cherubim were outward looking, and their complementary ministries were to fill the whole earth with the knowledge of the glory of the Lord, Hab. 2. 14, 20. This happy prospect awaits the appearance in glory of the greater than Solomon, along with His glorified people who are to reign with Him, when God's kingdom will have come indeed. Following reference to the ark, and the two cherubim, along with the associated details in the oracle, 1 Kings 6. 16-28, we read of multiplied forms of life, fruit, and beauty upon the wood-clad walls, of the floor overlaid with golden glory, and of the doors through which the living voice of the living Lord bursts out upon the whole earth, vv. 29-36.

Even where king and nation do evil, God's voice, though unpalatable, is heard; cf. 22. 8; 17. 24. The "word of God (the Lord)" comes through "the man of God", the distinct yet complementary ministries of Elijah and Elisha being specific examples of this. For God's house today to be the influence He intended it to be, we still need to hear what the Lord says, 1 Tim. 3. 14ff. Whilst the Lord alone has the words of eternal life, the speaker, too, must speak "as the oracles of God", 1 Pet. 4. 11, and the hearer must hear what the Spirit says.

May 25th

READING : **1 Kings 7. 1-12**

ONE THAT RULES WELL HIS OWN HOUSE

IT MAY SEEM strange at first that this sketch of the king's house complex should be set in the descriptive framework of God's house, 6. 1-38 and 7. 13-51. The Spirit thus insists on the intimate relationship between God's house and that of God's king, between God's government and God's governor. The king occupied a mediatorial role; he ruled for God. The king was not a source of blessing, but a channel of blessing, causing the people to sing the Lord's praises for all that *He* "had done for David, his servant, and for Israel his people", 8. 66. So it is to be with today's leaders. They are not to act as despots, "as lord's over God's heritage", 1 Pet. 5. 3; Mark 10. 42-45, but to stand before the people with delegated authority, Heb. 13. 7, 17, 24, as "stewards of God", Tit. 1. 7. Pray for kings, 1 Tim. 2. 2; pray for spiritual leaders, Heb. 13. 18f.

Ominously, much more time was given to the palace building project than to God's, 1 Kings 7. 1; cf. 6. 37f. The number 13, first found in a context of rebellion, Gen. 14. 4, hints at the future opposition of the kings' houses to the demands of God's throne. Compare the sad history of the churches, Rev. 2-3.

The five distinct units of the palace buildings are noted, and divided into two groups by the reference to "house", vv. 2, 8(3). The first three units, vv. 2-5, 6, 7, are clearly *public buildings*, essential in the more official aspects of administration. Solomon's own house, and the house of Pharaoh's daughter, v. 8, are clearly *private dwellings*. The two private dwellings are said to be "of like work", "like this porch", v. 8. God requires that what we are and do in our more personal and private life, matches what we are called to do, and the stand we take in public. How the Lord hates hypocrisy.

The literal building programme here is a simile for the dynasties, the various kings' houses that govern for God. If there are five "houses" in 7. 2-12, then there are just five "houses" *referred to as such* in our Books. Each occupies the stage for a period, but to David alone was it said "thine house and thy kingdom shall be established for ever before thee", 2 Sam. 7. 16, pointing to the time when the Lord shall "exalt the horn of his anointed (Christ)", 1 Sam. 2. 10.

May 26th

READING : **1 Kings 8. 31-50**

LORD, TO WHOM SHALL WE GO?

IT WAS beyond Solomon's capacity and resources to meet the need of those he led. God's house, as the people's prayers were directed toward it, was proposed as the answer to every need. The sevenfold array of anticipated problems suggest the whole range of matters, individual, vv. 31f, corporate, vv. 33-40, and in the world around them, vv. 43-53.

Priority is given to problems arising between individual saints, vv. 31f. Nip problems in the bud before the altar, and see that right is vindicated; ct. 11. 40; 14. 30, 25f; 21. 19-24.

Humiliation before Egypt, 14. 25f, Syria, 2 Kings 10. 32f; 12.17f, and Assyria, 18. 13-16, is proof enough that sin is the cause of defeat. Hezekiah found the answer through prayer in God's house, 19. 1, 14-35; cf. Asa, 2 Chron. 14. 9-15; Jehoshaphat, 20. 1-25. If you have suffered defeat, turn to God, 1 Kings 8. 33f.

Barrenness among us, vv. 35f, cries out for a return to Him, all too often ignored, as in Ahab's case, 17. 1; 18. 1f, 17f. But a turning to Him, as in Jehoshaphat's case, guarantees that the "valley shall be filled with water", 2 Kings 3. 11-20. Lord, open "the windows of heaven", Mal. 3. 10!

Famine and seige, 1 Kings 8. 37-40, as at Gilgal, 2 Kings 4. 38f, and Samaria, 6. 24 to 7. 20, forced each to know "the plague of his own heart". But the man of God, representing the house of God, provided the solution. Shall we not turn to Him when we suffer a famine "of hearing the words of the Lord"?

The stranger, 1 Kings 8. 41-43, like Naaman, 2 Kings 5, or an Ethiopian, Acts 8, hearing of God's exploits and personal fame, will not be disappointed if he turns to God. When last did the visitor admit, "God is among you of a truth"?

Battles there will be, 1 Kings 8. 44f, for there are many adversaries. Our campaign is against the world, the flesh, and the devil. We are to supplicate, and gain the victory.

Even defeat and exile are not irrevocable for those who return to the Lord with all their heart, vv. 46-50. The holiness that becomes God's house may demand exile or excommunication, but this is not an end in itself. Return, 1 Cor. 5. 4ff.

Who, but the Christ, the Son of the living God, is equipped to meet the range of our present needs?, John 6. 68f.

May 27th

READING : **1 Kings 8. 54-66**

BLESSED BE THE LORD

SOLOMON, at the dedication of the Temple, *opened* by blessing and thanking God, 8. 12-21, *followed* by prayer and supplication as he looked back over the past, vv. 23-30, and forward to the future, vv. 31-53, and *closed* with a great benediction, vv. 54-60, exhortation, v. 61, and time of sacrifice and rejoicing, vv. 62-66.

"Blessed be the Lord", v. 56. The chapter abounds with references to Him under six different titles, together with a frequent use of "the (my, thy) name". Such an unfolding of Himself leads to praise. They enjoyed the Lord in His fulness.

He is the giving God. He had given *a son*, 3. 6; 5. 5, *wisdom*, 3. 5, 12; 4. 29, *riches*, and *honour* to a unique degree, 3. 13. Despite sin, He gave *parts of the kingdom* to respective rulers, 11. 13, 36; 14. 7; 16. 2. He would give *rain* to the parched earth, 18.1, and even gave to the sinning Northern kingdom *"a saviour"*, 2 Kings 13. 5. Here, He had "given *rest* to his people", and freed from fear, and foes, they could at last enjoy their God-given inheritance; cf. Deut. 12. 9-14.

He is the faithful God. Israel's God, and ours, is a speaking God. His ark is placed in the oracle, v. 6, for He is the God that speaks with His mouth, v. 15, cf. vv. 20 (3), 24 (2), 26 (2), 53, the verb and noun also occurring four times in v. 56 ("promise(d)" here is the same word). He need not have made known "his good promise", but such is His nature that He would have them (and us) live in the joy and encouragement of it before it materialized. Think of the *magnitude* of His bounty suggested by *"all* that he promised", and *"all* his good promise". Ponder His attention to *minute detail* suggested by "there hath not failed *one word"*. Everything here is conditional, "promised by the hand of Moses", part of that old covenant closely associated with Moses' prophetic history of the nation; see Lev. 26; Deut. 28. God has since provided something better, having its guarantee in "the blood of the new covenant", the better covenant established on better promises.

Blessed be the God and Father of our Lord Jesus Christ, who has given us a living hope, an inheritance in heaven, blessed us now with all spiritual blessings, and all that pertains to life and godliness, and precious promises.

May 28th

READING : **1 Kings 11. 1-13**

RIVAL LOVES

THE KING that built God's house was the first to be tested by that which it represented. Solomon miserably failed, 9. 26 to 11. 43. The king should "not multiply horses to himself, nor cause the people to return to Egypt", neither "multiply wives to himself ", nor "greatly multiply to himself silver and gold", Deut. 17. 16f. Solomon disobeyed on all these counts, 1 Kings 4. 26; 10. 26, 28; 11. 3f; 9. 28; 10. 2, 10, 11, 14, 16ff, 21ff, 25, 27. "Some (trust) in chariots, and some in horses", Psa. 20. 7; cf. 33. 17; 147. 10; Isa. 31. 1, 3. For others, the cancer of materialism eats at the very vitals of spiritual life. Anything that breeds independence leads on to outright disobedience.

"Solomon loved *many* strange women". His heart was taken by storm at the carnal level, 1 Kings 11. 1, cleaving to them in love, v. 2. This is the more tragic for "the Lord loved him (Solomon)", 2 Sam. 12. 24, and earlier in his reign "Solomon (had) loved the Lord", 1 Kings 3. 3. Then, love for the Lord was evidenced in "walking in the statutes", as our Lord also taught "If ye love me, ye will keep my commandments".

Further, it was "many *strange (foreign)* women" that were loved by Solomon, 1 Kings 11. 1. This was flagrant disobedience to God's call for separation from the idolatrous nations all around His people, Exod. 34. 16. Union with "the daughter of Pharaoh", representing the house of bondage from which God's people had been redeemed, was but the first link in the chain of Solomon's enslaving. Drawn from the security of separation to the Lord, through pandering to the lusts of the flesh, "his wives *turned away his heart* ", 1 Kings 11. 3. The devil, taking advantage, enmeshed him still further so that "his wives *turned away his heart after other gods*", v. 4; cf. vv. 2, 5. The one who challenged others that their heart should be perfect with the Lord, 8. 61, is condemned, for "his heart was not perfect with the Lord his God". So Solomon went after false gods, 11. 5, and embarked upon a building programme of idolatrous houses, v. 7, even on the mountain before Jerusalem itself, 2 Kings 23. 13. Rival loves led to rival gods, and then to rival houses, but all started in Solomon's own house. Failure began in the private sector of his life. The ramifications were all too soon in evidence publicly. Is your home a sanctuary?

May 29th
READING : 1 Kings 12. 25-33
RIVAL HOUSES

PARALLEL political houses were within the framework of God's permissive will due to sin, 11. 31, 35; 12. 24, and dependence and obedience on Jeroboam's part would ensure for him a sure house, 11. 38. It was sheer unbelief, therefore, that led him to say that the kingdom would return to the house of David "if this people go up to do sacrifice in the house of the Lord at Jerusalem", 12. 26f. He did not believe God, and ceased to lean dependently upon the God who governed, and had raised him to power. He leaned upon his own understanding, Prov. 3. 5; ct. 1 Kings 6. 10; Psa. 125. 1.

Lack of trust led to positive disobedience; ct. 6. 12f. First, there were the *two calves of gold*, for which the wilderness departure provided a precedent, Exod. 32. 4, 8; 1 Kings 12. 28. *Two new rival houses* to that one alone acceptable to God were conveniently located in the southern and northern borders of the land, vv. 28f. One of the centres even bore the name Bethel (=house of God), and this, along with its historical associations, bolstered its claim to be a truly God-appointed centre, v. 29. To serve at these centres, Jeroboam "made priests" other than "of the sons of Levi", drawn from among those whose appetites they were to serve, v. 31. He even transferred his own feast of tabernacles to the eighth month, v. 32, rearranging God's calendar. Jeroboam has gone down in history as the great religious innovator, identifying the worship of the Lord with images (despite Exod. 20. 4-6), and then establishing his departure with the aid of new places of worship, new personnel to conduct the worship, and even a new calendrical programme for worship. This is the great sin of Jeroboam, 13. 34, wherewith he made Israel to sin, 14. 16. This refrain tolls throughout the sad history.

Israel's lampstand, that of the Northern kingdom, was finally removed at the exile to Assyria, because of the perpetuated sin of Jeroboam, 2 Kings 17. 22f. However, there is to be a rebuilding of the tabernacle of David in the future at the advent of great David's greater Son, Amos 9. 11f; Acts 15. 16. God has decreed that a united kingdom will re-emerge.

Is there weakness and division among God's people today? Walk humbly, dependently, and obediently with the Lord.

May 30th

READING : 1 Kings 13. 1-32

ALAS, MY BROTHER!

THE FEARLESS prophet-herald of the consequences of disobedience, vv. 1-10, was to have his own ministry applied to himself, vv. 11-32. An old prophet, hearing of his faithfulness, had his ass saddled, journeyed, and found him sitting, vv. 13f. Later, his ass was saddled, he went out, found the younger man's carcass cast in the way, and brought it back for honourable burial, vv. 27ff.

What caused the old prophet's appeal, v. 15, to succeed where the king's had failed?; ct. v. 7. First, it came at a time when the younger man was "sitting", v. 14. Having done all, he was to have kept riding, or at least "to stand", Eph. 6. 13. His earlier and firm "I will not go", v. 8, is weakened to "I may not return", v. 16. The Lord had "charged" him, v. 9, but now He had only "said to me", v. 17. This slowing down, and slackness regarding the terms of his commission, prepared the way for his downfall. Be warned!

"I also am a prophet as thou art", v. 18, was true. But this "old prophet" had the marks of decay about him, vv. 11, 25, 29 R.V. How had he come to settle at Bethel, and without even denouncing the departure there? Having heard the man's reason for declining, why did he seek to deflect him from his hesitant obedience? Why did he sink to lying to ensnare his more faithful colleague? Let the older ones ask "Are things as firmly held as once they were?" When a younger one's voice is heard, does your own stifled conscience disturb you? Do you feel a mixture of admiration and jealousy?

Not that the younger "man of God" should have allowed his personal and direct commission, v. 9, to be supplanted by a mediated message of "an angel", v. 18. The word "Bring him back" appealed to him, as his guard was down, "So he went back", v. 19; ct. v. 10. But "the prophet that brought him back", vv. 20, 26, condemned his coming back as an act of disobedience, v. 21f. A fitting epitaph for him now was "the prophet whom he had brought back", vv. 26, 23. Greater light and privilege bring greater responsibility, cf. James 3. 1, the strongest word for rebellion being reserved for this man of God alone in the Books of Kings, vv. 21, 26. Let us not "look back" nor "go back"—let us go on! Continue thou!

May 31st

READING : 1 Kings 14. 21-31

SHIELDS OF BRASS FOR SHIELDS OF GOLD

REHOBOAM, the foolish son of the wisest king, had, on his accession, added fuel to the fires of discontent lit by his father's oppressive administration, 12. 1-14. This resulted in the division of the kingdom, vv. 15-20. He was not permitted to subdue this breakaway by force, for the political division had Divine sanction, vv. 21-24; 11. 29-38.

Jerusalem is "the city which the Lord chose . . . to put his name there", 14. 21, emphasizing its uniqueness, privilege, sanctity, as also the Lord's purpose to unfold there all that He was personally to His people. When described as "the city of David", v. 31, it points to the Lord's irrevocable promises. So often in Kings this description is found in connection with the burial of those of David's line, as here. The mere mortals of David's line did not bring in the everlasting kingdom promised, neither can flesh and blood inherit the kingdom.

Rehoboam was not only his father's son, but his mother's also (an Ammonitess), vv. 21, 31, which further explains the shameful excesses of his reign. Judah's evil exceeded "all that their fathers had done", vv. 22-24, provoking the Lord to jealousy. Sharing one's heart with idols, and being on friendly terms with the world, is "enmity with God"; cf. James 4. 4f.

The section which our reading concludes (see analysis, p. 164) presents Egypt first as a trading partner, 10. 28f, then as an asylum for opponents of Solomon, 11. 17f, 21, 40 (2); 12. 2 (2), and now, finally, as Judah's attacker. God used Egypt to chasten Jerusalem, and to deplete thereby the treasures both of the Lord's and the king's houses, 14. 26. This is the first occurrence of this painful refrain in Kings. Sin spoils!

Rehoboam, like many after him, desperately tried to cover up the loss of glory. Instead of humbling himself, and giving God the glory due to His name, he sought to keep up appearances. The shields of gold, and the glory they represented, were replaced by shields of brass. It is now time for us to ask our hearts "How is the gold become dim"?, Lam. 4. 1.

How different in that glad future day when God's "glory shall be seen upon thee", Isa. 60. 2, 6, 9, 13, and God will glorify the house of His glory, vv. 6f. "For brass I will bring gold", v. 17. How long, Lord?

June 1st

READING : **1 Kings 18. 21-46**

HOW LONG HALT YE BETWEEN TWO OPINIONS?

THE CHAPTER conducts us through drought to downpour. The background is set, vv. 1-20, and when all are assembled, Elijah challenges the people and proposes the terms of the contest, vv. 21-24. Once the incapacity of Baal was established, vv. 25-29, Elijah drew near to the Lord, who answered the prophet's pleas by fire, leading to the people's confession, vv. 30-39. The slaughter of Baal's prophets, the supplication of Elijah, and the storm, round off the story, vv. 40-46.

The commission of Elijah, and the details of the contest, vv. 1, 36, are bound up with "the word of the Lord". Even the change of Jacob's name is the result of the Lord's word coming to him, v. 31. Yet the Lord, whose word comes out to men, is the same One that hears and answers them, vv. 24, 37. Oh to be in touch with the God of the oracle! From Baal there can be "no voice", no answer, no attention, vv. 26, 29. But the Lord not only answers by fire, He speaks by the "still small voice" also, 19. 12. Wait upon His word today!

Elijah repaired the altar, its twelve stones reminding of the sovereign grace that gave to Jacob the name Israel, v. 31. That altar was built "in the name of the Lord", unfolding His character as well as meeting His requirements. On the wood the bullock (pointing to the strong and untiring service of the Servant of the Lord) was placed. The people's only part was to pour out twelve barrels of water over wood and sacrifice alike, vv. 33b, 34, establishing that what was to happen was altogether of the Lord, v. 35. Elijah drew near to the Lord, the God of Abraham, of Isaac, and of *Israel*, v. 36, at the very time of the evening daily sacrifice in the temple. This was the hour when the Christ, nailed to a Roman cross, cried out "My God, my God, why hast thou forsaken me?", Mark 15. 34, and then, with a loud voice said "It is finished", 15. 37; John 19. 30. Surely, in His great sacrifice He experienced something indescribably worse than "the fire of the Lord". He exhausted the wrath of God against sin and sins.

Thus, Israel that day confessed "the Lord, he is the God". Were Elijah to appear today, how relevant his challenge would be, "How long halt ye between two opinions?". If the Lord is God, let us follow Him!

June 2nd
READING : **1 Kings 21. 1-29**

HAST THOU KILLED, AND TAKEN POSSESSION?

"Human Rights" is a lively topic today. Where there is no fear of God, nor recognition by rulers that they hold office under God, Rom. 13. 1-6, the "rights" of individuals are likely to be eroded seriously. Pray for kings, 1 Tim. 2. 1-2.

Our chapter records no mere "human rights" issue. Naboth's response to the king's "Give me", v. 2, was prompted by a deeper concern. "The Lord forbid it me, that I should give", v. 3. His inheritance had been given to his fathers by the Lord, so that he was not insisting upon his legal right alone, but declaring his unpreparedness to give up a Divine heritage. Would you be prepared to sell your spiritual inheritance?, ct. vv. 2, 6. Naboth was no Esau!

One who sells himself to work wickedness, and has a wife that urges him on, can know nothing of the preciousness of the Lord's inheritance. The coveted place was simply a convenient plot to convert from growing grapes to greens; read Deut. 11. 10ff. Ahab's sullen, sulking spirit construes personally Naboth's refusal which was based on principle, vv. 3, 4, 6; cf. v. 15. To the wicked and vicious Jezebel, the situation posed no problem. Her husband was king; he could do as he pleased. She would take the initiative on his behalf: "I will give thee the vineyard", v. 7, and later, "Arise, take possession of the vineyard", v. 15. Ahab readily responded as he "rose up to go down"! Beware of covetousness, which is idolatry, Col. 3. 5, and the brooding discontent that follows in its trail.

There is a higher throne than that of Ahab. With this we all have to do. From the golden throne within the oracle "the word of the Lord came to Elijah", vv. 17, 28. "Arise, go down to meet Ahab . . . in the vineyard of Naboth", v. 18. To the Lord, there had been no change of ownership. But there had been a crime of double enormity, v. 19. To such a sinner, the herald of God can never be welcome. Ahab said to Elijah "Hast thou found me, O mine enemy?", v. 20. Yet, apart from his ministry, the king would never have gone "softly" (gently, in penitence), vv. 27, 29. Judgment was inevitable. His house would become like those of the earlier dynasties, v. 22. But his repentance secured a reprieve for himself, v. 29. Be sure your sin will find you out, yet godly sorrow is never to be regretted.

June 3rd

READING : **2 Kings 2. 1-17**

WHERE IS THE LORD, THE GOD OF ELIJAH?

OUR READING describes the parting of two great men of God. The father-figure was swept up to heaven in a whirlwind, v. 11. He departed as swiftly as he had appeared, 1 Kings 17. 1. The younger man was left to be a prophet in Elijah's stead, 19. 16.

The Final Setting, 2 Kings 2. 1-8. It was "when the Lord would take up Elijah", v. 1. This hope was shared by one other only in the O.T., Enoch, Gen. 5. 24. The latter walked with God, and Elijah witnessed for God. Yet, for the church, an unnumbered multitude will rise to heaven without dying, 1 Thess. 4. 17. Happy prospect! Some said, "the Lord will take away thy master", vv. 3, 5, and for them the sadness of separation and loss was paramount. Even the disciples found it difficult to accept that the Lord's return to heaven would be to their advantage, and sorrow filled their hearts. Like Mary, they were ignorant of the boon to be theirs through the One who said, "I ascend", John 16. 5-7; 20. 16-17.

Elisha was determined to share every fleeting moment with Elijah before he "went up"; ct. v. 7. What present reward there was in this. He *felt the peace of God* enjoyed by his master, who was on eternity's borderland. He *followed the path of God* pursued to the last by his tireless mentor; he would not leave him, vv. 2, 4, 6. Keep me calm and committed, Lord!

The Fiery Separation, vv. 9-14. Elijah knew that when he was taken *up,* he would be taken *from* Elisha. He would make provision for that: "Ask what I shall do for thee", v. 9. Elisha claimed the firstborn's birthright, the blessing, and "double portion" of the inheritance, Gen. 27. 1-4, 35-37; Deut. 21. 17. He longed to be Elijah's spiritual successor, "a hard thing" to ask indeed, v. 10. But, so it would be "if thou see me when I am taken from thee"; cf. Acts 1. 10-11. As with the Lord Jesus, Elijah's assumption (taken up) was also an ascension (went up), vv. 1, 11; for another word see vv. 3, 5, 9, 10.

For many, yesterday's heroes can never be replaced. Whilst the disciple is not greater than his master, he can take the master's mantle and smite the waters, vv. 8, 14. Is not the God of Elijah still with those who are inseparable from the One who has ascended? Is not Jesus Christ the same for us today, as he was for those who led us yesterday?, Heb. 13. 7, 8.

June 4th

READING : **2 Kings 6. 8-23**

LORD, I PRAY THEE, OPEN HIS EYES

WE SEE the Lord's provisions to counter enemy incursions.

The Lord's Early Warning System: Averting Danger, vv. 8-10. Israeli's were to confess "A *Syrian* ready to perish was my father", Deut. 26. 5. So often that which we once were before grace called us threatens our spiritual existence.

That God is omniscient none of us doubts. But He would have His people aware also of Satan's manoeuvres, 2 Cor. 2. 11. It is "the man of God" He uses to alert the king, and he "saved himself there". Is not the man of God to save both himself, and them that hear him?, 1 Tim. 4. 16. We need, also, practical deliverance, "not once nor twice".

Timely Help in Present Need: Protection in Danger, 2 Kings 6. 11-18. The sphere of the supernatural is dismissed by many of the unconverted. The Syrian king can only suspect that military intelligence is being passed to the enemy. Even when told of the true "informer", the king believed that the Lord, who kept His servant informed about the Syrian general's schemes, could not safeguard that servant against his proposed capture, vv. 13-14. The darkness of night hid nothing from the man of God, whereas morning light brought terror to one not personally in touch, v. 15. Hence the "Fear not: for they that be with us are more than they that be with them", v. 16; Rom. 8. 35-39. The man that can banish fear in others, is the one who boldly draws near to the throne of grace, Heb. 4. 16. How speedily the Lord answered Elisha's request to "open his eyes", for until the servant saw he would remain unsure, 2 Kings 6. 17; cf. 2. 11-12. Take another look heavenward! If the Lord's people too frequently are unaware of the resources of the One who is for them, unbelievers are often dangerously oblivious of the One who is against them, 6. 18.

Many Times Did He Deliver Them: Removal of Danger, vv. 19-23. Elisha prayed for those in darkness, v. 20; ct. v. 17. Thus the Syrians became aware of their utter impotence and danger. Then the enemy were filled with delicacies! That "great provision" left the invaders satisfied, and surprised. They were sent away, their evil being overcome with good, Rom. 12. 20-21. Mercy routs the foe where might and messages fail!

June 5th

READING : **2 Kings 6. 24 to 7. 20**

THOU SHALT SEE IT ... BUT SHALT NOT EAT

WHAT SKIRMISHES could not achieve, a full scale siege would, or so the Syrian king reasoned, 6. 23, 24. The siege of Samaria and its sequel form the subject of our reading.

The King that leaned on the hand of a man. He was a caricature of what a king should be. He was *helpless*, 6. 27. He was *senseless*, proposing the removal of the head of the one peculiarly in touch with God among them, 6. 31. He was *restless*, despairing of the Lord's aid, 6. 33. He was *unbelievingly cautious*, causing an unnecessary extension of his people's distress, 7. 12-14. He depended upon man rather than God, 7. 2, 17. He could wear sackcloth on the flesh externally, while being controlled by the mind of the flesh inwardly, 6. 30, 31.

The Man of God that spoke the Word of the Lord. Wise elders wished to sit with him. He was unafraid, despite his knowledge of the king's threat, 6. 32, 33. He alone knew the day, the time, and the purpose of God to do the impossible, 7. 1; ct. 6. 25. The Lord revealed it; he was the faithful man of God who preached it, 7. 17, 18. Along with his "Thus saith the Lord" was a challenging "Hear ye", 7. 1. The next day all was fulfilled "according to the word of the Lord", 7. 16, 18. Is anything more sure than God's Word?

The Incredulous Captain that scoffed at the promise. With what scepticism he "answered the man of God", 7. 2, 19. He dared to fling his wild unbelief at the Lord Himself. The Lord did not need to "make windows in heaven", vv. 2, 19. They were there already. They could be used effectively to do the impossible *in judgment*, as the flood proved, Gen. 7. 11; cf. Isa. 24. 18, and *in blessing*, Mal. 3. 10. When the Lord makes known his purpose, no one except an infidel would say "might this thing be?", v. 2; cf. v. 19. Such scoffing cannot alter the course of events; cf. 2 Pet. 3. 4-7. The Lord only needs to allow the Syrians to hear the "noise" of His unseen hosts, cf. 2 Kings 6. 17; 7. 6, for a siege to be lifted with such haste as to free the beleaguered, and provide them with food and spoil in plenty, 7. 16, 18. But God's intervention was discriminating. While there was blessing for many, retribution stalked and trod down the infidel, vv. 2, 17, 20. So it has been; so it will be.

"Blind unbelief is sure to err, and scan His work in vain."

June 6th

READING : **2 Kings 9. 1-37**

THOU SHALT SMITE . . . THAT I MAY AVENGE

AHAB'S HOUSE, like the two preceding ones in the Northern kingdom, was to be destroyed, vv. 8, 9. Jehu was the Lord's instrument, anointed, vv. 3, 6, 12, and appointed to smite, v. 7. Yet, in the event, the Lord was settling accounts finally. "I will cut off", and "I will make" were the Divine pronouncements regarding His purpose. The Lord is longsuffering, giving ample room for repentance. His delay must never be construed as slackness. Men wilfully ignore at their peril the Lord's purpose finally to overthrow wickedness, and establish His kingdom by Divine power, 2 Pet. 3. 4-13.

"Is it peace?" The wounded Jehoram thought that Jehu must be bearing some urgent tidings from the battlefield. The king would know if all was well, 2 Kings 9. 17, 19, 22. He was oblivious of *his own* danger. How this is so with many today. Is it well with *your* soul? "What peace?", asks Jehu, v. 22, for there can be no peace when there is something between the heart and the Lord. "There is no peace . . . unto the wicked".

Fulfilling the Word. Jehu was the executioner of Divine wrath, not a traitor, v. 23. His bow was not drawn "at a venture", ct. 1 Kings 22. 34, but with determined and deadly accuracy, 2 Kings 9. 24. Equally deliberately, he cast Jehoram's body in Naboth's plot, v. 25f. Jehu remembered the word of the Lord, 1 Kings 21. 19, 29.

Jezebel, though a king's daughter, and a queen-mother in Israel, was a "cursed woman". Ruthless in implementing "royal rights", 1 Kings 21. 7, she exceeded this wickedness by pressing her own idolatrous worship of the Phoenician Baal upon Israel, 18. 19, setting herself in murderous opposition to the Lord's prophets, 18. 4; 19. 1-3. Her idolatries and witchcrafts led to that perversion of womanhood well epitomized in 2 Kings 9. 30. Even the church has not been free of such false prophetesses, Rev. 2. 20-23. She remained unrepentant, defiant to the end, 2 Kings 9. 31. She was thrown from the window to her death, vv. 32f. Mercilessly, Jehu trod her underfoot. In her case, the Lord brought about the fulfilment of His own word. Hence the details correspond perfectly with the prophecy, vv. 36f; 1 Kings 21. 23. Justice at last caught up with Jezebel at Jezreel. The Judge of all the earth will do right.

June 7th

READING : 2 Kings 10. 1-36

COME WITH ME, AND SEE MY ZEAL FOR THE LORD

THE PASSAGE completes the detailed account of the bloody revolution set afoot by prophecy, 9. 1-3; 1 Kings 19. 15-17. It was the affinity between the king's house and the house of Baal, which Ahab had built, 16.32, that led to the total overthrow of both, 2 Kings 10. 1-11, 17, 18-28.

What zeal, yea, what revenge! Jehu's outstanding quality was zeal. The word means "to become intensely red". How often the ardour of one's zeal is evident in the glow of the face! Jehu followed in the train of Elijah (ct. meaning of names) who said "being jealous I have been jealous", 1 Kings 19. 10, 14, *lit.* Earlier, Phinehas had been "jealous with my (God's) jealousy", Num. 25. 11 R.V.; cf. v. 13. Again, our Lord drove out those that defiled the temple, John 2. 17, for "the zeal of thine house hath eaten me up", Psa. 69. 9. There is nothing more nauseous to God than being "neither cold nor hot", Rev. 3. 16.

Come, see Jehu's zeal for the Lord. It was fearsome, red hot. In his role of a Divine executioner, he slew Jehoram, 2 Kings 9. 24-26. He trampled Jezebel under foot, v. 33. He called upon the elders of Samaria to behead the 70 sons of Ahab, 10. 1-10. He exterminated all that remained of Ahab's house, vv. 11, 17. He then destroyed Baalism with great energy, vv. 18-28. This was right in the Lord's eyes, according to all that was in His heart, and received His commendation, v. 30.

But there is a zeal that may seek a right thing in a wrong way; cf. Rom. 10. 2. Jehu went too far. He did all that was in the Lord's heart, but not in *the spirit* of the Divine commission. In him we see "jealousy (same word as zeal) is the rage of a man", Prov. 6. 34. Hence the Lord would visit "the blood of Jezreel upon the house of Jehu", Hos. 1. 4. How we need to be on our guard against the pursuit of truth apart from grace. Then, in all but annihilating Judah's royal line, he went beyond *the terms* of the Divine commission also, 2 Kings 9. 27-29; 10. 12-14; ct. vv. 10, 17. Conversely, Jehu did not go far enough. Had he been motivated by the Lord's glory and truth alone, he would have departed from the sins of Jeroboam, ct. v. 29, and walked in the law of the Lord with all his heart; ct. v. 31. We are not to pursue only that which suits our own disposition and interests in the cause of truth.

June 8th

READING : **2 Kings 11. 21 to 12. 21**

AT FIRST INSTRUCTED; FINALLY IMPOVERISHED

JEHOASH was a good king initially, 11. 21 to 12. 3. During that period, he knew the godly influence of Jehoiada, the high priest, v. 2. Jehoiada gave God His portion in the sanctuary, and the law of truth was in his mouth also, Mal. 2. 6-7. But the advantages gained through his godly instruction continued for the duration of Jehoiada's lifetime only. When Jehoash's prop was removed, his dependence upon the prop rather than on the Lord became evident. Good influence must develop in others the capacity to lead if the future is to be secured for God; see 2 Chron. 24. 17-22.

The one who had been hidden, and crowned, in God's house, 11. 2-3, 12, desired to see it repaired; see 2 Chron. 24. 7. Funds brought in through vows and free-will offerings were to be collected by the priests and channelled into repair work, 2 Kings 12. 4-5. Corruption and slackness among the priests led to Jehoash's stern rebuke, and a change in the arrangements, vv. 6-9. We must safeguard against abuses at the material level in the Lord's work; cf. 2 Cor. 8. 20-21. True liberality is promoted by putting the "chest . . . beside the altar", and on that side where the animals were slain, 2 Kings 12. 9. Giving is enhanced when the grace of God, and of the Lord Jesus, is specially vivid, 1 Cor. 16. 1-2; 2 Cor. 8. 9; 9. 15. Then, there will be "much money in the chest", 2 Kings 12. 10. But money in the chest does not further the Lord's work. Arrangements were made to prevent misappropriation, v. 10, while ensuring that the funds were put to work, vv. 11-14. Such was the faithfulness of the workmen that further safeguards on their use of the funds were unnecessary, v. 15. The Lord looks for faithfulness in the use of that which He has committed to us.

Jehoash's subsequent sin and departure, 2 Chron. 24. 17-24, was followed by the Syrian Hazael threatening Jerusalem, 2 Kings 12. 17. Jehoash stripped the treasures of the Lord's and king's houses to buy off the aggressor, v. 18. Asa earlier achieved the removal of Israel's threat by buying Syrian aid, rather than by looking to the Lord, 1 Kings 15. 18-19. At last that sin had come home to roost! The Syrian, once bought as an ally, now has to be bought off as an enemy. Our scheming will result inevitably in our own spiritual bankruptcy.

June 9th

READING : **2 Kings 14. 1-20**

WHY SHOULDEST THOU MEDDLE TO THY HURT?

THE OPENING summary of Amaziah's reign, 14. 1-4, provides another instance of a king whose commitment to right is referred to with decided reservations. In this he was like J(eh)oash his father, rather than David. It is important to follow the best examples set before us, 1 Cor. 11. 1.

Once established in his kingdom, Amaziah dealt firmly with those servants who had conspired against "the king his father", v. 5; 12. 20. The children of the assassins he treated leniently however, 14. 6; Deut. 24. 16. Such perfect blending of government and grace is a feature of the ways of God. We must approach life's situations with the light of the Scriptures.

Amaziah's success against Edom is dismissed quickly here; cf. 2 Chron. 25. 5-16; 2 Kings 14. 7. In renaming Selah Joktheel (=subdued by God), it appeared that he gave God the glory. The paragraph, opened by the ominous "Then", v. 8, indicates that this was not really the case, v. 10; 2 Chron 25. 14-18. Pride goes before a fall, and is hateful to God.

Amaziah, flushed with success, sought conflict with Israel, 2 Kings 14. 8. The pride of Amaziah was matched by the contempt of Jehoash of Israel, v. 9, who sought to dissuade Amaziah. Proud dreams of a subdued Israel, or even of a reunited kingdom, ignored the need for a humbling of the Davidic line "until he come whose right it is", Ezek. 21. 27. Because Amaziah would not listen, he was defeated crushingly at Beth-shemesh, 2 Kings 14. 11-12. The Israel whose expansionist policy under Baasha caused Asa to buy Syrian help against her, now, having experienced recent successes against Syria, came up to Jerusalem itself. Jehoash destroyed a part of its northern defences, and then depleted the treasures of the Lord's and king's houses alike, vv. 13-14; cf. 12. 17-18; 1 Kings 15. 17-21. This cycle is now completed with a certain poetic justice; see Outline, p. 164. Neither compromise nor pride is acceptable to God, and must bring judgment.

Amaziah lived, in many ways, after the pattern of J(eh)oash his father, 2 Kings 14. 3-4; he was cut off by assassins also, vv. 5. 19-20; cf. 12. 20-21. Taking the law into one's own hands, however the flesh may justify it, stands condemned in Scripture. We must know the spirit we are of, Luke 9. 51-56.

June 10th

READING : **2 Kings 16. 1-20**

THE GODS OF SYRIA WERE THE RUIN OF HIM

AHAZ was a particularly evil king, though son of a good king, 15. 34, 35, and father of one of the outstandingly good kings, 18. 1-8. Holiness is not hereditary!

The summary of his reign exposes the *religious* nature of his sin, 16. 1-4. He followed the example of the kings of Israel, and in some dire emergency even made his son pass through the fire. The high places knew his royal patronage, further deflecting the people from the one God-appointed centre. Neither did the king heed the counsel of Isaiah, terrified as he was by *political* adversaries, vv. 5-6; 2 Chron. 28. 17-18; Isa. 7. 1-9. Instead, he sent to Assyria saying "come up, and save me". He stripped the Lord's house and his own to buy their aid. Judah survived, but at the expense of their political independence. Even Ahaz owned himself to be the servant of the Assyrian king. The cost of compromise and fear is great.

Ahaz duly travelled to Damascus to greet his saviour and overlord. There, Ahaz became fascinated by a Syrian altar he saw, which was more glorious in man's workmanship, and more gigantic in size, than the temple's brazen altar. Details were transmitted to Jerusalem, where the priest weakly, if not wickedly, cooperated by making and installing it in the court. The law of truth was not in his mouth; ct. 12. 2; 2 Chron. 26. 16-21. We must resist departure from the Word of God, speaking truth in love.

The king, on his return, consecrated the new altar with his sacrifices. He offered upon it the whole range of sweet savour sacrifices, but remained strangely insensitive to his own sin and trespass, and that of the people, vv. 13-15. His religious departure was now accelerated out of all proportion, vv. 10-18. God's appointed means of approach to Him was moved aside, and Ahaz' Syrian-style altar replaced it as the new means of approach, v. 14. The king deflected priest and people alike, vv. 15-16. Other radical changes were made to the Divine appointments, v. 17, because Ahaz had looked for his salvation from the Assyrian rather than the Almighty, vv. 8, 18. It was a change of heart Ahaz needed. Change in that which God has ordered is not permitted. Heed Isaiah's warning: "If ye will not believe, surely ye shall not be established", 7. 9.

June 11th

READING : **2 Kings 17. 1-23**

SO ISRAEL WAS CARRIED AWAY

THE PENETRATING diagnosis of a nation's disease that led to its death is analysed for our warning here.

Because . . ., vv. 7-12. Assess the thanklessness toward their national Liberator, v. 7. Trace the departure involved, as they "walked in the statutes of the nations, whom the Lord cast out", v. 8, and "carried away", v. 11. As the Lord's people we are to be different, v. 15. Penetrate the darkness involved, as they practised evil in secret, v. 9. Does not the Lord know even the words spoken in the bedchamber?, cf. 6. 12; Heb. 4. 13. Weigh the disobedience involved, for they did what the Lord had forbidden: "Ye shall not do this thing", 2 Kings 17. 12. The elevenfold use of "and" here brings out the cumulative spell cast by idolatry. Fashions may change, but the face of evil remains carnal and devilish.

"Yet . . .", 2 Kings 17. 13. The Lord does not give up His sinning people, so evidencing His long-suffering. "Turn", He cried, through every prophet. Each one of these said the same thing; there was no uncertain sound, no differences of opinion. The hands of men delivered the challenge, but the hands were those of *"my servants* the prophets". O for more servants of the Lord, concerned for His Word and work, and not their "schools".

"Notwithstanding . . . but", vv. 14-17. The chain of sins is longer still here, its many links, "but" and "and" (16 refs), proving them to be "the bondservants of sin". The truth alone "shall make you free", John 8, 32, 34; cf. Rom. 6. 16-18. Sin's grip is tightened where indifference reigns, and the Lord's warnings are disregarded, 2 Kings 17. 14, 16. Hear ye Him!

"Therefore . . . So", vv. 18-23. Effect follows cause: judgment follows sin. The Lord had been provoked to anger by their idolatry, v. 11. Now, He was "very angry", v. 18. They were "removed", "rejected", "afflicted", "delivered" to spoilers, "cast . . . out", and "removed", vv. 18, 20, 23. They would not turn from evil, "So was Israel carried away out of their own land", v. 23b. It was Jeroboam whose innovations "drave Israel from following the Lord". That one act of disobedience, prompted by unbelief, cf. v. 14, caused many to become sinners. Keep us cleaving to Thyself, Lord!

June 12th

READING : 2 Kings 19. 14-34

THE ZEAL OF THE LORD SHALL DO THIS

ON TWO OCCASIONS Hezekiah was subjected to the blasphemous taunts of the Assyrian: (1) in a verbal tirade, 18. 17-35; (2) in a written text, 19. 8-13. Our passage treats Hezekiah's response to the second of these, and Isaiah's oracle to him.

"Lord, bow down thine ear", vv. 14-19. To turn to one of the Lord's servants is good, vv. 2-4, but to call upon the Lord is better! Can a nation have any greater asset than a king that prays? A lofty view of the Lord always promotes effective, and enormous petitions, v. 15. Hezekiah discriminated, as Sennacherib did not, between "the living God", and those that were "no gods", vv. 16-18. His plea was "save thou us . . . that . . . the earth may know that thou art the Lord God", v. 19. Let God's glory, not your good alone, govern your praying.

"I have heard", vv. 20-34. When the Lord heard, Isaiah was as near to Him, and as ready for service, as the day on which he was first commissioned; "Here am I; send me", Isa. 6. 8. The Lord's word was that Zion would defy the Assyrian, 2 Kings 19. 21. The enemy had dared to blaspheme the Holy One of Israel, vv. 22-24. The conqueror had been ignorant that he was God's instrument of judgment in the Near East, and because he claimed the glory, his own judgment was inevitable, vv. 25-28. He had acted like a beast; God would deal with him as with a beast, v. 28. To all such God says "I know" and "I will", vv. 27-28.

For the believing king there is a sign, vv. 29-31. This sabbatical year, see Lev. 25. 20-22, would be one in which they would enter into God's rest indeed. The enemy would not despoil that which grew of itself, nor that which would spring from it for the year following. If the promise seemed humanly impossible of achievement, its performance was guaranteed by "the zeal of the Lord". Is anything too hard for Him?

For the blasphemous king there would be shame. There are two reasons given for the salvation of Zion. The Lord acts "for mine own sake". His sovereign grace would unfold itself consistently with all He had revealed Himself to be, and He would be glorified. But He was also committed to Zion "for my servant David's sake", v. 34. David's greater Son is to come to save city and people alike. Rest on the promises of God!

June 13th

READING : **2 Kings 22. 8 to 23. 25**

MAKE THE BOOK LIVE TO ME, O LORD

REGARDING Josiah, Kings emphasizes those changes introduced in his 18th year when the Word was discovered.

The Book Found, 22. 8a, 13; 23. 2, 24, is variously described as "the book of the law", 22. 8a, 11, "the book of the (this) covenant", 23. 2, 21, and as "the book that Hilkiah the priest found in the house of the Lord", v. 24; cf. 22. 8. What neglect is suggested by this. What blessing accrued from its discovery. If such dramatic changes resulted from the discovery of Deuteronomy, with its call to remember the great lessons of the past, its insistence on exclusive loyalty to the Lord, and its warning that sin will bring suffering, what inestimable blessing will be ours if we discover the length and breadth of the Word?

The Book Read and Heard, 22. 8b, 10b, 11, 18; 23. 2. For some, remaining unimpressed and unaffected as they read, it is only "a book"; cf. 22. 8, 10. To others, its message is devastating as they hear it, v. 11. "Take heed therefore how ye hear", Luke 8. 18, for hearing that leads to response counts with God, James 1. 21-25. Josiah, in humbling himself when he heard, found this to be the secret of the Lord hearing him, 2 Kings 22. 18, 19. By obeying the Word, the Lord's ear is opened to our prayers. A softened heart brings in Divine guarantees, v. 20. Such preparation privately makes the leader a blessing to God's people publicly. He led them to the Lord's house, and read *all* the words of the book to them *all*, 23. 2.

The Book Followed, 23. 3, 16-18, 21-25. By means of the Word, Josiah separated the people from evil, vv. 16-17, 24. By the same Word, and with God's help they would walk after the Lord, v. 3, and "Keep the passover unto the Lord", vv. 21-23. Josiah's separation unto the Lord was total for he "turned to the Lord with *all* his heart, and with *all* his soul, and with *all* his might, according to *all* the law of Moses", v. 25. The Shema, Deut. 6. 4-9; 11. 13-21; Num. 15. 37-41, is the basic creed of the Jews, recited by them morning and evening. Josiah responded to this pithy statement of faith out of love for the Lord. It is opened by the first commandment of all, and there is a second like to it: "Thou shalt love thy neighbour as thyself", Mark 12. 28-34. Let love for God and man, the sum of the Scriptures, motivate our lives too.

June 14th
READING : 2 Kings 24. 8 to 25. 30
SO JUDAH WAS CARRIED AWAY

THE FINAL section of Kings opened with Ahaz buying Assyrian assistance with treasures from the Lord's and king's houses, and the radical changes he introduced into the temple court consequent upon this, 16. 8-18. It is closed when the treasures of those same houses, plus the golden temple vessels, were taken out to the Babylonian king, 24. 13, and subsequently the temple was burned, and the several massive bronze items of the court were broken up and carried away, 25. 9, 13-17; see p. 164. The prophecy of Jerusalem's denuding, pronounced following Hezekiah's folly, 20. 17-18, was fulfilled.

What a city of seige Jerusalem has been. In the times of Elijah and Hezekiah, 19. 30-31; 1 Kings 19. 14-18, a remnant of the nation was that in which the future lay. So it is here. There was a "gospel" then which was as unacceptable to many as is God's message for today. The judgment of sin was inescapable, 22. 16-17; 24. 2-4, 13, 20. Hope rested, therefore, in submitting to this Divine appointment. Even after Babylon's victory, Gedaliah's message was to those who remained "dwell in the land, and serve the king of Babylon; and it shall be well with you", 2 Kings 25. 24. The contemporary prophet, Jeremiah, said that the one who fell away to the besiegers, "he shall live", Jer. 21. 8-10; cf. 38. 17-20. Jehoiachin did so, 24. 12, and lived to see a change of heart toward him, 25. 27-30. Here was a five-fold expression of grace to one whose name, in strict justice, was to have been cut off forever, Jer. 22. 30. This hints at that Divine mercy which chose his grandson, Zerubbabel, 1 Chron. 3. 17-19, to lead those who returned later from Babylon to the homeland. The proportion of that mercy is demonstrated in the Messiah's genealogy, which is traced through one of his sons, Matt. 1. 11-12. Neither Israel's nor Judah's transgressions can thwart the determined gracious purpose of the Lord. God's strange work must remove from the nation all offence, and refine those He will bless. But the hope of the nation rests upon "the man that is my (God's) fellow", Zech. 13. 7-9; cf. Jer. 23. 5-6; Rom. 11. 25-32. It is ever true that those who say "Show us thy mercy", will not be disappointed. For, in Christ, "Mercy and truth are met together; righteousness and peace have kissed".

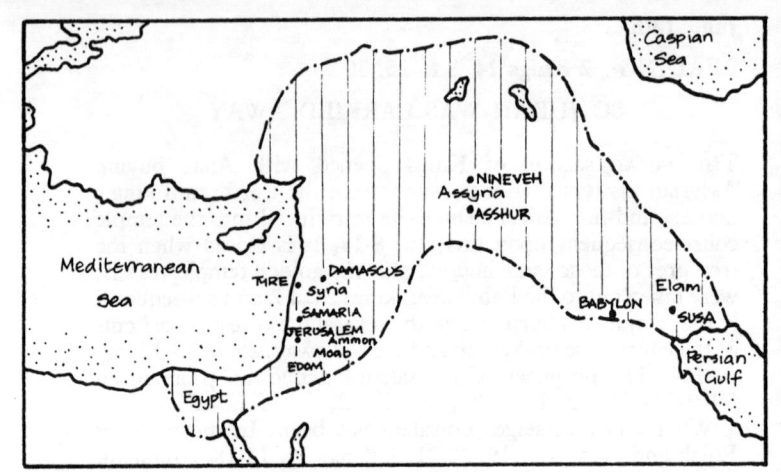

The Assyrian Empire

NOTE: — ASSYRIAN EMPIRE DID NOT INCLUDE EGYPT AS A PERMANENT FEATURE

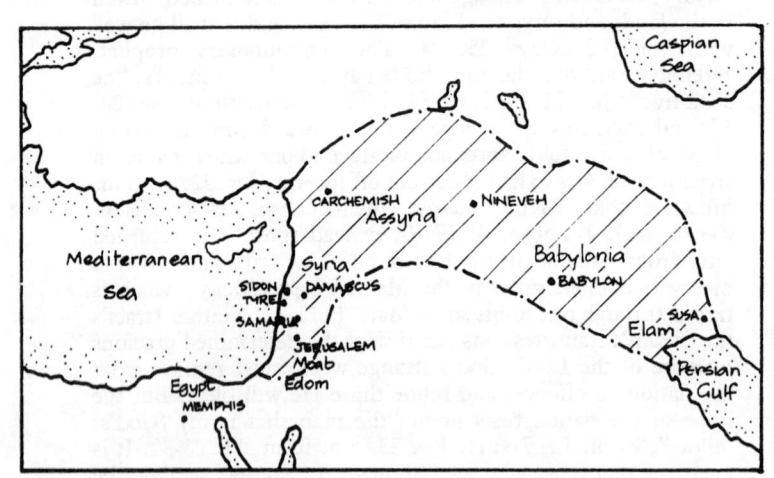

The Babylonian Empire

Introducing 1 Chronicles

THE BIBLE is largely a history book, but history as assessed from God's all-seeing and all-knowing viewpoint.

We ignore this history at our peril. It reveals the thoughts and actions of the same unchanging God to whom we all must give account, and it records the response to His kindness and warnings from "men of like passions", from men of the same nature as ourselves. Bible history is written to teach, and not merely to inform and entertain us. Whatever is written therein is designed to warn and instruct us so that we may be guided and encouraged thereby, 1 Cor. 10. 11; Rom. 15. 4.

A man's history depends largely on what kind of a man he is, and so partly on what kind of ancestors he has. Hence Chronicles starts with the genealogy of Adam, the man who fell. The present is rooted in the past. The history of Israel is the history of man, full of sobering lessons for us all. But one's history depends supremely upon the sovereign mercy of God; we find His gracious intervention often mentioned in Chronicles. Originally, the two books were but one, and they still close the canon in the Hebrew Bible. Commencing with Adam, and concluding with the return from the captivity, they embrace the whole of the O.T. story.

The writer of Chronicles has a different purpose from the authors of Samuel and Kings. In Chronicles, not the life of king Saul, but only his shameful death is recorded. Here David, the chosen of God, claims attention. Yet most of the personal details of his life are omitted, whether his triumphs over the bear, the lion, and Goliath, or his fearful sin with Bathsheba. It is his self-denying zeal for the temple and the service of God that dominates the story. The writer's concern is to show that the will of God for Israel, as for all men, is that man's life should be God-centred. True prosperity lies in simple obedience to His Word, particularly in giving Him the honour and worship which is His due.

An Outline

Genealogies: The People of God, 1. 1 to 9. 44.
Narrative: 1. David, chosen by God, 10. 1 to 12.40.
2. The ark of God, 13. 1 to 21. 30.
3. The house of God, 22. 1 to 29. 30.

June 15th

READING : **1 Chronicles 1. 1-7; 2. 1-7; 9. 1**

THE IMPORTANCE OF GENEALOGIES

WE MAY all learn much from our genealogies. We are all descended from Noah, the fearless preacher who found favour with God. Further, we may all claim descent from Adam, made in the image of God to have fellowship with Him. This is encouraging. Yet Noah became shamefully drunk, and Adam's disobedience brought lasting sorrow to his family.

Moreover, what we inherit, not only of character, but of natural possessions and privileges, often depends upon our "family tree". To claim the earthly blessings covenanted by God to Abraham and his descendants, an Israelite had to prove his lineage from Abraham. To claim the privilege of Levitical service and of holy priesthood, one's descent from Levi and then from Aaron had to be demonstrated, Ezra 2. 62; Neh. 7. 5, 64. So today, if we claim the enjoyment of God's present blessing, spiritual and eternal, we must be born again, be born from above, John 3. 3, 5. We must be assured and rejoice that our names are written in heaven, Luke 10. 20, to be members of a royal and priestly family, 1 Pet. 2. 5, 9.

The first promise of God was that the seed of the woman should bruise the serpent's head. So here the genealogies begin with Adam. Of Noah's family only sons of Shem are mentioned, for from his line came Abraham. Of Israel's sons the royal tribe of Judah and the priestly tribe of Levi have most attention. Judah's line comes first, for he was the chosen progenitor of Israel's God-given king, 5. 1-2. David's line had to be preserved for God's promises concerning the Christ to be fulfilled, Gen. 49. 10. Aaron's, the only priestly line recognized by God, is the most detailed one given, 6. 3-15, 49-53.

These records repeatedly remind us of the evil nature that we have all inherited. We have all forefathers like "Er, the firstborn of Judah, (who) was evil in the sight of the Lord", and "Achar(n), the troubler of Israel", 2. 3-7. So we must walk humbly. We note also some who "died without children". Let us rather seek to be "mighty men of valour . . . fit to go out for war", seeking by our prayers and testimony to win souls for Christ before we go, 2. 32; 7. 11. By God's grace shall we not be "of the house of them that wrought fine linen", or of those who "dwelt with the king for his work"?, 4. 21, 23.

June 16th

READING : 1 Chronicles 4. 9-10

THE PRIVILEGE OF PRAYER

SURELY, HERE are two verses well worth remembering, 4. 9f. Jabez is a picture of us all in his birth, and an example to us in his life. Like every man, he was born in sorrow. His name, meaning "sorrowful", would suit any of us, for the effects of Adam's sin are still with us, Gen. 3. 16; John 16. 21. But why is he described as "more honourable than his brethren"? What distinguished him from them? If we are known for nothing else, each can be noted for earnest prayer, James 5. 16. Prayer brings joy instead of sorrow, Phil. 4. 7f.

"Jabez called". *He was wholehearted*, like the psalmist who said, "Evening, and morning, and at noon, will I pray, and cry aloud, and he shall hear my voice", Psa. 55. 17. Don't be afraid to pray aloud, Jer. 33. 3. In his four petitions we see:

1. *Earnestness*. "Oh, that thou wouldest bless me indeed". Maybe he had not heard the high priest say, "The Lord bless thee, and keep thee", nor read Balaam's words, "I have received commandment to bless: and he hath blessed; and I cannot reverse it", Num. 6. 24; 23. 20. But Jabez longed to experience enrichment from his God. Sin and sloth hinder the enjoyment of God's blessings, Eph. 1. 3.

2. *Vision*. He asked "enlarge my coast". Israel never completely conquered the good land God had given them, though kings like David greatly extended their borders. We must widen our vision, and enjoy our inheritance of holy fellowship with God, and also bring others into its enjoyment. "Fight the good fight of faith, lay hold on eternal life".

3. *Dependence and Diffidence*. Cause that "thine hand might be with me". Man's true place is always one of dependence upon his Maker. A believer's place is that of the dependence of a sheep upon its Shepherd, a child upon its Father, or a servant upon his Master. With "no confidence in the flesh", we need the guiding, guarding hand of God.

4. *Humility*. Then, he desired "that thou wouldest keep me from evil, that it may not grieve me". This is humble recognition of need. Our Lord Jesus testified of the world that its works are positively evil, and He died to deliver us from it, John 7. 7; Gal. 1. 4. So we pray "lead us not into temptation, but deliver us from evil", Matt. 6. 13.

June 17th

READING : 1 Chronicles 9. 1, 10-27

MEN FOR . . . THE SERVICE OF THE HOUSE OF GOD

OUR READING provides the names and genealogies of "very able men for the work of the service of the house of God".

The house of God is where God dwells. It is where He can be found. The first reference in Scripture to the house of God occurs in the exclamation of Jacob, "Surely the Lord is in this place . . . this is none other but the house of God", Gen. 28. 16-17. God does not dwell today in material temples, but in and among His people.

In the New Testament, God's house is presented in three ways. (i) Peter wrote to believers scattered over a wide area of the Roman Empire as those who were "built up a spiritual house, an holy priesthood", 1 Pet. 2. 5. (ii) Paul instructed Timothy as to how men should behave themselves "in the house of God, which is the church (the assembly) of the living God, the pillar and ground of truth", 1 Tim. 3. 15. Here the local church at Ephesus was in view, 1. 3. (iii) The writer to the Hebrews spoke of God, "whose house are we, if we hold fast the confidence and the rejoicing of the hope firm unto the end", Heb. 3. 6. God insists on reality, which is shown by steady continuance in our bold confession of faith.

In 1 Chronicles 9 mention is made of the priests, who were privileged to work within the tabernacle and temple, and the Levites, who acted as porters or gatekeepers. To the tabernacle in the wilderness there was only one entrance, but to the temple courts there were four, suggesting universal and orderly access. In the Holy Jerusalem there will be twelve gates, providing for all twelve tribes of Israel, Rev. 21. 12-13.

It is our privilege to maintain in the house of God moral and spiritual conditions worthy of Himself. We should each gladly accept this responsibility, saying, "I had rather be a doorkeeper in the house of my God, than to dwell in the tents of wickedness", Psa. 84. 10. The Lord warned of wolves "in sheep's clothing", Matt. 7. 15. While delighted when others make professions of conversion, we must look for evidence of genuine faith when newcomers seek to join God's people; see Acts 9. 26-28; 20. 28-31. We must also take heed to ourselves lest we bring a carnal, self-seeking or worldly spirit into the holy presence of God.

June 18th

READING : **1 Chronicles 11. 1-25**

MIGHTY MEN OF VALOUR

THE DEATH of Saul, who was rejected by God because of his sin, was a turning point in the history of Israel, 1 Chron. 10. Our reading describes the anointing of David as king by "all the elders of Israel", vv. 1-3, his conquest of the stronghold of Zion, vv. 4-9, and the exploits of his mighty men, vv. 10-25.

Before the nation as a whole acclaimed David as king, many, chafing at Saul's tyranny, joined David as their leader in his rejection and exile. Outlawed in the wilderness, they waited with David for God to vindicate him. Though mercilessly hunted by Saul's soldiery, they accepted their suffering till God "slew" Saul, 10. 14. Their triumphs were over the heathen who were trespassing on the possession of God's people and from whose vicious influence God wished them to be delivered. They were carrying out God's judgments against these shamelessly evil nations. In the day of David's exaltation they came into their own.

So it will be with us: "If we suffer" with our Lord, despised and rejected now, "we shall also reign with him" in His kingdom, 2 Tim. 2. 12. He said to His disciples, "Ye are they who have continued with me in my temptations, and I appoint unto you a kingdom, as my Father hath appointed unto me", Luke 22. 28-29. We need to mortify (put to death) the evil deeds of the body, Col. 3. 5, and to bring into captivity every thought to the obedience of Christ, 2 Cor. 10. 3-5. We must quit ourselves like men and be strong, 1 Cor. 16. 13, contending earnestly for the faith once for all delivered to the saints and found in the Scriptures, Jude 3. Sometimes we will need the courage, like Jashobeam and Abishai, 1 Chron. 11. 11, 20, to trust God in the face of apparently overwhelming odds. Sometimes we may have to stand alone, like Eleazer, who preserved precious food for God's people, vv. 12-14, or face powerful alien influences, as Benaiah faced the Moabites and the Egyptian, vv. 22-23. Moab suggests the fleshly desires that war against the soul, 1 Pet. 2. 11, while Egypt suggests the worldly influences to which we were once in bondage, and which we must resist lest they enslave us again, 1 John 2. 15-17. Therefore let us "be strong in the Lord, and in the power of his might", Eph. 6. 10.

June 19th

READING : **1 Chronicles 13. 1-14**

STRIVING TOGETHER AND STRIVING LAWFULLY

THE ARK should have occupied the most holy place in the tabernacle of God, where the high priest was allowed to enter only once a year. God Himself dwelt between the cherubim above the ark. He said to Moses, "There I will meet with thee", Exod. 25. 22; cf. 2 Sam. 6. 2. The ark was the sacred symbol of the presence of God amidst His people.

David consulted "with every leader" to bring the ark from its place of neglect, 1 Chron. 13. 1. In the multitude of counsels there is wisdom. It is important, especially in local church matters, to have the fellowship of one's brethren. But all are not good counsellors. It seems that not one of David's advisers referred him to the Scriptures. His *objective* was good, his *spirit* was gracious, "Let us . . .", but his *method* was wrong; see Psa. 119. 24. The Philistines had returned the ark to Israel on a new cart without trouble, 1 Sam. 6. 7, so David used a similar method. This led to the calamitous end of Uzzah, 1 Chron. 13. 9-10. Good intentions must be governed by a reverence for God's Word. The godly must beware of worldly methods in God's service, however plausible. Zeal to put things right is needed; but beware of zeal without knowledge. Where God has left us instructions we must follow them. Even the Levites, who alone were permitted to carry the ark, were forbidden to touch it, Num. 4. 15. As the oxen stumbled Uzzah tried to steady the ark, and he died. "To obey is better than sacrifice", 1 Sam. 15. 22. All must learn the greatness of God's holiness, as did Ananias and Sapphira, though there are no doubt many liars in the world far worse than they, Acts 5. 1-11.

God is amazingly patient with us in our ignorance and disregard of His Word; if He does discipline us it is for our blessing, Psa. 94. 12. David learned his lesson. Three months later he confessed his error, submitted to the Word of God and experienced the help of God, 1 Chron. 15. 1-3, 26. He and his brethren could then strive together and strive lawfully. When we are humbly guided by God's Word we may count on God's help; see 2 Tim. 2. 5. God sometimes interrupts our joy to give us a purer joy; compare 13. 8-10 with 15. 25.

June 20th
READING : 1 Chronicles 15. 1-29
JOY IN ISRAEL

WHEN ALL Israel came "with one heart" to make David king in Hebron, we read that there was "joy in Israel", 12. 40. Our chapter records another occasion of joy and singing when the ark was brought up to its place in Jerusalem, 15. 25-28. This was the result of careful *preparation*. David wanted to find a place not merely for a sacred vessel, but for the Lord; see Psa. 132. 1-9. Hence he made diligent preparation, pitching a tent for the ark where God could be enquired of and worshipped in Jerusalem, 1 Chron. 15. 1, 3, 12. He confessed his error in not heeding the Scriptural order previously, and ensured that the ark was borne on the Levites' shoulders, "as Moses commanded according to the word of the Lord", v. 15. If we would know the reality of the Lord's presence in our midst we also must prepare: we must feed on the Scriptures so as not to appear before God "empty" but with full hearts; we must examine and judge ourselves before we gather, Deut. 16. 16; 1 Cor. 11. 28-31.

David also saw the need of *sanctification*, v. 12. The Levites were privileged to carry the ark and later to serve in the temple courts. Now all believers may draw near to God and serve Him. This implies a duty to sanctify ourselves, to set ourselves apart for His service. As to our persons we have been sanctified through the offering of the body of Christ once for all, Heb. 10. 10. As to our practices we must cleanse ourselves from all filthiness of flesh and spirit, perfecting holiness in the fear of God, 2 Cor. 7. 1. Let us pursue holiness — the sanctification "without which no man shall see the Lord", Heb. 12. 14.

Such prayerful preparation will lead to *jubilation* that Jesus Himself is given His place as Lord in the midst of His people. Believers today are "as sorrowful, yet always rejoicing", 2 Cor. 6. 10. Joy in the Holy Spirit is not achieved merely through musical or emotional appeals. It is experienced in the depths of one's spirit when we really bow our wills to Him. It is known after prayer, even if backs are bruised and bleeding, and limbs are cramped and cold, Acts 16. 25. It is joy in God and joy in our unchanging Lord, and consequently it is a joy unspeakable, 1 Pet. 1. 8.

June 21st

READING : **1 Chronicles 16. 1-36**

A PSALM OF THANKSGIVING

"Is ANY cheerful? Let him sing praise", James 5. 13 R.V. This was probably the happiest event in David's life. He had found a place for the Lord. To the God to whom he owed everything he had given the place of highest honour among His people, Psa. 132. 1-9. He therefore delivered a psalm to Asaph and his brethren for regular praise to God before the ark in Jerusalem. It was fitting that he should appoint this psalm, after such a triumphant recovery from the lawless days of the judges and the fearful failure of king Saul. There had been congregational praise at the Red Sea, Exod. 15. 1. But now Israel can look back over many centuries of God's mercies. First "the seed of Israel", 1 Chron. 16. 13, were called to celebrate His goodness, vv. 8-22; then "all the earth" was called — for He rules the nations, vv. 23-31; and finally the inanimate creation was called — for His lovingkindness is over all His works, vv. 32-33; cf. Psa. 145. 9.

It is a psalm of thanksgiving, although not an ascription of praise direct to God. We also often speak to one another in our singing. We do not use harps, psalteries, trumpets and cymbals because, unlike the Levites, we do not serve in a material sanctuary with a service appealing to the eye and the ear; see Heb. 9. 1. We enter into "the holiest" to offer up spiritual sacrifices, 10. 19. An Israelite priest functioned because he was of a certain tribe (Levi) and family (Aaron). We, however, must be born of the Spirit into the family of God before we are able to worship Him in spirit and in truth, for which we need no ear for music at all! Our Lord applied Isaiah's words to all the impressive God-given ceremony in His day: "Their heart is far from me . . . in vain they do worship me", Matt. 15. 7-9. How diligently would David's men practise on their instruments! May we give equal time to prayerful, spiritual exercises today!

Note the 15 references to the Lord, Jehovah, the eternal unchanging One. They remind us of the Red Sea song, "Who is like unto thee, O Lord, among the gods (mighty ones) . . . glorious in holiness, fearful in praises, doing wonders?", Exod. 15. 11. He is incomparable. "For all the gods of the people are idols: but the Lord made the heavens", 1 Chron. 16. 26.

June 22nd

READING : **1 Chronicles 16. 23-36**

SAVE US AND GATHER US

THIS PSALM, v. 7, begins and ends with the call to give thanks unto the Lord, vv. 8, 34. One reason given is, "for he is good; for his mercy endureth for ever", v. 34. Note the repetition of this phrase in Psalm 136. The word for mercy, often translated "lovingkindness" or "goodness", means more than pitiful forbearance; it suggests God's steadfast love, His faithfulness to His people. It contrasts with their "goodness" which evaporated like the morning mist, Hos. 6. 4.

Thankfulness resulted from remembering the Lord's marvellous works in the salvation and preservation of His people, and His faithfulness to His people despite all their failures, vv. 12, 15. Israel expressed their thanks in song. How much more will they in the coming millennial day when they will be able to say, without fear of contradiction, "The Lord reigneth", v. 31. They and we must "declare his glory", v. 24, for His greatness is unsearchable. In contrast, the gods of the nations are idols — nonentities, things of nought, v. 26; cf. 1 Cor. 8. 4.

We sing to God and we testify to men. Finally came an exhortation to pray, v. 35. How often had back-slidden Israelites been carried off by enemies in the days of the judges! Even David's own family had later suffered this bitter experience, 1 Sam. 30. 1-6. "Save us . . . and gather us" is the appeal to God who will ultimately gather all Israel to their homeland, Jer. 31. 8-12. Satan may scatter the flock of God today, but the Lord gathers us, and our gatherings anticipate our final gathering to Him, 2 Thess. 2. 1. Israel prayed "Save . . . and gather" that they might praise Him. If we prayed and gave thanks more often in private we should more eagerly say, "Oh magnify the Lord with me, and let us exalt his name together". What a joy would the Lord's Supper and the prayer meeting be then!

"And all the people said, Amen", v. 36. This expression of agreement was normally used in church gatherings in apostolic days, 1 Cor. 14. 16. It is in merciful contrast to the twelvefold "Amen" that Israel had to pronounce on God's curses, Deut. 27. 15-26. Our "Amen" expresses heartfelt desire; God's "Amen" expresses heartfelt determination; see 2 Cor. 1. 20.

June 23rd
READING : **1 Chronicles 23. 1-32**

PRIESTS AND LEVITES

EARLIER CHAPTERS deal with David's desire to build a house for God and his charge to Solomon to do this, 17. 1; 22. 6.

The priests and the Levites were now appointed to daily service. The repeated mention of their names shows the importance of their work. The Levites had to facilitate the work of the sacrificing priests. All Israel had to contribute to their upkeep by gifts of firstfruits and by providing villages for their dwellings. The whole life of the nation centred in the worship of the Holy One in their midst.

Similarly our ministry to God and to men should lead to local church gatherings where Jesus is Lord in the midst of His people, and where the sacrifice of praise is offered to God.

Levites originally functioned between the ages of 30 and 50, Num. 4. 47, because they needed maturity of judgment and manly vigour to perform their duties. God wants the best of our energies, mental and physical. It is not for godly kings or for the royal priesthood called to reign with Christ, 1 Pet. 2. 9, to dissipate their strength in sensuality or to cloud their judgment with strong drink, Prov. 31. 2-5. The glory of young men is their strength, and that is to be given to God. Moses had appointed Levites at 25 years to serve a five-year apprenticeship, Num. 8. 24-26, but David, with God-given authority, instituted a settled order. Having been given the pattern of an incomparably magnificent temple, he appointed Levitical service to begin at the age of 20.

There are no such limits today; but we should consider well what is implied by them. God would not have a "novice" responsible for public service; see 1 Tim. 3. 6. God looks first for spiritual growth. Paul had to speak of the outstandingly gifted saints at Corinth as "babes", 1 Cor. 1. 5; 3. 1; cf. Heb. 5. 13. There had been very little spiritual growth by prayerful feeding on the Word of God.

As spiritual priests, we delight God's heart by prayer and praise, and then we bring His blessing to men, Num. 6. 23-26; 1 Chron. 23. 13. As spiritual Levites "always abounding in the work of the Lord", we labour, purifying "holy things", vv. 27-28. We must therefore keep ourselves pure, 1 Tim. 5. 22.

June 24th

READING : **1 Chronicles 27. 1-15**

IF WE SUFFER . . . WE SHALL REIGN

Despite king David's lamentable failures, there are remarkable parallels between his experiences and those of the Lord Jesus. David, hated and hunted by Saul as a partridge on the mountains, is typical of the Son of man who had nowhere to lay His head. David, defeating the Philistines and establishing his kingdom, reminds us of the coming of the Son of man in judgment, gathering out of His kingdom all that do iniquity or cause stumbling. David, reigning unchallenged with "no evil or adversary" to be dealt with, foreshadows in measure the coming kingdom of our Lord Jesus Christ.

Our reading today consists of a roll of honour containing the names of twelve divisional commanders whom David appointed when his kingdom was established. In chapter 11, all twelve are mentioned as leaders in making David king at Hebron, and the exploits of the first three are described in some detail. These men who suffered with David in his rejection now have their reward. As with David's men so with us: it is through much tribulation that we enter the kingdom of God, Acts 14. 22. We glory in tribulation because it is intended to develop our character, leading to more fellowship with, and usefulness to, our Lord, Rom. 5. 3-5.

We should also have in mind the day when the Lord shall come to be glorified in His saints and admired in all them that believe, 2 Thess. 1. 10. Each will then have his own reward and praise from God, 1 Cor. 4. 5. The Lord holds out to us not only the hope of having a place in the Father's house, but also the prospect of sharing His coming reign. Concerning His millennial reign the Lord said to His disciples, "in the regeneration when the Son of man shall sit in the throne of his glory, ye also shall sit on twelve thrones, judging the twelve tribes of Israel", Matt. 19. 28. We must be diligent to supply with our faith resolution, courage, virtue, etc., that we may secure an abundant entry into the everlasting kingdom of our Lord and Saviour, 2 Pet. 1. 5-11. With that day in mind, He said, "every one that hath forsaken houses, or brethren . . . or father, or mother . . . for my name's sake, shall receive an hundredfold", Matt. 19. 29; cf. 2 Tim. 2. 12. "Verily there is a reward for the righteous", Psa. 58. 11.

June 25th

READING : 1 Chronicles 28. 1-10

SERVE HIM WITH A PERFECT HEART

DAVID CALLED a national assembly to announce God's choice of Solomon as king and as the one to build His house. Just as Moses, when death drew near, encouraged Joshua, Deut. 31. 7-8, and as Paul before his departure exhorted Timothy to endure hardship as a good soldier of Jesus Christ, 2 Tim. 2. 3, so David urged Solomon, "Know thou the God of thy father, and serve him with a perfect heart and with a willing mind", v. 9. Elders do well to encourage younger men to continue the work of God.

We must know God, not only as the God of Abraham, Isaac and Jacob, or as the God of our father, but as *our* God; "O God, thou art *my* God", Psa. 63. 1. We must confess Him as One with whom we are personally acquainted. A true believer is described as one who has "known God", Gal. 4. 9. Paul's most scathing indictment of the carnal Corinthians who boasted in their knowledge was, "some have not the knowledge of God", 1 Cor. 15. 34. To know the Holy One makes us fear sin and moves us to serve Him. This is one object of our salvation, 1 Thess. 1. 9. God repeatedly commanded Pharaoh, "Let my people go that they may serve me", Exod. 8. 1, 20. So David urged Solomon to serve the Lord with all his heart; cf. 1 Sam. 12. 20.

In the Scriptures the heart is regarded as the source of man's feelings, thoughts and actions. Genesis 6. 5-6 speaks of the thoughts of men's hearts and the grief of God's heart. The word "heart" means the innermost man, the real man, not the outward appearance which can mislead; see 1 Sam. 16. 7. The deceit and fickleness of the human heart is discerned only by God, Jer. 17. 9-10; Heb. 4. 12. His understanding is infinite, Psa. 147. 5. We tend to be people of mixed motives, often pleasing ourselves, our brethren or fellow-men, while half-heartedly trying to please God. Serving with a perfect heart means with sincere wholeheartedness. Those who enthroned David were not of "double" or "divided" heart, 1 Chron. 12. 33; Hos. 10. 2. We pray, "Unite my heart to fear thy name", Psa. 86. 11. This is attained only by prayerfully allowing the light of God's holiness to shine upon us, Psa. 139. 23. May we each come to know Him and to serve Him better!

June 26th
READING : 1 Chronicles 28. 11-21
WORKING ACCORDING TO PLAN

DAVID GAVE to Solomon the Divine plan of the temple, vv. 11-19, and encouraged him to build, vv. 20-21.

In building the ark as the way of salvation, Noah was commended for doing all exactly as God commanded him, Gen. 6. 22. Moses was similarly commended for ordering the worship of God's people according to the pattern God gave him, Exod. 25. 40; 40. 16. Now David gave to Solomon "the pattern of all that he had by the spirit" together with the necessary materials for the holy vessels. God must be served and worshipped in a manner worthy of Himself, and He Himself must reveal this manner to us; cf. Isa. 55. 9.

Israel's instructions were for one nation worshipping at one earthly centre, Deut. 12. 11. Ours are for a world-wide testimony to all peoples in all places. God no longer pledges His presence in any material building. Yet the law of God's house is always absolute holiness, that is, distinctiveness and separateness from the world around, Ezek. 42. 20; 43. 10-12. It is the character and spirit of the worshippers that is vital. We must be holy in all manner of behaviour, 1 Pet. 1. 15.

We have no "order of service" given for our observance today, but in 1 Corinthians 11 to 14 and in 1 Timothy we have instructions about church gatherings and our service in general. Happy is he who acknowledges these as "the commandments of the Lord", and is liberated from the traditions of men to follow the traditions left by the apostles in the Scriptures, 2 Thess. 2. 15. Love will not find it irksome to attend to every detail, and will fear to go beyond what is written, 1 John 5. 3.

To follow Divine instruction needs courage, and David therefore urged Solomon, "Be strong and of good courage . . . my God, will be with thee; he will not fail thee nor forsake thee, until thou hast finished all the work", 1 Chron. 28. 20. God pledges His presence and support to those who seek to build for Him, 1 Cor. 3. 9-15. It is spiritual material which is required. David weighed the gold and silver, but God ponders and weighs the actions and spirits of men, 1 Sam. 2. 3; Prov. 16. 2. May we have *His* commendation!

June 27th

READING : **1 Chronicles 29. 1-30**

THE LORD LOVES A CHEERFUL GIVER

THE CHEQUERED history of king David ended on a triumphant note! He urged Israel to follow his example in preparing for the temple, and then led them in praising God, the Giver of all.

The giving by David and the people was *spontaneous*; notice the seven-fold repetition of "willing" and "willingly". David had been forbidden the privilege of building God's house, but this did not deter him from humbly preparing for it. Let us labour even when others enjoy the results; cf. John 4. 38. Our opportunities and our resources are limited, so let us give when and how we can. May we earn the commendation that we did what we could; cf. Mark 14. 8. "If there be first a willing mind, it is accepted according to that a man hath, and not according to that he hath not", 2 Cor. 8. 12.

David's giving was *urgent*, in view of a brief transitory life, "Our days on the earth are as a shadow", 1 Chron. 29. 15. Opportunities we miss will never recur in eternity. It was *lavish* giving — gold and silver and precious stones in abundance from David's own treasures. Yet, in the Lord's estimation, the widow who put two mites into the temple treasury gave more, because she lavishly gave all. It was *love's* giving; "because I have set my affection to the house of my God", v. 3. Yet David was not proud of his generosity, "But who am I, and what is my people, that we should be able to offer so willingly . . .?", v. 14. Who am I? "Dust and ashes", said Abraham, Gen. 18. 27. Why did David, secure on his throne and surrounded by his wealth, speak thus? Surely because he had a lively sense of the greatness of God and of the privilege of giving to Him. He had also a deep sense of his continual and increasing indebtedness to God. "For all things come of thee, and of thine own have we given thee". Paul challenged the complacent Corinthians, "What hast thou that thou didst not receive?", 1 Cor. 4. 7. When many were sad at the delay in building the second temple, the message came, "The silver is mine and the gold is mine, saith the Lord of hosts", Hag. 2. 8. That is, God had all the resources and wealth necessary. Let us then remember the words of the Lord Jesus, "It is more blessed to give than to receive", Acts 20. 35.

Introducing 2 Chronicles

SOLOMON HERE, as David in 1 Chronicles, is presented so that his *typical* proportions are more apparent. He builds the temple and bears the glory. Following "the great schism", when the northern 10 tribes repudiated the authority of Rehoboam, the remainder of the Book concentrates attention upon the 20 rulers of Judah. The history of the northern kingdom is hardly mentioned. The attitude of each king to the worship of Jehovah is uppermost in the writer's mind, giving a clearly *priestly* flavour to the record. Note the dominant place of the Levites. The history demonstrates the importance of man's response to Divine revelation. The law of God given by Moses was still valid; prosperity resulted from simple obedience to it, ch. 34; cf. Mal. 4. 4. The prophets of God are prominent. Their warnings must be heeded. There were sound sermons in abundance, e.g. 13. 8-12; 15. 1-7; 20. 14-17; 29. 5-11; 30. 6-9.

There is no mere repetition of the Samuel/Kings records. Chronicles emphasizes more the departure from, and then the revival of, Scriptural worship in Jerusalem, and of the religious reforms of Hezekiah and Josiah. Hence, "as long as he (Uzziah) sought the Lord, God made him to prosper", 26.5. Jehoshaphat sums it up, "Believe in the Lord your God, so shall ye be established; believe his prophets, so shall ye prosper", 20. 20; cf. 14. 11; 16. 8-9; 20. 12.

Repeated disobedience to God's Word, and alliances with the ungodly, resulted in moral deterioration. Even good kings failed, and wickedness brought defeat, 12. 1-5; 21. 10; 24. 23-24. Still God's longsuffering and goodness shine out, and with Him there is forgiveness, 12. 7; 30. 9; 33. 12-13. But at last "there was no remedy", 36. 16.

An Outline.

Solomon's reign: building the temple, 1. 1 to 9. 31.
Rehoboam: the division of the kingdom, 10. 1 to 12. 16.
From Abijah to Zedekiah: history of Judah
  until deportation to Babylon, 13. 1 to 36. 21.
Cyrus of Persia: charged to build house, 36. 22-23.

The book encourages the remnant returned from Babylon, reminding them of their privileges, and pointing the way to the blessedness which king David had once enjoyed.

June 28th

READING : **2 Chronicles 3. 14; 4. 1; 5. 1-14**

GLORY FILLING THE HOUSE

SOLOMON'S completion of the temple culminated in bringing in the ark, united praise, and the glory of the Lord filling the house. The glory-filled temple, as the appointed gathering centre for God's people, points us to the day when all nations will go up to Jerusalem to worship, Zech. 14. 16. But the elements common to it and to the tabernacle in the wilderness have lessons for us as God's dwelling today, 1 Cor. 3. 16. Let us consider three of these:

1. *The altar*, the place of sacrifice. As in the tabernacle, this is the first sacred vessel we meet inside the eastern entrance. God had said to Moses, "there will I meet with the children of Israel", Exod. 29. 43. Man must first come to God by way of the shed blood of Christ, who gave Himself for our acceptance "an offering and sacrifice to God", Eph. 5. 2. We meet God at the altar. "Then will I go unto the altar of God, unto God my exceeding joy", Psa. 43. 4.

2. *The veil*. We enter the immediate presence of God "through the veil, that is to say, his flesh", Heb. 10. 19-20, so that beautiful curtain speaks of the moral and official glories of our Lord's Manhood. From the blue, reminding us that He came down from heaven, to the fine linen, suggesting His perfect purity and righteousness, all speaks of One who is "altogether lovely", John 8. 23; cf. Rev. 19. 8.

3. *The ark*. This was the only vessel brought into the temple from the tabernacle. Placed in the oracle, the Holiest, it was covered by the blood-sprinkled mercy-seat of which God said, "there will I meet with thee, and I will commune with thee", Exod. 25. 22. We enter the Holiest by virtue of the blood of Jesus. The acacia wood, called "incorruptible" in the Greek O.T., speaks of Christ's sinless Manhood; the gold that wholly covered it, supremely precious and supremely glorious, bespeaks His Godhood. So "let us draw near", Heb. 10. 19-22.

Altar, veil and ark all speak of Him who is the Way as well as the Door. In coming to Him we come to God.

In God's temple, everything and everyone speaks of His glory, crying, "Holy, holy, holy, is the Lord of hosts" and "Worthy is the Lamb that was slain", Psa. 29. 9. He delights to find us "as one . . . in praising and thanking" Him.

June 29th
READING : 2 Chronicles 6. 12-25; 7. 1-3
A MONARCH'S PRAYER

SOLOMON PRAYS now as a king in the presence of his people. Prayer, whether in private or in public, is no occasion for personal display. Why then was a large bronze platform erected in the temple court? So that all present could see and share in Solomon's worship. Compare Nehemiah's pulpit of wood used when they read the Scriptures to Israel, Neh. 8. 4-5. A wooden structure, though temporary like Nehemiah's, would hardly have become Solomon's wealth.

Israel saw their acknowledged king kneel before the King of kings. This indeed spoke of submission. Our Lord Himself knelt in Gethsemane, before He fell on His face. Such an attitude becomes us. Then men saw Solomon stretch out his hands heavenwards, as Ezra did when confessing his people's sins, Ezra 9.5. This showed his earnestness in recognizing that every good gift comes from above. He had a lively sense of the greatness of Jehovah, the God of Israel. He repudiated the pagan notion that God was confined to a material temple. He exclaims, "heaven and the heaven of heavens cannot contain thee; how much less this house which I have built!", 2 Chron. 6. 18. Later, when Isaiah saw the Lord, he observed that the hem of His garment was enough to fill the temple, Isa. 6. 1. "Do not I fill heaven and earth? saith the Lord", Jer. 23. 24. Solomon still has the humble spirit of his earlier prayer, "I am but a little child", 1 Kings 3. 7. Note how often he refers to David and himself simply as God's servants.

The goodness and faithfulness of God are prominent in 2 Chronicles 6. 14-21. Reverence and humility are the keynotes. Then we see a true shepherd king showing compassionate concern for his failing flock, vv. 24-42. It is intercession for feeble folk who will need forgiveness. Solomon repeatedly speaks to God, not of "my people", but of "thy people". Pastors, like the Ephesian overseers, are to shepherd "the flock of God", Acts 20. 28 R.V.; 1 Pet. 5. 2-3.

After bringing in the ark, and the united praise, the house was filled with a cloud displaying the glory of God. After Solomon's prayer, that glory is associated with the fire that descended to consume the sacrifices, 7. 1-3. Compare the result of united prayer recorded in Acts 4. 23-31.

June 30th
READING : **2 Chronicles 10. 1-19**

CAUSES OF DIVISION

THIS CHAPTER records the sad division of Israel when the northern ten tribes broke off their allegiance to David's house, and separated from Judah and Benjamin.

The immediate causes of division among the people of God may be apparent, and seem simple. But underlying causes are more complex, often found in events taking place, and feelings aroused, long before an open rupture. In Israel we find:

1. *Inherited Prejudices.* Long before David's day, Ephraim were jealous of the other tribes, and only Gideon's graciousness allayed their unreasonable anger. Again they evinced their quarrelsome spirit in Jephthah's day, Jud. 8. 1-3; 12. 1-3. We find that Ephraim, though privileged, were envious of Judah, whence came God's chosen king, and where was His chosen dwelling-place. Thank God, that breach shall finally be healed; see Isa. 11. 13; Ezek. 37. 15-22. Still today unjudged feelings of envy or pride wreak incalculable harm.

2. *Solomon's Pride.* Solomon's self-indulgence led to his taking pagan wives in disobedience to God, and introducing heavy taxation and forced labour to build them palaces and heathen temples. Thus he had alienated many.

3. *Rehoboam's Self-confidence.* In his arrogance Rehoboam ignored the advice of the experienced counsellors who had imbibed Solomon's wisdom. Instead he listened to his younger friends, and answered his petitioners "roughly", forgetting his father's proverb, "A soft answer turneth away wrath", Prov. 15. 1. Then to send Hadoram, who supervised the forced levy, only added insult to injury, 2 Chron. 10. 18.

4. *Jeroboam's Ambition.* Here was an able man, whose desire for advancement God discerned, and promised to fulfil. But he despised God's goodness, and in his lust for pre-eminence did evil above all who preceded him, 1 Kings 11. 37; 14. 9.

Both the church at Corinth, where many errors urgently needed correction, and the delightfully healthy church at Philippi, needed the same appeal: "I beseech you, brethren, . . . that there be no divisions among you", 1 Cor. 1. 10; cf. Phil. 1. 27. Let us then put on that self-effacing and self-denying love, that binds all together in perfect harmony, Col. 3. 14, and "keep the unity of the Spirit", Eph. 4. 1-6.

July 1st

READING : **2 Chronicles 15. 1 to 16. 14**

ASA: SEEK THE LORD AND HIS STRENGTH

REHOBOAM, SOLOMON'S SON, "forsook the law of the Lord", and "he prepared not his heart to seek the Lord", 12. 1, 14. But his grandson, Asa, did what was "good and right" and "commanded Judah to seek the Lord", 14. 2, 4. For ten years he had peace; but the godly must always be prepared for opposition. A huge Ethiopian army attacked Judah, but God answered Asa's prayer, and they were defeated, 14. 9-15.

Then comes Azariah's exhortation echoing Psalm 18. 25-26. With the merciful, God will show Himself merciful; with the upright and pure, He will show Himself upright and pure; but with the perverse, He will show Himself contrary. Such warnings are to make us wary of our fickle hearts, and to encourage godliness; cf. 2 Tim. 2. 12. The result was

1. renewed destruction of idols, 2 Chron. 15. 8.
2. wholehearted seeking the Lord, vv. 12, 15. Note the same order in 14. 3-4. These two things go together; "cease to do evil; learn to do well", Isa. 1. 16-17.

It needs courage to put away idols that have long claimed our time and energy. Are there not idols in our hearts and homes that need drastic demolition?, Deut. 12. 3. Destruction of idols is linked with devotion to the altar, reminding us of our Lord's self-sacrifice for us, 2 Chron 15. 8. An idol is that which has the place of interest and affection in our life that God alone should have. Asa put God before family relationship in courageously removing the "queen-mother" from her influential place, and utterly destroying her idol too, v. 16.

But in "his old age" Asa failed grievously; he broke the covenant made to seek the Lord, 15. 12. He robbed Jehovah's house of treasure to persuade the idolatrous Syrians to attack Israel, 16. 2-4. This unequal yoke forfeited the help of God, despite initial success. Alliance with the unbeliever is bad; to seek his help in opposing our brethren is worse, 2 Cor. 6. 14. Thus Asa'a last years were marked by wars and disease. Despite Ahaziah's warning, "he sought not to the Lord, but to the physicians", and he sought in vain. So let us watch and pray, that we might "still bring forth fruit in old age", Psa. 92. 14. Let us "Seek the Lord, and his strength", and seek His face continually, 105. 4.

July 2nd

READING : 2 Chronicles 17. 1-10; 19. 4-11

JEHOSHAPHAT: TEACHERS AND JUDGES

THE FIRST thing we read of king Jehoshaphat is that he "strengthened himself against Israel". Israel, the northern nation, though still professing loyalty to Jehovah, indulged in idolatry and immorality, hastened on by departing from God's centre of worship. From this, Judah's good kings sought to preserve their people. Jehoshaphat was rightly concerned to protect the goodly inheritance Judah had from God. Today some profess to be Christians, and yet pursue religious ideas and practices foreign to, and often forbidden by, the Word of God. So we need to give heed to teaching, 1 Tim. 4. 13, 16.

The king wished his people to be preserved from error. So he sent princes, for it is princely work, and Levites, for it was their duty, to teach the law of God in the cities of Judah. They carried the book of the law with them; the appeal must always be, "what saith the scripture?". The Levites were not mere lecturers; they were men of conviction. God had ordered all to worship at the place of the Name, which was then Jerusalem. But Jeroboam had persuaded the northern tribes to worship at Dan and Bethel as being more convenient. So, rather than disobey God, many Levites left their homes in the north to dwell in Judah, 11. 13-14.

Our Lord's great commission was, "Make disciples (learners) . . . teaching them to observe all things whatsoever I have commanded you", Matt. 28. 19-20 R.V. So it is the duty of elders to see that the saints are well taught; and it is the duty of all to be teachable. However old we are we should still be learners, Job 34. 32; cf. Acts 17. 11. Our Lord Himself was here as a disciple, saying of God, "he wakeneth mine ear to hear as they that are taught", Isa. 50. 4 R.V. What less than the whole counsel of God will suffice?, Acts 20. 27.

Later Jehoshaphat appointed judges also in the cities of Judah to act impartially in the fear of God, 19. 5-9. The "saints shall judge the world . . . how much more things that pertain to this life?" When there is a matter between two brethren, the local assembly is the last court of appeal, Matt. 18. 15-20; 1 Cor. 6. 4. So all, and elders especially, must, like Solomon, pray for wisdom. The meek will God guide in judgment; the meek will He teach His way, Psa. 25. 9.

July 3rd

READING : 2 Chronicles 18. 1 to 19. 3

"FIRST LOVE" AND "FIRST WAYS"

WHY WAS Jehoshaphat's reign so prosperous? Because "he walked in *the first ways* of his father David", 17. 3-4. This meant earnestly keeping the commands of God. But contrast his helping "the ungodly" recorded in today's reading. Both Jehoshaphat's forefather David, and his immediate father Asa, started well, but fell into shameful sin in later years. How bright was the early history of David, killing the bear and the lion, and then Goliath, and twice showing mercy to his inveterate enemy, king Saul, when he could have slain him. Yet later he takes his ease while others lead his army, and he becomes guilty of murder and adultery. In his case God heard his penitential cries, and restored his soul. Good king Hezekiah, and good Josiah also, became guilty of sad mistakes after a life of valuable service to God.

Most of us remember the joy we had in testimony when first converted. Is such joy ours today? Or have we, like the church at Ephesus, left our *"first love"*? God said to Israel, "I remember thee, the kindness of thy youth, the love of thine espousals, when thou wentest after me". But then He cries, "my people . . . have forsaken me the fountain of living waters", Jer. 2. 2, 13. Have we lost our zest for prayer and the ministry of the Word? If so, what is the cause?

In Jehoshaphat's case, it was when God gave him great "riches and honour" that he became allied to king Ahab, who murdered Naboth and sought to kill Elijah also, 2 Chron. 18. 1. Prosperity brings snares. Jehoshaphat probably thought that his son Jehoram's marriage to Ahab's daughter would help to achieve the reunion of Judah and Israel. But what communion has light with darkness? This was an unequal yoke so much condemned in both Testaments, 2 Cor. 6. 14-18. "Evil company doth corrupt good manners", 1 Cor. 15. 33 R.V., and on his father's death his son murdered all his brothers.

How bright were the *"first ways"* of believers after Pentecost! But soon hypocrisy and petty jealousy spoilt the testimony. If we have "riches and honour", however little, let us beware of maintaining a respectability that fails to give bold testimony to our despised and rejected Lord. If youthful enthusiasm fails, God can restore.

July 4th

READING : 2 Chronicles 20. 1-30

"THEY CAME TO SEEK THE LORD"

JEHOSHAPHAT is now threatened by a powerful alliance of Moab, Ammon and Edom. Consequently there was:

Fear. The king had learned, "It is better to trust in the Lord than to put confidence in princes", Psa. 118. 9. So he called the nation to prayer. If the fervent prayer of one righteous man avails much, how much more the prayers of many? At times we also may well fear, for evil is rampant in the world, and found even in our own hearts. Yet we too can pray, "O our God . . . we have no might . . . but our eyes are upon thee". Then we say with David, "I sought the Lord, and he heard me, and delivered me from all my fears", Psa. 34. 4. Jehoshaphat's prayer was not perfunctory, but accompanied by

Fasting. This is voluntary abstinence from food to devote energy to spiritual exercises. The Lord spoke of it as something essentially personal to be kept secret, Matt. 6. 16-18. Yet at times the Lord's servants may make self-denying supplication together, Acts 13. 1-3. We debate reasons for ineffective testimony. Ought we not rather to cry, "sanctify a fast, call a solemn assembly . . . assemble the elders, gather the children"; see Joel 2. 12-17. The common danger enriched the

Fellowship. It is a privilege to share in the prayerful concern for our spiritual welfare that godly elders have. From all the cities of Judah came men with wives and children to pray. The women did not opt out because they were not, like the Levites, called to public work. Some must have made costly journeys. The presence of godly women makes a great difference to a prayer meeting. They also brought their children, for children need early impressions of the presence of God, and their little ones, "for of such is the kingdom of heaven". They did not leave them at home with the servants. We should seriously consider the needs of children in our gatherings; cf. Neh. 8. 2.

Then Jahaziel's message from the Lord is

"Fear not". Whatever our fears within, or our foes without, the message is, "the battle is not yours, but God's", 2 Chron. 20. 15. Thus prayer gives place to trustful praise, vv. 18, 19, 21. For deliverance comes in unexpected ways to those who pray: the allies quarrelled and Judah was saved.

July 5th

READING : **2 Chronicles 21. 1-30**

GOD OVER ALL, BLESSED FOR EVER

HERE WE FIND Jehoram at the outset of his reign slaying his brothers, and others who might be his rivals. He did evil like Ahab, *"for"* he had married Ahab's daughter, Athaliah, and learned Ahab's ways, v. 6. How important to choose the right partner in marriage! Keep your heart with all diligence; make quite sure of the will of God before you set your heart on a possible wife or husband, Prov. 4. 23. The influence of any unconverted relative may become a snare to a believer who does not watch and pray; but a wife's influence or a husband's is lifelong.

Bible history is different from secular history in two respects. First, it takes account of the unseen world; of God and His angels, and of Satan and evil spirits, all of which men generally ignore. We saw an example in chapter 18. Behind Ahab's false and flattering prophets were evil spirits; but behind the spirits was God ordering one of them to carry out his evil suggestion so as to execute God's judgment upon the king.

Secondly, Scripture recognizes the absolute sovereignty of God, His right in His infinite wisdom, to do as He will. Psalm 135. 6 puts it, "Whatsoever the Lord pleased, that did he in heaven, and in earth, in the seas, and all deep places". So Daniel taught the autocrat Nebuchadnezzar that ultimately God rules in the kingdom of men, and appoints as monarchs whom He will, Dan. 4. 17, 35. We say God "allows" it, but Amos says that God does it, even when evil (i.e. calamity) befalls a city, Amos 3. 6 R.V. Thus it was the Lord who stirred up the Philistines against Jehoram, and the Lord who smote him with disease, vv. 14-18. His judgment came *"Because"* Jehoram ignored the good example of his father and grandfather. God has good reasons for all that He does, though often beyond our ken, Isa. 55. 9. This is a great comfort to those who trust His wisdom and His love.

To recognize that God is in supreme control of all events does not make us fatalistic, for we may and must still choose, Deut. 30. 19; Luke 10. 42. So despise not the discipline of the Lord; those who are exercised thereby reap the fruit of more happy, holy lives, Heb. 12. 11.

July 6th

READING : **2 Chronicles 22. 1 to 23. 15**

A WOMAN'S INFLUENCE

SOMETIMES in this book we find the sons of good kings turning out badly. That shows the amazing perversity of the human heart. Yet sometimes the sons of bad kings become godly. That shows the amazing grace of God.

Amaziah's case is more easily understood. Not only was he the youngest son of the wicked king Jehoram, but his mother, Athaliah, "was his counsellor to do wickedly", v. 3; cf. 1. 4. She had evilly influenced her husband's conduct, and now misled her son. When he died, her lust for power was seen in her intent to destroy all the descendants of king David. We discern Satanic activity in this, for it was, like Herod's destruction of the babes in Bethlehem, an attempt to destroy the line from which Christ would be born. But God had sworn that there would never be lacking a man to sit on David's throne, 2 Sam. 7. 16; 23. 5; 2 Chron. 21. 7.

While much of Israel's sorrow resulted from an evil woman's ambition, how much we owe to another woman, Jehoshabeath, wife of the faithful priest Jehoiadah. Her compassion for little Joash, and her bravely defying the queen-mother and caring for him six years, completely outwitted Athaliah. The idolater, Athaliah, doubtless despised the house of Jehovah, not expecting to find a royal prince there, even if the priests allowed her entry.

Then comes Jehoiadah's careful preparation for installing Joash on the throne. Thank God there were many still loyal to David's line. They needed only a wise, courageous leader. Are there not many today who need a trumpet call to stand for the truth of God as seen in the Scriptures?, 1 Cor. 16. 13; Isa. 58. 1. We need to pray God to raise up godly men who will exhort their brethren to fear God more than men.

Athaliah and her mother Jezebel are examples of women who have sought to fill a place to which God has not called them, Rev. 2. 20. Sisters in Christ have two great privileges; their womanly work, and a sphere of influence. Doubtless God brought back Dorcas from the dead because of her valuable work. But, while little or nothing is recorded of their work, think of the sweet influence of Mary of Bethany, of Timothy's mother, and of Aquila's wife: what influence have I?

July 7th
READING : 2 Chronicles 26. 1-23
PRIDE GOES BEFORE . . . A FALL

KING UZZIAH did what was right as his father had done. But his father, Amaziah, after a good start, had a sad end; see ch. 25. "Be ye followers (imitators) of me", says Paul, but adds significantly, "even as I also am of Christ". Whom do we really follow? As long as Uzziah sought the help of God, he prospered. But did he seek the Lord as earnestly as Isaiah? — "With my soul have I desired thee in the night; yea, with my spirit within me will I seek thee early", 26. 9. Or was he largely influenced by Zechariah the seer alone?, 2 Chron. 26. 5. We need personal conviction and dedication. In his good works, recorded to his credit, Uzziah was marvellously helped till his heart was lifted up with pride.

Knowing Uzziah's presumptuous sin, we might label him a bad man, but God is generous in His judgment of His people. They "have kept thy word", said our Lord Jesus of His disciples, whose spokesman denied Him thrice, while they all forsook Him and fled. Are we as *kind in judging* our brethren as is our Lord whose eyes are as a flame of fire? As to what is right, we must *judge in the light of God's Word*. As to others' motives or overall faithfulness, "*judge nothing before the time, until the Lord come, who both will bring to light the hidden things of darkness, and will make manifest the counsels of the hearts*", 1 Cor. 4. 5; Luke 6. 37.

Yet in the judgment of His people God is impartial. Past good works do not excuse present disobedience. God resists the proud, so judgment falls on Uzziah. In prosperity beware of self-confidence. "I say . . . to every man that is among you, not to think of himself more highly than he ought to think", Rom. 12. 3. In his proud and persistent attempt to offer incense, Uzziah was usurping the place of the priests. To claim the privilege of priesthood as well as of kingship is to claim what God has appointed solely for His Son, of whom Melchizedec is a faint foreshadowing, Gen. 14. 18; Heb. 7. 1-4. We may begin with high ideals and honest endeavour to please God, but if prosperity comes, beware of pride bringing God's displeasure and maybe public shame. Let him who thinks he stands take heed lest he fall, 1 Cor. 10. 12.

July 8th

READING : 2 Chronicles 29. 1-29

HEZEKIAH: GOD'S INTERESTS FIRST

HEZEKIAH'S FATHER was a cruel idolater who deliberately shut up the doors of the house of God, 28. 24. But at the outset of his reign Hezekiah set about undoing the evil work of his father and reopened the doors of the temple. *This was his "first" concern.* "Honour thy father and mother" is the first commandment with a promise of blessing attached for the obedient, Eph. 6. 2. A son should honour his father, but the Lord Jesus said "He that loveth father or mother *more than me* is not worthy of me", Matt. 10. 37.

Hezekiah first bade the priests and Levites who had failed to stop the spiritual rot to sanctify themselves. This meant setting themselves apart as peculiarly called to the service of Jehovah, and as suitable to serve the God whose name is Holy. Such was their diligence that the cleansing of the house of God was completed in 16 days. Like them, we must keep ourselves pure personally if the house of God (today His people viewed collectively) is to be clean. "Pure religion" is to keep ourselves unspotted from the world around, unclean in its thoughts, pleasures and literature, James 1. 27. Paul's first letter to the church at Corinth was a call to personal purity, and to cleanse the assembly of God from moral and doctrinal evil. May God give us grace resolutely to respond! In such matters we need a sense of urgency. When the house was cleansed, Hezekiah *"rose early"* to order the sin-offering for the nation, and the burnt-offering, with the praise that accompanied it by the command of God in David's day, 2 Chron. 29. 20-25.

Then all the congregation bowed and worshipped, that is reverence; the singers sang, that is an expression of thankful joy; the trumpeters sounded, that is exultation, glorying in the Lord, vv. 28-30. Today there is no more offering for sin, but, knowing that our body is the temple of the Holy Spirit and the assembly is the temple of God, we may offer the sacrifice of praise continually, Heb. 13. 15. With far greater privileges than Israel had, we enter the presence of God owning that we draw near only by virtue of the blood of Jesus. Can we enter without a sense of gratitude and awe moving us to praise and worship?

July 9th

READING : 2 Chronicles 30. 1 to 31. 1

REVIVAL AND JOY IN JERUSALEM

OFTEN A REVIVAL among the people of God stems from the diligence of one devoted soul. Kings who, like Hezekiah, achieved such revival in Israel, were characterized by three things: reverence for the Word of God, concern for all the people of God, and devotion to the house of God.

First, Hezekiah revived the worship of God according to "the commandment of the Lord by his prophets", 29. 25. He calls the nation to celebrate the Passover "as it was written", and "according to the law of Moses", 30. 5, 16. Later the worship was ordered "as it is written in the law of the Lord", 31. 3. Would to God that we stood in awe of His Word! Then we could expect revival.

Secondly, sacrifice was to be made "for all Israel", 29. 24. When calling the nation to keep the Passover, he sends to "all Israel", from Beer-sheba in the south to Dan in the far north, though he did not rule over the northern kingdom. While some mocked, many from other tribes "humbled themselves and came to Jerusalem", 30. 4-18. The joy of this reunion and dedication made this Passover outshine every observance since Solomon's reign. The priests were not prepared, so, rather than wait another year, the need to obey God's command encouraged them to hold the feast in the *second* month instead of in the *first* as originally commanded. They had Scriptural support for making allowance when circumstances really made it impossible to observe the original order, Num. 9. 10-13. Would to God that we had a genuine concern for all the saints to observe the commandments of God together! Then we could expect revival.

Thirdly, Hezekiah's concern for the house of God meant that there was now a Scriptural rallying-place for all Israel. Jehoshaphat had destroyed "the high places" which Israelites had made for the worship of idols. But Hezekiah diligently "destroyed them all", including those dedicated to Jehovah, 31. 1, for God had commanded that every Israelite was to sacrifice only in the one place of His choice, Deut. 12. 11-14. When the Levites "taught the good knowledge of the Lord" and people made confession, "there was great joy in Jerusalem". Devotion to God, His Word and His people brings joy.

July 10th

READING : **2 Chronicles 32. 24-31**

"THE LORD TRIETH THE RIGHTEOUS"

HEZEKIAH HAD come through many a test. He first overcame the disadvantage of having a wicked father. Then, when he invited his Israelite brethren to join in the Passover feast, some mocked him; but scorn did not shake his resolution. Later, threatened by the boastful army of Assyria, then the dominant world power, he calmly made preparation and encouraged his troops: "With us is the Lord our God to help us". Then he and Isaiah "prayed and cried to heaven" and God wrought a marvellous deliverance. Thus Hezekiah "was magnified in the sight of all nations", v. 23. Now comes another test.

Today's reading says that "In those days" of triumph Hezekiah had a fatal illness; but he "turned his face to the wall" seeking God's mercy, and God caused the shadow on the sundial to go back as a sign that he would recover, 2 Kings 20. 1-11. Then came Babylonian ambassadors with a present asking about the miraculous sign, and "Hezekiah hearkened unto them". Were they also seeking his help against the mighty Assyrians? He had promised God to "go softly", to walk humbly all his life, but, moved by flattery, he showed the heathen all his treasures. He apparently forgot that these resources were valueless apart from the help of God, and so earned Isaiah's stern rebuke, Isa. 38. 15; 39. 6. Many a good man has been spoiled by prosperity and flattery when other temptations have failed to bring him low. His "heart was lifted up" like Uzziah's, for pride is common to every human heart. We are assured that God will not allow us to be tried above that we are able to bear, but we do well to pray "lead us not into temptation", 1 Cor. 10. 13; Matt. 6. 13.

In this matter God left Hezekiah, "to try him, that he might know all that was in his heart", 2 Chron. 32. 31. In such trials, God demonstrates, and we learn, the frailty of our fickle, foolish hearts. God led Israel through the trying circumstances of the wilderness to humble them by revealing their real attitude to His commands, Deut. 8. 2, 16. So we continually pray, "Hold thou me up, and I shall be safe", Psa. 119. 117, and then say, "When he hath tried me, I shall come forth as gold", Job 23. 10.

July 11th

READING : **2 Chronicles 33. 1-25**

MANASSEH : GRACE ABOUNDING

HERE ARE two things that beggar description, the wickedness of the human heart, and the exceeding grace of God that overcomes it. Indeed, we could entitle the story of Manasseh as John Bunyan did his autobiography: "Grace Abounding to the Chief of Sinners"; cf. Rom. 5. 20. Despising his father's God, Manasseh blatantly built altars to false gods, erecting an idol even in the temple. He resorted to spiritist mediums, and the cruelty and sexual immorality that accompany idolatry. Worse, the people followed him. With a father like Hezekiah, Manasseh must have known the commandment, "Thou shalt not make unto thee any graven image": his disobedience was defiant, Exod. 20. 4-5. God mercifully reproved him, but because "sentence against an evil work is not executed speedily, therefore the heart of the sons of men is fully set in them to do evil". Manasseh and his people "would not hearken", Eccl. 8. 11; 2 Chron. 33. 10. Not till he was carried in chains to Babylon did he humble "himself greatly", then God graciously restored his soul, vv. 12-13.

Moreover, Manasseh publicly repudiated his former way of life; he gave evidence of true repentance (an example to those who profess conversion but show little evidence of walking in newness of life), Luke 3. 8. How encouraging for those who pray for wayward children! Doubtless Hezekiah had not only instructed Manasseh, but often prayed for him, Isa. 38. 19. He never saw that prayer answered. Yet answered it was, long after his death. So pray on.

God is amazingly good and ready to forgive, yet we reap what we sow. The evil that men do lives after them. Manasseh's conversion was evidently too late for him effectively to recall the nation to holiness. The high places were not removed, and his son Amon "trespassed more and more". "For the grace of God . . . hath appeared" and, being pure grace, it carries with it salvation for all kinds and conditions of men, Tit. 2. 11. Each one of us must say, "by the grace of God I am what I am". The chief of sinners is with Christ, yet many today who, like Bunyan, know God and know themselves, gratefully feel that that title applies to them also, 1 Tim. 1. 15.

July 12th

READING : **2 Chronicles 34. 1-21**

JOSIAH'S YOUTHFUL ZEAL

JOSIAH SHINES as a bright star in the ever darkening night of Judah's declension and departure from God. Coming to the throne after two wicked kings, "while he was yet young", aged 16, he began to seek God. Most true conversions to God take place in youth, so that life may be devoted to Him. "The glory of young men is their strength", and happy are they who devote their youthful energy to the Lord, Prov. 20. 29; Psa. 96. 7. Those who seek fellowship with God must deal with things which grieve Him. So four years later Josiah personally supervised the destruction of the shameful images in the land. Note his drastic treatment of the idols. God had commanded, "ye shall overthrow their altars, and break their pillars, and burn their groves with fire; and ye shall hew down the graven images", Deut. 12. 3. Josiah obeyed. He slew the heathen priests, for they did far more harm than murderers. A murderer takes one's physical life only; but a false priest or prophet ruins one for all eternity. Then Josiah burned their bones on their altars as was prophesied of him three centuries before; see 1 Kings 13. 2; 2 Kings 23. 16, 19-20. How helpless were their false gods!

We also must deal courageously with that which hinders our devotion to our Lord; surely the love of Christ constrains us to do so. We must "kill" covetousness, common to us all, the greed for earthly things which is idolatry, Col. 3. 5. The Lord Jesus spoke of cutting off one's hand, and plucking out one's eye, rather than permit that which leads to sin and breaks our fellowship with Him.

After six years of cleansing the land Josiah's zeal was unabated. He was growing in grace. Appreciating the importance of the house of God he arranged to collect money for its repair, making it worthy of the Holy One. But he had more to learn. Youthful enthusiasm must be tempered by an accurate knowledge of the Word of God. A copy of the law was discovered and handed to Josiah. Finding therein how serious was Israel's sin in the sight of God, the king rent his clothes in humiliation and so postponed God's judgment. Pray God He will raise up young men like Josiah today who will turn neither to right nor left, 2 Chron. 34. 2.

July 13th

READING : **2 Chronicles 35. 1-26**

WISDOM AND FOLLY

As in every true revival, a reverent appeal to the written Word of God marked Josiah's reformation in Judah. He and the nation pledged themselves to complete obedience, 34. 30-33. At the very end of the Old Testament period God says, "Remember ye the law of Moses my servant, which I commanded unto him in Horeb for all Israel", Mal. 4. 4. This involved the observance of the feasts of Jehovah. Josiah bade the priests prepare for the first feast, the Passover, "according to the word of the Lord" and "as it is written in the book of Moses". The seven-day feast of unleavened bread followed. Hezekiah's Passover was greater than any since Solomon's. He gave animals for sacrifice, and for the people to eat during the week. But Josiah gave many more, 2 Chron. 35. 7. No king kept such a Passover as his, v. 18. Josiah's preparation was so thorough that he had no need to alter the date as Hezekiah did. While other offerings eaten by the people were boiled, the passover lambs were roasted in accord with the Scripture, v. 13; Exod. 12. 9 (figure of Christ enduring fiery judgment for us, 1 Cor. 5. 7-8). Finally, though the northern tribes were in bondage to Assyria, many came to Jerusalem, so "all Judah and Israel" kept the feast.

"After all this" good king Josiah fell. Pharaoh's army was using the coastal route on Israel's border to reach Assyria. Josiah zealously sought to protect his territory, though Egypt had no quarrel with him. He forgot Solomon's advice, "Go not forth hastily to strive", and the danger of meddling with other people's quarrels, Prov. 25. 8; 26. 17. We must contend earnestly for the faith today, but let us not dissipate our energies in unnecessary contention. Josiah ignored Pharaoh's conciliatory message, and disguised himself to do battle. This was not acting with faith in God. Had he forgotten Ahab's death at Ramoth-Gilead? One can understand wicked king Ahab disguising himself in battle, or king Saul when he visited the witch of Endor. But not Josiah; it was something quite out of character in such a godly man. So Israel's bright star sets in a cloudy night, and we await One who will never fail, the Bright and Morning Star Himself, Rev. 22. 16.

July 14th

READING : **2 Chronicles 36. 1-23**

"TILL THERE WAS NO REMEDY"

THIS CHAPTER first describes the incorrigible wickedness of Judah's last four kings, their priests and people, calling down judgment from God, and leading to bitter captivity in Babylon. But the last thing recorded is the faithfulness of God seventy years later in moving Cyrus to have the house of God built in Jerusalem again.

Judah had forsaken God their Saviour, following their pagan neighbours in a mad pursuit of pleasure and so of riches. Thus they became slaves to various passions, Tit. 3. 3. A man cannot be a slave to two masters at the same time; he cannot serve God and mammon. Covetousness led them to disobey God's command to leave the land fallow every seven years. This was a specific reason for the exile; it was "until the land had enjoyed her sabbaths", 2 Chron. 36. 21; Lev. 25. 4; 26. 34.

The deportation to Babylon was "to fulfil the word of the Lord" through Jeremiah. God had already withdrawn from the temple, so that it was an empty shell ready for destruction, Ezek. 11. 23; Jer. 7. 14. Yet He still rose early to send gracious warnings to His people, 2 Chron. 36. 15. This is vivid anthropomorphic language describing the God who never slumbers nor sleeps. One rises early to deal with urgent matters; God's first interest in the universe is the wellbeing of His people. Indeed, He rose "daily" for nine centuries for their sake, Jer. 7. 25. But Jerusalem despised His messengers, as later they despised and rejected His Son; cf. Matt. 21. 33-46. Disregard of God's messengers is disregard of God.

Judgment came also because of Manasseh's sins; he "filled Jerusalem with innocent blood", 2 Kings 24. 3, 4. God commanded that if a man shed blood, his blood was to be shed; but when the rulers themselves were murderers, judgment was not executed and the land was polluted in the sight of God, Num. 35. 31-34. (Sobering for us today!) A shepherd, like David, thinks first of his sheep. But from Solomon onward king after king thought first of himself, and even the best failed. Israel's history, under judges or kings, is one of dismal failure. It is the history of mankind. All calls for Him whose right it is to reign.

Introducing Ezra

EZRA is one of seven books which are closely linked together — three historical, three prophetic, and one both historical and prophetic. The three historical are Ezra, Nehemiah and Esther; the three prophetic, Haggai, Zechariah and Malachi; and Daniel is both historical and prophetic, see Table, p. 372. All have to do with the work of God after the close of the 70 years captivity predicted by Jeremiah, in which the land of Israel was to make up for lost sabbatical years. For 490 years the seventh year's sabbath had not been observed; the land had had no rest, cf. Jer. 25. 11-14; 2 Chron. 36. 21; Dan. 9. 2.

During the 70 years the people were in bondage, first to Babylon, then to Persia, see Maps 4 and 5. Babylon was the fountainhead of idolatry. It was to cure His people of idolatry that God gave them up to serve the Chaldeans, "that bitter and hasty nation", cf. Hab. 1. 6. They there learnt the wickedness of forsaking the Guide of their youth, and were cured effectively of idol worship. The result, in the days of Ezra and Nehemiah, was a gracious revival, which gave to His Word a place of importance in their lives it had not held before. Ezra was a lineal descendant of Phinehas, the grandson of Aaron, and therefore he was a priest, cf. 7. 11; 10. 10, 16. He was also a scribe, cf. 7. 6, 11. He does not appear in any significant way in the book until after chapter 6, when he leads a company of exiles back to Jerusalem. His book can be divided around two returns, one under Zerubbabel, that occupies the first six chapters, and the other under Ezra. The rebuilding of the temple largely concerned Zerubbabel. The sacrifices were renewed, and the temple foundation laid, cf. ch. 3. Then there was opposition and the work stopped, ch. 4. The Lord raised up two prophets, Haggai and Zechariah, to challenge His people. The work began once more, the temple was completed, and the Passover celebrated.

Some 60 years elapsed before the events of chapter 7, and then the heart of Ezra was stirred to return with a second group of exiles and with the vessels of the Lord's house. Between chapters 6 and 7 the events of the book of Esther may be inserted. Ezra returns to effect the reformation of the people of God.

July 15th

READING : **Ezra 1. 1-11**

GOD OVERRULING — MAN INTERCEDING

THE PURPOSES of God may seem to tarry, but they are never abandoned. There is a very real sense in which they never tarry for a moment. The chosen nation had been scattered, its national home lost, its national consciousness to an extent dimmed. Yet God was preparing for the return to the land of a people who had left it idolatrous, but who would return monotheistic, and rebuild and hold the fort till His Son, their Messiah, should come. Meanwhile He was overruling in the affairs of men to produce an unlikely instrument, Cyrus.

God constantly in human history has compelled kings and rulers to carry out His sovereign will. Nebuchadnezzar was described as God's "servant", Jer. 25. 9, who, though a heathen, and seeking to pursue his own wicked devices, was made to serve God's purposes. Similarly, Cyrus, another heathen king, is referred to as "my shepherd", Isa. 44. 28, and is used by God to bring His lost sheep of Israel back to their land whether he aims at obeying the will of God or not. So God is seen working out in history His supreme purposes in spite of the ignorance, and sometimes even by means of the malice, of men. Was not this the case in the crucifixion of the Lord? "He makes the wrath of men to praise Him".

The return is seen to be due to the Divine overruling, yet that is not all. In Babylon, Daniel and other pious souls had given the Lord no rest, and had ever asked Him to bring His people back from captivity. Daniel had seen that the fulfilment of Jeremiah 25. 11-14 must be near, and so he prayed, cf. Daniel 9. Here is the starting point of the work of God recorded in Ezra — an aged prophet on his knees in Babylon. The seventy years of affliction were nearly over, and that knowledge drove Daniel to his knees, and brought him to prayer and confession. He confessed the failure of his nation, and acknowledged their sin as his own. "We have sinned", he says, just as both Ezra and Nehemiah were to associate themselves in confession with the nation's sins later, cf. Ezra 9. 6ff; Neh. 1. 4ff. The outcome of Daniel's prayer we have in the opening verse of Ezra: "The Lord stirred up the spirit of Cyrus, king of Persia". Our God has willed to act when His people pray.

July 16th
READING : Ezra 3. 1-13
THE WORK OF RESTORATION

THE LEADERS in this return were evidently conscious of the matters of real importance. As far as possible they restored the Divinely-appointed order of worship, and immediately commenced the work of re-building the temple. Consider how they set about the work.

They were united, "as one man", v. 1. The children of God should be characterized by unity, cf. Psa. 133. 1; Acts 2. 1, 41-47; 4. 24, 32. How essential this is to the receiving of the Lord's blessing. Then *the Word of God was obeyed.* Their first concern was to do all "as it is written", vv. 2, 4. Faith keeps strictly to the Word of God. They were going to carry out God's instructions as given to Moses. Their authority was the Word of God. We cannot walk by faith except as we yield unhesitating obedience to His Word. It was to keep the Word of God that *the altar was built.* The first action when back in the land was to approach their God in the way appointed. The new start which God was giving would have been invalidated without that altar, which meant forgiveness for the past, and renewed consecration for the future. Instructed by the Scriptures, they offered up burnt offerings and sin offerings, and thus confessed themselves to be guilty sinners, and that only by the shedding of blood could they be forgiven and brought back to God. Burnt offerings were offered before ever the house was built, v. 6. These speak of Christ as well pleasing to God, and of the believer's heartfelt appreciation of what Christ and His work are to God. There must be true appreciation of Christ Himself, and of His work, before there can be any proper entering into the truth of the house of God.

Finally *the foundation was laid,* v. 10. There was fellowship in the work — they were "together", v. 9. Working together led to praising together, vv. 10, 11; cf. 1 Cor. 3. 9. Some, unduly occupied with the past, wept as they saw the foundation, whilst others, who were younger and needed maturity to match their zeal, shouted. There is room for both; for weeping over past failure to hold the truth committed to us, and to shout for joy as we think of the matchless grace of God rising above all our failures. If the world cannot understand, they should realize something is happening for God.

July 17th

READING : **Ezra 4. 1-24**

OPPOSITION BY ALLIANCE!

THE ENEMY of our souls can afford to leave us alone if our lives for God are inactive and unaggressive, but if we begin to build God's temple, then we may expect opposition. If we are not experiencing testing and trial, it may be because we are doing little to destroy evil and to promote good. The opposition soon made itself felt as those who returned set about re-building the temple, vv. 1, 2. As always when a work for God takes place, there were adversaries. So it was in the days of the early church, as soon as the Spirit of God had begun His blessed work, cf. Acts 4. 1-3; 5. 1-9, etc.

The enemy's first approach, and he was to try others, was to propose co-operation, v. 2. Who were these who offered help? Samaritans. For their history we need to go back to 2 Kings 17. 24, 32, 33, 41. They were a hybrid race, who worshipped idols and added the worship of Jehovah to that of their own false gods. They are like so many today who make a profession of Christianity, but who have never really owned Christ as Lord, and who know nothing of His saving work. They come with their right-sounding words, but the Bible calls them "adversaries", Ezra 4. 1.

Zerubbabel, then, was asked to admit into partnership such as were really enemies of the work. The proposal to help seemed so harmless, and it might have seemed to human reasoning that there was only advantage to be gained from acceptance. Yet we must beware of any proposal to allow the ungodly to assist in God's work, cf. 3 John 7. If we accept their help, we shall find that they are our adversaries still, and their intention is to impede our work for the Lord.

The proposed alliance and help were refused by the leaders of the remnant. Men who have not submitted to our God have no part in His work of building His temple, or His church. If the Temple of the true God was to be re-built, it was to be done by those who accepted His claim to be the only living God, creator of heaven and earth. God must be our God before we can build a House for Him. The cause of Christ in the world is to be maintained by those who have first given "their own selves to the Lord", cf. 2 Cor. 8. 5. True co-operation in the Lord's work is not possible with those who do not know Him.

July 18th
READING : Ezra 7. 1-28
"A READY SCRIBE"

EZRA was a descendant of Phinehas to whom had been granted an everlasting priesthood, cf. Num. 25. 12, 13. He was a man of spiritual exercise. As a scribe Ezra must have had a good knowledge of the Word. He was learned and experienced in the Law, and skilled in teaching it, "a ready scribe"! "Ready" does not apply to his pen, but to his mind. How did he apply his mind to the service of God? Verse 10 gives the answer.

He "set his heart to seek the law of the Lord", R.V. He really wanted to be instructed of God — he "set his heart". There was fixity and stability of purpose. As a teacher, he begins by himself seeking to understand the truth.

He would not only seek the law of God, he would do it. He let it govern his own life. He would not attempt to teach what he had not tried to perform. He would test the effect of his doctrine on himself before venturing to prescribe it for others. Teaching, if it is to be of any value, must be conveyed through those who exemplify it. Here lies the secret of the tremendous influence Ezra exerted on coming to Jerusalem.

Being an exponent of the law himself in his life, he would *"teach in Israel statutes and judgments"*. This necessarily came last — after the study and meditation, after the application to his life. To teach statutes and judgments they must be understood first. The only way to understand Scripture is to be prepared to do it, cf. John 7. 17. We only effectively teach it if our own lives are in accordance with what we say. To the Ephesian elders the apostle Paul claimed to have illustrated in his life what he taught with his lips, cf. Acts 20. 20, 35, I "have showed you", he says. Concerning the greatest of all Teachers it was said that He was *"mighty in deed and word"*, Luke 24. 19.

Ezra's ministry was just the ministry needed by the returned company — a competent, sober man, of sound judgment, a man mighty in the Scriptures, an able instructor of his brethren. He earnestly prepared his own heart to seek the law of the Lord, and he did not traffic in unfelt truth. He was personally right with God, and so was prepared to set others right. Am I "a ready scribe" like Ezra? We need those who take heed to themselves, and to their teaching, cf. 1 Tim. 4. 12-16.

July 19th

READING : **Ezra 8. 1-36**

GUARDING THE DEPOSIT

THE VESSELS of the Lord were to be returned to Jerusalem. There would be dangers on the way, so Ezra proclaimed a fast, and asked the Lord for protection, vv. 21, 23. The fasting was an outward sign of deep humiliation, and an expression of their dependence. The need of guidance as well as protection was fully recognized by the gathered company, and they trusted the Lord for both. Ezra knew the Lord was his best defence, and he would not ask for a military escort, v. 22. To have done so would have belied what he said to the king, and would have been to make a tacit confession of some doubt in his own heart as to the ability and willingness of God to protect his enterprise. He had no such doubt, and therefore he made no such request. God never fails those who act in full dependence upon Himself.

The journey took about four months. Their health and security were marvellous during so long a journey. Such a body of people, with so large a quantity of treasure, may have been an easy prey to marauding tribes, yet they arrived safely at their destination. Nothing but the care of a supervising and almighty Lord could have brought them safely there. They had committed themselves to Him, and they were protected by the God whose presence rendered an escort of soldiers needless. What have we to fear when we have God's protecting hand over us?, cf. Rom. 8. 31, 38f.

Faith in God, however, did not make Ezra careless. He had a considerable trust committed to him — the precious vessels of God's house. He felt his great responsibility, and prepared carefully, Ezra 8. 24-30. So it is with us. We, too, have a precious deposit, as 2 Timothy 1. 12, 14 tells us. There are two deposits here. We deposit ourselves with God, whilst He deposits with us His sacred truth. He has made us stewards of His precious truth. We are to safeguard this holy treasure throughout our journey until we reach the place of manifestation when all will be weighed once more in the balances of the sanctuary. Will we have lost anything on the way? Will we have kept what He has committed to us? In the house of God account was rendered, as all God's people will give account one day at the judgment seat of Christ, 2 Cor. 5. 9-10.

Introducing Nehemiah

THIS IS the last book in Old Testament history; it covers a span of 25 years (445-420 B.C.). The spiritual condition of the time may be grasped by reading Malachi.

In Ezra we have the return of the remnant, and their rebuilding of the temple and its worship. In Nehemiah the record is given of the rebuilding of the walls of Jerusalem, and the restoration of the civil conditions of the people. Restoration begins at the heart of things and spreads outwards. The heart has to be right with God, and established in His dwelling place. The work of His service in the world can then go ahead.

For every need God has His man. Ezra had returned when there was a need for the people to be challenged, and his ability as a "ready scribe" was essential. Now the walls are to be rebuilt, and Nehemiah, a man of practical bent, is required. He arrived at Jerusalem about twelve years after Ezra, with the rank of governor of the province. He had authority to rebuild the walls of the city, and so safeguard the rebuilt temple.

The secret of Nehemiah's efficiency lay in his constant bringing of all his problems to God. He was a man of prayer — many times he is seen at prayer in the book, viz. 2. 4; 4. 4-5; 5. 19; 6. 14; 13. 14, 22, 29, 31; cf. 1. 5-11. He habitually turned to God, seeking His wisdom and strength. He demonstrates the strength that comes from humble dependence upon God. True to God and his principles, Nehemiah overcame all enemies and surmounted all obstacles. He was a simplehearted man, characterized chiefly by humility and purity of nature, and revealing the mighty power that can be exercised by one who has no purpose in life, and no power, that is not centred in God. He was prudent, as his preparations for defence while rebuilding the walls show, ch. 4. He was disinterested and unselfish, and used his wealth for the benefit of others, whilst others were using the conditions of the day to increase their wealth at the expense of their poorer brethren, ch. 5. He was a man of profound piety, connecting everything, great or small, with the will of God, in whose presence he lived.

The first seven chapters of his history seem to be dominated by Builders and the Walls, whilst from chapter 8 it is the Book, and Worship, and the demands of obedience.

July 20th

READING : **Nehemiah 2. 1-20**

THE SAD CUPBEARER

NEHEMIAH dwelt in the palace, and seemed to be a favourite with the king. But like Moses his heart was with his lowly brethren, and his spirit was zealous for the testimony of his God. Though he had never seen Jerusalem, the city of his fathers, he loved her, and his feelings would have been summed up in the words of Psalm 137. 5, 6. His brethren had come and given him an unhappy report of the state of Jerusalem, and he had wept, Neh. 1. 4. He was not the last to weep over Jerusalem. A far Greater was to do so, cf. Luke 19. 41. Meanwhile Nehemiah prays and confesses the sins of his people, and asks the Lord to grant mercy with the king.

Four months elapsed before God opened the way for him to take action. He carried the burden of the knowledge four months before the king asked him why he was sad, four months in which doubtless he continued to pray. It was forbidden for royal servants to appear before the king gloomy and unhappy. It was ill-omened, and might suggest plotting at the royal court, cf. Esth. 4. 2. Nehemiah had not been sad before, and the king notices it and asks him why.

Nehemiah was a courtier in the throne room of the King of kings, and he immediately turns from the king of Persia to seek counsel above. This was an instantaneous, arrow-like prayer. Prayer was his constant resource, and he cast himself upon God. This is our privilege, too. Whatever our experience, the heart which is in touch with God will always turn to Him, even in the smallest matters. The man who can thus find God in a moment must be in the habit of frequently resorting to the Divine presence. Nehemiah did not answer until he had prayed. He walked with God because he talked with God. Are we living so truly, and so simply, in touch with the Lord so that we can, at any moment, and in any circumstance, refer the cause to Him for His guidance and His help?

Instructed of God, Nehemiah asks the king to be sent to rebuild Jerusalem. He could have looked on from afar off, and bewailed the failure of his people, but he was a true builder, and he would go. We need to be in touch with God to be true builders. Paul claimed to be "a wise masterbuilder", cf. 1 Cor. 3. 10. What sort of builders are we? 1 Cor. 3. 12.

July 21st

READING : **Nehemiah 3. 1-32**

BUILDERS

GOD has seen fit to occupy a whole chapter in recording the names, and activities, of the leaders of families and townships who engaged in the work of rebuilding. Why should so much space be given to men who would otherwise be forgotten? It is because no service for God is forgotten. No work done for His glory is overlooked by Him, and He delights to place on record the smallest service. Some of the individuals are distinguished, e.g. Baruch, the son of Zabbai, worked "earnestly", v. 20, the daughters of Shallum worked with their father, v. 12, and some of the priests "sanctified" their work, v. 1.

Consider some of the builders. Eliashib himself, v. 1, though he co-operated, had very little sympathy with the work of Nehemiah, as his connection with Tobiah shows, cf. 13.4. Separation had broken down. Next to him built the men of Jericho, the city of the curse. They had experienced God's redeeming grace, as also Christ "has redeemed us from the curse of the law being made a curse for us". So they are now serving in newness of spirit, v. 2. Next, and apparently alone, Zaccur builds, but his labour is not forgotten of God. Meremoth built two sections, vv. 4, 21. Meshullam co-operated, but he seemed to be a close ally of Tobiah, for Tobiah's son married his daughter, cf. 6. 18. The Tekoites did an extra piece, v. 27, but their rulers did nothing, v. 5. Their rulers probably liked to talk and direct, but would not bend their necks to the work. They have not been without their successors! The men of Gibeon were there, v. 7. They were descendants of the wily deceivers who had tricked Joshua, cf. Josh. 9. 3ff. They remind us of what we once were, and of what grace has made us. Goldsmiths and apothecaries were little used to hard work, but God did not forget their blisters, v. 8! Rephaiah was a ruler, a man of wealth, but he did not delegate his work to a servant, he did it himself. Jedaiah worked over against his house. Many of God's people can do little in the way of public service, but are to keep the testimony at home. Then there was Shallum, ruler over half part of Jerusalem, doing his share as also his daughters, cf. Phil. 4. 3. Their work, whatever it was, has a place in the records, and similar devotion will find mention and reward in a coming day.

July 22nd
READING : Nehemiah 4. 1-23

PROBLEMS

WHEN A WORK is undertaken for God, opposition will soon show itself. It will come through external circumstances, and from internal foes. It did so here. The external problems were two. There was firstly *contempt*, vv. 1-3, and secondly *conspiracy*, vv. 7, 8. Contempt took the form of derision and scorn. Mockery is something we find in the New Testament still being used as a weapon against God's servants, cf. Acts 17. 18; 26. 24. We must not be surprised to find it used against us. The Lord felt the cruel cut of scorn, cf. Luke 22. 63; 23. 35-37. Whatever scorn has been directed against us had, first of all, been poured out on our beloved Lord. The scorn was a cloak for something else—Sanballat was angry, v. 1. Nehemiah was not easily discouraged. He kept praying, organizing, encouraging and building.

Mockery failing, conspiracy was tried. They plot to use force. Mutual enemies become mutual friends to make mutual cause against the people of God, cf. Luke 23. 12. The very fact that a work is of God will arouse the opposition of the enemy, and here the wall was going up and the work of God was being done. The people had a mind to work, however, and so they prayed, set a watch and continued, cf. Mark 14. 38.

Then came internal problems. There was first of all *rubbish*, which was a source of discouragement, v. 10, and secondly there was *fear*, created by looking at dangers, vv. 11-14.

There was much rubbish which hindered and caused the strength of the workers to fail. We cannot build on top of rubbish. It must be cleared away, and a solid foundation laid, cf. 1 Cor. 3. 11. But to do this they needed strength, and it was decayed, Neh. 4. 10. The remedy is found in Isaiah 40. 31.

The fear which beset them arose from looking at circumstances rather than at God. They were so timid that Nehemiah virtually stands alone again, though never alone, cf. 2 Tim. 4. 16, 17. The answer was to bring them back to a consciousness of the greatness of God, Neh. 4. 14. If He is remembered, and kept before the heart, defeat is impossible. "God is our refuge and strength, a very present help in trouble", Psa. 46. 1. This God is our God, who gave His Son, raised Him from the dead and set Him at His right hand as our Helper in all trouble.

July 23rd
READING : **Nehemiah 6. 1-19**

FURTHER PROBLEMS

SATAN makes another attempt to stop the work. Mockery had been tried and had failed. So, too, had force. Why not try invitation? Nehemiah is invited to come down to meet Sanballat, v. 2. "Come down", they say, "down to our level". Anyone who seeks to do a work for God is always being persuaded to lower the standard, and here lies the snare of the devil's friendship. But how can the Lord's servant come down? Nehemiah was "doing a great work, so that I cannot come down", v. 3; cf. Matt. 27. 42. If you realize the greatness of that which God has called you to do, you will not leave it.

Conciliatory methods had failed to corrupt Nehemiah — *insinuation* might now succeed. They resorted to lying misrepresentation, cf. Acts 24. 5. The charge, indirectly, was that Nehemiah was unauthorized, cf. Mark 11. 28ff., and directly, that his aim was self-aggrandisement and rebellion against the king. If the world cannot persuade us to compromise, it will misrepresent our motives. By discrediting the messenger, Satan may discredit the message. Such may not be easy to bear, but the wise course of action is to leave it with the Lord.

A Jew is now hired to alarm Nehemiah, v. 10. *Intimidation* will be tried. Nehemiah was warned of his own murder. He should flee to the temple, but he was not a priest, and to enter the temple and hide there was not permissible for him. They were trying to trap him into a sin against the law of his God. Shemaiah was the man used. He had not taken his place with the workers. He was at home, v. 10. Such a man, if not in fellowship with God and His things, would prove a ready tool for the conspirators. Satan finds something for his idle hands to do. Nehemiah's reply was "Should such a man as I flee?".

The wall was finished, v. 16, but the opposition was not. The enemy succeeded, by *infiltration*, where he had failed previously, vv. 17-19. Betrayal on the part of the leaders was worse than opposition from without. What led to this? Marriage alliances with the enemy, cf. 2 Cor. 6. 14-18. An unequal yoke had been entered into. Nehemiah was not deceived by the fair words of the transgressors. He had God-given insight to discern the subtlety of his foes. So "we are not ignorant of his (Satan's) devices", 2 Cor. 2. 11.

July 24th
READING : Nehemiah 8. 1-18
"BRING THE BOOK!"

IN EVERY genuine revival amongst God's people, the Word of God has had a large place. Every true revival must begin with the Word, and believing submission to it, cf. 2 Chron. 29. 35; 31. 3, 4; 34. 14ff. The immediate result of the work of restoration was a great hunger for the Word of God. Here we have a united people waiting on God, Neh. 8. 1. They were before the water gate, which intimates something of the cleansing, refreshing, reviving power of the Word of God.

Their cry is "Bring the book". It is an acknowledgment that the Author of the Book is the All-wise, and All-Sufficient One, whose Word is a safe guide in every time of confusion. Whenever God's people are thus ready to hear the Word of God, there must be blessing and Divine illumination.

The attentive people were solemnized by the reading of the Word of God, v. 3. Subjection to the Word followed, vv. 5-8. Who that has any conscience at all, can fail to be touched by the reverence thus shown for the Word of God? There was no flippancy, but there was a holy subjection to God, and a hallowed reverence for His Word.

What a lesson verse 8 is to preachers! This should be the objective of all who are called to preach and teach the Word of God. The task of the teacher is clear-cut, and well defined. It is to interpret the Word of God in plain and simple language. What God says in His Word is infinitely more important than anything man can say. It ought to be noted that the Word "distinctly" is translated "with an interpretation", R.V. marg. It was expository preaching, the need for which is undiminished, but is too often sadly lacking in the churches to-day.

They were moved to tears, v. 9, and well they might be, for no one can face the demands of God's holy law without a sense of condemnation. Their awakened conscience told them how guilty they, and their fathers, had been in refusing to obey the Word of God. Their tears of penitence testified to the self-judgment that was going on. Joy took the place of sorrow, v. 10, and was followed by obedience, vv. 14-16. The reading of the Word, and the revival that followed, produced a wholehearted keeping of the feast of Tabernacles, not celebrated in this fashion since the days of Joshua, v. 17.

July 25th
READING : **Nehemiah 13. 1-31**

THE MAN WHO UNDERSTOOD

NEHEMIAH had been away from Jerusalem. It was a sad state of affairs he found when he returned. Coming to the city he "understood", v. 7. He saw things from the Divine standpoint, and therefore he was not deceived — he understood. He understood what had gone wrong and why. The man who views events as one in fellowship with God will understand. The causes of failure do not change. To follow Nehemiah in his dealings with them will help us to "understand".

There had been mingling with other nations — separation had broken down, vv. 4-9. Indeed, Tobiah the Ammonite, the inveterate enemy of God's people, was comfortably ensconced in the temple court in defiance of Deuteronomy 23. 3. Eliashib, the priest, was allied to him. He whose work it was to instruct others in the law had failed to keep it himself, cf. Matt. 23. 2, 3. We need to be careful that we do not let the ties of relationship weaken the straightforwardness of our testimony for the Lord. God's purposes demanded a holy people, and Nehemiah did the only thing that could be done with corruption that had invaded God's house — he threw it out.

Then, the people had failed in stewardship towards priests and singers, and for the upkeep of the temple, vv. 10-14. They had failed to keep the promise regarding the sabbath, vv. 15-22, and the sabbath day was being desecrated by all sorts of traffic and business. They had pledged themselves not to marry heathen women, and they had failed to keep their word, vv. 23-29. It was not only the ordinary people either, cf. v. 28. Has a daughter of Sanballat captured your heart, and stolen its loyalty from the Lord Himself?

Note what is said about the children, vv. 23, 24. Children had been born, and were witness to the corruption that had been brought in. Too readily they followed the speech and example of the parent who knew not God. Nehemiah acted very firmly, v. 25. Against this background Nehemiah four times calls to be remembered, vv. 14, 22, 29, 31. His whole commission involved controversy and opposition, but he was conscious that if remembered for good by his God, all earthly disparagement would count for little. Let us then aim at being remembered for "good" when we stand before the Lord.

Introducing Esther

THE AHASUERUS whom we meet in this book is almost certainly to be identified with the king known as Xerxes to the Greeks. He was king of Persia in the years 486 to 465 B.C. Thus the events fall between the prophecies of Haggai and Zechariah and the rebuilding of the temple in Jerusalem (520 B.C.) and Ezra's journey to Jerusalem in 458 B.C. Our book, then, is to be placed between chapters 6 and 7 of Ezra. Only about 50,000 Jews acted upon the decree of Cyrus in 536 B.C., and returned to Jerusalem. All the others, deported to Babylon or born in captivity, elected to remain there. Many of them must have been owners of property, and many must have been engaged in commercial enterprises which were profitable.

This is one book in the Bible which does not directly mention God's name, though the heathen king is mentioned some 187 times. The book is never quoted in the New Testament. It makes no reference to prayer, or to any of the sacred observances of the Jewish law. But the fact that God's name is not mentioned is a testimony to the book's inspiration. Had its selection been left to mere man it would probably not have found a place in the canon. Yet the book describes the sovereign control of events by the power of God. God is certainly out of sight, unrecognized, but He is all the time at work, furthering His purposes. Here we have the reality of the providence of God, i.e. that over all the affairs of human life God has a part. God sees, knows, and cares for His own. He may be out of their sight, but they are never out of His, cf. Psa. 121. 3, 4. He may be behind the scenes, but He moves every scene that He is behind. As for His people, it is the story of those who were away from the land, and had not returned under Zerubbabel.

Along with their preservation from destruction, as purposed by Haman, was bound up that of the whole of the Jewish people in Persia's 127 provinces. God's purposes and promises to Israel were at stake, and the frustration of Haman's evil design was really God's overthrow of Satan's murderous attempt to thwart the Messiah's advent.

At the feast of Purim, celebrated annually to commemorate this deliverance, the whole book is read with joy. Try it!

July 26th
READING : **Esther 2. 2-11, 21-23; 3. 1-6**

MORDECAI THE JEW

MORDECAI was a Benjamite, a descendant of Saul, 2. 5. His work was thus to end the war against Amalek, cf. Exod. 17. 8, a work entrusted to Saul, cf. 1 Sam. 15. 3. He had brought up his kinswoman, Esther, as his daughter, and when she was likely to be elevated to be queen, his concern for her did not cease as his walking before the court of the women's house proves, 2. 11. His constant aim was to guide her in the difficult path of her new career. Later he receives the highest honours that the king can bestow, but he never seeks them for himself, and he would be content if his desires for the good of his people could be achieved by the queen, whom he has counselled from her childhood. Such self-effacement is rare and beautiful.

Whilst following his humble occupation, Mordecai overhears the plot of two eunuchs to murder the king. He tells Esther who in turn informs the king, 2. 21, 22. The event was recorded, and would later be used in God's providential dealings for the good of His people, cf. 6. 1-11.

The enemy of God's people was Haman the Agagite, cf. 1 Sam. 15. 8. Agag was a descendant of Amalek, therefore Haman was an Amalekite. Mordecai refused to do obeisance to him, Esth. 3. 5. Haman was claiming some sort of Divine honours. Mordecai was made of stern stuff. He was not going to bow down before one so haughty and depraved as Haman, even though he was the king's favourite. Certainly Mordecai now proclaims that he is a Jew, 3. 4. Do people with whom you work know that you are a Christian? If not, some crisis sooner or later will force you to admit it, or else make you ashamed.

Did Mordecai have a "Thus saith the Lord" for not bowing down? Here was an act of oriental prostration which meant religious homage, and Mordecai knew but one God. Refusal to bow down had brought the three Hebrew youths into the fiery furnace, cf. Dan. 3, and Mordecai was proving a worthy companion of theirs. Furthermore, a faithful Jew could not do reverence to one with whom Jehovah was at war. We have no rights to be liberal at our Master's expense. He would not bow, and he left the results with God. And what results! In a moment Haman is tumbled from his high position, and Mordecai exalted. God honours those who honour Him.

July 27th

READING : Esther 4. 1-17

"IF I PERISH, I PERISH"

THE PICTURE of Esther is a singularly fine one. A beautiful woman, occupying a place of grave peril at the court of an Eastern despot, she makes a great venture on her people's behalf in their hour of peril. Mordecai is persuaded that deliverance will come from some quarter, and he suggests that Esther has been raised to her high position for saving her people, v. 14. If she does not act now, and holds her peace, deliverance will come from another source. But Esther acts and does so in the spirit of conscious dependence upon God, with a complete readiness to sacrifice her life. She had "come to the kingdom for such a time".

Mordecai had owned he was a Jew, 3. 4. She will do so, too. She scorns to forget her humble origin in all the splendour of her recent advancement. She is not spoiled by her great elevation. She does not forget all obligations and interest beyond the obligation to please the king. She still renders submissive obedience to her guardian. She will own her despised and hated people before the king. She will plead the cause of the oppressed even at the risk of her own life. She knows the danger of what she is doing, v. 16. Accustomed to obey, she was strengthened by the voice of her own conscience. She knows that what she is called upon to do is right. She recognizes that her new privileges brought new responsibilities. She accepted that she had been raised up to save her people. Here was a faith reserved and reticent, but real and powerful. When she saw God's purpose for her, she acted with the promptitude and the obedience of the founder of her nation. Moses esteemed "the reproach of Christ greater riches than the treasures in Egypt", cf. Heb. 11. 24-26. There was a difference. Moses lost his position when he identified himself with his people. Esther retained hers, and turned it to good account.

Esther's faith measured up to Mordecai's expectation. She will approach the king in order to save her people even if for her the result is death. Does it not remind us of One who did more than say "If I perish, I perish"? He gave Himself, and took upon Himself the curse of a broken law, and became accursed for us, Gal. 2. 20; 3. 13.

July 28th

READING : **Esther 6. 1-14**

A KING'S SLEEPLESSNESS

IN THE DEALINGS of God, vast issues follow apparently trivial things. A sleepless night in itself is a trivial and passing thing. In the case of Ahasuerus it was another of the forces by which God moved to preserve His people. Why could he not sleep? God would not let him. The king's sleeplessness altered the course of history, and the future of the Jews. A sleepless night—how commonplace and insignificant! Yet God uses the commonplace and insignificant to achieve His great purposes — Shamgar and his ox-goad, Jud. 3. 31, a woman and her tent peg, Jud. 4. 21, a millstone, Jud. 9. 53, pitchers and trumpets, Jud. 7. 20, the jaw bone of an ass, Jud. 15. 15-17, sling and five stones, 1 Sam. 17. 39, 40, five loaves and two small fish, John 6. 9. So a baby's cry saved a nation, Exod. 2. 6, and a boy's careful listening an apostle, cf. Acts 23. 16ff.

God can use the sleeplessness of a king to the advantage and honour of His people. God put it into his heart to order the book of the chronicles to be brought up so that they might be read to him, not to produce sleep, but to spend the sleepless night in a profitable way. Once more we see the hand of God directing the reading to the record of Mordecai's discovery of the plot against the king's life, and how he had saved the king. The deed of Mordecai had been unrewarded through the wise purpose of the Lord, and is now brought to light through the same wisdom. In that memorable sleepless night the machinations of revenge, so finely spun in the dark by Haman, are suddenly arrested, and their exposure becomes assured. He who shall "neither slumber nor sleep", Psa. 121. 3, 4, the ever-watchful King of Israel, was present in the royal bed-chamber that night, cf. Dan. 2. 1; 6. 18. "The king's heart is in the hand of the Lord", Prov. 21. 1.

The rediscovery of Mordecai by Ahasuerus may well serve to teach us how important it is to get better acquainted with the One who has saved us. Would that we searched "the book of records" more, so that we should become more aware of what He has done for us. Then it will not be said of our blessed Lord, as it was said of Mordecai, "There is nothing done for him", Esth. 6. 3. We, too, may inquire "What honour have I brought to Him who has done so much for me?".

Introducing The Book of Job

JOB IS ONE of the oldest books in the Bible and deals with one of the oldest problems, the mystery of suffering. It is the first of five poetical books developing five leading themes in sequence: Job — the mystery of suffering; Psalms — the sanctuary; Proverbs — sonship; Ecclesiastes — man's life "under the sun"; Song — rest and love "under his shadow".

The Bible speaks of Job as a real historical character, Ezek. 14. 14; James 5. 11. He lived in the land of Uz. This is thought to be the area along the border between Israel and Jordan, east of the Dead Sea, 1. 3; Lam. 4. 21. Historically the book seems to lie somewhere between the flood and the calling out of Israel as a nation. The flood is referred to in the book as a comparatively recent event, 22. 15-17, but there is no mention of Moses or the law. The fact that Job lived 140 years after the events recorded in the book, points to the longevity of men in the patriarchal period, 42. 16.

The Theme. Fundamentally the book is a theodicy, a vindication of God's governmental dealings with His people. It faces the question, why do the righteous suffer. How can their sufferings be reconciled with belief in a God of love and justice?

The book has a historical introduction and conclusion. The central part is composed of a series of debates between Job and his critical friends. Then God reveals Himself and the problem is settled. An interesting and important theme is the role of Satan in the suffering of the saint. He can go a certain distance in God's permissive overruling providence but no further.

An Outline of the Book:

Historical introduction. Job's test	1. 1 to 2. 13
False comfort of his three friends	3. 1 to 31. 40
Elihu's speeches	32. 1 to 37. 24
God's intervention	38. 1 to 42. 6
Historical conclusion	42. 7-17

Consider thoughtfully Job's faith in God, 19. 23-27. Satan's malice, chs. 1-2, his friends' "wisdom", e.g. 4. 8-11, his own soul's laments, e.g. 9. 25 to 10. 22, and lyrics, e.g. 9. 4-12, and the divine oracle, chs. 38ff; each have their place in Job's schooling.

July 29th
READING : Job 1. 1 to 2. 10
THE TESTING OF JOB

THE BOOK OPENS with five scenes alternating between earth and heaven. Job is introduced as a perfect and upright man who feared God and hated evil. He had a delightful family, he was wealthy and had a burden for his family. When they had a feast, he offered burnt offerings for them in case they had cursed God in their hearts, 1. 1-5.

Then the scene changes to heaven. Satan is seen as having access to the presence of God. Elsewhere he is called "the accuser of our brethren", Rev. 12. 10. Here he accuses Job of self-seeking in his apparent piety. He infers that he is a hypocrite. He tells God that He has protected him with three hedges, around himself, his house and all that he has. He challenges God to remove the hedges and "he will curse thee to thy face", v. 11. Satan is permitted to deprive Job of his wealth and his family, and takes his departure, vv. 6-12.

Then the scene changes to earth. There were four heavy blows on Job in a single day, two from his enemies and two from what men would call "acts of God", lightning and the wind, vv. 13-19. Four messengers of doom tell him that his wealth and his family have been destroyed. We can understand his grief, but stand challenged by his worship, vv. 20f.

Again the scene changes to heaven. In the first interview with God, Satan is cynical; here he is callous, 2. 1-6. He said "all that a man hath will he give for his life", touch his bone and his flesh, and he will curse thee to thy face". The Lord replied: "he is in thine hand; only spare his life", 2. 6 R.V.

Back on earth, Satan is permitted to smite Job with a loathsome disease over all his body, vv. 7-8. As a final blow his wife says: "curse God, and die", v. 9. But in spite of it all he was not moved from his earlier reaction: "The Lord gave, and the Lord hath taken away; blessed be the name of the Lord", 1. 21; cf. 2. 10.

It is easy to thank *God the Giver*, but to thank *God the Taker* shows a character stayed upon God in spite of appearances. Job was never permitted to know the sinister character of Satan actively working behind the scenes to undermine his faith in God. In our own testings we often remain in ignorance as to "why". Have faith in God, and praise His name!

July 30th

READING : Job 2. 11-13; 9. 1-35

JOB AND HIS THREE FRIENDS

THREE OF Job's friends, Eliphaz, Bildad and Zophar, when they heard of his calamity, came to visit him. They sat for seven days and nights without saying a single word. Instead of acting like friends they behaved like judges. At first they are reserved and courteous, but finally severe in their judgment. There are three rounds of debate; each one speaks and Job replies. In the last round Zophar drops out, leaving Job in his distress. The debates begin after Job's bitter outburst recorded in chapter 3. There are 16 speeches in all; three by Eliphaz, three by Bildad, two by Zophar, with Job's replies to each of them.

Eliphaz with a great show of dignity argues from *experience*. He frequently uses the term "I have seen". His experience is based on a terrifying dream. But Job's trial was of a more practical kind, as he passed through the crucible of suffering. Eliphaz ends by calling Job a hypocrite, 15. 34.

Bildad in his speeches falls back upon *tradition*. "For inquire, I pray thee, of the former age", and attend to the researches of their fathers. "Shall not they teach thee, and tell thee?", 8. 8-11. He argues that suffering is always a result of hidden sin, therefore Job is a sinner. He, too, uses the hateful word "hypocrite".

Zophar the *legalist* is hard and merciless. As well as a hypocrite, he calls Job a liar, 11. 3. He is harsh and dogmatic.

All this goaded Job into defending himself. It never dawned on his three friends that suffering could be anything but retributive. They illustrate the humbling fact that, apart from God-given light, man cannot properly understand himself nor the purpose of life in the context of God's ways. In justifying himself and his philosophies, he will either condemn God or his fellows. Do not preach at the troubled one: pray with him.

How precious are the words "whom the Lord loveth he chasteneth, and scourgeth every son whom he receiveth", Heb. 12. 6. In his defence Job declared himself innocent of their charges. He longed for God to take up his case, saying "my desire is, that the Almighty would answer me", 31. 35. God did answer him in His own good time, but not in the way that he expected.

July 31st
READING : Job 19. 1-29
JOB'S FAITH IN A COMING REDEEMER

OUR READING forms Job's reply to Bildad's second address. In it Job censures his "friends" as they sustain their campaign of reproach, vv. 1-5, complains that God was counting him an adversary, vv. 6-20, claims their pity in light of his confidence in his Redeemer, vv. 21-27, and urges them to beware of continuing their pursuit of him, vv. 28-29.

In the midst of debates between Job and his critical friends, there is one of the most amazing statements concerning his faith in God. When we consider the early age in which it was uttered, it is all the more remarkable. His friends had said some true things, but at the same time they were cruel and even malignant in their assessment of Job's sore trial. Their dark black logic had condemned him as a sinner who was trying to cover up the wickedness for which he was suffering. Job had reacted with indignation and self-justification. He longed for a Daysman, one who could "lay his hand upon us both", 9. 33. Bildad, at the end of his second speech, infers that Job does not know God, 18. 21. This statement calls forth Job's magnificent testimony.

"Oh that they (my words) were printed in a book! . . . For I know that my redeemer liveth, and that he shall stand at the latter day upon the earth: and though after my skin worms destroy this body, yet in my flesh shall I see God".

There are seven great truths in the statement in verses 23-27 that are worth careful study and meditation.

The Book: Job had no Bible. His longing for a written authoritative revelation.
I know: Absolute assurance. No doubt or uncertainty.
My: Personal appropriation. His faith and trust.
Redeemer: The "Goel", Kinsman-Redeemer-Avenger.
Liveth: Resurrection. Heb. 7. 25; Rev. 1. 18.
Stand at the latter day upon the earth: The Two Advents.
Though worms destroy this body, yet in my flesh I shall see God:
Bodily resurrection.

It is only the Divine Spirit of God who could have put these precious words into the heart and mouth of Job. "My Redeemer, O what beauties in the lovely Name appear: None but Jesus in His glory, shall the honoured title wear."

Aug. 1st
READING : Job 33. 6-30
ELIHU'S SPEECHES

AFTER JOB has silenced his three friends, the young man Elihu speaks. He is a most interesting character. He alone in the book has a genealogy, 32. 2. His name means "God is He" or "God Himself". He was descended from Buz, who was a nephew of Abraham, Gen. 22. 21. Job had expressed a desire for a "daysman", or mediator, to act between him and God, 9. 33. This is the position which Elihu takes. He claims to be speaking by inspiration of the Spirit of God, 32. 8, 18; 33. 4. In some respects he is a picture of that One of whom it is said: "There is . . . one mediator also between God and man, himself man, Christ Jesus", 1 Tim. 2. 5 R.V.

He challenges Job as to four statements he made about himself. "I am clean, without transgression; I am innocent, neither is there iniquity in me", 33. 9 R.V. He also takes up the four charges he makes against God. "Behold, he findeth occasions against me, he counteth me for his enemy, he putteth my feet in the stocks, he marketh all my paths", vv. 10-11.

In answer to Job's statements about himself and about God, Elihu shows four ways in which God speaks to man to reveal to him his true condition as a sinner, and to take pride from man, v. 17. Here we have the gospel in a nutshell. He speaks (1) in a dream, v. 15; (2) by preservation in danger, v. 18; (3) in serious illness, vv. 19-22, and (4) by a messenger or preacher, v. 23. These are methods which God still uses. When the sinner confesses "I have sinned, and perverted that which is right, and it profited me not", v. 27, then God steps in, "Deliver him from going down to the pit: I have found a ransom", v. 24. There are four results for the one so delivered: (1) he becomes a child; (2) he prays; (3) he sees God's face, and (4) he has a righteous standing before God, vv. 25-26.

Job later learned these important lessons when God spoke to him out of the whirlwind, with the same blessed results, 42. 5-6. The great principles of the gospel are the same in our day as they were in Job's day. First there must be repentance, then confession, followed by faith's acceptance of God's remedy, the ransom paid. By these means alone is found God's answer to the question, "how should man be just with God?", 9. 2.

Aug. 2nd

READING : **Job 38. 1-14; 40. 1-5; 42. 1-6**

GOD'S INTERVENTION

Job's three friends, having finished their caustic remarks, concluded that Job was a hypocritical sinner suffering on account of wickedness in his life. Elihu on the other hand had taken a different position, insisting that suffering is not for specific sin, but is God's chastisement and discipline of His children. Job is silent.

Then God speaks out of the whirlwind. Elihu had closed his discourse on the lofty theme of the majesty and the justice of God. The moment has now come for divine intervention. The words of Jehovah fill four chapters with a brief interlude at the opening of chapter 40. About 70 questions are asked for Job to answer if he could. All are concerned with the mighty power displayed in creation. It covers the primeval revelation recorded in Genesis 1-2, and in the same order. The earth, seas, light, the stars and the constellations, then animals and birds ending with behemoth and leviathan (perhaps the hippo and the crocodile). This is the revelation of God's eternal power and Godhead, Rom. 1. 20. Whereas the dark pagan world had deliberately turned away from God into idolatry and immorality, this revelation caused Job to confess: "Behold I am vile; what shall I answer thee? I will lay mine hand upon my mouth", 40. 4. Job had silenced his friends, then God silenced him! Self-justification disappears. This is a critical point in Job's experience. This is the end which the Lord had in view when He permitted all these testing disasters to come upon him. It is the revolutionary effect of coming into God's presence, and hearing His voice. He says: "I have heard of thee by the hearing of the ear: but now mine eye seeth thee. Wherefore I abhor myself, and repent in dust and ashes".

Job now sees himself in a totally new light. Formerly he had boasted of his righteousness and purity; now he sees the self-conceited depths of his fallen nature. This spirit of self-judgment is wrought in all those to whom God reveals His majesty and glory and holiness. Abraham said "I am but dust and ashes", Gen. 18. 27. Isaiah said, "I am undone", Isa. 6. 5. Daniel declared "my comliness was turned in me into corruption", Dan. 10. 8. And Peter confessed "I am a sinful man, O Lord", Luke 5. 8. Have we had this experience?

Aug. 3rd

READING : **Job 42. 7-17**

JOB'S RESTORATION

THE COMMENT of James on Job's traumatic experience is, "Behold, we count them happy which endure. Ye have heard of the patience of Job, and have seen the end of the Lord; that the Lord is very pitiful, and of tender mercy", James 5. 11. As far as the record goes, Job never knew about the dialogue between God and Satan, or of the reason for his trial. Peter had a testing experience, Luke 22. 31-32, and also Paul, 2 Cor. 12. 7-9, but they knew that Satan was behind it. Satan is increasingly active today, and it is very possible that he is responsible for many things that happen to God's people.

We can see clearly now that when Job was in affluence, his possessions intact, and his family around him, he had no true idea of himself, and therefore little true idea of God. But he had learned a lesson, utterly surprising to himself, discovered in the furnace of affliction through which he had passed. In New Testament language we too have to learn the lesson of Romans that "in me (that is, in my flesh,) dwelleth no good thing", 7. 18.

There are a number of things involved in "the end of the Lord" for Job as mentioned by James. First, he had a new conception of the majesty and glory of God, and of his own unworthiness in His sight. Then he had a different attitude to his friends. Instead of bitter sarcasm and anger to the men who had misunderstood and misjudged him, he acts in kindness and grace. The Lord "turned the captivity" of Job, his troubles passed away, when he prayed for his friends. Instead of harsh words, he engages in priestly intercession. There was a mellowing process in his experience which only comes out of the school of suffering.

God now comes in and blesses Job, restoring to him twice the possessions which he had lost, giving him again seven sons and three daughters. It may be asked, why should his property be doubled and not his family? Surely the answer is that for the cattle and herds there was no after life, but his children that had died were to live again, and he was given another family on earth. So actually they were doubled too! How blessed to know that those who die in the Lord are with Christ which is very far better.

Introducing The Psalms

THE BOOK of Psalms is the hymnbook of the Jewish people. When David brought the ark of God to Zion, he organized the Levitical choirs and the ministry of song, 2 Sam. 6; 1 Chron. 15. Asaph, Jeduthan and Heman were choir masters. This leadership continued in the Asaph family Neh. 7. 44.

The Psalms are divided into five books and have been compared with the first five books of the Bible as follows:

Psa. 1-41	corresponding to Genesis.	Foundation truths.
Psa. 42-72	corresponding to Exodus.	Redemption.
Psa. 73-89	corresponding to Leviticus.	The Sanctuary.
Psa. 90-106	corresponding to Numbers.	The Wilderness.
Psa. 107-150	corresponding to Deuteronomy.	Review and Summary.

The first book, with two or three exceptions, contains the psalms of David; the second a series by the sons of Korah and another series by David. The third has two minor collections, one by Asaph, the other by the sons of Korah. In the fifth there is a group of pilgrim songs, the Songs of Degrees. The close of the first four sections is marked by a doxology. Psalm 150 at the end of the collection is itself a doxology.

There are several groups of psalms with a distinct theme: *Messianic* — these are related to the Person and work of Christ; *Prophetical* — Psa. 42-49 predict the future history of Israel; *Hallel Psalms* — Psa. 113-118 were used at the three yearly feasts; *Songs of Degrees* — Psa. 120-134 record the return from Babylon; *Imprecatory Psalms* — about 15 psalms fall into this category. They speak of God's judgment on His enemies.

The Psalm titles are full of meaning, perhaps indicating the festival at which they were to be used, the type of music, the author and the theme. The word "Selah" may indicate a musical rest, or a pause for contemplation.

The New Testament contains 243 quotations from the Old Testament, of which 116 are from the Psalms. The seven quotations in Hebrews 1-2 are an example. They reinforce and expound the great sevenfold statement in Hebrews 1. 1-3 concerning the Person and work of Christ. Then, our Lord Himself in resurrection expounded to the disciples the things which were written in the law of Moses, and in the prophets, and in the Psalms concerning Himself, Luke 24. 7, 44.

Aug. 4th

READING : **Psalm 1. 1-6**

THE BLESSED MAN

PSALMS 1 and 2 form an introduction to the whole book. Both speak of Christ. In Psa. 1 He is the Blessed Man — His moral glory; in Psa. 2 He is the Anointed King — His official glory.

The expression "the Blessed Man" occurs seven times in the Psalms. He is *the Forsaken Man* of Psa. 22, *the Perfect Man* of Psa. 37. 37, and *the Man of God's right hand* in Psa. 80. 17.

In Psalm 1 there is a contrast between the Blessed Man, vv. 1-3, and the wicked man, vv. 4-6. One prospers, v. 3, but the other perishes. Associated with the blessed man is a book, a tree, and a river. One's mind goes back instinctively to the garden of Eden. The first man Adam miserably failed and was expelled from paradise. This Blessed Man had a book, the law of God in which He meditated day and night. His delight was in the Word. It was hidden in His heart as in an inner shrine, Psa. 40. 8. Morning by morning His ear was opened to hear as the Learner and He was not rebellious nor turned away back, Isa. 50. 4-5. Then He was like a tree planted by the rivers of water yielding fruit. This reminds us of the true Vine of John 15 yielding fruit, more fruit and much fruit. The rivers of water suggest those which come down from the throne, and flow through the inner parts of the believer to a thirsty world, John 7. 37-38.

There are three things the Blessed Man will not do — walk or stand or sit with those opposed to God. Note the downward trend, walking followed by standing, then, finally, sitting. That was Peter's mistake when he sat at a fire and denied the Lord. It started with walking afar off, Luke 22. 54f. But this Blessed Man is a separated Man. In contrast to Peter, Enoch walked with God, Gen. 5. 24, Elijah stood before the Lord, 1 Kings 17. 1 and David sat before the Lord, 2 Sam. 7. 18. They were the blessed men of their day.

However, the ungodly are not so, but are like the chaff carried away by the wind, and ultimately burned in the fire. The psalm ends with two contrasting ways, and two destinies. One results in spiritual prosperity, the other perishes, v. 6. This is a theme emphasized in every part of the Word of God. All true happiness is found in godliness, but sorrow and tragedy are the fruits of wickedness.

Aug. 5th

READING : **Psalm 2. 1-12**

THE ANOINTED KING

THE SECOND Psalm expounds the official glory of the Messiah. It projects our minds into the future when He will sit upon the throne with every enemy under His feet.

The Psalm has 12 verses, divided into four stanzas of three verses each. There are four speakers, one in each section. In the first stanza, vv. 1-3, it is the voice of rebellion, man in revolt against the Lord and His Anointed. There is a fourfold description of opposition: the gentile nations, "the peoples", which include Israel, Gen. 25, 23; Acts 4. 25-28, the kings, representing organized government, and then judicial authority. All are joined together against Almighty God and His Christ. They issue an ultimatum: "Let us break their bands asunder, and cast away their cords from us". It is the breakdown of order at the end of the age, 2 Thess. 2. 6-8.

The second stanza, vv. 4-6, is the response of the Lord to man's rebellion. "He who sitteth in the heavens shall laugh; the Lord shall have them in derision. Then shall he speak unto them in his wrath, and vex them in his sore displeasure." "The wrath" is a technical term used in the Book of Revelation for the great tribulation. The bowls or vial judgments are the wrath of God, the concentrated anger of the Almighty poured out on the Antichrist and his followers, Rev. 15. 7. The climax of all this is: "Yet have I set my king upon my holy hill of Zion", Psa. 2. 6. This is God's unalterable purpose, and nothing upon earth or in hell can thwart it. In the first stanza He is the Anointed. Here, He is King.

The third stanza, vv. 7-9, is the revelation of the Son. "I will declare the decree: "the LORD hath said unto me, Thou art my Son; this day have I begotten thee". This is one of the great decrees of the Godhead in eternity past, here revealed for the first time by the Son. The eternal Sonship of Christ is one of the great basic doctrines of Scripture. It is quoted and expounded three times in the New Testament, Acts 13. 32-33; Heb. 1. 5-6; 5. 5. He is destined to rule as Heir over the nations and sit upon the throne as King, vv. 8-9.

The fourth stanza, vv. 10-12, is the voice of the Spirit to the kings and judges of the earth to submit, and be reconciled to Him while there is time.

Aug. 6th

READING : **Psalm 8. 1-9**

THE FIRST AND THE LAST ADAM

THE PSALM is completely enclosed in an ascription of worship, vv. 1, 9, reinforced by the praise of babes and the young in Christ, v. 2; cf. Matt. 11. 25; 21. 15f. In verses 3-4 there is a contrast between the immensity of the starry heavens, and the frailty and littleness of man. But all the time Almighty God had him in mind and decided to visit him, first in the paradise of Eden and later at the incarnation in Bethlehem. The first man Adam was given dominion and sovereignty over God's creation, Gen. 1. 26. This included the fish in the sea, birds in the air, and the animals of the forest. Man was God's vicegerent. But unfortunately, on account of man's sin and disobedience, that rule over creation has been forfeited. But in God's purpose Paradise Lost will be Paradise Regained by the second man, the Last Adam our Lord Jesus Christ.

The psalm looks back to Genesis 2 and forward to Hebrews 2. Man in innocence was made in the image of God. In Genesis 2. 19-20 he names the animals and exercises his dominion, but in Genesis 3 all is upset by the fall and its terrible consequences. The crown of sovereignty has fallen from his head, and his sceptre is in the dust. The writer in the Epistle to the Hebrews sadly says: "we see not yet all things put under him", 2. 8. What we do see is a groaning creation under the curse. Man is afraid of the lion and the snake, and even of a dog or a mouse! The first Adam and his posterity have sadly failed in the original mandate that was given to him. But Hebrews 2. 9 introduces another Man: "But we see Jesus". Hebrews 2 outlines four great epoch-making events, fulfilling the prophecy of Psalm 8. 4-8. Two of these are now history and two remain as prophecy.

(1) Made for a little time lower than the angels, with a view to the suffering of death, Heb. 2. 9 R.V. The incarnation and crucifixion of Christ.

(2) Crowned with glory and honour, vv. 7, 9. Resurrection and glorification. The fallen crown recovered.

(3) Set over . . . hands. Sovereignty regained, v. 7.

(4) All under His feet, v. 8; 1 Cor. 15. 27; Eph. 1. 20-22.

Well might the psalmist repeat the ascription of praise, "O Lord, our Lord, how excellent is thy name in all the earth!"

Aug. 7th

READING : **Psalm 16. 1-11**

CHRIST IN RESURRECTION AND EXALTATION

THIS PSALM is quoted by Peter, Acts 2. 31-32, and by Paul, Acts 13. 35. Both apostles interpret it as referring to the resurrection and exaltation of Christ. It is one of six psalms with the title "Michtam". The word means "golden". It is truly a goldmine of precious teaching concerning our Lord.

The psalm is in two parts:
(1) The pathway of faith. The dependant Man, vv. 1-7.
(2) The pathway of life. Resurrection and exaltation, vv. 8-11.

The first part presents five attitudes of our Lord in His pathway on earth. It has been called a Divine pilgrim's progress. But unlike Bunyan's pilgrim, this One has no bypath meadow.

(a) *His attitude to God,* vv. 1-2. It was an attitude of complete dependence upon, and subjection to, the will of His God. It was a voluntary position which He took in incarnation. He never acted independently. He exclaims: "Thou art my Lord (Adonai); I have no good beyond thee", v. 2 R.V.

(b) *His attitude to the people of God,* v. 3. "As for the saints that are in the earth, they are the excellent in whom is all my delight", R.V. These are the nobility of heaven!

(c) *His attitude to pagan idolatry,* v. 4. Under differing "foreign" influences the land was dotted with pagan shrines. He never entered any of them.

(d) *His attitude to material things,* vv. 5-6. He was perfectly satisfied with His portion, His lot, His cup, and His goodly heritage. Is there a reference to the Levite?, Num. 18. 20.

(e) *His attitude to the voice of God,* v. 7. Here we have a piece of soul-history. Whole nights were spent in communion with His Father, Isa. 50. 4; Mark. 6. 46; Luke 6. 12.

The second part of the psalm, vv. 8-11, speaks of the period between His death, burial and resurrection: "thou wilt not leave my soul to Sheol; neither wilt thou suffer thine holy one to see corruption", v. 10 R.V. At His incarnation He is called "that holy thing", Luke. 1. 35. Here He is called "thine Holy one". Both are gloriously true. He is the impeccable Son of God. The psalm ends with His exaltation to God's right hand. Joy is mingled with sorrow down here, but there will be fullness of joy up there "in thy presence".

Aug. 8th

READING : **Psalm 19. 1-14**

GOD'S THREEFOLD REVELATION

THE PSALM describes three ways in which God reveals Himself:

(1) in creation, vv. 1-6; (2) in the Scriptures, vv. 7-11; (3) to the seeking soul, vv. 12-14. This is the order of progressive revelation in Romans 1-3. First to the heathen world without a written revelation, then to the world of education and culture, and to the world of religion represented by the Jew.

David was evidently a student of the stars and the Scriptures. The solar heavens are preaching sermons. The Bible says the stars are innumerable, Gen. 15. 5. It is difficult for our minds to grasp their immensity and their majesty. Betelguese, in the Constellation of Orion, is so huge, that the orbit of the earth round the sun could be contained inside it. The beauty, and precision, of creation displays the Creator's eternal power and Godhead.

God's second revelation is in His Word, vv. 7-11. David only had the first five books of the Bible, and we can be thankful to God that today we have the complete and final revelation in the written Word. The psalmist uses six titles and seven attributes to describe it, and six results from obeying it. It is called the law, testimony, statutes, commandment, fear and judgments. They are expounded in detail in Psalm 119. The attributes are: perfect, sure, right, pure, clean, true and righteous. The results are: conversion, making wise, rejoicing the heart, enlightening the eyes, warning and reward. The Word is compared to gold and honey, its preciousness and its sweetness, v. 10.

God's final revelation is to the seeking soul, vv. 12-14. David had looked up to heaven and found perfection there; then into the Word, and he found perfection there; but as he looks into his own heart he sees failure, and sin described as errors, secret faults, and even presumptuous sins. He prays that he may be saved from the great transgression, the deadly sin of rebellion or apostasy. Then he expresses the great desire of his heart, "Let the words of my mouth, and the meditation of my heart, be acceptable in thy sight, O Lord, my strength (Heb. Rock), and my redeemer", v. 14. The Rock is for safety, and the Redeemer is for salvation and liberty.

Aug. 9th

READING: **Psalm 22. 1-31**

THE PSALM OF THE CROSS

THERE ARE four psalms that speak of the death of Christ, each looking at it from a different standpoint:

Psalm 40 is the burnt offering.	God's purpose
Psalm 22 is the sin offering.	The passion
Psalm 69 is the trespass offering.	The penalty
Psalm 118 is the peace offering.	The prophetic programme

Perhaps the most important is Psalm 22 on account of the wealth of detail given, and the universal results that issue from the sacrificial death of Christ on the cross.

The psalm was written by David in the eleventh century B.C. It contains 33 items describing death by crucifixion. The fact that this cruel and painful method of execution was invented by the Roman army many centuries later, vividly demonstrates that the details of the psalm are inspired.

The psalm divides into two parts. The change comes in the centre of verse 21, where the suffering Saviour cries "thou hast heard me". Everything previous to this refers to suffering; everything after it is expressed in unbroken song. Each part has three sections:

(1) Suffering from a threefold source:
    (a) Divinely from God, vv. 1-6a. The holiness of God.
    (b) Physically from man, vv. 6b-18. The hatred of man.
    (c) Diabolically from Satan, vv. 19-21a. The hostility of Satan.

(2) The second section reveals three circles of blessing as a result of His death and resurrection:
    (a) My brethren, v. 22; John 20. 17; Heb. 2. 12.
    (b) Seed of Jacob, seed of Israel, v. 23.
    (c) All the ends of the world, v. 27.

The psalm begins and ends with two cries of Christ on the cross: "My God, my God, why hast thou forsaken me?", v. 1, and "They shall come and shall declare his righteousness unto a people that shall be born, that he hath done this", (Heb. = it is finished), v. 31.

The blessings of Calvary will embrace even the establishment of His kingdom. The rejected Man of Calvary will one day be King of kings and Lord of lords.

Aug. 10th

READING : **Psalm 23. 1-6**

THE GREAT SHEPHERD OF THE SHEEP

PSALM 23 is the best known and most loved of all the psalms. The three Psalms, 22, 23 and 24, cover the past, the present and the future. Psalm 22 presents the Good Shepherd who gave His life for the sheep. Psalm 23 describes the Great Shepherd who tends with unwearied care the flock for which He died. Psalm 24 points to the Chief Shepherd who will come in glory, and occupy the hill and the house.

Psalm 23 seems to recall a number of outstanding events in David's life. Verses 1-2 remind us of his early life when he was a shepherd, 1 Sam. 16. It was at that time, while tending the flock, that he had the encounter with the lion and the bear, 17. 34-36. It was the delightful time in his life when he learned to use the personal pronoun "The Lord is *my* shepherd". But, in contrast, he had a dark day when he committed a great sin, and needed repentance and restoration, 2 Sam. 11. Psalm 23. 3 could well refer to that time, "He restoreth my soul". Verse 4 reminds us of the valley of Elah, which to him was like treading the valley of death. He went down to meet the giant Goliath, not with the equipment of a soldier, but with the rod and staff, the sling and smooth stone of a shepherd. These he had already proved, 1 Sam. 17. After this great victory, Saul invited him to his house and table, but, on account of jealousy, his host became his bitter enemy and tried to take his life, 1 Sam. 18-19; Psa. 23. 5a. This was a very difficult period of his life. But then he had a distinguished day, "Thou anointest my head with oil", v. 5b. On three occasions David was anointed as king: first in the house of his father Jesse by Samuel, 1 Sam. 16. 13; secondly, over the tribe of Judah when Saul was dead, 2 Sam. 2. 4; and the third time over all the tribes of Israel, 2 Sam. 5. 3.

The climax of David's life was when God made a covenant with him concerning his house, a throne and a kingdom in perpetuity. It was then that his cup overflowed, and he could say: "Who am I, O Lord God? and what is my house, that thou hast brought me hitherto?", 2 Sam. 7. 18. Looking back over his life he could say, "Goodness and mercy have followed me all the days of my life", and anticipating the future, when life is past, "I will dwell in the house of the Lord for ever".

Aug. 11th

READING : **Psalm 24. 1-10**

THE KING OF GLORY

It is very likely that Psalm 24 was written at the time when David brought up the ark of God to Zion, Jerusalem became the centre of worship, and David occupied the throne as king, 2 Sam. 6. But the psalm points forward to a coming day when the King of glory will occupy the throne of world dominion. Throughout human history there have been many aspirants to sit upon that throne, but all have failed to meet the challenge and the qualifications of verses 3-4: "Who shall ascend?" First, officially, he must be both a king and a priest! Then it is reserved for Him "that hath clean hands, and a pure heart; who hath not lifted up his soul unto vanity, nor sworn deceitfully". These are moral qualifications. All the former candidates have waded to power through blood and oppression, and most have been moral degenerates. There is only one Person in all the universe who qualified, Jesus of Nazareth, the King of glory.

He has another credential. He is the creator and sustainer of the universe, vv. 1-2. There is a third qualification suggested. He is "the Lord mighty in battle", v. 8. First in the wilderness when He defeated Satan, Matt. 4. 1-11; then on the cross when He "death by dying slew", John 19; and ultimately at Armageddon, Rev. 19. 19-21. He is the Kinsman-Redeemer, and the mighty conqueror of all His enemies.

The latter part of the psalm, vv. 7-10, gives a dramatic picture of the coming of the King of Glory to take possession of the throne and of the temple. David's ascension to his throne on Mt. Zion is a lovely preview of what will happen in that day. After the total victory of Armageddon, the deliverance of Israel, and their repentance and conversion, Zech. 12-14, the Conqueror and His retinue approach the city, whose gates are bolted and barred against the enemy. There is the twofold challenge, and the twofold answer. The gates are thrown open and He enters to occupy the hill and the house. Then, "he shall build the temple of the Lord . . . and he shall bear the glory, and shall sit and rule upon his throne; and he shall be a priest upon his throne", fulfilling Zechariah 6. 12-13.

Present day events seem to point to that day when the King of glory will be upon the throne of world dominion, Isa. 9. 7.

Aug. 12th
READING : Psalm 32. 1-11
DAVID'S REPENTANCE AND FORGIVENESS

THERE ARE two psalms associated with David's great sin in 2 Samuel 11. Psalm 51 describes his conviction and repentance after the first shock of discovery. In Psalm 32 the joy of forgiveness is expressed.

We would gladly draw the curtain over this tragic episode in David's life. After many great victories, his guard is down. He is not a young man. He broke three of the commandments: the 7th—adultery; the 6th—murder; the 10th—coveting his neighbour's wife, Exod. 20. 13, 14, 17. Then he attempted to cover up what he had done — guile. The Word of God describes all in detail. It all emphasizes the fact that there is no perfect man, but with God there is forgiveness, when there is genuine confession and repentance. David's conviction is outlined, vv. 1-4. He uses four words: transgression, sin, iniquity, guile. Then follows his confession, v. 5. Again he uses the words: transgression, sin, iniquity. There is now no attempt to cover up. He uses three words to describe God's grace to him:

Forgiven, vv. 1, 5.	The work of a father.	Luke 15. 11-32
Covered, v. 1.	The work of a priest.	Lev. 16; Luke 18. 13
Imputeth not, v. 2	The work of a judge.	Rom. 4. 5-8

David's experience illustrates God's way of forgiveness and salvation in every age.

Verses 7 and 10 speak of a hiding place, and a twofold circle of protection, suggesting an inner fortress surrounded by two walls or moats. The forgiven soul is compassed about by songs of deliverance, v. 7, and encircled by mercy, v. 10, eternally secure. The first part of the psalm, vv. 1-7, outlines the fundamental principles of the gospel; the second part, vv. 8-9, gives us guidance for the way ahead. Note the contrast between the intimate guidance with the eye, and the impulsive horse that must be restrained with bit and bridle. The horse would be too quick, like Moses when he slew the Egyptian, Exod. 2. 12, and the temperamental mule would be too slow, like Jonah when he fled from God's call to go to Nineveh, Jonah 1. 3. Be guided with God's eye upon you, v. 8 R.V.

There are three stages of joy in verse 11: glad — inward inarticulate joy; rejoice — outward exuberant joy; shout — the triumphant outburst of victory.

Aug. 13th

READING : **Psalm 40. 1-17**

THE PERFECT SACRIFICE

HISTORICALLY the first part of the psalm, vv. 1-5, could be applied to David's experience in various periods of his life, e.g. when he was hunted by Saul, 1 Sam. 19-20; when he fled to Gath, 1 Sam. 21; or when his son Absalom rebelled against him, 2 Sam. 15. We do not know the exact circumstances, but, like many of God's choicest servants, he sunk in the deep pit of depression. There his cry went up, and he was brought up out of the horrible pit, and his feet were placed upon the rock and the new song put in his mouth. For the believer today, this elevating experience ends by being caught up, 1 Thess. 4. 17.

The great central section of the psalm, vv. 6-8, is a tremendous revelation of the Person and work of the Messiah, quoted and expounded in Hebrews 10. 5-10. It is in five parts with the incarnation in the centre.

(1) The inadequacy of the Levitical sacrifices, v. 6.
(2) The opened ear of the Servant, v. 6; cf. Exod. 21. 6.
(3) The incarnation, "Lo, I come", v. 7.
(4) The fulfillment of the messianic prophecies, v. 7.
(5) The law written in the inner shrine of His heart, v. 8.

The writer of the Epistle to the Hebrews quotes the Septuagint version of the psalm. The change of "Mine ears hast thou opened" to "a body hast thou prepared me" is not a discrepancy. The Holy Spirit sanctions the translation. It is an evidence of the work of the inspiring Spirit of God. It is an allusion to the Hebrew servant of Exodus 21. The pierced ear is an evidence that the whole body is dedicated.

The third section of the psalm goes back to David's personal experience, vv. 11-17. Once again he is in the valley of depression. Life is often like that. After the uplifting experience of occupation and communion with the Lord, he goes back to introspection, and contemplation of himself. He will not find any comfort there, v. 12. The reason may be persecution and scorn from a hostile world, vv. 14-15. But there is a glorious remedy in praise and thanksgiving, vv. 16-17. Comfort comes with the delightful thought: "But I am poor and needy; yet the Lord thinketh upon me", v. 17. Not only is His arm outstretched for our deliverance, but His thoughts and purpose are occupied with us in love.

Aug. 14th

READING : **Psalm 45. 1-17**

THE KING-BRIDEGROOM AND HIS BRIDE

THE WRITER of Psalm 45 introduces his subject by a magnificent eulogy of the Person and the scene he is about to describe. He finds it difficult to control his feelings. His heart is like a bubbling fountain, his mouth is that of an orator, his theme is the musical composition of a poet, his tongue is the facile pen of a scribe. Every faculty is employed to extol the glories of the King-bridegroom and his bride, v. 1.

The psalm has been applied to some contemporary event, such as the marriage of Solomon and the daughter of Pharoah, but as Perowne has remarked, "A greater than Solomon is here". Hebrews 1. 8-9 settles the messianic interpretation. The quotation of verses 6-7 of the psalm, and its application to Christ make any other interpretation inconsequential. Here we have the King and His bride coming forth, after His marriage, to deal with His enemies and to reign over the nations, Rev. 19. 11-16.

There is a threefold glory of the King-Bridegroom, vv. 1-8. First, *His moral glory*. He is "fairer than the children of men: grace is poured into thy lips", v. 2. The glory of His Person and His ministry, what He is and what He said. Second, *His official glory*. He has a sword, a sceptre, a throne, and is anointed with the oil of gladness, vv. 3, 6, 7. Third, *His divine glory*. He is addressed as God, v. 6, and in Hebrews 1. 8 as Son. This can only refer to one glorious Person, God's beloved Son!

Then, there is the threefold beauty of the Bride, vv. 9-15. First, *her adoration*, v. 11. She is exhorted to forget her own people, and her father's house. Her old life is a thing of the past. She is now united to One who is King of kings and Lord of Lords. He "is thy Lord; and worship thou him". Second, *her adornment*. Her dress is of wrought gold and a garment of needlework, vv. 13-14. The gold would symbolize a robe of glory and righteousness, Rom. 3. 22, and the needlework the righteous acts of saints, Rev. 19. 8 R.V. Thirdly, *her nuptial joy*, Psa. 45. 15. "With gladness and rejoicing shall they be brought: they shall enter into the king's palace". The psalm ends with the promise of a numerous posterity who would be given positions of prominence in the kingdom, Luke 22. 28-30.

Aug. 15th

READING : **Psalm 46. 1-11**

THE REFUGE, THE RIVER AND THE REDEEMER

PSALMS 46, 47 and 48 are closely related. They form a trilogy of praise in which some great deliverance of Jerusalem from the enemy is celebrated. But it is also a beautiful picture of a coming day, when Christ shall come and deliver the beleaguered city of Jerusalem, and establish His throne and kingdom. It has thus a primary historical interpretation, a secondary prophetical fulfilment, and a practical spiritual application to us.

There are three stanzas divided by the musical rest, "Selah", in verses 3, 7 and 11. *The first stanza*, vv. 1-3, commences with "God is our refuge and strength, a very present help in trouble", v. 1. It reminds us of Luther's great hymn: "A mighty fortress is our God". The words of verses 2-3 could be applied to the results of nuclear war. Revelation 6. 12-17 describes similar conditions during the tribulation period. God will have a safe place for His people during that terrible time, Rev. 12. 14.

In the first stanza there is a roaring and troubled sea, but in *the second stanza*, vv. 4-7, there is a quiet river of rest. It is described in Ezekiel 47. 1-5. It issues from under the threshold of the house and has four depths, to the ankles, to the knees, to the loins, and then becomes waters to swim in. Best of all "God is in the midst of her; she shall not be moved: God shall help her, and that at the dawn of morning", v. 5 R.V. marg. Verse 6 reminds us of the raging of the nations, Psa. 2. 1, and of the melting of the elements in 2 Peter 3. 10. Then comes the outshining of His glory when He comes to reign, Zech. 14.4. The section ends with the presence of the Lord of Hosts, the God of Jacob, the One who revealed Himself to the patriarch at Jabbok, Gen. 32. 28.

The third stanza, vv. 8-11, invites us to come and see the devastation on the earth after the events described in vv. 1-3. Ezekiel 39. 11-16 gives us a graphic picture of it. Then, "He maketh wars to cease unto the end of the earth; he breaketh the bow, and cutteth the spear in sunder; he burneth the chariot in the fire", Psa. 46. 9. What a glorious day that will be for our poor troubled earth! The Prince of Peace on the throne and the government upon His shoulder.

Aug. 16th
READING : **Psalm 68. 1-35**

GIFTS FROM THE VICTORIOUS CHRIST

HISTORICALLY, the psalm refers to the day when David moved the ark from the house of Obed-Edom to Mt. Zion, 1 Chron. 15. Psalms 24 and 132 are associated with the same event. The Psalm has its historical roots in the Old Testament, and its doctrinal fruits in the New Testament. The messianic reference is in the centre, v. 18; Eph. 4. 8. In the background four great victories are celebrated. First, *the victory over the Egyptian* and the march to Sinai, vv. 1-8. It opens with a quotation of the words of Moses at the exodus when Israel came out of Egypt: "Let God arise, let his enemies be scattered", v. 1; cf. Num. 10. 35. The *second victory, that of Deborah and Barak over the Canaanite*, is recorded in Judges 4-5. It is graphically described in verses 9-19 of the psalm. The storm which immobilized Sisera's chariots, v. 9, the women in charge of communications, v. 11 R.V., the retreat, the rout, and the spoils of war, vv. 12-13, are all poetically portrayed. It is at this point that the messianic passage is introduced. "Thou hast ascended on high, thou hast led captivity captive: thou hast received gifts for men; yea, for the rebellious also, that the Lord God might dwell among them", v. 18. The apostle Paul selects three clauses, and applies them to the ascended Christ, Eph. 4. 8.

Thou hast ascended on high. The ascension of the Victor.

Thou hast led captivity captive. The defeated enemy.

And gave gifts unto men. Spiritual gifts to the church.

Paul uses the victory over the Canaanites as an illustration of the victorious Head of the Church in ascension, giving gifted men for the teaching and edification of His people.

The third victory, that over the Jebusites and Philistines, is climaxed by the bringing up of the ark to Zion, vv. 20-28; 1 Chron. 15. 25-28. One result of the victory was the uniting of all the 12 tribes of Israel into one nation. The two southern tribes, Judah and Benjamin are linked together with the two northern tribes, Zebulun and Naphtali. Together they make Mt. Zion the political and religious centre.

The final victory lies in the future with the ushering in of the kingdom, with its centre at Jerusalem, and David's Son and Lord upon the throne, vv. 29-35. "Blessed be the Lord . . . even the God who is our salvation", v. 19 R.V.

Aug. 17th

READING : **Psalm 69. 1-36**

THE PSALM OF THE TRESPASS OFFERING

THE TITLE of the psalm is "To the Chief Musician upon Shoshannim". The word "Shoshannim" means lilies. The four psalms that have this title were traditionally associated with the passover season. In Scripture the lily is found in four places corresponding to the four psalms where we find the title.

The lily of the valley—the cross. Psa. 69.
The lily of the field—Solomon in all his glory. Psa. 45.
The lily among thorns—trial and tribulation. Psa. 80.
The lily in the garden—testimony and victory. Psa. 60.

While much of the psalm describes David's experience of rejection and suffering, yet there are seven quotations from it in the New Testament referring to the Messiah, so we are on safe ground in applying it to the Saviour. The keyword is in verse 4, "Then I restored that which I took not away". He paid the price, and suffered the penalty, for sin. He added the fifth part thereto, making reparation for the sins of the world. His sacrificial death was the fulfilment of the guilt offering, Lev. 5. 1 to 6. 7.

He did not take away man's innocence, his fellowship with God, or the dominion which was committed to him before the fall. But in his great work of redemption, reconciliation and restitution, He has restored all that Adam lost at the fall.

The infinite value of the atonement: Propitiation was for the whole world, 1 John 2. 2. He gave Himself a ransom for all, 1 Tim. 2. 6. The sacrifice and the value of the precious blood was infinite, but it is only effective to those that believe, Rom. 3. 22. The 20% added in the trespass offering makes the doctrine of a limited atonement unscriptural. Revelation 22 is higher than Genesis 2; not simply man in innocence, but in perfect conformity to the image of Christ. The image and the likeness restored. It will all be realized through the Man who went through the deep waters and the overflowing flood, v. 2. He was the One who was hated without a cause, v. 4; John 15. 25. He could say: "Reproach hath broken my heart", Psa. 69. 20, and "They gave me also gall for my meat; and in my thirst they gave me vinegar to drink", v. 21.

The psalm ends with a song, v. 30, and a seed, v. 36. It has a glorious climax and conclusion! We love His name!

Aug. 18th

READING : **Psalm 73. 1-28**

SPIRITUAL DEPRESSION AND ITS CURE

THE FIRST 11 psalms in this third section of the book are by Asaph. He was a Gershonite Levite, and is first mentioned in 1 Chron. 6. 39, where he is introduced as one of three great leaders of song appointed by David. In 2 Chron. 29. 30 he is called "Asaph the seer", and there we are told that the words of some of the psalms of praise sung by the Levites in the days of Hezekiah were of his authorship.

Here in Psalm 73 he recounts a difficult experience in his life which is all too common among God's people today. He begins by laying a foundation which held him steady all through his deep trial. "Truly God is good to Israel, even to such as are of a clean heart", v. 1. But as he compared the prosperity of the wicked with the suffering of the godly, he was perplexed and upset, vv. 2-3. When he considers this problem, his faith is severely shaken. The wicked seem to have no fear of death, v. 4. They get away with violence, corruption and oppression, vv. 6-8. They are proud and defy Almighty God and nothing seems to happen. Their business prospers, and their riches increase, vv. 9-12. In contrast the people of God suffer, and the "waters of a full cup are wrung out to them", v. 10. Not only in ancient times, but in our own day, how often this has happened! Herod feasting in his palace, and John in the dungeon underneath it, finally being executed at the whim of a wicked woman, Mark 6. 20-29. What must be the feelings of godly people in the prisons and labour camps of Siberia? In verse 15 Asaph will not speak while under this deep cloud of depression, in case he would cause other saints to stumble. It might lead them into the same dark valley in which he found himself.

But he finds the solution to his problem in verse 17. He goes into the sanctuary, and in God's presence he sees the end of the ungodly. They have their "heaven" in this life. In God's own time conditions will be reversed. A day of recompense and righteous judgment lies ahead. The saint who cries: "How long, O Lord?", will have an answer, Rev. 6. 10.

His faith and his serenity are recovered in the sanctuary, and at the end his response to his opening, "God is good", v. 1, is "it is good for me to draw near to God: I have put my trust in the Lord God, that I may declare all thy works".

Aug. 19th

READING : **Psalm 78. 1-20, 59-72**

A CRISIS IN ISRAEL'S HISTORY

APART FROM Psalm 119, Psalm 78 is the longest in the collection, and is one of the most important. It gives an historical outline of the history of Israel covering many centuries. The introduction, vv. 1-8, speaks of four generations, and the responsibility of the fathers to teach these truths to their children and grandchildren, cf. 2 Tim. 2. 2.

In Psa. 78. 9-11 we are reminded of the battle recorded in 1 Samuel 4, when the ark was captured by the Philistines. It was a dark period in their history, which resulted from the failure of Eli the high priest and the disgraceful conduct of his two sons Hophni and Phinehas, 1 Sam. 2. 12-17. Then follows the deliverance of Israel from Egypt, and the miracles associated with it, Psa. 78. 12-14. This summarizes the book of Exodus. It is followed by the wilderness experiences recorded in the book of Numbers: the smitten rock, v. 20, the manna, v. 24, and the quails, v. 27. The whole sad story of rebellion and murmuring is repeated again and again. Three times we find the words "turned back", vv. 9, 41, 57, and the wrath and anger of God is mentioned ten times. The climax is "So he forsook the tabernacle of Shiloh, the tent which he placed among men . . . Moreover he refused the tabernacle of Joseph, and chose not the tribe of Ephraim: but chose the tribe of Judah, the mount Zion which he loved. He chose David also his servant, and took him from the sheepfolds . . . to feed Jacob his people", vv. 60, 67f, 70f. To trace all the details of this great change from Ephraim to Judah, and from the tabernacle at Shiloh to mount Zion, one would need to read the book of Judges, parts of Joshua, and the early chapters of 1 Samuel. There we get the historical account, but in the psalm the inner and spiritual reasons for the change.

As we consider the tragic history of Israel, the lessons are applied to us in two passages in the New Testament. In 1 Corinthians 10. 1-10 we are warned against committing the same sins, and told that "all these things happened unto them for ensamples, and they are written for our admonition", v. 11. Again, Hebrews 3-4 remind us of the sad fate of a whole generation who died and left their bones in the wilderness, 3. 17. These are red lights of warning to us today.

Aug. 20th

READING : **Psalm 80. 1-19**

THE SHEPHERD OF ISRAEL

AFTER the sad story of Israel's history, and the change of the centre of gathering from Shiloh to Zion recorded in Psalm 78, Asaph gives himself to prayer, Psa. 80. Three times he uses the words: "Turn us again, O God . . . cause thy face to shine; and we shall be saved", vv. 3, 7, 19. In Psalm 78, three times Israel has turned back, vv. 9, 41, 57. They were heading in the wrong direction. Notice the increase in intensity in Asaph's prayer. First "O God", v. 3; then "O God of hosts", v. 14; finally "O Lord God of hosts", v. 19. He asks God to return, v. 14. When the backslider returns, then God returns! His face does not shine while the sinner continues on his wicked way.

There are four lovely pictures of Christ in the psalm:

(1) The Shepherd of Israel, v. 1.
(2) The Lord of the vineyard, called "the branch", v. 15.
(3) The Man of thy right hand, v. 17.
(4) The Son of man made strong for Thyself, v. 17.

In Psalm 77. 20 the people of Israel at the Exodus are led forth "like a flock" by a great shepherd, Moses; at the end of Psalm 78 they are fed and guided by another great shepherd, David; but at the end of Psalm 79, and at the beginning of Psalm 80, they are under the care and rule of the greatest shepherd of all, our blessed Lord Himself.

The vine is introduced in verses 8-16. It is brought out of Egypt, and planted in the land, vv. 8-10; Isa. 5; Jer. 2. 21. Its boughs were unto the sea (Mediterranean), and its branches unto the river (Euphrates), v. 11, the boundaries of the land as promised to Joshua, Josh. 1. 4. Much is said about boughs and branches, but the principal reason for which they exist, fruit, is not mentioned. Instead of grapes there were wild grapes, Isa. 5. 2. The boar out of the wood (Assyria and Babylon) destroyed and devoured it, Psa. 80. 12-13. In verses 11 and 15 there is a transition from boughs and branches (plural) to the Branch (singular — lit.="Son", as Gen. 49. 22 R.V. marg.) The Branch is a title of the Messiah, our Lord Himself, see Isa. 4. 2; Zech. 3. 8; 6. 12. He is the true vine, replacing the degenerate vine, John 15. 1. He is also the Man of God's right hand, and the Son of man, Psa. 80. 17. All the hopes of Israel, and of the church, are centred in Him.

Aug. 21st

READING : **Psalm 84. 1-12**

LONGING FOR GOD AND HIS HOUSE

THE PSALM is by or for the sons of Korah. There seems to be a reference in verse 10 to the rebellion of Korah, Dathan and Abiram recorded in Numbers 16. Here the sons of Korah, spared by divine grace, say they would rather be doorkeepers in the house of God than to dwell in the tents of wickedness, cf. Num. 16. 27. The psalm appears to have been written at a time when the temple and its services were established, and pilgrimage thereto was a part of the national life. It expresses the longing of the pilgrim in a distant part of the land, as he thinks of the joy of going up to worship in the temple at the yearly feasts. The psalm is in three parts:

(1) *The homesick vision of the house of God*, vv. 1-4. His longing is reminiscent of 42. 1-2. His whole being cries out, not only for the material place, but for God Himself. He uses the illustration of the sparrow and the swallow. One has a house, and the other a nest, in the temple precincts. One is always there, rain or shine. The other is migratory, and when the cold winter blasts come, it takes off for sunnier climes. He pronounces a benediction on those that dwell in the house, like the priest and the Levite. They are continually occupied with the ministry of praise.

(2) *He is on his way to Jerusalem and the temple*, vv. 5-8. His strength for the pathway is from God Himself, v. 5. Notice the R.V. change "in whose heart are the highways to Zion", v. 5b. He has been over this way before. He knows the road. He has a heavenly guide. The map is engraved on his mind and heart. But he has to pass through the deep valley of Baca. In the dry season it is parched and dry, but he knows where to find water in the oasis spring. Then the early rain comes, and the pools are full, v. 6. The pilgrim bands increase as they get nearer to their destination, v. 7.

(3) *He arrives at the place of desire and worship*, vv. 9-12. After the long weary journey the pilgrim has finally arrived, and sees the face of God's anointed high priest. For us today, we have our Great High Priest, the risen glorified Son of God. "The Lord will give grace and glory", grace for the way, and glory at the end. On the way, the Lord is a sun to shine upon us, and a shield to protect us.

Aug. 22nd

READING : **Psalm 89. 1-37**

THE DAVIDIC COVENANT

THE AUTHOR of the psalm is Ethan the Ezrahite. His other name was Jeduthan, 1 Chron. 25; 16. 41-42. He was one of Solomon's wisest counsellors, 1 Kings 4. 31. He must have known what God said to Solomon about his sin and idolatry, and how the kingdom would be taken from his son, 1 Kings 11. 9-13. This throws light on his impassioned appeal to Jehovah in the latter part of the psalm, vv. 38-51.

The psalm is in two main parts: (1) The Davidic covenant, based on God's faithfulness, vv. 1-37; and (2) Its present failure, but future fulfilment, vv. 38-52.

The covenants which God made with His people is one of the major themes of Scripture. Four are related to Israel alone: the covenant made with Abraham, Gen. 15, a seed and a land; the covenant made at Sinai, Exod. 19. 25, the law; the Levitical-Phinehas covenant with its priestly privileges and responsibilities, to be given perfect expression in a future temple, e.g. Ezek. 40-45; the covenant made to David was the promise of a kingdom, a dynasty, and a throne given to him and his posterity in perpetuity, 2 Sam. 7. 8-17.

Psalm 89 is occupied principally with the covenant made to David. In verses 3-4 it is mentioned concisely, but in verses 19-37 it is expanded and expounded. It is based on two of God's attributes: His faithfulness and His loving kindness. Each of these attributes is mentioned seven times. Both are great covenant context words and take us back over the past and look forward into the future. In verses 27-29 there is a very precious reference to the Messiah who comes from David's line: "Also I will make him my firstborn, higher than the kings of the earth". The "firstborn" is a title that can refer only to Christ. Paul uses it in relation to creation, Col. 1. 15, and resurrection, v. 18. It is used again as one of the great titles of the risen Christ, Rev. 1. 5.

There is a warning in verses 31-33 concerning David's seed. History records failure all along the line, and chastisement has been administered, but the covenant stands and is irrevocable, vv. 34-37. In these exciting days of the 20th century we see the groundwork being laid for the fulfilment of God's purpose in relation to David's throne, Son and sceptre.

Aug. 23rd

READING : **Psalms 90. 1 to 91. 16**

WILDERNESS DEFEAT AND TRIUMPH

These two psalms form the introduction to the fourth book of psalms. The title of Psalm 90 is "A Prayer of Moses the man of God". The two psalms cover the history of the nation of Israel in their desert wanderings, recorded in the book of Numbers. They are in sharp contrast to each other. Psalm 90 tells of the 600,000 men who died in the desert on account of unbelief. Psalm 91 describes the experience of Caleb and Joshua, the two survivors who lived to enter the promised land. Both psalms commence with God as the dwelling place of His people. Psalm 90 ends with a sevenfold prayer; Psalm 91 ends with a sevenfold promise. One is full of dark pessimism; the other is replete with encouragement and faith.

The book of Numbers has been called "The story of a lost generation". Moses was the emancipator and leader of the people, and in this prayer he summarizes the sad story. "Thou carriest them away as with a flood", 90.5. After the worship of the golden calf about 3000 died, Exod. 32. 28; at the Korah rebellion 14,700, Num. 16. 49; at Baal Peor 24,000, Num. 25. 9. "So teach us to number our days, that we may apply our hearts unto wisdom", 90. 12. Oh! that "the beauty of the Lord our God (might) be upon us", v. 17.

What a contrast in Psalm 91! "He that dwelleth in the secret place of the most High shall abide under the shadow of the Almighty", v. 1. There is a *fourfold protection*, in the four names for God: El Elyon, Shaddai, Jehovah, Elohim, vv. 1-2. A *fourfold provision:* a refuge, a fortress, under His wings, a soldier's shield and buckler, vv. 2-4. A *fourfold peril:* the enemy, v. 5; sickness, v. 6; wild beasts, v. 13; Satan, vv. 11-12. This is the passage which Satan used at the temptation of our Lord in the wilderness. But he left something vital out, "to keep thee in all thy ways". Then he added "at any time" to the Word. Satan is never more dangerous than when he is taking away from or adding to the Scriptures.

The last three verses give a sevenfold promise. It is the answer to the sevenfold prayer of 90. 12-17. They were fulfilled in the lives of Joshua and Caleb, and could be experienced in our lives too. Set your love upon Him, you that know His name. Call upon Him; His promises are for you.

Aug. 24th

READING : **Psalm 102. 1-28**

THE UNCHANGEABLE ONE

THIS PSALM is quoted and applied to the Lord Jesus in Hebrews 1. 10-12. In first part of the psalm, we see the rejected and lonely Man of Sorrows, vv. 1-24. In the latter part of the Psalm we see the unchanging Eternal God, and the answer of the Almighty God to the Eternal Son, vv. 25-28.

There are three main subjects in His prayer:

(i) *His Lament*. It is a dialogue between the Father and the Son. It reminds us of the "strong crying and tears" of Gethsemane, Heb. 5. 7-8. The words "I am" occur five times in Psa. 102. 1-11.

(ii) *His Loneliness*. He is like the pelican in the wilderness, the owl of the desert, and the sparrow alone on the housetop, v. 6f. We see this *in His homelife*. He had four brothers, and also sisters, Mark 6. 3. But John 7. 5 tells us: "For neither did his brethren believe in him". Apparently it was only after His resurrection that they came to have saving faith, Acts 1. 14. He was lonely *in His prayer life*. He often went to the desert to pray, Mark 1. 35. On at least two occasions He spent a whole night in prayer alone, Matt. 14. 23; Luke 6. 12. In Gethsemane He and the disciples were divided into three groups. First eight disciples, then Peter, James and John. But He went further, and kneeled down and prayed, Luke 22. 41. He was alone *in His agony*. Finally, on the cross he cried, "My God, why hast thou forsaken me?". He was alone *in His death*.

(iii) *His Life*. Cut short in the midst of His days, v. 24; Dan. 9. 26; Isa. 53. 8. Instead of the normal lifespan of 70 years, Psa. 90. 10, He was "cut off" at 33 years of age.

The answer of Almighty God, vv. 25-28. There is a tremendous contrast between the opening, and the closing verses of the psalm. The lonely Man is now the glorified Lord of the universe, the Unchanging One. The Bible declares that the earth as we see it today, and which seems so permanent, is like an old and tattered garment that one day will be discarded. It is becoming more and more ragged and threadbare. It will pass away, and give place to a new heavens and a new earth. But speaking to the Messiah He says: "Thou art the same". The present need of the churches is met by Jesus Christ, the same yesterday, today and forever!

Aug. 25th

READING : **Psalm 103. 1-22**

THE FATHER AND HIS CHILDREN

THE SYRIAC version suggests that Psalm 103 was written in David's old age, after his experience of sin and forgiveness. David was a man of prayer, but there is not a word of prayer in the psalm, all is praise and worship. It is in three parts:
 (1) A Solo, vv. 1-5. The individual. "Bless the Lord".
 (2) A Chorus, vv. 6-18. Others join in. Note pronouns.
 (3) The Symphony, vv. 19-22. Angels, creation.

The Solo, vv. 1-5. David mentions five reasons for praise: Forgiveness. He enjoyed this as recorded in Psa. 32. 1, 5. Healing. Note its inclusiveness, spirit, mind, and body, v. 3. Redemption. Daily preservation from evil and Satan, v. 4. A crown of loving kindness lined with tenderness, v. 4. Renewal. His youth renewed like the eagle's, v. 5; Deut. 32. 11. "David selects a few of the choicest pearls from the casket of divine love, threads them on the string of memory, and hangs them round the neck of gratitude", Spurgeon.

The Chorus, vv. 6-18. God's mercy is based on righteousness and love. There are five illustrations of God's love to man.

The Astronomy of love, v. 11. As heaven is high above earth.

The Geography of love, v. 12. As far as east is from west.

The Paternity of love, v. 13. As a father pities his children.

The Anatomy of love, v. 14. He knows our frame.

The Eternity of love, v. 17. From everlasting to everlasting.

Jehovah, the covenant keeping God is mentioned here four times, vv. 6, 8, 13, 17. The section begins with the God of all space and ends with the God of all time. All these blessings are for them that fear Him, vv. 11, 13, 17.

The Symphony, vv. 19-22. The symphony begins with God's throne in heaven, His overall kingdom, His angels, the heavenly hosts, His ministers that do His pleasure, then it is climaxed by all nature. It reminds us of the paean of praise in Revelation 5. 13 "And every creature which is in heaven, and on earth, and under the earth, and such as are in the sea . . . heard I saying, Blessing, and honour, and glory, and power, be unto him that sitteth upon the throne, and unto the Lamb for ever and ever". The whole psalm emphasises the truth that to know God is to worship Him. "Bless the Lord, O my soul".

Aug. 26th

READING : **Psalm 107. 1-43**

FOUR PICTURES OF SALVATION

THE PSALM outlines four graphic illustrations of the gospel.
A traveller lost in a desert, vv. 4-9.
A prisoner shackled in a dungeon, vv. 10-16.
A sick man on a death-bed, vv. 17-22.
A mariner in a storm, vv. 23-32.
In each case there is a desperate condition, then a cry for help, followed by a glorious deliverance.

(1) *A traveller lost in a desert*, vv. 4-9. Every continent has a desert with either shifting sand or blinding snow, with paths wiped out, and a mirage that leads to nowhere. It is a terrible thing to be lost with a guide that is himself lost! This world is like that. Men are lost, Luke 15; 2 Cor. 4. 3. When all hope is gone, then a cry leads to deliverance. He is led forth by a right way to a city, Psa. 107. 7; John 14. 5f; Heb. 11. 10.

(2) *A prisoner shackled in a dungeon*, vv. 10-16. Think of the prison population of any large city, its maximum security area, solitary confinement, and in some cases its death row. Man is a prisoner of sin and Satan, condemned already, and waiting for the sentence to be carried out, John 3. 18. Many are shackled by drugs, drink and depravity. But when there is the cry of repentance and faith, the chains are broken, and the captive is freed, Psa. 107. 14.

(3) *A sick man on a death-bed*, vv. 17-22. The sick man here is called a fool, v. 17. Sickness is often caused by self-indulgence, a strong body ruined by sin. Sin is called a disease, and the sinner described as sick, Isa. 1. 4-6; Job 33. 19-24. When the cry of distress goes up, the Good Physician draws near and deliverance comes.

(4) *A mariner in a storm*, vv. 23-32. There are few things more frightening than the wind and waves in a hurricane! Life is like a voyage at sea, bound for the great haven of eternity. In the storms and cyclones of life, man needs a compass, a pilot, and an anchor of the soul, Heb. 6. 19. There is One who is Master of wind and wave, and who can say to the storm, "Peace, be still", and there can be a great calm, Mark 4. 39.

The appendix, vv. 33-43, applies the lesson in a practical way, "Whoso is wise, and will observe these things, even they shall understand the lovingkindness of the Lord", v. 43.

Aug. 27th

READING : **Psalm 110. 1-7**

THE MELCHIZEDEK PRIEST-KING

PSALM 110 is quoted 14 times in the New Testament, more frequently than any other Old Testament passage, and in each case is applied to the Lord Jesus Christ. We have also the authority of our Lord Himself, who said it was written by David under the inspiration of the Holy Spirit, Matt. 22. 41-46. His statement emphasized two points: first, that David was the author of the psalm; and second, that David, inspired by the Holy Spirit, called his Son his Lord. The Pharisees got the point, and made no attempt to dispute it.

The psalm gives three majestic pictures of Christ, ending with a delightful appendix, v. 7.

(1) Priest exalted to God's right hand, v. 1. Expectant.
(2) King-priest to rule, vv. 2-4. Resplendent.
(3) Judge dealing with his enemies, vv. 5-6. Triumphant.
(4) The appendix. The drink, and the uplifted head, v. 7.

There is the magnificent statement of His deity at the beginning, v. 1, and an exquisite touch of His humanity at the end, v. 7.

The command in verse 1 of the psalm "Sit thou" covers the high priestly work of Christ at God's right hand today, but it continues until His enemies are put under His feet and made His footstool. That would extend to the rapture, the tribulation period, and His appearing in glory. Then God gives the second command: "Rule thou in the midst of thine enemies", v. 2. This would refer to the millennial reign of Christ, which will last for 1000 years, Rev. 20. 1-6. At that time He will be manifested as the King-Priest after the order of Melchizedek.

"Thy people are freewill offerings in the day of thy power", v. 3 R.V. marg. This statement would indicate a Jewish remnant which will welcome Him when He comes to reign. At His first advent "He came unto his own, and his own received him not", John 1. 11. But when He comes in glory, a remnant of Israel, divinely illuminated, will receive Him, Zech. 12. 10-14; 13. 1. Verses 5-6 could refer to His victory at the battle of Armageddon, Rev. 19. 17-21; cf. Ezek. 38-39.

The uplifted head of the conquering Christ is in contrast to the wounded head of the arch-enemy, v. 6f; cf. Gen. 3. 15.

Today is your opportunity to offer yourself willingly to Him.

Aug. 28th

READING : Psalm 118. 1-29

THE CONCLUSION OF THE HALLEL

This is the final messianic psalm. It outlines the history of anti-Semitic persecution throughout the ages, ending with the coming of the Messiah to set up His kingdom.

It is also the final song of the Egyptian Hallel, celebrating the deliverance of Israel from Egypt, Psa. 114. 1. The Hallel consists of six Psalms, 113-118. They were sung at the three yearly feasts, Passover, Pentecost and Tabernacles. It is very likely that this psalm was the hymn sung by our Lord and His disciples after the institution of the Lord's supper.

The psalm must have been very much in the Saviour's mind in the last week of His public ministry. It is referred to four times in Matthew's Gospel, 21. 9, 15; 21. 42; 23. 39. It is also referred to by Peter, Acts 4. 11; 1 Pet. 2. 7, and by Paul, Eph. 2. 20.

Verses 5-18 give an outline of Israel's sufferings throughout the centuries, climaxed by the great tribulation, Matt. 24. 21. Four times the words "All nations (or "they") compassed me about" appear, vv. 10-12. The stage is being set today for this ultimate encirclement of the nation, but it will result in the total defeat of the forces of evil, Rev. 19. 11-21.

The last paragraph of the psalm, vv. 19-29, has been called "a precious messianic jewel". There are seven items:

The opened gates of the city, and the temple, vv. 19-21.
The rejected stone, made the head of the corner, vv. 22-23.
The day which the Lord hath made, v. 24; cf. Zech. 13. 1.
Blessed be He that cometh in the name of the Lord, v. 26.
National conversion. The great illumination, v. 27.
The festal sacrifice, v. 27. The Feast of Tabernacles.
The final benediction, vv. 28-29.

If it is true, as seems most likely, that this was the hymn sung in the upper room at the celebration of the passover, and the institution of the Lord's supper, what a solemn light it throws on the thoughts in the mind of our Lord that night as He went out to Gethsemane and the cross. He was truly the festal sacrificial Lamb, bound to the horns of the altar, not with the cruel nails but with the cords of love. All the hopes of Israel, and of the people of God of every age, are firmly based on that sacrifice. Hosanna! Save now!

Aug. 29th

READING : Psalm 119. 1-24

THE WORD OF GOD AND THE SAINT'S WALK

PSALM 119 is the longest in the book, and is one of the most important. It is all about the Word of God, and its effect on the believer's life and walk. Its key verse could be: "Wherewithal shall a young man cleanse his way?, v. 9.

The psalm is an alphabetic acrostic. The Hebrew alphabet has 22 letters, and the psalm has 22 stanzas with a different letter of the Hebrew alphabet at the head of each one. Each stanza has 8 lines, and each line begins with the same letter. Each letter has a pictorial meaning. For example: Aleph means an ox, Beth a house, and Gimel a camel.

Ten terms are used in the psalm to describe the Word: law, testimonies, ways, precepts, statutes, commandments, judgments, word, sayings, truth. These terms are not synonyms, but, like the colours in the rainbow, give various aspects of the power and authority of the Word of God. In the New Testament, Christ is the Alpha and Omega, the first and last letters of the Greek alphabet; but in Psalm 119 He is the Aleph and the Taw of the Old Testament. He is the living Word, and the written Word is all about Him.

Stanza One: Aleph — the ox. The ox is the clean sacrificial animal with the divided hoof. This is the keynote of this section, vv. 1-8. It emphasizes the way, and the walk, of the believer, vv. 1, 3, 5. The Moravian motto shows an ox standing between a plough and an altar with the caption, "Ready for either!" Are you ready for patient, sacrificial service?

Stanza Two: Beth — a house. The word is seen in Bethel, Bethlehem, Bethany, etc. After the work and obedience of the patient ox, we are introduced to the house. The house suggests fellowship and order. At the door stands a young man with the question, How can I cleanse my way? Here is a clean house and holiness becomes it, 93. 5. The holiness that is required in the house is gained through the Word, v. 9.

Stanza Three. Gimel — a camel. The camel is a picture of the desert and pilgrimage, Gen. 24. 61. The psalmist exclaims: "I am a stranger in the earth", v. 19; 1 Pet. 2. 11. On the journey of life, do I make God's Word the "men of my counsel"?, v. 24 marg.

Aug. 30th

READING : **Psalms 120. 1 to 122. 9**

PERSECUTION, PRESERVATION AND PEACE

PSALMS 120-134 form a group of fifteen psalms, each headed "A Song of degrees", or, as in the R.V., "A Song of Ascents". They have been applied in different ways. Some think that the tribes going up to Jerusalem sang them on their way to the annual feasts. Others believe that they were used when Israel returned from their captivity in Babylon, Psa. 126. 1. They seem to be arranged in groups of three. In each group there is a rising movement. The first begins at a distance; the second marks the road and its difficulties; the third generally ends in Zion, or the house of God.

The first, Psalms 120, 121, 122, deals with their national life.

The second, Psalms 123, 124, 125, their social life.

The third, Psalms 126, 127, 128, their family life.

The fourth, Psalms 129, 130, 131, their devotional life.

The fifth, Psalms 132, 133, 134, their spiritual life.

Psalm 120. The subject of this psalm is *persecution*. It opens with a cry of distress, v. 1. The source of the trouble is lying lips, and a deceitful tongue, v. 2. Two names are mentioned from which the persecution comes, Mesech and Kedar, v. 5. The first, Mesech, is found in Genesis 10. 2. He is the progenitor of a race linked with Tubal, Magog, and other northern nations. Broadly speaking it could refer to Russia, Ezek. 27. 13; 38-39. Kedar was a son of Ishmael, Gen. 25. 13; cf. Jer. 49. 28-29. These two, Russia and the Arab world, are Israel's typical enemies. How graphic, and up to date are the words "I am for peace: but when I speak, they are for war".

Psalm 121. The theme here is *preservation*. The word "keepeth", or "keeper", is used six times, vv. 3, 4, 5, 7, 8 ("preserve" is the same Heb. word). The psalmist looks not to the hills for help, but to the Lord Himself, vv. 1-2. Note R.V. and marg. There are five areas of preservation: his foot, v. 3; from sunstroke and moonstroke, v. 6; from all evil, v. 7; his soul, v. 7; from the hazards of travel, v. 8.

Psalm 122. Whereas in Psalm 120, there is distress, persecution and war, here it is *peace* at last. Seven things are mentioned about Jerusalem, the city of peace: its house, v. 1, gates, v. 2, walls, v. 7, thrones, v. 5, palaces, v. 7, testimony, v. 4, and *peace*, vv. 6, 7, 8.

Aug. 31st
READING : Psalms 126. 1 to 128. 6
IDEAL FAMILY LIFE

THESE THREE psalms have as their background the return of Israel from their captivity in Babylon. The historical record is in Ezra and Nehemiah.

Psalm 126. Israel had been under God's hand of discipline for a determined period of 70 years, Dan. 9. 2; Jer. 25. 11, 12. The Psalm describes their feelings when deliverance came, vv. 1-2a. It was like a dream. Then we have the reaction of the nations: "The Lord hath done great things for them", and Israel's reply: "The Lord hath done great things for us; whereof we are glad," vv. 2-3. Then, their prayer, and the sowing and reaping in a land that had been abandoned for two long generations, vv. 4-6.

Psalm 127. This is the central psalm in the "Songs of degrees". It is "for Solomon". It was originally directed to the man who wrote the book of Proverbs. Whilst it is true that the returned exiles were engaged in rebuilding the temple, yet verses 2-3 seem to refer to the building of a home. The house, the city, the watchman, the bread of sorrows, the sleepless nights, all point to this. "Except the Lord build the house, they labour in vain that build it", v. 1. The building of a godly home is most important. The Bible lays down the principles. Marriage in the Lord, 1 Cor. 7. 39, is a lifetime commitment, v. 39a. There is to be no unequal yoke, 2 Cor. 6. 14. It is based on mutual love and respect, Eph. 5. 22-25. Children born into such a home are the fruit and joy of the parents, Psa. 127. 3-5.

Psalm 128. Psalm 127 is the home in relation to the city. Psalm 128 is a rural home. Four parties are mentioned, the husband, wife, children and grandchildren. The husband (1) fears the Lord, v. 4, (2) walks in His ways, v. 1, (3) labours with his hands, v. 2, and (4) happiness is the result, v. 2. The Bible has much to say about the husband in the home. He is the head, and God will hold him responsible for leadership, and kindly discipline in the home, Eph. 5. 23; 6. 4. If the husband is the head, his wife is the heart. She is like a fruitful vine, and the children like olive plants around the table, v. 3. The godly home is God's masterpiece, and is a most attractive and pleasant place, built upon the foundation of the Word. The greatest joy is to see one's children walk in truth, v. 6.

Sept. 1st

READING: **Psalms 132. 1 to 134. 3**

UNITY AND SERVICE IN THE HOUSE OF GOD

THESE three psalms form the conclusion to the Songs of degrees. They outline the spiritual principles by which blessing can be granted by God to His people in any age.

Psalm 132. The psalm opens with a solemn vow, made by David in his early life, concerning the ark of God. It had lain in obscurity for many years since it was captured by the Philistines, 1 Sam. 4. 22, then, later, returned by them to Kirjath-jearim, 1 Sam. 7. 1-2. Here it remained for many years. David had heard about it at Ephratah (Bethlehem), probably from his parents, and vowed that he would never build his own house until he had found a place for the ark, vv. 3-5. He found it at the "fields of the wood" (Kirjath-jearim), v. 6. The psalm was written when David brought it to Mt. Zion, 2 Sam. 6. Psalms 24, 68 and 105 also are associated with this period. The ark of God symbolized the presence of God among His people. It is a picture of Christ, as the gathering centre.

Psalm 133. Not only was the ark brought to Jerusalem, but all the 12 tribes were united under David, first at Hebron, then at the new centre, Jerusalem, 2 Sam. 5. 1-10. This beautiful psalm celebrates that unity. Two illustrations are used to describe it. It is like the oil of priestly consecration poured on the head of Aaron the high priest, which ran down from his head to his beard, and on to the collar of his robe, Exod. 30. 23-25, 30. It would thus fall in fragrance near the two onyx stones graven with the names of the 12 tribes of Israel, which were upon the shoulders of the ephod, Exod. 28. 9-12. That fragrant oil united the head, and the body. Then it is like the dew of Hermon which is the highest peak in Israel, with its white crown of snow against an azure sky, acting like an air conditioner in the hot season. The night breezes from the Mediterranean, blowing over it, are distilled, as also over the bare limestone hills of Zion in the south, and the silent dew refreshes every blade and petal and flower. The oil suggests the fragrance of unity, and the dew its freshness. It is "there (that) the Lord commanded the blessing, even life for everyone".

Psalm 134. The Levites in their nightly service in the house of the Lord, pronounce the benediction, "The Lord . . . bless thee out of Zion", to conclude these lovely "Songs of Ascents".

Sept. 2nd

READING : **Psalms 146. 1-10; 150. 1-6**

THE HALLELUJAH CHORUS

THE LAST five psalms each begin and end with the word Hallelujah, translated here "Praise the Lord". The Psalter begins with "Blessed", Psa. 1. 1, and ends with "Hallelujah", Psa. 150. 1. Each of these last five psalms increases in praise and joy, until the sublime finale in Psalm 150. All creation, and the whole universe, are called upon to praise the Creator, Sustainer and Redeemer of every living and inanimate thing!

Psalm 146 commences with the *individual:* "Praise the Lord, O my soul . . . I will sing praises unto my God while I have any being", vv. 1-2. Specifically, he mentions the oppressed, the hungry, the prisoner, the blind, the bowed down, the righteous, the stranger, the fatherless and the widow. All have every right to praise the Lord.

Psalm 147 treats *Jerusalem and the outcasts of Israel.* The Lord builds up Jerusalem and He gathers together Israel, v. 2. God has glorious purposes of grace for Israel. The psalmist links the broken heart, v. 3, with the stars v. 4. The Lord is vitally interested in both. He notices the beast in the forest, and the young ravens in the nest crying for food, v. 9.

Psalm 148 commences with the *heavens*, the angels and the heavenly hosts, vv. 1-2. Then, in successive steps, the solar system, and the clouds, vv. 4-5, the mountains and hills, the trees, the beasts, creeping things and flying fowl, vv. 9-10, and mankind, from kings and princes to old men and children, vv. 11-12, are all exhorted to praise the Lord.

Psalm 149 opens with a new song to be sung in the *congregation of the saints*. Israel and the children of Zion have a special right to be joyful, for "the Lord taketh pleasure in his people; he will beautify the meek with salvation", v. 4. They have the high praises of God in their mouth, and a two-edged sword in their hand, v. 6. When the righteous judgment of God is meted out to their enemies, again they praise the Lord.

Psalm 150. The volume of praise has increased in intensity until, in Psalm 150, the word "praise" occurs 13 times. In the N.T. the word "hallelujah" only occurs in Revelation 19. 1-6. There it is used four times as a fitting introduction to the marriage of the Lamb, v. 7. The last occurrence of this great word is: "Alleluia: for the Lord God omnipotent reigneth".

Introducing Proverbs

THIS IS the first book in the Bible prefaced by the name of the author. Solomon sought wisdom more than any other gift, cf. 2 Chron. 1. 10-12, and God honoured his request by granting him a larger measure of it than was enjoyed by any of his contemporaries. To communicate a portion of what he had received was the aim of his collection.

The theme, then, is wisdom. It takes for granted God's own unerring wisdom, and seeks to instruct man what His wisdom really is. The wisdom in this book is not human sagacity, or cleverness, or ability, but the application, to the smallest details of human life, of the wisdom that built the heavens and the earth, and maintains them in being. The perfectly wise man is the one who, in his whole being, lives and thinks and acts in right relationship to the All-Wise God. So the book contrasts the fear of Jehovah, and the folly of self-will. The former is declared to be the foundation of wisdom, and the latter is denounced as the cause of suffering and death.

Here God has condescended to become our Teacher on the practical affairs belonging to all the relations of life. Proverbs becomes for practical ethics what the Psalms is for devotion. Whereas the Psalms warms our hearts towards God in holy affection, Proverbs teaches us, apart from the duty of a right relationship to God, how to live before men prudently, honestly and discreetly, demonstrating therein a love to our neighbour. The Lord has clothed His instruction in this striking and compressed method of the proverb. The proverb is a short sentence, conveying some moral truth or practical lesson in a concise, pointed form. These proverbs are, not so much popular sayings, as the distillation of the wisdom of those who knew the law of God, and were applying its principles to the whole of life. There are, also, many exhortations to prudence and virtue, and there are eulogies on true wisdom, the first nine chapters being formed primarily of these latter. There is ample evidence that our Lord loved this book for there are echoes of its language in His teaching. Compare, e.g., teaching regarding love for the chief seats, Prov. 25. 6, 7; Luke 14. 8-11, and wise and foolish housebuilders, Prov. 14. 11; Matt. 7. 24-27.

Sept. 3rd

READING : **Proverbs 1. 1-7**

THE FEAR OF THE LORD

VERSE 7 stands out as the keynote of the book, and of the subject of which it treats. It is found elsewhere in the Old Testament in 9. 10, in Psalm 111. 10 at the end of a choral chant, and in Job 28. 28 after a poetic passage of great beauty. The expression "the fear of the Lord" occurs a further thirteen times in Proverbs and plays a prominent part in the Old Testament. "Fear" here is not slavish dread, the fear that "hath torment", 1 John 4. 18, but childlike reverence, a worshipping submission. That fear or reverence is the prerequisite of all religious truth. "The Lord" is "Jehovah", the Self Existent One who has revealed Himself by name as "I am that I am", Exod. 3. 13-15. The "beginning" is the foundation, the first and controlling principle, the principal part. Therefore, in all knowledge, all understanding of life and its interpretation, the fear of the Lord is the principal thing, apart from which we grope in darkness and miss the way. Without the knowledge and fear of the Lord, the One Triune God, the wisdom which affords guidance for the whole of life cannot begin to be acquired. The beginning of wisdom is not to be found in keen insight, nor wide experience, nor the learning of the schools, but in the spirit of reverence and awe.

There can be no real attainment of wisdom or knowledge which does not start with a recognition of God. Our own understanding is untrustworthy; cf. 3. 5. After all, our ways are not His ways, neither are our thoughts His thoughts, Isa. 55. 8. The only true basis of understanding in this world is to have the knowledge of God. For example, if the universe, of which we form a part, is a thought of the Divine mind, a work of the Divine hand, a scene of the Divine operations in which God is realizing a vast spiritual purpose, it is clear that no attempt to understand the universe can be successful which leaves God out. And He is the God who has revealed Himself. To meet man's need, God must be the God who reveals Himself. He did so to Moses in the desert, but He has done so supremely, and finally, in the Person of His Son concerning whom it is said, "No man hath seen God at any time; the only begotten Son . . . he hath declared him", John 1. 18.

Sept. 4th

READING : Proverbs 3. 1-10

TRUST

THE HEART of this passage is found in verses 5 and 6, but the childlike trust to be seen there is in fact rooted in sound teaching in verses 1-4, and expressed by bold obedience, e.g. v. 9. There are three negative commands here. We are told to *"forget not"*, v. 1. Sometimes forgetfulness has serious consequences. We easily forget what we only hear; we remember best what we turn into deeds. We are exhorted to *"lean not"* in verse 5. We are to depend only on God, not upon ourselves. *"Be not wise"* is the warning of verse 7. To fear the Lord means to recognize His authority, and to obey His commands. To be wise in our own eyes means to act independently of God.

Now let us consider the heart of the passage, vv. 5, 6. The Object before us is the Lord, and we are to trust in Him. There are other repositories of trust referred to in Proverbs. We are told that the man who trusts in his own riches shall fall, 11. 28; that the man who trusts in his own heart is a fool, 28. 26, for the "heart is deceitful above all things, and desperately wicked", Jer. 17. 9. But the man who trusts in the Lord, "happy is he", 16. 20. What is meant by "trust"? It is the characteristic Old Testament word for "faith". The English word "faith" only occurs twice in the Old Testament, Deut. 32. 20; Hab. 2. 4, and in both cases means "faithfulness". The word "trust" occurs 152 times, and is used to render Hebrew words signifying *refuge*, or *to take refuge*, Isa. 30. 3; Ruth 2. 12; Psa. 2. 12; *to lean on*, or *to have confidence in another*, Psa. 28. 7; Prov. 11. 28; *to believe*, Job 4. 18; Micah 7. 5; Gen. 15. 6; Psa. 106. 12; *to devolve on*, Psa. 22. 8; and *to stay oneself upon*, Job 35. 14. The teaching of trust is to be complete, both in degree, and in extent: "with *all* thine heart" and "In *all* thy ways". At the same time we are not "to rely on" our own understanding. Our own understanding is not adequate. We are to acknowledge Him by seeking His wise aid, cf. 16. 3; Psa. 37. 5; Jer. 9. 23, 24, and the promise is secure — He shall direct.

Those paths will not be found in the counsels of the ungodly, Psa. 1. 1, but God will open a straight path through the wilderness for our feet, cf. Isa. 40. 3, where the same phrase is used, and also Hebrews 12. 13.

Sept. 5th

READING : **Proverbs 4. 10-19**

THE PATH OF THE JUST

THERE ARE two paths here. There is "the path of the wicked", which is dark and leads to everlasting darkness, v. 14, and there is "the path of the just", its light shining unto the perfect day, v. 18. The thought of two ways is found elsewhere. Psalm 1 speaks of the "way of the righteous" and the "way of the ungodly". In Matthew 7. 13, 14 we have a broad way that leads to destruction, and a narrow way that leads to life. We need to be sure that we are on the right path.

The right path is called "the path of the just". But who are the just or the righteous? "There is none righteous", Paul tells us, Rom. 3. 10, and this is certainly true as far as we as sinners are concerned. Yet it is possible for a sinner to be reckoned right before God, for God has through the cross of Christ secured a way whereby He can be just, and yet justify the sinner, who has righteousness reckoned to him on the exercise of faith, cf. Rom. 3. 25-26; 4. 22-24. Having placed his faith in the Saviour, he is now on the right path.

The way is narrow — it is a path, cf. Matt. 7. 13, 14, but it leads to life and light. It is a path of light, of growing light, that leads to "the perfect day". It is "the light of dawn", R.V. marg, which shines more and more until the full blaze of noonday, until "the standing firm of the day". As the sun climbs the heavens, shining brighter and brighter, from the first faint glimmer of dawn till it reaches its meridian height and appears to stand there firm and motionless, so is the path of the righteous. His sun stands still at last in the heavens, and hastens not to go down for the whole of the everlasting day.

It is certain that the first part of the figure ought to be the picture of every Christian life in the present — a steady growth in the knowledge of God, and in the likeness of our Lord Jesus Christ, going from "strength to strength", Psa. 84. 7, and "from glory to glory", 2 Cor. 3. 18, as we behold the glory of the Lord, and are changed into the same image by the Spirit of the Lord.

The just have the Lord for their light, "The Lord is my light", Psa. 27. 1. This light, involving the knowledge of the Lord, should become clearer and clearer till the perfect day when they "shall see him as he is", 1 John 3. 2.

Sept. 6th

READING : Proverbs 5. 1-23

WIPING OUT THE PAST

AT THE END of this chapter, vv. 21-23, the reader is told that God's eye is upon man, and He will cause sin to bring its punishment. Here the rebel rapidly becomes a victim of his own rebellion, the reason being that he had not heeded the Divine discipline, v. 23. The final scene in his life is here described. He has sinned so long that he is "tied and bound" hand and foot, with "the chain of his sins", and cannot get free even if he has the wish to do so.

How did he come to such a pass? His evil deeds became evil habits. Anything done once becomes easier to do again. It is so very much easier to form a bad habit than a good one. As the habit grips harder, the poor pleasure, for the sake of which the deeds are done, diminishes. Once we step on the slippery road, we find ourselves on an decline well-greased, from which it is difficult to recoil and withdraw. We dare not believe that we can do a doubtful thing once without the danger of repetition. The craving increases as fast as the pleasure from gratifying it diminishes.

The problem is that our evil deeds can imprison us for ever. Our evil past holds us in its firm grip. It is then we silence our conscience and ignore all that which within us "thirsteth . . . for the living God". Is it that we would have responded to God long ago but for some pet sin we refuse to give up? Furthermore those evil deeds work their own punishment. Life is full of consequences of evil doing. Even now we reap as we have sown. "Every transgression and disobedience receives its just recompense of reward", and the full tale waits for eternity.

He is "holden with the cords of his sins", and he cannot break these cords himself. They cling too tightly to men. We cannot blot out the past. We cannot extirpate the evil that is part of ourselves. What we cannot do, Christ can do. He can cancel the past, and set the prisoner free. He gives us new life, and the power to fight the old evil habits. It was that assurance of forgiveness and liberty that gave rise to the apostle John's burst of praise in Revelation 1. 5 R.V. "Unto him that loveth us, and loosed us from our sins". Yes, "He breaks the power of cancelled sin, He sets the prisoner free".

Sept. 7th
READING : Proverbs 6. 1-19
SEVEN THINGS GOD HATES

A GOD WHO is righteous must be in opposition to that which is wrong and sinful. Seven things are enumerated here, vv. 16-19, as detestable to Him, and the seventh is worse than all, seven here as elsewhere representing completeness.

God hates *the look that is proud*, v. 17. Here is the elevation of self to a level that is neither justified nor deserved. It is hateful to God because it renders men unfit to receive His grace. Till they acknowledge their weakness, they will not seek for His strength; cf. 1 Pet. 5. 5; Matt. 5. 3. It ranks with gross vices, and the chief sins. It is the chief crime of Satan; cf. Isa. 14. 12-18. God hates *the lying tongue*, Prov. 6. 17. We can lie to make ourselves appear better than we are. Ananias and Sapphira did so, Acts 5. 1-9. Whether we lie for personal advantage, or from weakness, God hates it. It is a sure sign of God's hatred against lies that they recoil on the head of the liar. The father of lies is the devil; cf. John 8. 44; ct. Heb. 6. 18; Titus 1. 2. Notice that the picture here is of habitually speaking lies — it is far gone. Hateful to God are *hands that shed blood;* cf. Matt. 5. 21, 22. So hateful are they to Him that He could not let David His chosen servant build Him a house, because this charge could be laid against the great king, 1 Chron. 28. 3. *The devising heart* is likewise detested, Prov. 6. 18. The imaginations of man's heart are evil continually. The thoughts and desires of man are in view; cf. 2 Cor. 10. 5. There is much that lies deep in the wicked imaginations of man's heart, that we may wonder at the forbearance of our God. He hates *feet which are swift in running to mischief*, cf. Rom. 3. 15, but feet can be used for good, too; cf. Rom. 10. 15; Eph. 6. 15. *The false witness* is a destroyer of justice between man and man — he is likewise detestable, for what is a witness but a person whose duty and responsibility it is to tell the truth. Finally, as the blessing of heaven falls upon the peacemaker, so the hatred of God comes upon *the man who sows discord among brethren*. On the other hand, God surely must be pleased with the opposite of these things — the modest look, a truthful tongue, hands that help the weak, a heart that plans kindnesses, feet that are swift to do God's bidding, witness to the truth, and the promotion of harmony among the brethren.

Sept. 8th

READING : **Proverbs 7. 1-24**

THE WORD OF THE LORD

OUR GOD regards and cares for His people as the apple of His eye. To Israel in the wilderness He said, through the farewell song of Moses, that "the Lord's portion is his people . . . kept . . . as the apple of his eye", Deut. 32. 9, 10. To the returned remnant, through Zechariah, the Lord again assured His people under the same figure: "he that toucheth you toucheth the apple of his eye", Zech. 2. 8. David could confidently pray, "Keep me as the apple of the eye, hide me under the shadow of thy wings", Psa. 17. 8. In Proverbs 7. 1-4 we are asked to make God's Word as the apple of our eye, that is to say that God wants us to treat His Word as He treats us. What is meant by this phrase, "the apple of the eye"? It is an emblem of that which is the tenderest and dearest, and therefore guarded with the most jealous care. Hence, in these few verses, we have repeated injunctions: "keep", "lay up", "keep", "Bind", "write". The Word of God is to be our treasure, infinitely precious to us, supremely valued and appreciated. But more than that, its truth is to be grasped by us, hence the words "keep", "lay up". These words encourage all to get a firm grasp on Biblical truth. And truth, once grasped, has to be practised; cf. James 1. 22-25. The best advice is useless against strong temptation unless it is thoroughly taken to heart, and translated into practice.

It is through the Word that God speaks to us. We speak to Him in prayer. The writer of the Proverbs has something startling to say on this; cf. Prov. 28. 9. How tragic if we have no time to hear what God says to us in His Word. True it is that we shall never *find* time to read and study God's Word — the enemy will see to that. We have to *make* time. Do we do so?

Do I, like Job of old, esteem "the words of his mouth more than my necessary food"?, Job. 23. 12. Thinking lightly of the Word of the Lord leads to lack of vision, Prov. 29. 18, and where there is lack of vision the people perish. One further step from lightly esteeming the Word of the Lord is to despise it, and that carries its own severe penalty; cf. 13. 13. Let us be found amongst those who love, honour, and obey His Word, and are able to say "O how love I thy law! It is my meditation all the day", Psa. 119. 97.

Sept. 9th

READING : Proverbs 8. 1-36

WISDOM

WISDOM cries in the open air, in the public paths, in the entry of cities, where the crowd surges, vv. 1-3, and this is where the Gospel must be proclaimed. She calls to the sons of men, vv. 4, 5, and has excellent things to say, vv. 6-9. Indeed, her words are priceless, vv. 10, 11; having no material equivalent, they cannot be bought. Wisdom is herself better than gold or silver, leading to righteousness, enriching all who love her, v. 21, and coming from eternity, vv. 22-29.

This wisdom is not an abstract attribute or quality, but a Person. We see here Christ, who is both the power and wisdom of God. There, in that Divine Man, in His gentle love and deep and weighty words, in His power to give life to them that find Him, we have the highest embodiment of the wisdom of God, who was before all worlds, yet stoops to each lowly and obedient heart. All that is said here of wisdom is true of Christ. He scattered His gospel like seed, vv. 1-7, in the busy haunts of men; drew all men, without partiality, unto Himself, vv. 4, 5. He is Himself the Truth, being able to say, like wisdom, with absolute truth "All the words of my mouth are in righteousness; there is nothing crooked or perverse in them", v. 8 R.V., whose teaching is "plain" and "right", who is of incomparable worth, vv. 9-11. He stands detached from nothing in this world, and with what force He might claim that even kings rule by Him we shall only know when the kingdoms of this world have become His in their entirety, vv. 12-21. He loves us even when we do not love Him, v. 17, and will reward with His presence all who seek Him diligently, v. 17 R.V. He is better than gold or silver, v. 19; he leads us in the way of righteousness, v. 20; cf. 1 Cor. 1. 30, enriching for eternity those who obey Him, Prov. 8. 21. Coming from eternity, He is Himself eternal, whose absolute pre-existence is declared for us, Col. 1. 15, 17.

He, too, could say that His delight was with the sons of men. If His delight had not been with us, how could ours have ever been with Him? It is not merely that He delights in us because He has redeemed us. No, He redeemed us because He delighted in us. What new meaning lights up life when we realize that the delight of the Son of God is centred in us.

Sept. 10th

READING : Proverbs 13. 1-25

PARADOXES

How can one be rich, and yet have nothing? Or how can one be poor, and yet have great wealth? Yet verse 7 says that these conditions can exist. Furthermore the Bible furnishes illustrations of the statements made. For example, there was Haman who could recount to his family of "the glory of his riches", Esther 5. 11, but who could say "Yet all this availeth me nothing", v. 13. He had great riches, but they were ashes as long as Mordecai lived.

Consider another illustration towards the end of the New Testament, the church at Laodicea, Rev. 3. 14-22. Here was a church which was rich. The Lord Jesus said, "thou sayest, I am rich", yet He continued to say, "and knowest not that thou art . . . poor". What a tragedy! They assumed that outward prosperity was synonymous with spiritual success. They were really spiritual paupers. Their souls were starving in the midst of their abundance. They could meet all claims, save the claims of God. The Lord would teach them, "I counsel thee". He says that true wealth is Himself possessed in all the aspects of His perfection. He opens the door of the storehouse of all His infinite riches and says, "If you are aware of your poverty, I have riches". How different the words of the Lord Jesus to the church at Smyrna! "I know . . . thy poverty (but thou art rich)", 2. 9. Theirs was complete poverty, total destitution. There was peculiar honour in being thus near and like Himself who had "not where to lay his head". "I know thy poverty for I have shared it. I know thy riches for I have given them". Destitute and stripped of their belongings, they were still rich in all the treasury of glory, in spiritual possessions, in grace and its glorious fruits.

Poor but rich was what the apostle Paul claimed to be, "as poor, yet making many rich; as having nothing, and yet possessing all things", 2 Cor. 6. 10. He was not well endowed with worldly wealth. Dispossessed of all things that could bring him earthly gain and prosperity, such as privilege of race and social prestige, he had suffered their loss for Christ, and had in his grasp the most wonderful possession, cf. 1 Cor. 3. 21, 22, and it was given to him to make many rich through the preaching of the unsearchable riches of Christ.

Sept. 11th

READING : **Proverbs 15. 1-24**

THE TONGUE

THERE ARE two ways of answering angry words, mildly or angrily. The answer of the children of Reuben to the rest of the Israelites, and to Phinehas, was an example of a soft answer; cf. Josh. 22. 15, 21-30. Trouble could have otherwise ensued. Another example is the answer of Gideon to the angry men of Ephraim when "they did chide with him sharply". His answer esteemed them better than himself, and their anger cooled; cf. Jud. 8. 1-3. Then there is the gracious example of Abigail, when her "soft answer" turned away David in his wrath from avenging himself; cf. 1 Sam. 25. 23ff.

What sorrows and grievances hard words can cause! Consider the reply Rehoboam gave to the people when they had pleaded for some alleviation of the burden his father had placed upon them; "My father made your yoke heavy, but I will add thereto; my father chastised you with whips, but I will chastise you with scorpions", 2 Chron. 10. 14. What distress was caused to Jonathan by Saul his father's angry words regarding David; cf. 1 Sam. 20. 30-34. How many times has an angry answer marred fellowship and friendship. Even the greatest of men have had their failures here. Even a Paul and a Barnabas had angry words over the suitability of a fellow-worker, and "the contention was so sharp between them that they departed asunder one from the other". A sharp "paroxysm" indeed, and they never sailed together again; cf. Acts 15. 37-41. What a dangerous member the tongue is! "Behold how great a matter a little fire kindleth!".

The tongue is capable of uttering wisdom or crass folly. Which does our tongue employ?, Prov. 15. 2. It can be a "wholesome" tongue, v. 4. "Wholesome" means "gentle" or "soothing". Soft sayings soothe, but wild words wound. We can heal hurts with gentle words, or we can aggravate them with words that wound. Did we ever use words that were meant to wound?, cf. 12. 18. Are we going to be hearers only, or doers?; cf. James 1. 22. If our passage today is to be of any use to us, we must act upon the plain advice given. Is someone very angry with you, annoyed with you? Will you lose your temper, too, and so dishonour your Lord? Or are you going to give a "soft answer (that) turneth away wrath"?

Sept. 12th

READING : **Proverbs 21. 1-31**

"THE LORD LOVETH A CHEERFUL GIVER"

"It is more blessed to give than to receive", Acts 20. 35, is the only one of the Lord's recorded sayings quoted in the New Testament which is not found in the Gospels. It concerns giving. No doubt Solomon himself was generous, and gave freely to the Lord's temple and its services; cf. 1 Kings 5 to 8. He was the son of the most generous contributor to God's house that ever lived.

In giving, the character of the giver is important. If God is going to accept anything from us, we must first of all be right with Him. First of all, we must accept His Gift to us, that Greatest of all Gifts, His Beloved Son. What we are colours what we give. Proverbs 21. 26, 27 present the righteous and the wicked, and verse 25 introduces a picture of the slothful which continues into verse 26. The sin of covetousness marks the slothful, and the grace of benevolence the righteous. The wish of the slothful man passes into restless, covetous, distasteful desire. The righteous, free from that desire, gives without grudging. The slothful covets, that he might consume it on his own lusts, James 4. 2, 3, while the righteous gives to all who need, remembering that he is a steward, Luke 16. 10, not an owner, and that blessing will attend on him for so doing, Acts 20. 35. As for the wicked, Prov. 21. 27, his sacrifice is an abomination, even when he brings it in a mere formal spirit, because of the moral character of the offerer; cf. Isa. 1. 13-15. The r.v. margin has the rendering "to atone for wickedness", Prov. 21. 27, but generosity will not atone for sin. Only the blood of the Saviour can do that. The true motive for giving is gratitude at the remembrance of God's amazing grace towards us in Christ; cf. 2 Cor. 8. 9. To give of our substance honours the Lord, Prov. 3. 9, and that is a motive. The priority in giving is first to give our own selves, 2 Cor. 8. 5, then our substance, 2 Cor. 8. 2. To withhold from giving is unjust. The r.v. margin of Proverbs 11. 24 speaks of withholding what "is justly due". The generous will look for opportunities to be benevolent, they have "a bountiful eye", 22. 9. And they will be rewarded, not only in the life to come, but in the present; they will have no lack, 28. 27, indeed, there will be increase, 3. 10. Our God is no man's debtor.

Sept. 13th

READING : Proverbs 24. 10-12

IF THOU FAINT . . . FORBEAR . . . SAYEST

THESE THREE verses provide a section in which our mettle is tested by exceptional strain, v. 10, and by avoidable responsibility, vv. 11, 12. Before these two tests the man with the shepherd's heart will stand firm, but the hireling will flee, pleading bad conditions, v. 10, hopeless tasks, v. 11, and pardonable ignorance, v. 12.

First a word to test our courage, v. 10. The proverb could mean that our faltering in the day of trouble indicates that our strength is small. It could, however, mean that because of our fainting our strength will be small. Want of courage will cause want of strength to meet the emergency. So we need the exhortation not to be weary nor to lose heart in doing right, 2 Thess. 3. 13. "Let us not be weary", says Paul, "in well doing; for in due season we shall reap, if we faint not", Gal. 6. 9. J. B. Lightfoot translates "be weary" by "turn cowards, lose heart". A promise is given by Paul as an encouragement to persevere, for he recognized that some incentive is needed in well-doing. Active Christian service is tiring, exacting work. We are tempted to become discouraged, to slack off, even to give up. So he tells us "in due season *we shall reap*, if we faint not".

Secondly, a word to test our compassion, v. 11. "Deliver those that are drawn unto death, and those who totter to the slaughter, stop them", *lit*. This last clause carries the idea of strong desire and repeats the entreaty of the first — "deliver", i.e. save them from their doom. The words present a contrast to verse 10. Instead of fainting in the day of adversity, we are to help others to the uttermost of our power. If souls are in danger of death by unjust judgment, we may deliver them by giving a true witness; cf. 14. 25. If they are about to be "slain" we may deliver them by rendering help like the Samaritan, and by not passing by. That man being "slain" is our neighbour!

Finally, a word to test our concern, v. 12. Can we be indifferent to the needs of men and plead ignorance? We are too much inclined to answer after the manner of Cain, "Am I my brother's keeper?", Gen. 4. 9, when we might give aid to those who need it. To plead ignorance as an excuse for avoiding duty cannot deceive God.

Sept. 14th

READING : Proverbs 31. 10-31

MRS. PRICE-ABOVE-RUBIES

HERE IS the picture of a good woman. She is a diligent worker, cf. vv. 13, 15, 19. She is a woman of unflagging industry. She is the house-manager, and her husband "shall have no lack of gain", v. 11 R.V. "She considereth" and then "buyeth", v. 16. She is shrewd but not hard, thrifty but not austere, vv. 22, 24. She behaves uprightly, and "Strength and honour are her clothing", v. 25. Her husband has no cause of complaint against her. A man's influence in the life of his town is not always traced to the true source, his wife. Behind a good man there is usually a good woman, and this is so here. She seeks her husband's good, v. 12. Not only when she comes to him as a young bride, but when age has mellowed her, she does him good. She has an interest in her husband, vv. 11, 12, 23. She is his stay and confidence. "The heart of her husband trusteth in her", v. 12 R.V. She is his natural confidante and counsellor. Absolute trustworthiness shines through this picture. The husband comes home from sitting with the elders of his town, and he seeks her confidence and advice. He has no fear of her betraying his secrets.

"Her children arise up, and call her blessed", v. 28, and so she must have been an exemplary mother. Her family were certainly well clothed, and well fed, vv. 15, 21, 27. It is good to be praised by friends and associates, but the sweetest praise comes from one's children. They are the ones who have spent days and years in close contact, and have noted the flaws as well as the strength of the mother. A child's praise is a rich compensation for many hours of devotion and personal sacrifice on the part of the mother.

She has "a good report of them without", of her neighbours in particular. She helps the poor, and proves a friend in need. She has an interest in others. She is one who cares for the needs of those who are less blessed than herself. She senses the needs of other people, and does something about them, v. 20.

This Book of wholesome loving, aptly ends with the picture of the united family joining in the praise of one who, under God, can do most to build up the character extolled in its pages. Her character and outlook are based on the fear of the Lord, the condition of all excellence.

Introducing Ecclesiastes and the Song of Solomon

THE BOOK OF ECCLESIASTES has been regarded in various ways. To some, it is a discussion of the subject "Life without God". To others, here is the diary of a cynic pointing only to the pessimistic evaluation of life as "vanity and vexation of spirit". To some, it is a profound unveiling of the unsatisfied yearning of the human heart. For others, it is a sermon for the natural man in language he understands, intended to lead him from self to God. For yet others, it is Solomon the Prodigal re-exhibited by Solomon the Preacher.

Compare the conclusion to the Book, 12. 13, 14, with 1. 12 to 2. 1. The "matter" referred to in the conclusion was a long experiment, which the preacher made, in search of the supreme happiness. Ecclesiastes records the successive stages of this search. We are taken back to those days of vanity, the Preacher standing before us, in turn as the man of science, the man of pleasure, etc., until, in concluding the matter, he turns from all these "lying vanities" and emerges penitent. So Solomon re-enacts the scenes of his search after happiness.

THE SONG OF SOLOMON is set in the form of a dialogue. There are interjections from other persons, e.g. the daughters of Jerusalem, 5. 9; 6. 1, but, in the main, the conversation is between Solomon and the Shulamite. Some have discerned another character here, a shepherd as well as a king, but these are descriptions of the same person. The words "my love" and "my beloved" are constantly repeated, the latter being used by the Shulamite, and the former by her companion, her bridegroom. The love and communion enjoyed by these two picture the relationship between the Lord and Israel, Christ and His Church, and Christ and the individual believer.

"Dry wells send us to the fountain", wrote Samuel Rutherford, and this is true in the contrast between these two Books. The Song shows how blessing and satisfaction can be possessed, and in this provides a contrast to Ecclesiastes, with its repetition of "vanity and vexation of spirit". As in Ecclesiastes all is emptiness, in the Song all is fulness. The world and the Lord are contrasted. In the one Book the heart is too large for its object; in the other the Object is too large for the heart. "Now none but Christ can satisfy".

Sept. 15th

READING : **Ecclesiastes 1. 1-18**

"ALL IS VANITY"

VANITY is one of the key words of this book. The writer employs phrases which recur throughout — "vanity", "what profit", "under the sun", "vexation of spirit". Summed up, they point to the emptiness of life when it is wholly conditioned in material things. Vanity here does not have the modern sense of pride, but has the meaning of emptiness; cf. 6. 12. It denotes that which passes away, more or less quickly, and completely like a "light wind". The R.V. translation of vanity in Isaiah 57. 13 is "breath". It is that which leaves no adequate result behind it, and therefore which fails to satisfy the heart and mind of man which crave for something permanent. In this Book it is applied to all works on earth—pleasure, grandeur, wisdom, etc., brought together under ten "vanities": 2. 15-16, 19-21, 26; 4. 4, 7, 16; 5. 10; 6. 9; 7. 6; 8. 10, 14.

"Vanity of vanities" means vanity in its highest degree, and "all its vanity" without exception. These things are not in themselves vain, for God makes nothing vain, 1 Tim. 4. 4, 5. But they become vain when put in the place of God, and made the end instead of the means; cf. Psa. 39. 5, 6; 62. 9; Matt. 6. 33. They are vain also because of the vanity to which they have been subjected by the fall; cf. Rom. 8. 20. Paul explains the place of vanity in the Divine providence, by tracing its origin to the subjugation and corruption of creation by sin, as a consequence of the fall. Its removal is declared to be reserved until after the manifestation of the glory of the children of God.

"Vanity of vanity, all is vanity" is a true description of life when it is lived under certain conditions, but it is not true of what life necessarily must be. The believer in the Lord Jesus would reject this to be true of life as he finds life, for he finds his life in Christ, and it is not vanity, emptiness or nothingness. To him, in every way life is real, rich and full. For "godliness is profitable unto all things", 1 Tim. 4. 8. The Preacher is, of course, saying that things in themselves bring no satisfaction to the soul of man. To live on earth without recognizing the supreme wisdom, which begins and continues in the fear of God, to deal only with what is "under the sun", is to find nothing that really satisfies, to be left at last without any reality, to be left with nothingness.

Sept. 16th
READING : Ecclesiastes 5. 1-7

"FEAR THOU GOD"

THE FEAR of the Lord is the beginning and maintenance of true wisdom. The fear of this chapter is the fear of the slave, rather than the reverential fear of the son. It lacks the note of confidence, of trust and love, yet, there is advice given here which is good. There is preparation here for the sanctuary, and we must remember that God is to be found in the assembly of His saints. There is the Eastern practice which drops the sandals at the palace door; the devout worshipper, having taken off his travel-stained shoes, will try to divest himself of secular anxieties and worldly projects in the house of God. These things are to be left behind. Then, "to keep the foot" was to walk in the right way, the way of reverence and obedience; cf. Psa. 119. 101.

The advice is, firstly, to come ready to hear God's Word, Eccles. 5. 1, and to be quiet before Him. Sometimes, dull hearing may be produced by uninspired speaking, and messages which lack the freshness of the Spirit. Sometimes, much of the impatience and inattention of hearers may be because of the longwindedness, or wordiness of the preacher. Sometimes, however, the remedy lies not in the greater power of the preacher, but in the greater piety of the listener. We should come with purpose, and prayerfully; James 1. 19-25.

Secondly, he advises a few sincere prayers rather than rushing through many, v. 2. In praying, the Lord Jesus said, do not use vain repetitions as the Gentiles do, expecting to be heard because of their much speaking, Matt. 6. 7-8. Is it a case that lengthy prayers stifle the spirit of the prayer meeting?

Thirdly, he advises honesty with God, though others may make grand promises without fulfilling them, Eccles. 5. 4-7. "Be not rash", he says, but remember at whose throne you are kneeling, v. 2. Be not wordy, he adds, but let your words be few and emphatic, as of one favoured with an audience from heaven's King. A vow should not be made hastily as the experience of Jephthah, Jud. 11. 30-35, and of Saul, 1 Sam. 14. 24-28, shows. When the vow is made, it must be kept; cf. Psa. 76. 11. Do we make vows in singing our hymns of praise which we never keep, or never intend to keep? Our God requires truth in the inward parts, and our yea to be yea, Matt. 5. 37.

Sept. 17th

READING : Ecclesiastes 12. 1-7

REMEMBERED

WHO is to be remembered? Thy Creator. This word occurs again only in Isaiah 40. 28 and 43. 15. It is plural in its form, as Elohim is plural, and as "the Holy One" is plural in Proverbs 9. 10; 30. 3; Hosea 12. 1. This expresses the majesty of God, and hints at Triunity. *When?* In thy youth, not simply because the majority of conversions occur in youth, but that a whole life can be dedicated to God, rather than its few closing years. And *why?* For if you do not remember Him then, your next opportunity to do so will be in old age, Eccles. 12. 2-7. How foolish to calculate on a time which many will not see! How foolish to calculate on a time which, were it really to come, you could turn to no account!

Consider what old age brings. The darkening of the lights of heaven denotes a time of affliction and sadness, in which gloom becomes harder to disperse, v. 2. The strong arms (the keepers of the house) have withered, the active limbs (the strong men) can do no more. The teeth (the grinders) are few, and eyesight fails, v. 3. Deafness becomes an affliction (the doors shut), appetite fails (the sound of the grinding is low), sleeplessness comes (rising at the song of the bird), and the voice becomes tremulous, v. 4. There is fear of heights, the hair is white, the weakened mind cannot bear worry, the will to live ceases, and death comes, v. 5. Or again, we see the aged man with his bent back (the silver cord loosed), his weakened mind (the bowl broken), his broken breathing (the pitcher broken), his weak heart (the wheel broken at the cistern). And then death, v. 7.

A dissipated youth is sure to be followed by a cross and a joyless old age. But the Creator remembers, in their old age, those who, in their youth, remembered Him. Some of these features listed, therefore, would not be recognized in an aged believer. It could not be truly said by him, "I have no pleasure", v. 1, and though there may be clouds, he will surely have long and sunny intervals, and beyond this cloud region he has the most blessed prospects. Old age and feebleness need not bring unhappiness to the believer who knows that His Saviour is with him now, and has prepared for him a home hereafter; cf. John 14. 2, 3. Indeed, "the path of the just is as the shining light, that shineth more and more", Prov. 4. 18.

Sept. 18th

READING : **Song of Solomon 1. 1 to 2. 7**

THE SONG OF SONGS

SOLOMON composed 1005 songs, cf. 1 Kings 4. 32, but this is the *most excellent* of them all. The phrase "song of songs" indicates this, and has to be compared with the phrase "Holy of Holies", the most holy place, or "King of kings and Lord of lords". The Song speaks of Solomon, and we are made to look upon him as a monarch in great glory. In this he foreshadows the Lord Jesus Christ in all the triumph of His resurrection and ascension. In this Book we know Him as the King, 1. 12, and the believer's position is by His side, as the object of His supreme affection. Here is a Book of spiritual communion.

Its dialogue is between the king and the Shulamite, 6. 13, and between "the altogether lovely one", 5. 16, and "the fairest amongst women", 1. 8, the bridegroom and his bride. The bridegroom refers to her as his "love", and the bride refers to him as her "Beloved". To understand the book it will help to know who is speaking in the verses, and so the simple guide is that when the words "my beloved" are used, it is the bride speaking, and when the words "my love" are used, it is the bridegroom.

If this guide is followed in the first canticle, i.e. 1. 1 to 2. 7, the order of speaking would be as follows:

1. 2-7 the bride speaks in the company of the daughters of Jerusalem. Verses 8-11 the bridegroom responds — note the phrase "my love", v. 9. Verses 12-14 the bride responds, and receives the bridegroom's reply, v. 15. The bride speaks in verse 16, and then continues down to and including 2. 1. The bridegroom in 2. 2 acknowledges that she is a "lily", and to this the bride responds by calling him a citron tree, and she continues down to verse 7. In verse 7 she again addresses the daughters of Jerusalem, and the verse should read "that ye stir not up, nor awaken love, until it please", R.V. She does not wish her communion with her beloved to be disturbed.

It is the bride who refers to herself as "the lily of the valleys", and "the rose of Sharon", 2. 1. These are lowly flowers of the field, and befit herself. Her beloved acknowledges the comparison, v. 2, but as for him, he is the great citron tree, in whose shadow she rests, that which is capable of yielding both shelter (shadow) and sustenance (fruit).

Sept. 19th

READING : **Song of Solomon 2. 8-17**

THE LITTLE FOXES

AT THE END of the last canticle the bride was left enjoying the sweetness of communion in the arms of her beloved. Such communion, so deep and blessed, would surely never be interrupted. Alas, experience shows how easily *communion* with one's Lord may be broken. Our *union* with Him is eternal, and cannot be broken. But just as the young deer may be disturbed by the crackle of a twig, 2. 7, so a chance look, a hasty word, a foolish tale, may disturb and mar our peace and communion.

The Shulamite has returned to her own home, and has moved away from nearness to her beloved. He comes seeking her. The canticle has two movements, viz. 2. 8-17, the seeking bridegroom and the unresponsive bride, and 3. 1-5, the seeking bride and the responsive bridegroom. The affections of the bride are spoken to by the voice of her beloved. She knows his voice, cf. John 10. 4, and the voice proclaims he is coming. Could anything awaken the affections of the believer like the news that his Lord is coming? Her affections, however, are not sufficiently awakened to go out to meet him. He tries to draw her forth to himself. He does so first by *self-revelation*, v. 9. He reveals himself to her bit by bit, as the Lord did to those two on the Emmaus road, until their hearts burned within them, Luke 24. He then tells her of *deepest affection*, she is his "love, his fair one", v. 10. He speaks of a *new creation*, vv. 11-13a, based on spring resurrection, of which she is a part. He appeals to his loved one to stand on resurrection ground. He assures her of her *secure position*, v. 14, she is in the clefts of the rock. Yet all these, her blessings, do not draw her forth in gratitude to him. What is wrong? Ah, there is *broken communion* which prevents her yielding fruit, the little foxes have done their damage, v. 15. The fox's tail had touched the delicate vine blossom, and when, later, the farmer came seeking fruit, there was none. Oh the little foxes that mar our fruitfulness for our Beloved!

Sad her response, vv. 16, 17. She comforts herself by reminding her own heart of her union with him, v. 16. She is saved and secure, she cannot be lost. Furthermore, she knows where to find him if she needs him. So, careless of his longings, she lightly dismisses him, and the grieved bridegroom departs.

Sept. 20th

READING : **Song of Solomon 3. 1-5**

FOUND — OUTSIDE THE CITY

THE DAY has cooled, and the shadows have fled, but the beloved does not return. It was dark, and she was alone. It might have been vastly different. Responding to him, she could have gone forth with him in the sunshine, "leaning on his arm". The partial view through her window she could have exchanged for the warmth of his embrace. But he is gone. She is alone. The sense of his nearness is lost. Foolish bride, but how many times have we been like her? Yet her conscience is wakening, and her affections are beginning to be re-kindled as she turns her thoughts now to him. She refers to him four times as "him whom my soul loveth". She is going to seek him. When a believer's love is awakened it is only the Lord who can satisfy the heart. Though her love is awakened, she does not immediately find him. There are reasons for this.

First of all, she was *seeking her beloved in the wrong way*, v. 1. "On my bed . . . I sought him", she says. "On my bed?" How can one seek the Lord and retain one's ease? The symbol of the Beloved is not a bed, but a cross. When the Lord Jesus calls a man to follow Him, He offers him a cross; cf. Luke 14. 27.

Secondly, she *sought him in the wrong place*. She sought him in the city, v. 2, with the same result. She "found him not". He is not to be found in the city, but amongst the lilies, by the footsteps of the flock, by the shepherds' tents, the mountain of myrrh, the hill of frankincence, the bed of spices. The city had no room for Him. There was no room when He was born, Luke 2. 7, and afterwards there never was any room, "his own received him not". Foxes had holes and the birds had nests, but He had nowhere to lay His head. And the city held no attractions for Him. The Gospels do not record a single night that He spent within the walls of the city of Jerusalem, the city of the Great King. In the momentous week in which he suffered, every evening he went outside the city. "And every evening he went forth out of the city", Mark 11. 19 R.V.

Lastly, *she sought him of the wrong people*, the watchmen, v. 3. They were responsible for the execution and maintenance of law and order. They were concerned with law, and did not know the beloved. But she passed them by. She was on her way out of the city, and there she found him, cf. Heb. 13. 13.

Sept. 21st

READING : Song of Solomon 5. 2 to 6. 3

THE ALTOGETHER LOVELY

THERE HAD BEEN relapse before, 2. 8-17, and sadly it has happened again. Her chamber door is barred, 5. 5, an evidence that his return was neither eagerly desired, nor expected. He stands outside the door, and seeks admittance; cf. Rev. 3. 20. He reminds her of how dear she is to him, "my sister, my love, my dove", and how he has suffered for her, "my head is filled with dew, and my locks with the drops of the night", Song 5. 2. His appeal to her echoes from the darkness of Gethsemane, and the awful solitude of Golgotha.

The bride, however, does not know how to shake off her lethargy, v. 3. To respond to his appeal called for energy and sacrifice. Then the beloved puts in his hand by the hole in the door, v. 4. It was as simple an act as the Lord's look on Peter, cf. Luke 22. 61, but it began the work of restoration. Our hearts, too, surely respond when He stretches out to us His nail-pierced hand!

She rose to open to him, but he had gone, v. 5, though the door-way was filled with the fragrance of his presence. She seeks him now. To those to whom she appeals he is unknown, vv. 7-9. Is her beloved really more to her than another beloved? Her heart must be searched, as Peter's was at the lakeside; cf. John 21. 15-17. Then the reality of her love is shown. She needed no premeditation to speak of the beauties of her beloved. Oh to be ready always to speak well of Him.

In her description are there not seen some of the glories of our Beloved? She describes the spotless character of His person, and the character of His sacrifice, v. 10; His Divine majesty in the head of most fine gold, the vigour of manhood in the bushy black locks, v. 11; the purity and perfection of His vision, v. 12; the beauty and winsomeness of the cheeks upon which the traitor's kiss was implanted; His lips into which grace was poured, v. 13; the rings of His hands reminding us of His authority, cf. Gen. 41. 42, and Sonship, cf. Luke 15. 22; the preciousness of His person, v. 14; the strength and stability, steadfastness and continuance of His reign founded on Divine righteousness, v. 15; cf. Psa. 45. 6. There is no deterioration here; ct. Dan 2. 31-33. He is all glorious throughout. He is altogether lovely. This is our Beloved.

Sept. 22nd

READING : Song of Solomon 8. 5-14

"LEANING ON THE EVERLASTING ARM"

THE FINAL canticle is also the briefest. In it the bride is seen coming up from the wilderness, leaning on her beloved. She is displayed before the world in company with him, but in dependence on him, leaning on him. In 2. 8 we have seen her *listening to her beloved*, "the voice of my beloved", she said, a voice that proclaimed his approach seeking her fellowship and love. Alas, then she had failed him. Here in 8. 5, however, she knows his nearness, and is seen *leaning on her beloved*. Leaning is the picture of weakness clinging to strength; cf. 2 Cor. 12. 9, 10. We can be strong in the Lord's strength only when, in conscious weakness, we lean upon Him. The final verses of the Song tell us of the bride's *longing for her beloved*, v. 14. Her love can only be gratified by his return, "Make haste my beloved". Does it not bring an echo from the last words of John when, having seen visions of heavenly splendour and millennial glory, what he desires above them all is the Lord he adores. "Even so, come, Lord Jesus", Rev. 22. 20.

She had been in the wilderness, a pilgrim and a stranger. That is *where she was*, and *what she was*. Does it not remind us of our position, in the world but not of it, having here no abiding city, looking for a city which hath foundations whose Builder and Maker is God?, 1 Pet. 2. 11; Heb. 11. 10, 13-16. That causes us to consider *where she was going*. She was going "up from the wilderness". That was not her rest. Then we must notice *how she was going*, "leaning upon her beloved", in conscious dependence on him.

The bridegroom is heard speaking, v. 5b. He claims her from her very birth. Before she knew him, he knew her. "I awakened thee", R.V. The first impulse of our new life came from Him. He quickened us who were dead in trespasses and in sins. She is reminded that all her blessings from her birth she owes to her beloved. All that we are, and all that we ever shall be, we owe to Another. We are truly debtors to grace alone. Realizing this, she makes her request, "Set me as a seal upon thy heart", v. 6. Never again can she rest in her love to her beloved. She realizes all her blessing depends on His love, not on her own. We can trust His heart, though we cannot trust our own. His love has been proved, vv. 6, 7.

Introducing Isaiah

THE BOOK of Isaiah is an incomparable literary masterpiece. The following facts confirm our belief in the unity of the Book.

1. *The title, "the Holy One of Israel"* is used 23 times (cf. also 5. 16; 6. 3; 10. 17; 29. 23; 40. 25; 43. 15; 49. 7; 57. 15), though elsewhere it is found only at 2 Kings 19. 22 = Isa. 37. 23; Jer. 50. 29; 51. 5; Psa. 71. 22; 78. 41; 89. 19. The uses of the title are dispersed throughout the book, more being found in chapters 40-66 (13 times) than in the chapters 1-39 unquestioningly attributed to Isaiah.

2. *The quotations of Isaiah in the N.T.* specifically attributed to him are drawn from the *whole* book. Only the Psalms are quoted more frequently. We shall note examples from the chapters whose authorship has been questioned, i.e. 40-66. **40. 3** is attributed to Isaiah by Matt. 3. 3; Luke 3. 4; John 1. 23; **42. 1-4** by Matt. 12. 17; **53. 1, 4, 5** by John 12. 38; Rom. 10. 16; Matt. 8. 17; Acts 8. 30; **61. 1, 2** by Luke 4. 17; **65. 1, 2** by Rom. 10. 20.

3. *The fact of inspiration.* Isaiah wrote prophetically in both general and specific terms, concerning both the more immediate and more distant future. By means of Divine revelation, he is as at home predicting the Babylonian event as when he unfolds the birth of Immanuel, or the Messianic kingdom. He prophesied the overthrow of Babylon before it had emerged, freshly, to be a great power, ch. 13. Over two centuries before the event, he named Cyrus who would be God's anointed instrument for Babylon's overthrow, 44. 28; 45. 1. Through this 8th century B.C. prophet, there is forecast the first advent of the Messiah, chs. 7, 53. Fulfilment of these, and many other of his prophecies, is a grand proof of inspiration, Deut. 18. 21-22. With confidence we await the second advent and kingdom of the Messiah, so clearly revealed by Isaiah also, chs. 2, 9, 11, 12, 24-27, 35 and 40, 55, 60-63, 65-66.

4. *The contents.* The book has two main parts, linked by the historical hinge, chs. 36-39. Deliverance from Assyria dominates the first part (cf. 36-37), the return from Babylon the second part (cf. 38-39). His ministry is contemporary and mainly condemnatory in 1-39: in 40-66 it is prospective and mainly consolatory.

Sept. 23rd
READING : Isaiah 1. 1-31

SPIRITUAL DECLINE

IN THE GOODNESS of God, Uzziah's long reign of 52 years was marked by prosperity. This ought to have led the people to a loving obedience, thankfulness and praise. Alas, prosperity is often followed by a spiritual decline. Prosperity and living in luxury undermined the morals of the nation, and led the way to its subsequent collapse. In this situation, Isaiah comes upon the scene to warn of a like peril to that which befell their northern neighbours. Let us take a practical warning from this, and guard against spiritual decline through the pursuit of material things; cf. Prov. 30. 8-9; 1 Tim. 6. 6-11.

The spiritual condition of Judah is described in this chapter. The people were guilty of rebellion against their Guardian, of irreverence for the Holy One, and of backsliding, Isa. 1. 2-4. Jerusalem is called a harlot city, v. 21, and its inhabitants are addressed as people of Sodom and Gomorrah, having but narrowly escaped the fate that overtook the cities of the plain, vv. 9-10. Jerusalem was no longer a city of righteousness, but one of violence; the rulers practised bribery and corruption, and failed to administer justice on behalf of the poor and defenceless, vv. 21-23. The people were spiritually sick, a nation of spiritual lepers. Yet, like the Laodicean church, Rev. 3. 17, they knew it not.

Only true repentance could avert judgment overtaking them. Jehovah pleads with the people to face the facts. If they repented, there would be cleansing; otherwise, He would purge them in judgment, vv. 16-20. He has their highest good in mind, however, and the blessing intended for His people will be realized ultimately when Jerusalem will be called "The city of righteousness", v. 26.

God's ways with Israel are pertinent, 1 Cor. 10. 11. He disciplined them because He loved them. So it is with us, for "whom the Lord loveth he chasteneth", Heb. 12. 6. Our relationship, as sons, is more privileged than that of Israel; our Father deals with us accordingly. Let us, then, be in subjection to Him, lest the benefits of discipline are lost on us, and His efforts with us be wasted. As far as Judah was concerned, further correction seemed futile, v. 5.

Sept. 24th

READING : Isaiah 2. 1 to 4. 6

WALKING IN THE LIGHT OF THE LORD

CONTINUING the theme of future blessing in 1. 25-27, Isaiah directs the people beyond their present state to the glorious time when Zion will be re-established as the centre of world-wide blessing and peace, 2. 2-4. The threat of war will not exist, because nations will no longer be aggressive. We live in an age when men are taught and trained in the use of destructive weapons, conventional, nuclear and biological. In that day it will not be so, "neither shall they *learn* war any more", v. 4. Agriculture and husbandry will be the pleasurable employments, as the references to "plowshares" and "pruninghooks" indicate. This will be "the industrial revolution" reversed. Today, industry and commerce require factories whose chimneys pollute the air we breathe. Not so then. Well might we cry, "Thy kingdom come"!

This state of tranquility will be brought about by Him who is referred to as "the branch of the Lord", 4. 2. In that day, Jerusalem will not only have Jehovah's presence with her, symbolized by the cloud and smoke by day, and the pillar of fire by night, but also His protection, which the covering of glory suggests, vv. 5-6. In view of all this, one senses the fervour with which the prophet makes the invitation, "O house of Jacob, come ye, and let us walk in the light of the Lord", 2. 5. The appeal appears to have been unheeded, the people preferring to walk in the ways of pleasure and idolatry like the nations around, vv. 6-9. How true this is of our day and age when men refuse the gospel invitation, choosing the pleasures of sin, loving darkness rather than the light.

Another evil is exposed in 3. 16-26, namely, the vanity of the daughters of Zion. The women who please the Lord are those who spend more time on inward adornment and less on their outward appearance, 1 Tim. 2. 9; 1 Pet. 3. 3-4.

The glory of God's majesty, particularly in judgment, is seen in the section 2. 10 to 3. 26. Those who refuse to walk in His light will one day seek to flee in fear from His glorious power, 2. 19; cf. Luke 23. 30; Rev. 6. 16. Seeing that we are children of light, let us walk in the light of the Lord, and so enjoy a life of increasing illumination, John. 8. 12.

Sept. 25th
READING : Isaiah 5. 1-30
THE WELLBELOVED'S VINEYARD

ISRAEL IS likened here to a vineyard. The fence implies that Israel was protected, and also separated from the other nations, Num. 23. 9. The gathered-out stones remind us of the previous occupants of Canaan who were dislodged when Israel took possession of the land. That it was planted with a choicest vine recalls Israel's first love and holiness to the Lord, Jer. 2. 2, 3, 21. The building of the tower and winepress would indicate that the husbandman intended the vineyard to be profitable. However, it proved to be a complete loss, because, through its own fault, all it produced was wild (stinking) grapes, v. 4. If the vineyard speaks of Israel, it follows that "my wellbeloved", v. 1, refers to none other than Jehovah. It is a title expressive of His love for His people about which there could be no question, Jer. 31. 3.

The fruit for which the Lord looked, v. 2, was justice and righteousness, v. 7, but instead of these, He found the very opposite, oppression and other evils which are denounced under a series of six woes, vv. 8-25.

The first woe is directed against the land speculators, vv. 8-10, who lived in splendid isolation, and had no scruples about the poor peasants they ousted from the land; cf. 3. 14; Mic. 2. 1-5. Their property will go to rack and ruin, and their fields will yield but little increase.

The second woe is against drunkards, vv. 11-12. Inflamed with wine and strong drink, they make merry in song. Fuddled in mind, they fail to appreciate the works of God's hands.

The third woe is upon the defiant sceptics, vv. 18-19. These who so love iniquity and sin are likened to a bullock harnessed to a cart. In their unbelief, they challenge the Holy One to reveal Himself.

The fourth woe is to the clever who, with their "new morality", consider old values out of date, v. 20.

The fifth woe refers to the self-satisfied, v. 21.

The sixth woe is directed against the moral cowards, who accept bribes and pervert justice, v. 22-23.

The Lord Jesus is the True Vine, and His disciples the branches. Are we fruitful? Do we disappoint or glorify Him?

Sept. 26th
READING : Isaiah 6. 1-13

ISAIAH'S VISION

In the year king Uzziah died, Isaiah received the vision recorded in our chapter. According to John 12. 41, it was the glory of Christ which the prophet saw. By contrast to Uzziah's reign, the reign of Christ will not be cut short by death, 9. 7; Rev. 11. 15. The knowledge of the coming of the Messiah must have been a source of encouragement to the faith of the prophets, who longed for a kingdom of righteousness and peace. Isaiah's longing for better times seems implied in verse 11, "Then said I, Lord, how long?".

The effect of the vision upon Isaiah produced a sense of self-abasement, "Woe is me! for I am undone; because I am a man of unclean lips", v. 5. Similar reactions were aroused in others who witnessed Divine majesty and power; cf. Job 42. 5-6; Luke. 5. 8. The sight of the king, the Lord of Hosts, and the holy deportment and purity of lip of the seraphs, made the prophet to see himself as a leper like the rest of the people among whom he lived, and like Uzziah, who died a leper, 2 Kings 15. 5. In the last chapter, we observed how the prophet denounced the sins of the people with a string of woes; here he laments alike his own as well as the people's uncleanness. His "Woe is me" is a contrast to the seraph's "holy, is the Lord of hosts".

What need there is for reverence in our lives and service before God! If the seraphim, attendants of the Divine throne from eternity, still stand in awe in God's presence, so ought we to seek to serve Him with reverence and godly fear, Heb. 12. 28. We have liberty to enter the Holiest, 10. 19, but not license for laxity.

Isaiah's ministry may be compared with the Lord's. We read, "Then said I, Lo, I come", words which apply to Christ, Psa. 40. 7. Here we read, "Then said I, here am I; send me", Isa. 6. 8. Again, Isaiah is told that his ministry would not be heeded or understood, vv. 9-10. John states the same fact to be true of the Lord's ministry, John 12. 40. Conversely, however, what a contrast between the two persons. The Lord never had to lament over any sin in Himself, and grace was poured into His lips, Psa. 45. 2. His lips are likened to lilies dropping sweet smelling myrrh, Song 5. 13.

Sept. 27th
READING : **Isaiah 7. 1 to 9. 7**

IMMANUEL

CHAPTER 7 BRINGS us to the days when Ahaz reigned in Judah, and he "did not that which was right in the sight of the Lord his God", 2 Kings 16. 2. In view of his idolatry, it is not surprising that God allowed Rezin and Pekah, kings of Damascus and Israel who had formed an alliance, to declare war on him and Judah. They inflicted heavy losses on Judah, 2 Chron. 28. 6, and panic gripped the house of David, Isa. 7. 2. The aim of the alliance, it appears, was to set up a vassal king in Jerusalem, v. 6, to strengthen their stand against the threat of Assyria. It seems there were those in Judah who were prepared to support this end, 8. 6, 9-12. As for Ahaz, he looked to the Assyrians, and sold himself in the process, 2 Kings 16. 7; 2 Chron. 28. 16.

Faced with this situation, Isaiah urges trust in Jehovah as the right course to take, 7. 9; 8. 13, 19. It was the course he and his family took, 8. 17-18. The attempt of the enemy to replace Ahaz with another king, not of David's line, could not possibly succeed.

Isaiah's son, Shear-jashub, was present with his father before the king. His name means "the remnant shall return", and was an assurance to the king that Judah would survive, 7. 7. The description, "smoking firebrands", 7. 4, implies that Rezin and Pekah were almost finished.

Ahaz, hypocritically, declined to ask for a sign, v. 12. He did not want to believe God; he had decided to rely on Assyria. God, however, gave him a sign; the sign of Immanuel (God with us), v. 14. This was a further confirmation that God was with Judah, 8. 10. The prediction was intended to convince Ahaz that God, and not Assyria, would establish the throne of David.

Reference again to the birth of Immanuel in 9. 6-7 provides another assurance that the throne of David will be established. Though unoccupied for centuries, it is yet to be filled by Him who is both truly Man and the mighty God. The government of the world will rest upon the shoulder of Him who bore the cross for us.

The God that is *with* us, is also *for* us, and "If God be for us, who can be against us?", Rom. 8. 31.

Sept. 28th
READING : Isaiah 9. 8 to 10. 34
THE LORD'S ANGER

DAVID WROTE "The Lord is . . . slow to anger, and plenteous in mercy", Psa. 103. 8. In contrast, we find in these chapters a statement of Divine anger repeated four times, "For all this his anger is not turned away, but his hand is stretched out still", 9. 12, 17, 21; 10. 4. This is not the hand stretched out in salvation, 59. 1, but in judgment, Ezek. 16. 27. Judah had provoked the Holy One of Israel to anger, 1. 4. Consequently, God raised up the Assyrian nation to be the rod of His anger against His sinful people, 10. 5. The nation in whom Ahaz put his confidence becomes the nation's scourge. The progress of the invading Assyrians towards Jerusalem is graphically described in 10. 28-32. God is sovereign over nations of men, and employs them to carry out His purpose, discarding them when that purpose has been served. Filled with ambitious pride, the Assyrian knew not that he was but a tool in the hand of the Almighty, 10. 5-11, and that his downfall was predicted, 10. 12-19.

We live in a godless world of political instability, where nations vie with each other for world supremacy. Let the believer be at peace in the knowledge that God is still on the throne, and that He still rules in the kingdom of men, Dan. 4. 25.

An answer to the question, "wilt thou be angry for ever?", Psa. 79. 5, is provided in Isaiah 10. 25, "For yet a very little while, and the indignation shall cease". The removal of Sennacherib's forces from Jerusalem in the days of Hezekiah, ch. 37, was a partial fulfilment of 10. 24-25. However, the prophecy looks forward to an ultimate consummation of God's purpose for Israel. The relief afforded here by the departure of the Assyrians was not permanent. A similar fate befell Judah as had previously befallen the ten tribes of the northern kingdom. Nebuchadnezzar came and took Judah into captivity. Not until Israel looks on Him whom they pierced and confess their guilt, will His hand be withdrawn finally.

We bless God for the fact that the wrath of God no longer hangs over our heads, and that we shall never come into judgment, John 3. 18; 5. 24; cf. Psa. 103. 10.

Sept. 29th

READING : Isaiah 11. 1 to 12. 6

MILLENNIAL BLESSEDNESS

HE WHO is called Immanuel in chapter 7, here is referred to as "a rod out of the stem of Jesse". He is David's greater son; David's Lord as well as David's son, Psa. 110. 1; Matt. 22. 42-45. Jesus Himself said, "I am the root and the offspring of David", Rev. 22. 16. His competence to take up the reins of universal government is because He possesses the sevenfold fulness of the Spirit of Jehovah, vv. 1-2; cf. John 3. 34.

Chapter 11 records some of the effects of Christ's reign. First, there will be *no miscarriage of justice*. He will judge, not after the outward appearance but in true righteousness. The decisions He makes will be equitable, and the wicked will be punished, vv. 3-5. The "wicked" or "wicked one", v. 4, may refer to the man of sin whom the Lord will destroy at His coming, 2 Thess. 2. 8.

There will be *no wildness in the animal creation*. Adam lost his dominion over the beasts of the fields through sin. Through His death, Christ will restore that lost dominion to redeemed humanity in the millennium, Heb. 2. 5-8. Dangerous beasts, with their lust for blood gone, will pasture peacefully with domesticated cattle. Infants will be exposed to no danger, because of the harmlessness of beasts, reptiles and insects, vv. 6-8. This scene of gentleness is the result of the earth being full of the knowledge of the Lord, v. 9. How the beasts responded to the Lord's control, Mark 1. 13; Luke 19. 30, 35.

There will be *no national independence*, v. 10. During the times of the Gentiles, none of the nations has achieved world domination. But Christ will achieve global supremacy. In that day, He will set up an ensign under which *all* the Gentiles shall rally, vv. 10, 12; cf. Gen. 49. 10.

There will be *no Jewish exiles*, vv. 11-12. The outcasts of Israel and Judah will return to the land, no longer in unbelief, but in recognition of their Messiah who gathers them.

There will be *no division in Israel*, vv. 13-16. Judah and Ephraim will be reconciled, all envy and strife having gone. Instead, they will sing a song of praise to Him whose anger has been turned away, ch. 12. How good and pleasant for brethren to dwell together in unity!, Psa. 133.

Sept. 30th

READING : Isaiah 13. 1 to 16. 14

THE BOOK OF BURDENS (1)

A "BURDEN" is a Divine utterance, usually of judgment, which weighed heavily on the spirits of the men who gave them. The office of the prophet was neither easy nor popular. Preaching the judgment of God should never be a delight.

The burden of Babylon, 13. 1-14, 27. Babylon was the first of four great empires destined to dominate the world scene during the times of the Gentiles. Babylon and its king were represented by the head of gold in Nebuchadnezzar's dream image, Dan. 2. 38. Its principal sins were pride, ambition and luxury, 13. 11, 19; 14. 4, for which its downfall was predicted, 13. 17-22; 14. 4-23. The mention of Lucifer, 14. 12, refers partly to the king of Babylon who boasted of his successes, Dan. 4. 30. Pride, however, is a particular sin of Satan, who is the real force behind the king. Satan's influence is detected in the motive for the building of the tower of Babel, Gen. 11. 4. He it is who will master-mind the Babylon of the future, whose judgment is described, Rev. 18. Lucifer means "morning star", a title which rightly only belongs to Christ. From the first to last mention of Babylon in Scripture, it is seen to represent all that is antichrist. "Pride goeth before destruction, and an haughty spirit before a fall", Prov. 16. 18.

The burden of Palestina (Philistia), 14. 28-32. Israel did not completely drive out the Philistines. They were a constant source of oppression. Uzziah inflicted a decisive blow on them, 2 Chron. 26. 6-7, but under the weak Ahaz they regained their lost prestige, over which they rejoiced, Isa. 14. 29. Judgment, however, was coming upon them and they would howl. "Rejoice not when thine enemy falleth", Prov. 24. 17.

The burden of Moab, 15. 1 to 16. 14. Moab was one of the off-spring resulting from the incestuous relationship between Lot and his two daughters. The daughters of Moab first caused Israel to commit whoredom, Num. 25. 1. In the calamities to fall upon the nation within three years, Isa. 16. 14, the daughters of Moab were to be like a bird cast out of a nest, v. 2. Here pride and haughtiness were the sins for which they were judged, 16. 6; Jer. 48. 26, 29.

Oct. 1st
READING : Isaiah 17. 1 to 21. 17
THE BOOK OF BURDENS (2)

THE BURDEN OF DAMASCUS, 17. 1-14, includes Ephraim (the ten tribes), presumably because of the alliance between the two kings, 7. 4-9. Their glory will depart, v. 3; cf. 1 Sam. 4. 21. The worship of Baal with its groves and sun images, Isa. 17. 8, was the downfall of Ephraim. Saul of Tarsus later witnessed a glory greater than that of the sun outside Damascus.

The burden of Egypt, 18. 1 to 20. 6. Ethiopia, allied to Egypt, is included in this burden, 18. 1. Egypt and Assyria were rival powers with Israel wedged in between. In the days of Ahaz, Judah looked to Assyria for help against Syria and Israel. Judah's hope was disappointed, for in the days of Hezekiah the Assyrians marched on Judah and Jerusalem. In those, and subsequent days, Judah looked to Egypt for help against the northern aggressors, and again was disappointed. Egypt was a bruised reed, 36. 6, and herself was to be led away captive, 20. 4. By his symbolic act, Isaiah demonstrated, personally, the folly of leaning on Egypt for help. It is better to trust in the Lord than to put confidence in man and princes, Psa. 118. 8-9. Egypt will be torn by internal strife, Isa. 19. 2; be given over to necromancy, v. 3; and be subject to a cruel lord, v. 4. The main industries on which their living depended, fishing and weaving, were to fail, vv. 5-10. Their political counsel will be ineffective, vv. 11-14, and mass unemployment will be throughout the land, v. 15. Surely, these things have a message for us to-day. The passage also points to a day yet future when Egypt will look to Israel, along with whom they are destined to be blessed, vv. 18-25.

The burden of the desert of the sea, 21. 1-10, is a further oracle against Babylon, announcing its fall, v. 9, by the Medes and Persians, v. 2. *The burden of Dumah*, 21. 11-12, refers to Edom. A long night is predicted on this nation. An eternal night will be the portion of those who, like Esau, the father of Edom, sell their spiritual birthright for a mess of pottage. *The burden of Arabia*, 21. 13-17, concerns the wild aggressive descendants of Ishmael, Gen. 16. 12. Their strength and glory will fail and be diminished, Isa. 21. 16-17. Among those who hate peace, we must seek to live at peace, Psa. 120. 5-7; Rom. 12. 18.

Oct. 2nd

READING : **Isaiah 22. 1 to 23. 18**

THE BOOK OF BURDENS (3)

THE BURDEN OF THE VALLEY OF VISION, 22. 1-25, applies to Jerusalem as verses 9-11 make clear. Under the threat of an Assyrian invasion, the people made every effort to defend themselves. Houses were demolished to repair the breeches in the city wall. To safeguard the city's water supply, subterranean passages in the rock were dug, vv. 8-11. Isaiah exposes the failure of the people to see the Assyrian threat as a Divine visitation on Jerusalem, which would have caused the people to look to the Lord their Maker, instead of relying on their own resources, v. 11. The crisis called for true repentance, the signs of which are "weeping" and "mourning", v. 12, but they feasted, thinking only of the present, v. 13; 1 Cor. 15. 32. The prophet is moved to tears, Isa. 22. 4, as it was also revealed that these would die of their sins, v. 14. Isaiah is like the Lord who wept over the Jerusalem of His day, because its people knew not the day of their visitation, or the dreadful fate that was to overtake them, Luke 19. 41-44.

Shebna was the treasurer in charge of the house of David. He used the office to secure himself, as a "nail that is fastened in the sure place", Isa. 22. 25. He was removed from office, and replaced by Eliakim who had the interests of the people at heart, v. 21. Eliakim is a type of Christ, who also is referred to as "a nail in a sure place", v. 23. Unlike Shebna, He will not be removed, and all the government of the house of David will hang upon Him, v. 24; cf. Zech. 10. 4. Christ has the keys of hades and death, Rev. 1. 18, and also the key of the house of David, Isa. 22. 22.

The burden of Tyre, 23. 1-18, completes the book of burdens. Tyre was a mercantile nation whose merchants were of repute, v. 8. She imported gold, silver, copper, etc., from Chittim (Cyprus), and from as far off as Tarshish, v. 1. Materialistic in outlook, her pride was to be brought low, first by an Assyrian, and later by a Chaldean siege, v. 13. After Divine visitation, she does not change, v. 17. Verse 18 points to a day still future when her outlook will be different. "The silver is mine, and the gold is mine", Hag. 2. 8. Let us beware of materialism, and seek to lay up instead treasures in heaven, Matt. 6. 20-21.

Oct. 3rd

READING : **Isaiah 24. 1 to 27. 13**

SONGS OF PRAISE

WE HAVE NOTED the fact of Divine intervention in the affairs of nations. In a crisis, men fear; when it passes, they relax and self-indulgence recurs. Divine correction, in general, fails to change men's ways, 26. 10. This makes necessary a major judgment that will effectively sweep the earth clean, Acts 17. 31.

Isaiah 24 directs attention to that day which will precede Christ's reign in Zion, v. 23. The heavens will be cleansed as well as earth. He will "punish the host of the high ones that are on high", v. 21. Consequently, the devil and his host will be imprisoned in the abyss, cf. Rev. 20. 2-3, or earth would be infected again.

In chapter 25 the prophet sings praise to Jehovah for what He has done, vv. 1-4, and for what He will do, vv. 6-10. He will eliminate all need; remove the veil of blindness from all peoples as well as Israel; abolish death, and banish sorrow, vv. 6-8. The phrase "in this mountain" occurs three times, and emphasizes that Zion will be the centre of universal blessing to all peoples. Yes, "this is our God; we have waited for him", v. 9.

Chapter 26 speaks of the restoration of Israel in their land, and the song they will sing then. The song expresses their trust in Jehovah, and the peace that will be their portion, vv. 1-4. Having been dominated by Gentile lords, they will at length own Jehovah as supreme Lord. As Noah and his family came through the flood, so many of Israel will come through the tribulation of those days. Others will be martyred, but will be raised again, vv. 19-21. We, too, have been set free from the bondage of sin and Satan. Let us, therefore, acknowledge no other lords besides Him who died for us and rose again; cf. v. 13; Rom. 6. 12-14; 14. 9.

Chapter 27, the song of the restored vineyard, should be compared with the song of the Wellbeloved's vineyard, 5. 1-7. There the vineyard was abandoned, and overgrown; here it is tended and protected. There it was a picture of Israel's scattering; here of Israel's re-gathering, vv. 12-13; cf. Deut. 30. 4; Matt. 24. 31. Prior to that day, the trumpet will sound for us, 1 Thess. 4. 16-17. What a gathering that will be! May we live daily in expectation of this event.

Oct. 4th
READING : Isaiah 28. 1 to 33. 24
CHAPTERS OF WOE

IN THE DAYS of Isaiah, Judah and Jerusalem lived under the threat of an Assyrian invasion. However, the fearful events of those days foreshadowed worse calamities in the future when the land will be overrun, and the city will be surrounded by Gentile forces, Luke 21. 20.

The scourge of unbelief plagues the history of Israel. Only a part of the first generation out of Egypt entered Canaan because of unbelief, Heb. 3. 19. Only a remnant will enjoy the blessing of Christ's reign, 28. 5; 29. 22-24; 30. 19-21; 33. 2, 15-17. The apostates in Israel will have been consumed beforehand, 28. 17-22; 29. 20-21; 33. 13-14. In these chapters, unbelief is everywhere apparent. The rulers were scornful of the prophet's words, 28. 9-14. They entered into an evil covenant, 28. 15, but it would not save them from "the overflowing scourge". They considered the city of David to be invincible, calling it, "Ariel" (Lion of God), but it will be brought down, 29. 4. They trusted in Egypt, yet only to be let down, 30. 1-7; 31. 1-4. They looked to the wisdom of men, 29. 14, which Jehovah would bring to nought.

The prophet urges Judah to trust in Jehovah, referring to Him as a sure foundation stone who could be relied upon, 28. 16. Their safety lay in quiet confidence and waiting for Him, 30. 15-18. As a protecting eagle, He will defend Jerusalem, 31. 5, breaking the Assyrian's power, 30. 31-33; 31. 8-9; 33. 1, and establishing a kingdom in righteousness, 32. 1-20. The path of faith is the path of safety. Abraham, the father of faith, went down to Egypt in a crisis and consequently, exposed himself to danger. We must beware also of mistrusting God when in straitened circumstances.

The king who will reign in righteousness, 32. 1, is the same One of whom the Psalmist said, "Thou lovest righteousness, and hatest wickedness", Psa. 45. 7. Many thrones have been established by lawlessness; His will be established by righteousness. Saul, the people's choice, proved to be a failure, but God gave David, a king of His choice, to be the prototype of Christ. Of this One God said, "Yet have I set my king upon my holy hill of Zion", Psa. 2. 6. Israel's hope is "Thine eyes shall see the king in his beauty", 33. 17; cf. 1 John 3. 2-3.

Oct. 5th

READING : **Isaiah 34. 1 to 35. 10**

THE CURSE REMOVED

CHAPTER 35 provides yet another preview of the millennium. Verses 1-2, convey a picture of joy and luxuriant growth. The barren places of earth will be transformed into places of fertility, beauty and fragrance, just like Lebanon, Sharon and Carmel. The curse having been lifted, earth will yield her increase in abundance, Amos 9. 13. There will be abundant resources of water, Isa. 35. 6-7; drought and famine will be unknown. Sickness and disease will disappear before Christ's power, as they did when He was among men in lowly guise. The miracles which the Lord did when He was here were signs of His Messiahship. They were powers of the age to come (millennial age), Heb. 6. 5. Those Jews who repeatedly asked for signs exposed their spiritual blindness in failing to link the Lord's works with this passage.

We pause to consider a thrilling fact. This coming age of peace and plenty cannot be until we, the sons of God, are manifested in glory. Creation personified eagerly awaits that time, Rom. 8. 19-22. Do we live in eager expectation?

Chapter 34, by contrast, describes the dreadful day that will precede the reign of Christ. It will be a day of the Lord's indignation and fury, v. 2, and of vengeance, v. 8. With His sword He will execute righteous judgment on a godless world, whose armies will be gathered together in defiance against Him; cf. Rev. 19. 11-21. Strange appearances in the sun, moon and stars will add terror to that day, v. 4; cf. Matt. 24. 29; Rev. 6. 12-14.

Moses feared when God shook the earth at Sinai. How much more fearful it will be when God shakes heaven and earth, Hag. 2. 6, 21; Heb. 12. 21, 26-28.

Idumea (Edom) is singled out for mention, as being representative of all the nations that will be opposed to God and Israel. The traits of Esau are reproduced in his descendants, the Edomites. The Edomites were Israel's inveterate enemies, and they will be destroyed. In that day of doom, like their father, they will find no place of repentance, Heb. 12. 17. A birthright despised is a blessing departed.

Thank God that we live in a day of grace when forgiveness may be sought and found.

Oct. 6th

READING : Isaiah 36. 1 to 37. 38

DELIVERANCE FROM THE ASSYRIANS

HEZEKIAH "trusted in the Lord God of Israel", so that there was none like him before or after his days, 2 Kings 18. 5. He was a good son of a bad father. Ahaz, his father, sold himself and Judah to the Assyrians. He also abandoned the worship of Jehovah, 2 Kings 16. 10-18. Hezekiah restored the worship, and rebelled against the king of Assyria, refusing to be a vassal king. Consequently the king of Assyria marched on Judah. There were two occasions when the Assyrians came against Jerusalem; compare carefully 2 Kings 18. 1-37; 2 Chron. 32. 1-21; Isa. 36-37. The first is noted in 36. 1; the second, in 36. 2 to 37. 13. At the first encounter, the city was besieged. Although Hezekiah took every precaution to withstand the enemy, in the end he had to admit defeat, and pay a big tribute imposed on him. It appears that, for all Hezekiah's knowledge of God's power, he also relied on his own defence measures, 2 Chron. 32. 1-8. There is always a danger of not *wholly* trusting the Lord, and this was a lesson he had to learn.

The second encounter was some years later when Sennacherib sent Rabshakeh to Jerusalem. Rabshakeh's blasphemous speech to the elders, 36. 4-10, then to the people, vv. 13-20, met with no reply. There is "a time to keep silence, and a time to speak", Eccles. 3. 7. Hezekiah advised silence; compare the Lord Jesus, who never returned reviling but committed Himself to the righteous Judge, 1 Pet. 2. 21-23. In the face of this fresh crisis, Hezekiah humbles himself and casts himself entirely upon the Lord, 37. 1-4, who assures him, by Isaiah, of His Divine help, vv. 6-7. When, subsequently, he received the letter from Rabshakeh, he did not ignore it in self-confidence. Although assured of deliverance, he took it to the Lord in prayer. The prayer is marked by sincerity and a desire for the glory of the Lord, 37. 20. The Lord had heard all the words of the Assyrian general, and replies with like derision and scorn. Sennacherib and his forces are dismissed contemptuously as nonentities. Unlike their former operation, they would not be allowed to besiege Jerusalem, or even shoot an arrow at it, 37. 21-35. Rely on the Lord's almighty defence.

The zeal of the Lord Almighty is our sure guarantee that He will perform His promises, v. 32.

Oct. 7th

READING : **Isaiah 38. 1 to 39. 8**

HEZEKIAH'S SICKNESS AND RECOVERY

THE EVENTS recorded in chapters 38 and 39 took place before the Assyrian siege of Jerusalem. Two facts appear to confirm this. The first is that Hezekiah is promised deliverance from the Assyrians, 38. 6, and the second that Hezekiah showed the Babylonians the treasures of the palace which were later stripped to meet the huge tribute imposed on him at the time of the siege, 2 Kings 18. 14-16.

Hezekiah's sorrow at the prospect of death is understandable. He was only 39 years old, and he did not have an heir to the throne. His writing, after his healing, 38. 9-20, shows a lack of knowledge of the future state. We know "Jesus Christ, who hath abolished death, and hath brought life and immortality to light through the gospel", 2 Tim. 1. 10, transforming death for the believer into "sleep", 1 Thess. 4. 14. Unlike Hezekiah, Paul longed to be with the Lord whom he loved, Phil. 1. 23.

To heal Hezekiah, a lump of figs was prescribed—a simple remedy. God can make small things effectual, 1 Cor. 1. 27-29. When it comes to assuring him, however, God did a big thing. He made the sun go back ten degrees. It often requires a bigger effort on God's part to convince a man, than to remove his problem. Life and death are in the hand of God, Psa. 90. 12.

God answered Hezekiah's prayer and extended his life by fifteen years. Answered prayer, however, is not always the blessing it is thought to be. After three years, Manasseh was born. He grew up to be evil and undid all the good work of his father; cf. 1 Sam. 8. 3.

How easy it is to forget God's benefits towards us; see Isa. 39; Psa. 103. 2. In the affair with the envoys from Babylon, Hezekiah was guilty of ingratitude and pride, 2 Chron. 32. 25. Why did he evade telling the prophet what was discussed?, Isa. 39. 3-4. Did he arrange an alliance with Babylon against Assyria? God foretold that his present friends would become Judah's future foes.

A fitting conclusion to the first half of Isaiah is "let not the rich man glory in his riches: but let him that glorieth glory in this, that he understandeth and knoweth me", Jer. 9. 23-24.

Oct. 8th

READING : **Isaiah 40. 1-11**

THE SERVANT OF JEHOVAH INTRODUCED

IN THIS second section of Isaiah the Person of the "Servant of Jehovah" predominates. The term is applied to the nation of Israel, 41. 8, and then to the Messiah, 42. 1. From this point on, much of the material is occupied with the suffering and the glory of God's Servant. There is a magnificent introduction. The people are told to keep silence, 41. 1. Let God speak!

There are three voices in 40. 1-11:

(1) The voice of Jehovah, vv. 1-2. A message of comfort.
(2) The voice of John the Baptist, vv. 3-8; John 1. 23.
(3) The voice of Jerusalem announcing the Messiah, v. 9.

The first voice is one of comfort that comes from the forgiveness of sins. The message of a pardoning God.

The second voice is that of the forerunner of the Messiah. He has a ministry of smoothing and straightening the path for the revelation of the glory, Mark 1. 3. Then there is a contrast between the flesh, man's corrupt nature which is like burnt grass, and the Word of God which stands forever, vv. 6-8. It is a preview of John's ministry of repentance, redemption and retribution. John was a voice, but Christ is the Word, John 1. 1, 23.

The third voice is a call to Zion to cry from the mountain top to the cities of Judah, "Behold your God", v. 9. The Servant is the Divine Messiah. His hand and His arm are mentioned, v. 10, and then He is revealed as a Shepherd with a fourfold ministry, v. 11. Each of these ministries has a counterpart in the New Testament: He shall

(1) feed His flock like a shepherd. It is a ministry of feeding, Mark 6. 31-44. The commission to feed the people of God was given to Simon Peter, John 21. 15-17. Then he passed it on to elders in the assembly, 1 Pet. 5. 1-4;

(2) gather the lambs with His arm. It is a gathering ministry. The lambs represent new-born babies in Christ, 1 Pet. 2. 2; Psa. 50. 5;

(3) carry them in His bosom. It is a ministry of comfort, Isa. 46. 4; 2 Cor. 1. 3; Rom. 15. 4; Acts 9. 31;

(4) gently lead those that are with young. It is a ministry of guidance, especially encouraging to those that have the responsibility of working among young people.

Oct. 9th

READING : Isaiah 40. 12-31

WAITING ON THE LORD

FROM the contemplation of the ministry of the Servant-Shepherd, v. 11, the prophet turns to consider the God of creation. There is a magnificent revelation of the Triune God, a truth ignored or denied by many till the present day. The Scriptures teach One God in three co-equal Persons—Father, Son and Holy Spirit. In verse 10 men are exhorted to "Behold your God", who is the Shepherd in His fourfold ministry, v. 11, the Spirit in His omniscience and omnipotence, v. 13, and the Everlasting God, the Lord, the Creator of the earth, v. 28.

There are four facts relating to His power in creation:

(1) The relation of the depth of the ocean to the height of the mountains. There is balance between the two, v. 12.

(2) He sits upon the circle of the earth, v. 22. This is the only place in Scripture where we find this expression; cf. Job 22. 14; Prov. 8. 27. Not just the horizon but the earth. While the Bible is not a scientific textbook, yet it is in conformity with true science.

(3) He stretches out the heavens as a curtain, and spreads them out as a tent to dwell in, v. 22. A remarkable description of the atmosphere and the stratosphere.

(4) The starry hosts, each one with a number and a name, v. 26, are compared with puny man, and the utter foolishness of his worship of idols of wood covered with gold, vv. 18-20.

Then discouraged Israel is introduced. "Why sayest thou, O Jacob . . . My way is hid from the Lord, and my judgment is passed over from my God?", v. 27. The answer is a tremendous galaxy of titles of Almighty God, v. 28, and a precious promise to the faint and weary. It takes in both young and old. They "that wait upon the Lord shall renew their strength; they shall mount up with wings as eagles; they shall run, and not be weary; and they shall walk, and not faint", v. 31. The threefold promise indicates three stages of life. Mounting up with wings suggests the young believer; the middle years of running and not being weary indicate the mature busy service for the Lord. But last of all we have to slow down to a steady walk. Those that have to adjust merely to walking instead of flying or running are promised that they will not faint. Waiting on the Lord is not lost time.

Oct. 10th

READING : **Isaiah 42. 1-12**

THE SERVANT'S CALL AND COMMISSION

THE FIRST paragraph of this chapter, vv. 1-12, is the first of four "Servant Songs" in this section of Isaiah. The others are: 49. 1-13; 50. 1-11; 52. 13 to 53. 12. This first one outlines the presentation, the pathway on earth, and the programme of the Messiah. It is in four parts with a conclusion.

(1) *His Coming*, v. 1, as "mine elect, in whom my soul delighteth; I have put my Spirit upon him". This takes us to the Jordan and His presentation to Israel, Matt. 3. 13-17. There is a manifestation of the Holy Trinity. The voice from heaven. "This is my beloved Son", with the Spirit descending upon Him like a dove. There are three notable references by Isaiah to the Holy Spirit and the Messiah: His incarnation, 11. 2; here His baptism; His public ministry, 61. 1.

(2) *His Character*, vv. 2-4. There are four moral qualities: His softness, sympathy, success and steadfastness. These suggest the ingredients of the meal offering, Lev. 2. 1-2, 13.

(a) Softness, v. 2. "He shall not cry, nor lift up, nor cause his voice to be heard in the street". There was nothing of the noisy agitator, or the revolutionary, about Him. He was quiet, calm, and undisturbed by hostile treatment.

(b) Sympathy, v. 3. "A bruised reed shall he not break, and the smoking flax shall he not quench". He will gently straighten out the former, and blow into a flame the latter.

(c) Success, v. 4. "He shall not fail nor be discouraged". In spite of seeming failure, His life and death resulted in complete success and victory.

(d) Steadfastness, v. 4. Jacob, David, Elijah and Jonah all had periods of discouragement and failure, but He, never. He steadfastly set His face, Luke 9. 51.

(3) *His Call*, v. 6. A covenant to the people, Israel, and a light to the Gentiles. The Abrahamic, Gen. 15, the Davidic, 2 Sam. 7, and the new, Jer. 31; Heb. 8, covenants will all be fulfilled in and through Him.

(4) *His Commission*, v. 7. He is the Illuminator of blind Israel, and the Emancipator of the shackled heathen.

The Conclusion, vv. 9-12, looks forward to a new day, and a new song, when all of God's purposes for Jew and Gentile will be carried out by His Servant.

Oct. 11th

READING : Isaiah 44. 28 to 45. 25

PROPHECY OF DELIVERANCE BY KING CYRUS

ISAIAH 45 is one of the most remarkable prophecies in Holy Scripture. Isaiah lived many years before the 70 year exile of the people of Israel in Babylon. He warned king Hezekiah about it, 39. 5-7. The northern kingdom was taken into captivity first, 2 Kings 17. 4-6. Then the southern kingdom of Judah and Jerusalem was invaded by Nebuchadnezzar, the temple destroyed and the people exiled to Babylon, 2 Kings 25.

In the second unit of his prophecy, chs. 40-56, Isaiah predicts the return of the people to their own and, the rebuilding of the temple, and the re-establishing of the worship in Jerusalem. From the human stand-point, the person responsible for this is a Persian king called Cyrus, Ezra 1. 1-4. The amazing thing is that Isaiah, under the inspiration of the Holy Spirit, gives the name of the king Cyrus and remarkable details of his character and conquests, and this about 200 years before it happened! No wonder this amazing prophecy has been attacked by sceptics and modernist critics.

A number of passages in this section of Isaiah refer to Cyrus, although only two mention him by name. In 44. 28 the Lord says of Cyrus, "He is my shepherd, and shall perform all my pleasure". Then in 45. 1 we read, "Thus saith the Lord to his anointed, to Cyrus, whose right hand I have holden, to subdue nations before him". "I girded thee, though thou hast not known me", v. 5. All of this points up to that which Daniel said to king Belshazzar: "the most high God ruled in the kingdom of men, and that he appointeth over it whomsoever he will", Dan. 5. 21. The two remarkable titles given to Cyrus, "my shepherd" and "his anointed", are unique, and elsewhere applied to the Messiah. But surely the lesson is that God, in His sovereignty, can take up a heathen monarch, and use him for the carrying out of His purpose.

After the recital of the victories of Cyrus, God again takes up the theme of the salvation of Israel, Isa. 45. 9-17. His sovereignty is emphasized in the clay and the potter, v. 9; Rom. 9. 20-21. He is a just God and a Saviour, Isa. 45. 21. Then the invitation "Look unto me, and be ye saved, all the ends of the earth", v. 22, knowing that one day "unto me every knee shall bow, every tongue shall swear", v. 23; Phil. 2. 10.

Oct. 12th

READING : **Isaiah 49. 1-26**

THE SERVANT IS A SOLDIER

ISAIAH 40-66 is divided into three sections of nine chapters each. The first two sections, chs. 40-48 and chs. 49-57, end with similar words, "There is no peace, saith the Lord (my God), unto the wicked". The middle section, chs. 49-57, in many ways is the most important. It gives three pictures of the Servant: as a *soldier* with his weapons, a sword and a polished arrow hidden in a quiver, ch. 49, as the *scholar* in God's school, ch. 50, and as the *sufferer and sacrifice* for sin, ch. 53. Between chapters 41 and 53, the servant is mentioned 20 times. His rejection, suffering and ultimate exaltation are referred to again and again.

Chapter 49 is addressed to the coastlands, a people from afar. It tells of success among the Gentile nations, v. 6, but discouragement with regard to Israel, v. 5. Israel as a servant is replaced by the Ideal Servant, the Messiah, vv. 3, 6.

The Soldier-Servant is described in 49. 1-3, with His ministry of conflict when He came to His own people; cf. 63. 1-4; John 1. 11-12; Rev. 19. 15. Verses 4-6 express His discouragement on account of His rejection by Israel, "I have laboured in vain, I have spent my strength for nought . . . yet shall I be glorious in the eyes of the Lord, and my God shall be my strength". As a result, the Gentiles come into blessing, v. 6; Luke 2. 32. Paul quotes "In an acceptable time have I heard thee, and in a day of salvation have I helped thee", v. 8, and applies it to his work among the Gentiles, 2 Cor. 6. 2.

Then Israel too will be regathered, restored, and come into blessing. "Behold, these shall come from far: and, lo, these from the north and from the west; and these from the land of Sinim" (the east, perhaps China), v. 12. In the meantime Israel says, "The Lord hath forsaken me, and my Lord hath forgotten me", v. 14. But the gracious tender reply is, "Can a woman forget her sucking child, that she should not have compassion on the son of her womb? yea, they may forget, yet will I not forget thee. Behold, I have graven thee on the palms of my hands; thy walls are continually before me", vv. 15-16. The rest of the chapter speaks of that recovery and regathering. Recent events in the Near East seem to indicate that the stage is being set for that great event.

Oct. 13th

READING : Isaiah 50. 1-11

THE SERVANT IN GOD'S SCHOOL

THE CHAPTER opens with Israel in the position of a woman who has been separated from her husband on account of unfaithfulness. She is also bankrupt. But it is all one-sided. She is the delinquent, and no bill of divorce has been issued. This is the condition of Israel at the incarnation, v. 2.

Before speaking of His voluntary submission to the will of His Father, the Servant reminds us of His mighty creatorial power, vv. 2-3. While He was the Servant in His humiliation, at the same time He was the Son with all the attributes of the Godhead.

The word "learned" in verse 4 really means a disciple, or one who is instructed. Morning by morning He was wakened, and His ear opened to hear His Father's voice, Psa. 40. 6. He never acted independently, but always in happy fellowship and intimacy with His Father, and the Holy Spirit. He did not *learn* to obey. His will was *always* that of complete conformity to that of His Father. But "learned he obedience by the things which he suffered", Heb. 5. 8. Some of these sufferings are detailed in this chapter.

First, was the lesson of *sympathy*, "that I should know how to speak a word in season to him that is weary", v. 4. "Jesus therefore, being wearied with his journey, sat thus on the well", John 4. 6. He experienced weariness so that He could sympathize with those that are tired, and He certainly had a word in season for the woman at the well.

Then, there was the lesson of *submission*. "The Lord God hath opened mine ear, and I was not rebellious, neither turned away back", v. 5. His whole life was lived in view of Golgotha. In the garden of Gethsemane He would say, "not my will, but thine, be done", Luke 22. 42.

This is followed by the lesson of *silent suffering*, "I gave my back to the smiters, and my cheeks to them that plucked off the hair", v. 6; John 19. 1. Then, *steadfastness*, "therefore have I set my face like a flint", v. 7; Luke 9. 51, 53.

The chapter ends with a contrast between staying upon God in the dark, and self-willed guidance. Those that light their own little fire, and walk in the light of it, will ultimately end up in the dark, and lie down in sorrow, vv. 10-11.

Oct. 14th

READING : **Isaiah 52. 13 to 53. 6**

THE SUFFERING SERVANT

THIS GREAT passage is the peak and climax of Old Testament prophecy. It is a poem of five stanzas of three verses each. Except for the last, there is a different speaker in each stanza. Jehovah introduces the Servant in the first stanza, and it is He who speaks the final words of vindication and victory in the last one, 53. 10-12. In the central three stanzas, it is the voice of repentant Israel, 53. 1-3, believers of Jew and Gentile, vv. 4-6, and the prophet himself, vv. 7-9.

The first stanza, 52. 13-15, presents the *Person* of the Servant. It is an introduction and summary of chapter 53: His exaltation, v. 13; His humiliation, v. 14; His manifestation, v. 15. The three words, exalted, extolled, and very high, might indicate the three steps to the throne: His resurrection, ascension, and His seating at God's right hand. Before the dark valley of suffering and death, we are reminded of the glory, Isa. 6. 1-3. In His humiliation, 52. 14, His face and His form were marred more than any man's, not recognizable as a man! At His manifestation in glory, nations and kings will be shocked and stunned into silence, v. 15; Rev. 19. 11-16.

The second stanza, 53. 1-3, is the confession of repentant Israel, Zech. 12. 10 to 13. 1. It describes the Servant's *pathway* on earth, His birth, childhood, His presentation to Israel and their reaction, v. 2; John 1. 11. He was rejected, despised, and esteemed as nothing, v. 3. All was fulfilled in detail, and was climaxed by His death upon the cross.

The third and central stanza, vv. 4-6, will be Israel's confession in a coming day. The vicarious atoning death of the Saviour is the central theme of Holy Scripture, and of Christianity itself. It will be the song of the redeemed of both Jew and Gentile throughout eternity, Rev. 5. 9-14.

Four great words in verse 5 describe the *passion* of God's Servant, the Messiah. The words rendered "wounded" (or pierced) and "bruised" are the strongest terms to describe a death of violence and agony. The "chastisement" which brings peace was the judgment of God's righteous wrath upon His sinless soul. The word rendered "stripes" denotes not a scourging but a "bruise" (as marg. and the Septuagint); cf. 1 Pet. 2. 24, a stroke of Divine judgment.

Oct. 15th

READING : Isaiah 53. 7-12

THE SUFFERING AND THE GLORY

IN THE FOURTH STANZA, vv. 7-9, the prophet speaks. There is a series of remarkable prophecies, all fulfilled on the day of the crucifixion: His trial before the Sanhedrin, v. 7, His execution, v. 8, and His burial, v. 9. His silence before His accusers is mentioned in Mark 14. 60-61; Luke 23. 9; His death or "cutting off" in Daniel 9. 26, and His burial in John 19. 38-42. The Hebrew word for "death" is plural, v. 9. In this plural, the Holy Spirit conveys the fact that His death was more comprehensive than that of a Roman execution. It is the plural of majesty, many deaths rolled into one. There is a remarkable statement concerning His burial: "And they made his grave with the wicked, and with the rich in his death", v. 9 R.V. Here we have a unique instance of men's evil intention, but of God's over-ruling intervention. The enemy intended to bury Him in a common grave with the malefactors, but in God's purpose, His Holy One, Psa. 16. 10, was buried in a clean place outside the camp, Lev. 6. 11. Two rich men, Joseph and Nicodemus, provided the place, and the perfume respectively. He was given the burial of a king, 2 Chron. 16. 13-14.

In the first four stanzas of this great prophecy we see the physical, visible sufferings of the Servant of Jehovah at the hands of man, but *in the fifth and final stanza* we see the deeper sufferings at the hands of Jehovah Himself, vv. 10-12. "Yet it pleased the Lord to bruise him", v. 10. Three times His soul is mentioned. First, "when thou shall make *his soul* an offering for sin"; this is the guilt or trespass offering, Lev. 5. 15; 6. 7. Three blessings are linked with it: "He shall see his seed, he shall prolong his days, and the pleasure of the Lord shall prosper in his hand". The last clause in verse 11 points to the sin offering, Lev. 16. 22, "he shall bear their iniquities". Here again three blessings result: "He shall see of the travail (birth pangs) of *his soul,* and shall be satisfied: by his knowledge shall my righteous servant justify many", Rom. 5. 18-19.

The passage concludes with the drink offering: "he hath poured out *his soul* unto death", v. 12; Num. 15. 1-11; 28. 7-15. Again a threefold blessing climaxes all.

Oct. 16th

READING : **Isaiah 54. 1-17**

GOSPEL BLESSINGS FOR ISRAEL

THE CHAPTERS which follow the crucial passage of the Suffering Servant are directly related to it. We have seen how the great work of redemption was accomplished in chapter 53. Now we are to see the results, first for Israel, ch. 54, and then for the Gentile, ch. 60.

Up to the end of chapter 53, we read of the Servant in the singular; from that chapter onwards we read of "servants" in the plural. In the ten further references to the "servants" in the remainder of this prophecy, we learn of their qualifications and responsibility to follow the example of the supreme Servant, our Lord Jesus Christ.

Chapter 54 opens with the blessings for Israel resulting from the sufferings of her Messiah, and the first word is "Sing". There is no song today on account of her rejection of His claims. She is now in the position of "Lo-ammi", Hos. 1. 9, "not my people". But there is a day coming when the glorious promises of Isaiah 54 will be fulfilled. Paul asks the question "Hath God cast away his people?", and he answers: "God forbid", Rom. 11. 1. "Even so then at this present time also there is a remnant according to the election of grace", 11. 5. And "blindness in part is happened to Israel, until the fulness of the Gentiles be come in. And so all Israel shall be saved: as it is written, There shall come out of Sion the Deliverer, and shall turn away ungodliness from Jacob", 11. 25-26. Then shall verses 2-3 of our chapter be fulfilled, "spare not, lengthen thy cords, and strengthen thy stakes". Unfortunately the stakes are being pulled up today but it will not be forever! There is a promise of a permanent building with foundations, and a structure of precious stones, vv. 11-12: no longer the flimsy transient tent on the desert sand. For "behold, I will lay thy stones with fair colours, and lay thy foundations with sapphires. And I will make thy windows of agates, and thy gates of carbuncles, and all thy borders of pleasant stones". And this in spite of a gathering of enemies against her, v. 15. The promise stands, "No weapon that is formed against thee shall prosper".

The One who promises all this is the Redeemer, vv. 5, 8, and it is based on a covenant of peace, v. 10.

Oct. 17th

READING : **Isaiah 55. 1-13**

GOSPEL BLESSINGS FOR THE GENTILE

ISAIAH 53 to 55 present a beautiful outline of the blessings of the gospel. Chapter 53 is the basis and foundation in the atoning vicarious death of the Saviour. Chapter 54 the blessing goes out to Israel, and in chapter 55 the joyful invitation is extended to the Gentile. Our chapter opens with a call to *everyone* that thirsteth, v. 1. It reminds us of the Lord's conversation with the Samaritan woman at the well.

The Lord is presented in a fourfold way in Isaiah 55. First, as a *Merchantman* with three things for sale: water, wine and milk. But, amazingly, all are offered freely, without cost. The only condition is for the buyer to have a thirst, vv. 1-2. Water is plural, living waters, indicating everlasting life, Rev. 22. 17; wine would speak of the joy of salvation, Psa. 104. 15; and milk is for nourishment of the new life, 1 Pet. 2. 2. The offer is sealed with an everlasting covenant, even "the sure mercies of David", v. 3. The apostle Paul connected these words with the resurrection of the Lord Jesus, Acts 13. 34.

Secondly, as a *Witness* to the peoples. Gentiles are definitely in view since the word "people" which occurs twice should be in the plural, v. 4. As the Witness, He makes God known to men, John 5. 31-37; Rev. 1. 5.

Thirdly, He is the *Leader*, v. 4; Heb. 2. 10; 12. 2. To Matthew, Philip and Simon Peter He gave the command "Follow me", and they rose up, left all, and followed Him, Matt. 9. 9; John 1. 43; 21. 19. This is the pathway of the disciple.

Fourthly, He is the *Commander* of the peoples, v. 4. Many times in His upper-room farewell discourse, the Lord mentions His commands, John 13-16. "A new commandment I give unto you, That ye love one another", John 13. 34.

Verses 6-11 teach us how all these blessings in the gospel are to be obtained. First, by seeking the Lord, and calling upon Him, v. 6. Then, by forsaking evil, and genuinely repenting, v. 7. Finally, by the operation of the Word of God, which is like the rain which comes down from heaven, v. 11. Verses 12-13 look forward to a day when creation's groans will be turned into joy, Rom. 8. 21-22, "and it shall be to the Lord for a name, for an everlasting sign that shall not be cut off ".

Oct. 18th

READING : **Isaiah 59. 20 to 60. 22**

THE REDEEMER COMES TO ZION

THE CLOSING section of the book, chs. 58-66, is mainly occupied with the glorious future which God has in store for Israel, when she will be God's channel of blessing to the world. Chapters 58 to 59 go back over the past, reminding them of their sin and backsliding, and its results: "your iniquities have separated between you and your God, and your sins have hid his face from you, that he will not hear", 59. 2. But God in His sovereign mercy takes the initiative. "And he saw that there was no man, and wondered that there was no intercessor; therefore his arm brought salvation . . . and His righteousness, it sustained him", 59. 16. "When the enemy shall come in like a flood, the Spirit of the Lord shall lift up a standard against him. And the Redeemer shall come to Zion, and unto them that turn from transgression in Jacob, saith the Lord", 59. 19-20; Rom. 11. 26. This magnificent passage points forward to the appearing of Christ in glory, to deal with His enemies and bless a truly repentant Israel.

Chapter 60 opens with the command, "Arise, shine; for thy light is come, and the glory of the Lord is risen upon thee". This indicates a revival of the nation, and an enlightenment. The veil that lies upon their mind and heart will be lifted, and Israel will be God's witness to the nations. They are destined to shine amid the gross darkness that covers the earth and peoples at that time, v. 2; Rev. 17. 3-14. The Gentiles are mentioned three times in Isaiah 60, vv. 3, 5, 11, along with the names of Midian, Ephah, Kedar and Nebaioth. These are children of Abraham by Keturah, Gen. 25. 4, 13. Isaiah declares that all will assist in bringing Israel back to the land, possibly by air, 60. 8, and by ship, v. 9. The rebuilding of the sanctuary is predicted, "The glory of Lebanon shall come unto thee, the fir tree, the pine tree, and the box together, to beautify the place of my sanctuary; and I will make the place of my feet glorious", v. 13. The city and the central shrine will be called "The city of the Lord, The Zion of the Holy One of Israel", v. 14. The assurance of the Blessed One to accomplish all this is: "Thou shalt know that I the Lord am thy Saviour and thy Redeemer, the mighty One of Jacob", v. 16.

Looking at the Near East today, we see the day approaching.

Oct. 19th

READING : Isaiah 61. 1-11

THE TWO ADVENTS OF THE MESSIAH

Isaiah 61. 1-3 forms a separate unit. It was from this passage our Lord read in the synagogue at Nazareth at the commencement of His public ministry, Luke 4. 16-30. He ended abruptly in the middle of a sentence with the words "to preach the acceptable year of the Lord". He then said, "This day is this scripture fulfilled in your ears. And all bare him witness, and wondered at the gracious words which proceeded out of his mouth". But when He continued to speak of God's grace to Gentile outsiders, like the widow of Sarepta and Naaman the Syrian, their wonder turned to anger, and it resulted in the second attempt on His life. The first was at Bethlehem by Herod, Matt. 2. 13-18, and the second in His hometown Nazareth. Thus, early in His life and ministry, was He rejected by man and the nation, John 1. 11. The real reason was His claim to be the Messiah, and the Servant of Jehovah of Isaiah 61. 1-2. Luke emphasizes the relation of the Holy Spirit to our Lord. He was "full" of the Holy Ghost, 4. 1; "led" by the Spirit, v. 1; and the Spirit of the Lord was "upon" Him, because He had "anointed" Him to preach the gospel to the poor, v. 18. As a result "his word was with power", v. 32. His ministry as the Servant of Jehovah was sixfold: "to preach the gospel to the poor . . . to heal the brokenhearted, to preach deliverance to the captives, and recovering of sight to the blind, to set at liberty them that are bruised, to preach the acceptable year of the Lord". This is a summary of our Lord's ministry recorded in the Gospel by Luke. In the meantime, during this period of grace, "the day of vengeance of our God" is postponed. This is why our Lord did not read these words at Nazareth. That day is to come later; see Isa. 63. 4.

The theme of 61. 4-11, which continues into chapter 62, is the restoration of Israel at the appearing of Christ in glory. The wasted desolate cities will be rebuilt, 61. 4. The people shall be named "Priests of the Lord" and "Ministers of our God", v. 6. The nation of Israel will then be a kingdom of priests, who will go into God's presence on behalf of all the other peoples of the earth. They will also be God's messengers to them. Again all of this is based on an everlasting covenant, v. 8.

Oct. 20th

READING : Isaiah 62. 1-12

JERUSALEM THE JOY OF THE WHOLE EARTH

THERE ARE two cities in Scripture which are in vivid contrast, Babylon and Jerusalem. Babylon represents all that is corrupt in religion, but Jerusalem is destined to be the earthly centre of God's purposes in blessing for Israel, and for mankind.

The name Jerusalem means "City of Peace". The city is also called symbolically "Salem" (peace), Heb. 7. 2, and "Ariel" (the lion of God), Isa. 29. 1, 2, 7. It is first mentioned as the city of Melchizedek the king-priest, Gen. 14. 18. It was here on mount Moriah that Abraham offered his son Isaac on the altar, Gen. 22. David captured the city from the Jebusites, 2 Sam. 5. 7. His son Solomon built the temple where God had chosen to place His Name, Deut. 12. 5, 11, 14, 18, 21.

It is ironic that, although the name of Jerusalem means "peace", no city in history has seen more war and bloodshed. It has been besieged more than 30 times and has been plundered and burnt by Babylon, Persia and Rome. It was here that our Lord was crucified. But the greatest holocaust is yet to come. It shall be a "burdensome stone" for all peoples, Zech. 12. 3; 14. 2, but Israel shall be saved out of trouble, Jer. 30. 7.

Isaiah 62 is occupied with the deliverance and the restoration of Israel at the appearing of Christ in glory. "For Zion's sake . . . and for Jerusalem's sake I will not rest, until the righteousness thereof go forth as brightness, and the salvation thereof as a lamp that burneth", v. 1. That Salvation will be none other than the Person of Christ. "Thou shalt also be a crown of glory in the hand of the Lord, and a royal diadem in the hand of thy God", v. 3. The wasted cities will be rebuilt, 61. 4. The people shall no more be termed forsaken but "Hephzibah" (My delight is in her) and the land shall not be termed desolate but "Beulah" (married), v. 4. The Jerusalem that is here described is very different from the "Sodom" of Isaiah 1. 10; cf. Rev. 11. 8. This city has experienced God's hand of discipline, but righteousness and peace will emerge. The watchmen upon the walls shall never held their peace day or night, Isa. 62. 6. It will be the "arm of his strength" that will accomplish all this, v. 8. The message to Israel is: "Say ye to the daughter of Zion, Behold, thy salvation cometh; behold, his reward is with him, and his work before him", v. 11.

Oct. 21st

READING : **Isaiah 63. 1-19**

THE DAY OF VENGEANCE

In Isaiah 61. 1-3 we read, in the most beautiful language, the mission of grace and mercy of the Servant of Jehovah, read by our Lord at Nazareth, Luke 4. 18-19. There He preached the glad tidings of the gospel of God's love and salvation. But in the future there remains "the day of vengeance of our God". Where the gospel is refused, judgment falls. This is the subject in Isaiah 63. 1-6. It is God's strange work, 28. 21. The passage is often misinterpreted, and applied to the agony of Christ in Gethsemane. But the winepress is that of the wrath of God, and the blood on His garments is that of His enemies, Rev. 14. 19-20. It is a vivid and terrible picture of what will happen at the battle of Armageddon, Rev. 16. 16. Israel will be the focal point, the carcase with the vultures gathered around to pluck her clean, Matt. 24. 28. The armies of the nations, from the west and the east, Rev. 16. 12-14, and from the north and south, Dan. 11. 40, will be gathered together against Israel and Jerusalem. But, at the critical moment, the heavens will open and the Rider on the white horse will appear followed by the armies of heaven. He "treadeth the winepress of the fierceness and wrath of Almighty God. And he hath on his vesture and his thigh a name written, KING OF KINGS, AND LORD OF LORDS", Rev. 19. 11-16. Isaiah and the apostle John complement each other in describing the tremendous scene and its aftermath, while Daniel 11. 40-45 and Zechariah 14. 1-5 supply further details.

In Isaiah 63. 7-19 there is a résumé of some of the history of Israel. It expresses the feelings of a godly remnant of the nation during the terrible days of judgment and vengeance on an ungodly world. They confess the national sins and departure of the past, v. 10, and do not hide their weakness and failure of the present, v. 17. But they "mention the loving kindnesses of the Lord", v. 7, and confess Him as their Saviour, v. 8. The deliverance from Egypt in the time of Moses is appealed to as a parallel to their expected deliverance, v. 9. Mixed with their doubt and fear is the consciousness of their relationship with God, and that He is their Father and Redeemer, v. 16. It will be a tremendous comfort to them, as it is for us today, to be able to say, "We are thine", v. 19.

Oct. 22nd

READING : Isaiah 65. 17-25; 66. 22-24

THE NEW HEAVENS AND THE NEW EARTH

IN THE LAST few chapters of this magnificent prophecy there is a combination of God's condemnation of His people's infidelity and sin, and of His sovereign grace and deliverance where there is genuine confession and repentance. In chapter 64 there is the confession: "But we are all as an unclean thing, and all our righteousnesses are as filthy rags", v. 6. "But now, O Lord, thou art our father; we are the clay, and thou our potter", v. 8. Then, in 65. 9, the godly seed, the remnant, is introduced: "And I will bring forth a seed . . . and mine elect shall inherit it, and my servants shall dwell there"; cf. 6. 13.

There are two brief mentions of new heavens and a new earth. First, in 65. 17, "For, behold, I create new heavens and a new earth: and the former shall not be remembered, nor come into mind". Secondly, in 66. 22, "For as the new heavens and the new earth, which I will make, shall remain before me, saith the Lord, so shall your seed and your name remain". This is more fully revealed in the New Testament, Rev. 21. 1. But the emphasis by Isaiah is the establishment of the millennial kingdom. In the most sublime language, he refers to that glorious period when Christ shall be upon the throne, and reign for 1000 years, Rev. 20. 1-6; Isa. 2. 2-5; 11. 6-9. Then the animal kingdom will be transformed: "The wolf and the lamb shall feed together, and the lion shall eat straw like the bullock; and dust shall be the serpent's meat. They shall not hurt nor destroy in all my holy mountain, saith the Lord", 65. 25. Israel will be reborn nationally, 66. 7-9; Ezek. 36. 22-23. She will be regathered, and from her will go out God's messengers to declare God's glory among the Gentiles, Isa. 66. 19-20. Man's life span will be prolonged, 65. 20, but in spite of a perfect government and ideal conditions, sin will be present and death the result, v. 20. There is a delightful exhortation and encouragement to the godly citizen of the kingdom: "to this man will I look, even to him that is poor and of a contrite spirit, and trembleth at my word", 66. 2. In sharp contrast, the prophecy ends with a reference to those who have rejected the King, "their worm shall not die, neither shall their fire be quenched", v. 24; Matt. 25. 46. There are only two ways set before us, life and death, "therefore choose life", Deut. 30. 19.

Introducing Jeremiah and Lamentations

THE MAN. Jeremiah the prophet was of priestly stock, and lived in Anathoth, three miles north-east of Jerusalem, which was in Benjamite territory, and assigned to the Levites, Josh. 21. 18. It was re-populated after the exile. The length and the tragic character of his ministry assure him a special place among the prophets. He was a man deeply involved emotionally in his ministry, and was not ashamed of his tears.

THE TIMES. Jeremiah's ministry extends from the latter half of Josiah's reign, through the reign of Zedekiah to the captivity in Babylon, in 587 B.C.; read 2 Kings 22-25. Thus he saw something of the effects of Josiah's reforms, when many godly values that had been lost to the nation were restored. But he also saw the gradual decline in the spiritual life of Judah, after Josiah had been killed. He witnessed against the religious and social evils of his times faithfully, until the temple and the city were destroyed, and the people were taken captive to Babylon. They were times of religious declension and departure.

THE MESSAGE OF JEREMIAH. The prophet emphasizes four main themes:

1. *The Nation had forsaken its God* — treachery and spiritual adultery were its sins. The covenant of Sinai was broken.

2. *The Leadership of Judah had failed.* Priests were profane, prophets were false. The shepherds had deserted the flock.

3. *There was but one hope for survival* — surrender to the king of Babylon. Judgment was inevitable. God could no longer tolerate the rebellion of His people.

4. *There would be a return and restoration of the nation after 70 years.* A new covenant and the rule of the Messianic King were God's ultimate purpose for the nation.

AN OUTLINE OF JEREMIAH. There are four main sections:
Concerning the People and the City, chs. 1-25.
Character and Course of Jeremiah's Ministry, chs. 26-45.
Concerning the Surrounding Nations, chs. 46-51.
Concluding Historical Details, ch. 52.

LAMENTATIONS. A collection of poetic laments over the destruction of Judah. Written by Jeremiah, it expresses the deep soul-sadness of one who loved his people, and saw them fall. Perhaps the most tragic language of the Old Testament.

Oct. 23rd

READING : **Jeremiah 1. 1-19**

CALL AND COMMITMENT OF THE PROPHET

JEREMIAH was God's man for his own times. Throughout the darkest days of Judah's final decline, he spoke fearlessly the Word of God to the people. The book of Jeremiah consists, of course, of the words of 'Jeremiah', 1. 1, but we notice that he is the man "to whom the word of the Lord came", v. 2. This emphasizes the inspiration of the Old Testament Scriptures. God's Word was given through holy men of God, 2 Pet. 1. 21.

Jeremiah was a man *chosen* and *called*, vv. 4-5. Before he was aware of it, even before he was born, he was known, sanctified and ordained to be a prophet to the nations. His emergence during Judah's last times was no accident. God planned his appearance in history for that particular time of need. Here is wonderful evidence of Divine omniscience which sets each servant of God in his own times.

Jeremiah was also a man *commissioned*, vv. 6-8. God had something to say to His wayward people, and it was to His chosen servant that He entrusted the message. Jeremiah's diffidence was rebuked. He was sent to speak the words that God would have him speak. His commission was stamped with the authority of the royal command. He was assured of the presence of the God who sent him. Here is a challenging and comforting thought for all who would witness for the Lord. With Divine commands go Divine enablings.

Jeremiah needed to be a man *consecrated* to the service of his God, vv. 9-10. No unclean, sinful lips could bear the vital messages that he had to give. The hand of the Lord touched his mouth. After the touch, the Word was put into his lips. Compare Isaiah 6. 6-7. The preaching of any message, delivered in the name of the Lord, must be accompanied by the purity of the messenger. We must never overlook this.

Jeremiah became a man utterly *committed* to the message that he gave. He could not turn back, vv. 11-19. The vision of the almond (*lit.* "wake") tree in blossom taught an important lesson. The guaranteed effectiveness of His Word rested with the *watchfulness* of the Lord who would "perform it". This promise was to prove an incentive to Jeremiah to remain faithful; it far outweighed the reactions and rebellion of those who heard that word.

Oct. 24th

READING : Jeremiah 2. 1-19

CHALLENGE AND CONDEMNATION

JEREMIAH has been called the "prophet of doom", and, indeed, the tone of his Book is often dark and depressing. Sometimes he was brought to bitter tears as he bore the Lord's message, 13. 17. Yet there was a deep cause for the prophet's sadness. We read in chapter 2 of the conditions of the people to whom the Word of the Lord came. For them *there was a challenge from the past*, vv. 1-3. The Lord remembered the early affections of His people. In the barren and fruitless wilderness He was their first attraction; they went after Him. Israel's ways were then holy and the Lord's chief interest was in them. God could not forget those early days; they were precious to Him. God is hurt by our backslidings and waywardness. Although we can forget the blessedness of past fellowship with the Lord, He always remembers and treasures it.

There was also a challenge to the present conditions of His people. The Lord asked why His people had wandered so far away, v. 5. He had done nothing to deserve it. Both people and priests were so insensitive that they never asked after the Lord, vv. 6, 8. They handled His law and yet were blind to their true condition before Him. No other nation had so readily changed their gods, which were not gods at all, v. 11. The Lord penetrated through the outward façade of Israel's religion and laid bare their hypocrisy. Two evils had been committed. The fountain of living waters had been forsaken, and broken cisterns which held no water chosen instead, v. 13. An important lesson lies here. Backsliding in heart leads inevitably to a search for substitutes for lost spiritual enjoyment. Nature abhors a vacuum. Notice "two evils" had been committed. The broken cisterns had been taken as substitutes for the living waters, leading to disillusionment and dissatisfaction.

The prospect which Jeremiah held out for the future was bleak indeed. He could offer only condemnation; "Thine own wickedness shall correct thee, and thy backslidings shall reprove thee", v. 19. There is no hope of joy or freedom for the spiritual wanderer; he walks a self-condemned path. Backsliding "is an evil thing and bitter"; cf. Ruth 1. 19-21. It begins with a self-chosen forsaking of the Lord and it ends with great loss and barrenness of soul.

Oct. 25th

READING : **Jeremiah 7. 1 to 8. 3**

PROCLAMATION FROM THE LORD'S HOUSE

JEREMIAH WAS on the attack. The Word of the Lord had come to him, and he had been told not only what to say, but where to say it. He stood in the gate of the Lord's house, 7. 2. He attacked the people's confidence in the temple, as a guarantee of spiritual security, cf. Israel's earlier confidence in the ark of the covenant, 1 Sam. 4. 3. This incident highlights a very serious aspect of Judah's sin. It is described as spiritual "adultery", Jer. 3. 8; 5. 7. Judah's worship of pagan gods and their practise of Canaanite pagan rituals constituted adultery and treachery in the eyes of God. Yet, in spite of all this, they chanted, "The temple of the Lord", 7. 4, as if the possession of the temple was the hallmark of true devotion and faithfulness.

Notice the true character of the house of the Lord. Five times it is described as the place where God chose to put His name, vv. 10, 11, 12, 14, 30. It was therefore a place of holiness, a house where the presence of the Lord was known. In the light of this, how serious was the nation's sin! God questioned their actions with concern, "Will ye steal, murder, and commit adultery, and swear falsely, and burn incense unto Baal", v. 9. This house, called by God's name, was a den of robbers, v. 11; cf. Matt. 21. 13. We learn that a holy place demands a holy people. Otherwise claims as to its value and associations are empty, cf. 1 Cor. 3. 16-17.

Against these thoughts notice the call to obey, vv. 21-23. God made it very clear that in obedience lay the only hope for recovery. Without this, all their sacrifices and worship were empty forms. "Obey my voice, and I will be your God, and ye shall be my people." In the history of the dealings of God, with Israel, the call to obey came before the call to sacrifice, 1 Sam. 15. 22, 23. We need to grasp this important lesson today. Obedience will always lead to living and acceptable worship.

The inevitable end of these conditions could only be calamity. God could do without the temple buildings. He had forsaken the earlier shrine at Shiloh on account of His people's wickedness, v. 12; Psa. 78. 60. Where their abominations were found, and their polluted sacrifices were offered, judgment would fall, vv. 29-34. They would become a nation without a temple, priest and sacrifices. Contrast Hebrews 13. 15-16!

Oct. 26th

READING : **Jeremiah 9. 23 to 10. 25**

LIFE'S WORTHWHILE PURSUITS

JEREMIAH'S PROPHECIES are not all gloom and despondency. There are breaks in the clouds, and often the sun shines through. There were times when he spelled out the unswerving faithfulness of Israel's God, and the joy that was possible when relationships were right with Him. Today's reading shows the positive worth of knowing and understanding God.

Wherein should man's confidence lie? Jeremiah considered *the wisdom of the wise*. To the Hebrew mind this was of great importance. In king Solomon they had seen human wisdom reach a height that became famous in the nations around. All came to hear him and study his thinking. Yet can man boast with satisfaction in the qualities of his wisdom? Jeremiah said, "Let not the wise man glory in his wisdom", 9. 23.

He thought of the *might of the mighty* — the man of war. Faced with Babylonian strength, how strong was Judah? Could they boast in their might? God knew they were spiritually weak, and that was what really mattered. So "neither let the mighty man glory in his might". The same held true of *wealth*. Jeremiah faced similar social evils as Amos, and he knew that the rich often gained their wealth through oppressing the poor. They were boasting while the poor were languishing: "let not the rich man glory in his riches", v. 23.

Only in the knowledge of God is there any real ground for boasting: "let him that glorieth glory in this", says the prophet, "that he understandeth and knoweth me", v. 24. Jeremiah spoke of the true perspectives which give a solid foundation to life; judgment, righteousness, and lovingkindness are the delight of the One who is the Lord, v. 24. Jehovah is unique, "Forasmuch as there is none like unto thee, O Lord; thou art great, and thy name is great in might", 10. 6; cf. v. 16. Notice the contrasts between the true and living God and other "gods". Israel's monotheism was its greatest strength.

Let us reflect today that ours is the high privilege of knowing God through our Lord Jesus Christ. It is good to compare the teaching of 1 John 5. 20-21 with that of Jeremiah. We have a positive, personal knowledge and understanding that leads to permanent blessing; "This is the true (i.e. real) God, and eternal life". We need to keep ourselves from idols!

Oct. 27th

READING : **Jeremiah 15. 1-21**

SATISFACTION IN SUFFERING

THERE WERE two inevitable outcomes of Jeremiah's ministry. There was (a) the fulfilment of God's purpose to judge His wayward people and (b) the bitter persecution which followed Jeremiah's faithfulness in proclaiming the message. Notice carefully the tone of verses 1-11. How dark all seemed! The Lord announced that even the greatest of all intercessors, Moses and Samuel, could not turn away the coming judgment, v. 1. Instruments of retribution had been planned and prepared. The shameful corruption and evil of Manasseh's reign had left an unforgivable stain on the nation. Let us learn that there are situations created by His people's sins which even a loving God cannot alter.

There is deep sadness in the words of the prophet. We are confronted with a picture of lonely tragedy, "For who shall have pity upon thee, O Jerusalem . . . who shall go aside to ask how thou doest?", v. 5. Their sin isolated them from compassion and pity. Yet Jeremiah cared for them, and because he cared he suffered. Notice the pathos of his cry to the Lord, "know that for thy sake I have suffered rebuke", v. 15. There are other such cries in the Book; cf. 20. 14. It is interesting to compare Jeremiah's cries with Psalm 69. 7-9. In the Psalm we have foreshadowed the sufferings of Christ, Rom. 15. 3. In his sense of rejection and reproach for the Lord's sake, Jeremiah prefigured the Saviour.

In spite of the prophet's sorrow and sadness, his appreciation of God's Word became a source of strength, v. 16. We can link Jeremiah's joy in the Word of the Lord with the experience of the blessed man of Psalm 1. 1-2. In God's Word the prophet found an oasis of delight in a desert of despair. Notice his sense of *acquisition:* "Thy words were found". Jeremiah was a seeker — he sought for appropriate consolation in his sadness. By seeking, he found. It is noticeable that the Word of God furnished, not only the burden of judgment, but the basis of joy. He *assimilated* that which he found; the Word became his food and sustenance, sweet to his soul. His *appreciation* developed, and he was satisfied deeply in his heart. Spiritual growth and prosperity are always the outcome of the appropriation of the Word of God to our own circumstances.

Oct. 28th

READING : **Jeremiah 17. 1-27**

HEART SEARCHING AND A SANCTUARY

IT HAS BEEN SAID that the Book of Jeremiah is designed to reach the heart. An interesting study is to consider the prophecy with this theme in mind. There are three allusions in this chapter to the depths of Judah's sin. Each has to do with the heart. In verse 1 Jeremiah stated that the sin of Judah was engraved with an iron pen, with the point of a diamond, upon their heart. Here was *defilement*, a deep inner guilt. Idol worship was the outward display of an uncleanness that began in the heart.

In verses 5-6 the prophet turned his attention to the curse of misplaced trust and confidence. Instead of trusting in the Lord, confidence was put in man, and the arm of flesh. The source of this sad deficiency could be traced to the heart. Here was *departure* from the Lord. Outward attitudes again reflected the inward spiritual condition. Trust is a matter of the heart. "Trust in the Lord with all thine heart . . .", Prov. 3. 5, 6.

Yet again the prophet probed deeply into the seat of all evil. In verse 9, he stated that "The heart is deceitful above all things, and desperately wicked". Here was *deceit*. Wandering feet were directed by a deceitful heart. The Lord's penetrating eyes searched into the inner depths of men's feelings and thoughts. He knew Judah's wickedness. For us, also, it is true that nothing is hidden from the Lord, Heb. 4. 13. How carefully we need to walk before Him who has eyes "as a flame of fire", Rev. 1. 14.

With relief we pass from the *depths* of evil hearts to the *height* of God's glorious sanctuary. There is something wonderful for us to meditate on in this. Verses 12 to 14 take us out of the gloom of sinfulness up to the glory of the sanctuary. The "throne" conveys the ideas of elevation and authority. God rules from the beginning. To the sinful heart this realization brings fear. Yet the throne is a sanctuary! The place of condemnation becomes the place of communion. Instead of retribution there can be refuge. How beautiful this becomes when we link the thought with Hebrews 4. 14-16. Our great High Priest, Jesus the Son of God, has passed through the heavens, and the throne that once spoke terror to our hearts has become a "throne of grace". We can come with boldness.

Oct. 29th

READING : **Jeremiah 23. 1-32**

RENEGADE SHEPHERDS . . . RIGHTEOUS BRANCH

LEADERSHIP IN Judah had failed dismally. Jeremiah consistently condemned prophets, pastors and priests; see 5. 30-31. The implications of many of his messages were clear. If matters were wrong at the top, how could the people be right! Verses 1 to 2 speak of *pastors* who destroyed and scattered the sheep. They were shepherds who did not pasture the flock.

Jeremiah also attacked the *prophets* because of the false words they spoke, vv. 9-12. His heart was broken because of the prophets. The degradation and excess of their evil stirred the deep emotions of his being. Notice that the spiritual adultery and profanity practised by priest and prophet are set over against the "words of his (God's) holiness", v. 9. Jeremiah saw "folly" in the prophets, v. 13, and heard falsehood in their messages, vv. 16-17. It was no wonder, therefore, that as leaders of the people they completely failed, vv. 21-22. The Lord was against them, an assertion repeated three times, vv. 30-32. It is essential to reflect that if sound spiritual leadership is lacking, the spiritual well-being of God's people is set at risk. It was so in Jeremiah's day, and, sadly, it is so today. Let us pray continually for those who shepherd and care for the church of God, Acts 20-28; Heb. 13. 17.

In studying the ways of God we notice that failure on the part of His people, even of the leaders, does not defeat His ultimate purpose. Verses 3 to 8 make this clear. The scattered sheep, the remnant of the flock, are going to be regathered. Shepherds will be raised up who would feed the sheep, giving them confidence and satisfaction. We can think of John 10. 1-29 in this connection. There the failure of hireling shepherds is set over against the loving care of the Good Shepherd.

In verses 5-6 we have a significant Messianic prophecy. The prophet looked on the time when David's throne will be occupied by a righteous King. Notice the emphasis on righteousness. The King is a righteous Branch or Shoot. The suggestion is that something or Someone living would spring up out of that which was dead. Thus God's promises to Abraham and David would never be forgotten; cf. 33. 17. The nation's security and safety will depend on righteous rule, 23. 5. This is the significance of "The Lord Our Righteousness".

Oct. 30th

READING : **Jeremiah 26. 1-24**

COSTLY COURAGE

THE MINISTRY of Jeremiah was steeped in sorrow. Having launched out into his mission there was no turning back. Each message from the Lord brought increasing hostility from the people. He had been beaten and put in the stocks by Pashur, 20. 2. This persecution bit deeply into the prophet's consciousness. He felt abandoned and deceived, 20. 7-8. Today's reading highlights the course of his commitment, and its cost.

Verses 1 to 3 describe the *charge* given to Jeremiah. Note the categorical demand made upon the prophet's loyalty. No compromise was allowed for: "speak . . . all the words that I command thee to speak unto them; diminish not a word," v. 2. Why did God make such severe demands of his servant? It is obvious that God desired that His people should repent, v. 3. Only by hitting them hard, with faithful words, could the claims of God be driven home. His Word was like a hammer, 23. 29; it could break the rock in pieces! Compare Paul's charge to Timothy, 2 Tim. 4. 1-4.

The *challenge* of God's Word was repeated to the nation in its waywardness, vv. 4-7. The comprehensiveness of Jeremiah's audience is stressed. Priests, prophets, and people heard Jeremiah speak. They had been spoken to "early", emphasizing the relentless efforts of the Lord to break down the opposition. The appeal and threat had been disregarded.

The *courage* of Jeremiah stood out against the persecution. All the people were gathered together against him, v. 9. The unanimous verdict was given, "This man is worthy to die", v. 11. Did the prophet then cringe or compromise? No! He stood his ground, and did not give way. Subsequently, the decision was reversed, v. 16. Like the apostles many centuries later, Jeremiah spoke out boldly in the name of the Lord. Christian resilience is seen at its best when fires of persecution burn!

Such courage was *costly*. Jeremiah knew deep inward exercise as he stood before his God, 20. 7-11. Inside him a terrible struggle took place. Should he be quiet? Should he hold back from speaking? This would have been the easier course. But God's Word burned within him like a fire. He must speak. We too have to decide which will cost us more, compromise or courage?

Oct. 31st
READING : **Jeremiah 28. 1-17**

TEST OF TRUTH

HISTORICALLY, the ministry of Jeremiah covered a long period. From the latter years of Josiah's reign, through to the premature end of wicked Zedekiah in captivity, he witnessed a process of deterioration in spiritual things which could only end in disaster. In terse language the final course of events is spelled out, 25. 8-14. Israel would be desolate, and Judah would serve Babylon in exile for seventy years. The rise of Babylon as a dominant force among the nations was ordered in the providence of God. It marked the beginning of the "times of the Gentiles". Daniel's prophecy spans this period.

We look first at the *conflict* between a true message from God, and a false word from one who was inspired by Satan. Notice the timing of Hananiah's word. It came in the beginning of Zedekiah's reign. The shadows of imminent judgment were being cast over the land. Conditions in Jerusalem were worsening each day. Hopelessness and despair increased. How easily the people would clutch at any message of hope. So the false prophets gave the message, "I will break the yoke of the king of Babylon" saith the Lord, 28. 1-4. How wrong this was! Better no word at all than one that is false. Jeremiah knew this.

Inevitable *confrontation* took place, vv. 7-9. These verses are important. They state the criterion for evaluating the worth of the prophetic word. Prophecies of peace would only be seen to be genuine when peace came, v. 9. Jeremiah could say that his credentials were confirmed by fulfilment; the Lord had truly sent him; cf. Deut. 18. 19-22. We can be sure that the prophet remembered his vision of the almond tree, and the promise of the Lord, 1. 11. Truth spoken depends, for its credibility and fulfilment, upon the faithfulness of God. We remember that the Lord Jesus, the true Prophet, said He was the "truth".

The *condemnation* of the false prophet is made very clear. Jeremiah states the issue categorically to Hananiah, "The Lord hath not sent thee; but thou makest this people to trust in a lie", v. 15. Hananiah died the same year. Read in this connection 1 Timothy 4. 1 and 2 Peter 2. 1-2. Remember that those who refuse the truth lay themselves open to believe the lie, 2 Thess. 2. 11-12. We need the power of truth today.

Nov. 1st

READING : **Jeremiah 31. 1-40**

THE NEW COVENANT

JEREMIAH PRESENTS a picture of better things against a very dark background in his "Book of Comfort", chs. 30-33. We can gather many proofs of God's ultimate intentions for the blessing of His people. Notice the number of times the Lord says "I will", many of them linked with purposes of eventual good. Incredible sufferings still await the nation before these good things are realized; "it is even the time of Jacob's trouble; but he shall be saved out of it", 30. 7. This looks on to the great final tribulation under the beast, Rev. 13, when bitter trouble will be meted out to the nation before the Messiah appears.

Beautiful indeed is the promise of blessing, ch. 31. *God's unmistakable intention* to make them His people is stated, v. 1. "At the same time" refers back to 30. 18, when He brings back the captivity of "Jacob's tents". So the faithlessness of Judah will never thwart the faithfulness of Jehovah.

We also see *God's unchanging love*, 31. 2-3. These are wonderful words! Israel's affection was damaged by so many unworthy objects. Would Divine love change because of such fickleness? It was with stedfast love that He had drawn them to Himself, and would still draw them back to Himself again, Hos. 14. 4. Let us take comfort from these words — how often our love grows cold!

Again, we see in 31. 8-14 indications of *God's unfailing purpose*. This purpose is to regather His scattered people, and bring them home again to the land: "I will build", v. 4; "I will bring", v. 8. The immense scope of eventual restoration is suggested in these promises. Their sinfulness had brought judgment, and indescribable sorrow. Now God cannot do enough to redress these evils, and re-establish them.

Lastly, we read of *God's unbreakable covenant*, vv. 31-34. Jeremiah's great complaint against the people was that they had broken the terms of the covenant of Sinai, 7. 24-26. Every call of God to return to these commands had been disregarded. Now a new covenant would be made, not according to the old one. In it God would write His law on their hearts — spiritual appreciation. Knowledge of God would be their individual experience, and sins would be remembered no more. These speak of blessings that can never be lost; cf. Heb. 10. 15-18.

Nov. 2nd

READING : Jeremiah 32. 1-15; 33. 1-11

FAITH'S PROSPECT AND PRAISE

TODAY, we deal with two interesting thoughts. First we see a *vision* of a happy future for the land, a sign of restoration expected. Then we hear the *voice* of praise of the Lord for His goodness and His mercy. So we are lifted out of the *gloom*, the immediate story of disaster, and into the *glory*, the ultimate fulness of blessing for the people of God.

Chapter 32. 1-5 give us a picture of unrelieved *gloom*. Jerusalem was surrounded with the armies of Babylon. Jeremiah was shut up in prison. Zedekiah, having put Jeremiah away, pursues the foolish course which ends in captivity.

It is at this point that the word comes to Jeremiah, providing a challenge to his *faith,* and an assurance of a glorious *future*. Verses 6-16 describe a transaction designed to prove the prophet's faith, and his commitment to the future of his beloved people. It is well to remember that when Nebuchadnezzar moved against Jerusalem and eventually destroyed it, he had no knowledge of the rich promises of God bound up in Israel's inheritance. It was their land, Gen. 12. 1-7; 15. 7, 18-21. These promises will never be withdrawn, and will ultimately be fulfilled. In the millennial glory of the Messiah the climax will be reached. But Jeremiah was told to anticipate the future by purchasing his uncle's land. This was his by right of redemption. After the deeds of purchase were witnessed, they were put in an earthenware vessel. There is a pathos and a beauty about this action. The Lord said, "Houses and fields and vineyards shall be possessed again in this land", v. 15. We can remark here that every act of faith has its eye on the future, Heb. 11. 1. Was God able to substantiate His demand upon Jeremiah's faith?, see v. 27. Jeremiah might die in Egypt, but the exiles would return, and build the waste places again.

Chapter 33 is a heartening tonic to faith and hope. Consider the precious promise of the open-handedness of God to those who call on Him, v. 3. Untapped qualities of God's love are open to the call of faith. *Pardon* is promised to those who had sinned against God, vv. 6-8. Small wonder that the voice of *praise* and gladness is heard, vv. 9-11, referring to a glorious day in Israel's experience. All that God does contributes to His praise and His glory; cf. Eph. 1. 6, 9-14.

Nov. 3rd

READING : Jeremiah 36. 1-32

BURNING THE BOOK

THIS CHAPTER gives a significant insight into the transmission of the prophet's message from oral expression to the written word. The oracles of revelation were committed by Baruch to the Hebrew scroll. As it was read, so it would be unrolled. The exact contents of the scroll are not given to us. But the reason for its writing was the hope that Judah might repent, and turn from its evil ways, v. 3. God was ready to forgive. Reflect that God pursued every course open to produce *repentance* before *retribution* fell. Judgment is indeed His strange work!

Verses 4-8 tell us *the method* by which the ears of the people were reached. Publicly the word was read, the people heard! A special blessing is promised for those who read, and they that hear and keep the Word of God, Rom. 10. 17; 1 Tim. 4. 13; Rev. 1. 3. It seems as if this event took place at a time of national crisis. The king proclaimed a fast among the people, v. 9. Jehoiakim, weak man though he was, no doubt was keenly aware of the desperate nature of his times. We can believe that the word had particular relevance to such times, for it was then that they read the book publicly, v. 10. God speaks just when the message is needed. His timing is perfect.

Verses 11-24 tell us of *the movements* by which the scroll reached the king's chamber. Through the scribes and the princes, the impact of the word gradually spread. The intensity of the reactions of these men is striking. They enquired how the book came into being. Pronouncements were recorded, and these became proclamations of Divine truth, vv. 17-18. So it was that as Baruch and Jeremiah hid, the king heard the word. How foolish — piece by piece he burnt the roll! But having heard the message, he bore the responsibility of what he heard. It is important to remember how vital it is for us to pay attention to the Word of God. "Take heed . . . how ye hear".

The word was written again. *The meaning* of God's message was not to be lost. The Lord not only watched over His word, 1. 12, but He kept His messengers in safety, "the Lord hid them", v. 26. Verses 26-32 emphasize that God will say what He has to say in spite of man's rejection. Jehoiakim sealed his own doom when he burnt the roll of the book. Let us treat soberly and prayerfully every inspired utterance of our God.

Nov. 4th
READING : Jeremiah 38. 1-28

DELIVERED FROM THE DUNGEON

ONE OF the saddest features of Jeremiah's ministry was that in proclaiming the Lord's message, his motives were so much misunderstood. Regarding the ultimate issues between Judah and Babylon, his word was consistent. "If thou wilt assuredly go forth unto the king of Babylon's princes, then thy soul shall live, and this city shall not be burned with fire". The alternative was complete destruction, vv. 17-18.

Chapter 37 is interesting in this connection. It seemed that the attacking armies of Egypt would draw the Babylonian forces off from Jerusalem, and that they would depart, v. 9. Because Jeremiah affirmed his message, he was watched and accused of treason, v. 13. Denial made no difference, and he ended in prison, vv. 14-15. The princes seemed in a state of panic, and every move of the prophet was open to suspicion. He was hated for his faithfulness to the Lord's message. If they had been prepared to listen, there could have been peace.

The events of chapter 38 brought matters to a head. The prophet crystalized his message — surrender or die, vv. 1-3. At the request of the princes, he was put in the miry dungeon. The actions of Zedekiah remind us of the behaviour of Pilate when he dealt with the Lord Jesus. What dark days these were for the faithful prophet of God. Forgotten in the dungeon, he could have died. Remember he was suffering for righteousness' sake. He could have said, "They hated me without a cause"; cf. John 15. 25; Psa. 69. 4. His life was one of undeserved suffering. The Lord Jesus said, "If the world hate you, ye know that it hated me before it hated you", see John 15. 18-21.

There is something touching about the prophet's deliverance, vv. 7-13. An Ethiopian eunuch cared enough for the prophet to seek his rescue, and bring him out of the pit. Ebed-melech was not just any man. The reason why he could be so used of God is given in 39. 15-18. He is promised deliverance in the day of destruction because he trusted in the Lord. God knew how far to go in testing His servant, and He had deliverance at hand when needed. Jeremiah would feel forgotten in the darkness, but his God, and ours, is faithful. In allowing us to be tested, God has His way of escape that we may be able to bear it, 1 Cor. 10. 13.

Nov. 5th

READING : **Jeremiah 51. 1-26**

THE DAY OF RECKONING

OUR STUDIES in Jeremiah's prophecy end with considering a very important feature of God's dealings with men. The burden of chapters 50-51 is the judgment of Babylon because of its cruelty to God's own people. The picture that emerges from the prophet's ministry is clear. The nation, a people who were chosen to be holy unto the Lord, having sinned and resisted His Word, were carried away captive to Babylon, and their city and temple were destroyed. This represented righteous judgment! The instrument used to carry this out was the pagan nation of Babylon. However, the last forecast of doom was not against Judah but against Babylon, 51. 64. This must be considered.

Abraham asked of God the question "Shall not the Judge of all the earth do right?", Gen. 18. 25. In the patriarch's mind was the issue of deliverance for righteous Lot, and destruction of unrighteous Sodom. God proved His justice in the matter. The Lord knew how to deliver just Lot and destroy the wicked cities of the plain with fire, 2 Pet. 2. 6-9. God's actions declare God's righteousness.

Today's verses are a commentary on this fact. *God remembers His people*, Jer. 51. 5. Though sin had filled the land, and judgment fell, Israel had not been forsaken of God. Love never forgets; time and circumstance could not destroy the deep affection of Jehovah for a people whom He had redeemed. Yet *God must act in righteousness*. Too little we appreciate the balances of judgment that lie in God's mighty hands, vv. 9-10. Babylon, in her lust for conquest, took full advantage of Judah's weakness. The evils of Babylon's cruelty are remembered in the "Doom Song", ch. 50. God's vengeance answers the pride of the heathen, 51. 11-14.

God's relationship with His people, v. 19, is affirmed against the background of His wrath with Babylon. Their Redeemer, the portion of Jacob, is strong. He will plead their cause — a touching assurance, 50. 34. Terrible *retribution* will be meted out to Babylon, 51. 24. They will be desolate, never to rise again, vv. 54-64. Study God's ways, Hos. 14. 9. Judah was called out of Babylon, 50. 8; 51. 6. Had they obeyed their God, they would never have been there at all. Solemn reflection!

Nov. 6th

READING : Lamentations 1. 7-12; 3. 19-32

FROM TRAGEDY TO TRUST

EACH CHAPTER of Lamentations is a poem, a tragic lament on the sufferings of Judah. There is so much of the spirit of Jeremiah in its language that it is difficult to deny that he is the author. The destruction of Jerusalem, and the desolation of Judah in 587 B.C., are bewailed in most vivid terms. Sin and rebellion were the cause, suffering and exile the result; both inspire heart-broken cries from the prophet.

We notice *the tragedy*. The prophet seems to take the place of the nation in the language of chapters 1 and 3. Personal complaint and personal confession seem to be wrung from the heart of one who reflects upon a nation destroyed. Notice the pathos of 1. 12: "Is it nothing to you, all ye that pass by? Behold, and see if there be any sorrow like unto my sorrow, which is done unto me". The judgments are attributed to Jehovah Himself. "The Lord (he) hath . . ." 1. 15, 17; 2. 1-2, 5, 7-8 etc. The hand of the Lord had been laid heavily on the sinning nation, and there was no relief. There is a sense of disgrace and loss. The precious things of God have been profaned, as precious metal, gold, that has become tarnished, 4. 1-2. The sins of prophets and priests have been answered, 4. 13. We often apply 1. 12 to the sufferings of Christ on the cross. It was there, in God-forsaken loneliness, He bore the judgment of our sins, not His own. Is it nothing to us that He should so suffer? Thank God, we can answer with gratitude, "the Son of God, who loved me, and gave himself for me", Gal. 2. 20. This, we can truly say, means everything to us.

We also notice *the note of trust*, 3. 19-26. In the remembrance of affliction there is the light of hope. These are precious verses. God's unfailing compassion ensures the grounds of preservation and security. Changing affection and allegiance are met by God's steadfast love and constancy. Man's failure only highlights the faithfulness of God, who cannot fail. Each returning morning displays the freshness of His sympathy and compassion. Wonderful God! How good that "The Lord is my portion, saith my soul; therefore will I hope in him", v. 24. Let us enjoy this today. It reminds us that, with God, we can move out of *tragedy*, through *trust* into *triumph*. We deal with a God who does not change, Psa. 102. 27; Mal. 3. 6; Heb. 1. 12.

Introducing Ezekiel

EZEKIEL had been a priest in Jerusalem, and when he was deported to Babylon, Daniel had already been there in captivity for nine years. In Jerusalem, he had been separated from the religious evil that dominated life in that city, and amongst the Gentiles he was faithful amidst idolatry and departure. He found the Lord to be "a little sanctuary", 11. 16. As being in contact with God, he was able to perceive "visions of God", 1. 1; his obedience to God enabling him variously to be silent, to speak, or to engage in action parables to men of his own nation in captivity with him.

The Book deals at length with God's judgment on Jerusalem and Judah, together with God's promises of the people's future regeneration and restoration. It can be divided with reference to the various positions of the glory of God.

In chapters 1-7, Ezekiel saw the glory of God by the river Chebar; the prophet received his commission, and his teaching and action parables centered on the forthcoming destruction of Jerusalem, where God's throne on earth had been situated.

In chapters 8-11, Ezekiel saw the glory of God in vision form in the temple in Jerusalem. A few years before this temple's destruction, the prophet saw the glory of God depart reluctantly and slowly, so as to stand on the mount of Olives, 11. 23. The throne of God and His glory had been associated with the temple since Solomon's dedication, 2 Chron. 5. 14. God's glory appeared to men as fire, Lev. 9. 23; 10. 2, but His glory left the temple so that it would not be engulfed with fire caused by men in the burning of the temple, 2 Chron. 36. 19.

In chapters 12-42 visions of judgment and then of restoration were granted to Ezekiel, with the glory of God on the mount of Olives or having ascended to heaven. In a sense, this glory remained on the mount, the stones being charged so as to cry out even if men were silent, Luke 19. 40.

Finally, in chapters 43-48 the glory is seen as having returned to the restored house from Olivet on the east, 43. 4.

The major prophets are prophets of restoration: Isaiah is the prophet of the restoration of Zion; Jeremiah of bridal affections; Ezekiel of the house and Divine glory, and Daniel of the kingdom of God with the Jews at the head.

Nov. 7th

READING : Ezekiel 1. 1-28

THE GLORY OF GOD BY THE RIVER CHEBAR

ISAIAH was prepared for prophetic ministry by seeing the glory of Christ in the temple, Isa. 6. 1-4; John 12. 41; Jeremiah was prepared by God touching his mouth, Jer. 1. 9; Daniel was prepared in the school of God, Dan. 1. 17, but Ezekiel was prepared for his prophetic ministry by seeing "visions of God", Ezek. 1. 1, receiving his commission in chapters 2-3.

For its richness in symbolic detail, this vision of the glory of God is unsurpassed by any other vision recorded in the Scriptures. Moses, Solomon and Isaiah had known of the glory of God associated with tabernacle and temple amongst God's people, but Ezekiel saw the whirlwind from the north far away in the land of his captivity.

A most unusual form of chariot is described, it being so unusual that its construction appeared to defy ordinary verbal description. The main support consisted of "four living creatures", 1. 5 (called "cherubim" in 10. 1), characterized by intelligence that was in submission to the instant command of the will of God. All the living creatures went straight ahead, not turning when they went, v. 12, suggesting that movement was only possible north-southwards and east-westwards, enabling any cardinal point to be reached.

Ezekiel also saw four wheels that rendered possible movement on earth, v. 15. The peculiar structure in verses 15-21 suggests that there was one wheel on each side of a square base, two for north-south movement and two for east-west movement. Vertical movement was also possible, v. 21, evidently by means of the wings of the cherubim.

These cherubim supported "the firmament", v. 22. Above this was "a throne", v. 26, and even higher than this was "the likeness of the appearance of a man", v. 26. In other words, here is symbolic language leading to One high and lifted up, the Controller of the universe, coming in righteous judgment amongst Israel and the nations, yet all is tempered with mercy as seen in "the bow that is in the cloud in the day of rain".

A vision such as this can never be forgotten. It was formative for Ezekiel's subsequent ministry, in just the same way as the light that Paul saw at his conversion formed his apostolic ministry afterwards, Acts 22. 6-9; 1 Cor. 9. 1; cf. 2 Pet. 1. 16.

Nov. 8th

READING : **Ezekiel 8. 1-18**

THE GLORY IN THE TEMPLE IN JERUSALEM

A YEAR LATER, Ezekiel was transported in the spirit to Jerusalem, v. 3, so as to be shown the evils taking place there, evils that demanded judgment. The throne of God was still there, but the time had come for the glory to depart. This reminds us of Revelation 1-3, where John first saw the glorified Lord in His capacity to discern, having eyes as a flame of fire. Then, in chapters 2-3, he saw the state of the seven churches from the Lord's point of view, ending with Laodicea being cast out, with only a faithful remnant remaining to sup with Him and to share His throne.

The lesson to be learnt is that God discerns all activity that takes place, whether in the temple, the local church, or in Christendom. It is no light thing for evil to be found in a sphere that God has chosen for Himself; so Ezekiel was shown four evils, each attaining greater depths of abomination. "That which is highly esteemed among men is abomination in the sight of God", Luke 16. 15.

(i) Verses 5-6: the "image . . . which provoketh to jealousy", v. 3. Since Solomon had erected his altars on Olivet, evil kings had become more daring; yet the Lord, as a jealous God, would guard His uniqueness and pre-eminence.

(ii) Verses 7-12: inside the temple, Ezekiel was shown seventy men before idolatrous forms painted on the walls, boasting in the thought that the Lord could not see them as hidden in the temple. Later, men will seek to hide from His judgment, but they will not be able, Rev. 6. 15-17.

(iii) Verses 13-14: Ezekiel saw women "weeping for Tammuz", an idol of the nations around them. The idolaters wanted to be like the nations, for they "transgressed very much after all the abominations of the heathen", 2 Chron. 36. 14.

(iv) Verses 15-16: with their backs to the temple, twenty-five men worshipped the sun in the east. Namely, men of the twenty-four courses, and the high priest, deliberately turned their backs upon God.

Thus the evils of the house were declared. Are we aware today of sins, including idolatry, that can exist in a local church? See 1 Cor. 5. 11; Gal. 2. 4; 5. 20. Our "members . . . upon the earth" can include idolatry, Col. 3. 5; 1 John 5. 21.

Nov. 9th

READING : **Ezekiel 9. 1-11**

BEGIN AT MY SANCTUARY

IN NEW TESTAMENT times, "judgment must begin at the house of God", 1 Pet. 4. 17. This was seen in Corinth, where many slept as "chastened of the Lord", 1 Cor. 11. 30-32, while the unbelieving population in Corinth remained untouched. Certainly in Revelation 2-3, the local churches were examined prior to the subsequent judgments on Israel and the nations.

The same applies here in Ezekiel 9; God would deal with His sanctuary first. He had dwelt in glory above the mercy seat, "thou that dwellest between the cherubims", Psa. 80. 1. But the glory had now risen above a cherub within the vail, and moved to the threshold of the house, Ezek. 9. 3.

The administration of mercy and judgment was in the hands of seven men — six with a "slaughter weapon", and a "man . . . clothed with linen", v. 2. Who these were is not explained, except that they "had charge over the city", v. 1. Yet these could not be human leaders in Jerusalem. We understand the six to be angelic ministers under divine command to administer judgment (see Rev. 14. 19), with the "man . . . clothed with linen" as a Christophany, the Lord Jesus prior to His incarnation, Dan. 10. 5-6.

Even at that dreadful time, there were godly men present, such as Jeremiah. The man clothed with linen put a mark on this faithful remnant, described as "the men that sigh and that cry", v. 4. This should characterize believers today, with "my new name" written on them — the opposite to those who receive "the mark, or the name of the beast", Rev. 13. 17. The Lord wept over Jerusalem; Paul over the church, Acts 20. 31, and so should we weep for others, whether in the church, or amongst the nations.

Judgment fell on all those without the mark of spiritual identification, v. 6. Ezekiel did not fully understand; so many were slain that he wondered if even a remnant would be saved. But "I have done as thou hast commanded me", v. 11, shows that God's people came through safely.

Today, "The Lord knoweth them that are his. And, Let every one that nameth the name of Christ depart from iniquity", 2 Tim. 2. 19. If judgment starts at the house, may we not be judged!

Nov. 10th

READING : Ezekiel 10. 1-22

THE GLORY OVER THE THRESHOLD

THE GLORY OF GOD continued its reluctant departure from the temple which it had occupied since Solomon's dedication. This departure initiated the times of the Gentiles, when God's throne would no longer be in Jerusalem. The glory had been in the most holy place within the vail, "there", 8. 4; it had retired "to the threshold", 9. 3; now it is "over the threshold", 10. 4; then over the east gate of the court, 10. 19, and finally it departed from the city to the mount of Olives, 11. 23. Thus would be fulfilled what God had said through Jeremiah: I will "do unto this house . . . as I have done to Shiloh", Jer. 7. 14, namely forsaken it, with the glory departing, Psa. 78. 60-61.

In this chapter, the glory of God departing from the temple merges with the glory seen above the firmament that was above the cherubim forming the chariot-throne. In spite of the tragedy being enacted, the glory is described as "brightness" appearing in the court, with the house "filled with the glory", v. 4. Only Ezekiel during the vision perceived all this.

In Isaiah 6. 6, the coal of fire was used for cleansing, but here in verses 2, 6-7 the coals of fire are to be used upon the city. The man clothed with linen in 9. 4 was acting in mercy, but here in 10. 7 the man used the coals for judgment. Today, many glibly speak of Divine love, but deliberately overlook judgment. John 3. 16-21 treats these two aspects of God's dealings — "not condemned" and "condemned already".

Ezekiel made it clear that the description of the Lord's glory in verses 8-22 was the same as that which he had seen in chapter 1 by the river Chebar in captivity. God's glory far outside the city was the same as His glory inside the city. In particular, in verse 13 the cry "O wheel" is strictly a command to the wheels to rotate rapidly — that is, there was to be no more delay. God's Spirit will not always strive with men; the time came when Divine judgment had to fall, Gen. 6. 3, 7.

Mercy reigns until judgment must fall — a lesson for today when the gospel is preached until opportunities cease. Little wonder Paul had to write, "woe is unto me, if I preach not the gospel", 1 Cor. 9. 16. But for Jerusalem in Ezekiel's day it was too late; the scene was drawing to a close when the report would come, "The city is smitten", Ezek. 33. 21.

Nov. 11th
READING : **Ezekiel 11. 1-25**

THE GLORY REMOVED TO THE MOUNT OF OLIVES

FINALLY, Ezekiel is taken to the east gate of the temple court, in order to see the concluding display of rebellion, judgment, and promised restoration prior to the glory of God leaving Jerusalem. The prophet saw twenty-five men, as in 8. 16, and recognized two of them whom he had previously known prior to his captivity. These men were self-satisfied, rejecting any thought of judgment to come — typical of many men today. They used the metaphor "this city is the cauldron, and we be the flesh", 11. 3, an expression implying safety as meat is safe within a boiling-pot. But they reckoned without the power of God. The city would not possess the safety of a cauldron, v. 11, for they would be brought *out* in judgment, v. 7. In other words, scriptural teaching about judgment to come takes complete precedence over the theories and doctrines of men. So Pelatiah died, v. 13, a token of what was to come.

But mercy is promised, both for that time, and for the future. As in Isaiah 1. 25-27; 2. 1-5, early tokens of restoration promises came before the main restoration chapters at the end of that prophecy; so too in Ezekiel. In Ezekiel 11. 14-21, there are early tokens of restoration promises before the main restoration chapters 40-48 at the end. (i) For the faithful ones in captivity, God would be "a little sanctuary", 11. 16, even though the sanctuary in Jerusalem was to be destroyed. It is the same today; believers are not concerned about temples made with hands, but are occupied with a spiritual temple, with the Lord amongst His people, 1 Cor. 3. 16. (ii) In Ezekiel 11. 17-21, the promised return to the land is not that which took place at the end of the seventy years captivity, but is still future, when Israel will enter into the blessings of the new covenant. Compare Jeremiah 31. 31-33 with Ezekiel 11. 19.

Then the glory of God finally left Jerusalem, v. 23, and the times of the Gentiles properly began. The mount of Olives had only recently been cleansed from the idols that Solomon had erected, 1 Kings 11. 7. Josiah's act of cleansing is recorded in 2 Kings 23. 13. No doubt the glory returned to heaven, until its unique manifestation in the Person of Christ when "we beheld his glory", John 1. 14. This vision was not kept secret, but was told to those in captivity; see Revelation 1. 11.

Nov. 12th

READING : **Ezekiel 16. 1-34**

THOU DIDST TRUST IN THINE OWN BEAUTY

THE PSALMIST may well desire to see the beauty of the Lord, Psa. 27. 4, and the bride may well testify of the beauties of her Beloved, Song 5. 9-16, but according to Divine grace God also perceives the beauty of His people. The Bridegroom testifies of His beloved, what He saw in her, 4. 1-7, and here in Ezekiel 16 God explains the beauty that He found — that He once found — in His chosen city Jerusalem; see Psalm 48. Alas that this description was being given *after* the beauty had been squandered by those upon whom it had been bestowed.

In this chapter, God provides Ezekiel with a very basic reason why Divine judgment had to fall upon Jerusalem. In highly figurative language, using material and human concepts to describe spiritual beauty, He describes Jerusalem prior to its being taken up as the place of God's choice, vv. 3-5. Before its capture by David, 2 Sam. 5. 7, it had been occupied by the nations, whose idolatry had to be cast out when God gave the command "Live", Ezek. 16. 6.

This change was brought about by David and Solomon, who established the tent on Zion, and the temple on Moriah, who introduced the service of God with the priests and Levitical singers, porters and treasurers. This was really the work of God through His servants. In verses 6-14, the repetition of "I", referring to the Lord God, stresses that the work was Divine, changing the city "from darkness to light, and from the power of Satan unto God", Acts 26. 18. The conclusion is that Jerusalem became "exceeding beautiful" and "thy beauty . . . was perfect through my comeliness, which I had put upon thee". Today, this answers to the believer's position as "in Christ", and as "a chaste virgin", 2 Cor. 11. 2.

The contrast from verse 15 onwards is grievous to the soul. Trusting in her own beauty, she appropriated the things of God for herself. "*My* gold, *my* silver, *mine* oil, *mine* incense, *my* meat, *my* children" were turned into instruments of idolatry, worse than heathen practice, Rom. 1. 20-23. This idolatry was likened to the activity of an unfaithful wife, yet the mercy of an "everlasting covenant" was promised, Ezek. 16. 60. This reminds us of the self-satisfaction of Laodicea, yet mercy promises blessings to the overcomers there also, Rev. 3. 17-21.

Nov. 13th
READING : Ezekiel 28. 1-19
TYRE AS A TYPE OF SATAN

ALTHOUGH Ezekiel was in captivity, he was not provided with details concerning the judgment of the great world empires such as Babylon. Rather, in chapters 12-24, many details are given regarding the judgments upon Jerusalem and Israel, while in chapters 25-32 the nations adjacent to the promised land are dealt with. In particular, chapters 26-28 are devoted to Tyre, while chapter 28. 1-19 is even more particular, being *typical* of the rise and fall of Satan. For Satan is the arch-cause of all deception, idolatry, and iniquity among the nations, and if these are to be judged, then so also is Satan. Cognate passages in the prophetic Scriptures are Isaiah 14. 12-15 (in a context dealing with Babylon), and Revelation 20. 1-3, 10. The death of Christ makes possible the ultimate destruction of Satan and his works, Heb. 2. 14; 1 John 3. 8.

Our passage is divided into two distinct parts, vv. 2-10 and 11-19. In both, *the ruler* of Tyre is addressed as typical of Satan (in chapters 26-27 *the city* of Tyre is addressed).

God denounces Satan's *aspirations and ambitions* in verses 2-6. He had said, "I am a god", claiming to have the heart of God, vv. 2, 6, and wanting to "be like the most High", Isa. 14. 14, reminding us of the future man of sin as energized by Satan 2 Thess. 2. 4, 9, and of Laodicea as increased with riches, Rev. 3. 17. Yet Satan will meet his end in judgment, Ezek. 28. 7-10. Although he has access now to God in heaven, Job. 1. 6; 2. 1; Rev. 12. 9, and is titled "the prince of the power of the air", Eph. 2. 2, one day he will be cast down to the earth, Rev. 12. 9. Later he will be confined to the bottomless pit, 20. 3, and finally be cast into the lake of fire, 20. 10.

In the second paragraph, Satan's *appearance and anointing* are described. He was "perfect in beauty", having been in "Eden the garden of God"; he was "the anointed cherub" upon "the mountain of God", walking "up and down" as if Eden was shaped like a pyramid. He was perfect in his ways from his creation. But then "iniquity was found" in him, v. 15, with his heart lifted up because of his beauty, v. 17; "he was a murderer from the beginning, and abode not in the truth".

Judgment was forecast: "I will cast thee to the ground", v. 17, his final end coming after the millennium, Rev. 20. 10.

Nov. 14th

READING : Ezekiel 33. 1-21

THE RESPONSIBILITY OF THE WATCHMAN

EZEKIEL was not to be a passive watcher of visions, and a receiver of messages from the Lord. In these visions and messages moral and spiritual implications *had to be passed on*, and a heavy responsibility rested upon the prophet to warn men to flee from the wrath to come; cf. Matt. 3. 7.

An ordinary picture is used by God in verses 2-6. When invasion by an enemy was imminent, a watchman with a trumpet was responsible to warn the defenders. Today, sophisticated radar and satellite equipment keep unceasing vigilance, with modern telecommunication and computer systems transmitting immediate information to national leaders when trouble is detected. But in O.T. days, a watchman on a vantage point, together with a trumpet, was all that was available. This elementary system could break down in two ways. (i) People may not bother to respond to the trumpet alert, v. 4; they would suffer in the subsequent invasion. (ii) The watchman may not blow his trumpet; he would be held responsible for the consequences before God, v. 6.

These simple observations are applied in verses 7-9. Ezekiel was a watchman, receiving messages of warning from God. There were two possibilities of failure. (i) The prophet may fail to warn men, v. 8, as did Jonah when he fled from the presence of the Lord, Jonah 1. 2-3. (ii) Men may hear, but not respond to the message of warning, v. 10. The prophet would have discharged his responsibility, but the men would suffer judgment from the Lord. In the O.T., under law, self-righteousness would not put away sin; but if a man turned from sin, then this would lead to life. These vital principles are developed in verses 12-16. The people complained "The way of the Lord is not equal", v. 17; they criticized the Lord for not saving everyone regardless of repentance or otherwise.

Today, evangelists are watchmen, sent forth to warn men that judgment is near if there is no repentance and faith, Acts 20. 21; cf. v. 26. As a watchman and as an ambassador of Christ, Paul would seek to persuade men, 2 Cor. 5. 11, 18-21. Our responsibility is to persuade men with the Word that works effectually, but avoiding mere embellishment and entertainment that grieve the Spirit of God.

Nov. 15th
READING : Ezekiel 37. 1-28
RESTORATION IN THE VALLEY OF DRY BONES

THIS CHAPTER is divided into two parts. The first part deals with the future national and spiritual restoration of Israel, vv. 1-14. The second deals with the unification of the nation in their land under Messiah, God's Servant and King, vv. 15-28.

Vision-parables in the O.T. were just as vivid as the Lord's verbal-parables in the N.T. The nation was dead — a death that lasted through the Babylonian captivity, and extends to the present day. Any revival that took place under Cyrus, when some of the captivity returned to rebuild the temple, Ezra 1. 3, and when later some returned to rebuild the walls and city, Neh. 2. 5, is not included in the vision. Rather, the vision takes the reader to the end of the times of the Gentiles, when Israel, like the broken-off branches will be grafted in again, so as to live once more, producing fruit for God, Rom. 11. 17-24.

Of course, the nation would never consider itself as dead, but Ezekiel saw it from God's point of view. In just the same way, the Pharisees thought that they could see, whereas they were really blind, John 9. 39-41. Today, the nation of Israel would think it strange if they were described as dead. But God's thoughts and viewpoint are not men's. A future miracle is described in verses 5-10; the state of death (as amongst the nations — the "graves" in verse 12) is changed to spiritual life (in the land, v. 14). The Lord described this as "they shall gather together his elect from the four winds", Matt. 24. 31.

The second part of the chapter, vv. 15-28, shows who will take part in this restoration. At the end of Solomon's life, his idols caused God to state that he would rend the kingdom out of Solomon's hand, reserving "one tribe" for David and Jerusalem, 1 Kings 11. 30-39. This took place in 1 Kings 12. 16-33, and remained so afterwards, with the northern ten tribes being taken into captivity in 2 Kings 17. 18. Only in the future will Judah and Israel be reunited in one kingdom, like the joining together of two sticks, Ezek. 37. 17, with "David my servant" as Messiah and Shepherd over them, v. 24. See Jeremiah 31. 31, where the new covenant is made with the united house of Israel and Judah.

Today, alas, divisions amongst Christians persist, but the desire of the Lord is "that they may be one", John 17. 22.

Nov. 16th
READING : **Ezekiel 43. 1-12**

THE RETURN OF THE GLORY

THE MESSAGE of the prophets is that judgment is a Divine necessity, and also that a future restoration of Israel is promised in Divine grace. Throughout the book of Ezekiel, glimpses of these restoration blessings can be seen, but in chapters 40-48 these are described in detail. In those far-off days of ruin, Ezekiel was permitted to testify of this restoration, but conditions had to be fulfilled so that the revelation could be appreciated: "behold with thine eyes, and hear with thine ears, and set thine heart upon *all* that I shall show thee", 40. 4. Only when a servant perceives *all* the details of the house of God and its service is this servant equipped to show the house to others. In fact, chapters 40-46 provide the details of the restored house and its service, and Ezekiel was told that this would be the dwelling place of God amongst His people during the millennial peace on earth, 43. 7. The prophet was under responsibility to "show the house", v. 10.

This house was unlike the house that was built in Jerusalem by the captives returning from Babylon, Ezra 3. 12-13, and unlike the temple that Herod had initiated and that had been in building for forty-six years, John 2. 20. For the glory of God did not return from Olivet to those structures. Rather, twenty years after having seen the glory of God by the river Chebar in chapter 1, Ezekiel again saw this glory, testifying, "the glory of the Lord came into the house by the way of the gate whose prospect is toward the *east* . . . the glory of the Lord filled the house", Ezek. 43. 4-5. The Lord Jesus has ascended to heaven from the mount of Olives, Acts 1. 9-12, and He will return again to this mount, Zech. 14. 4, after which His glory will move from the east into Jerusalem. What a different house this will be! Unlike the idolatry so often perpetrated in Solomon's temple by evil kings; so unlike the cold barren formalities that took place in Herod's arkless temple; rather "Upon the top of the mountain the whole limit thereof round about shall be most holy. Behold, this is the law of the house", 43. 12.

Today, local churches should have this same character: "ye are the temple of God, and . . . the Spirit of God dwelleth in you . . . the temple of God is holy, which temple ye are", 1 Cor. 3. 16-17. See Eph. 2. 21-22; 1 Tim. 3. 15.

Nov. 17th
READING : Ezekiel 47. 1-12

WATERS FROM THE SANCTUARY

THIS DESCRIPTION of the life-giving stream from the sanctuary forms one of the grandest passages in Ezekiel's prophecy, having no parallel in Moses' tabernacle and Solomon's temple. For David, such waters had been absent when he said, "my soul thirsteth for thee . . . in a dry and thirsty land, where no water is; to see thy power and thy glory, so as I have seen thee in the sanctuary", Psa. 63. 1-2. Jerusalem is situated about twenty miles from the Dead Sea, and throughout its existence, the brook Cedron has flowed on its eastern side, between the city and the mount of Olives, turning south-eastwards to flow into the Dead Sea. But the river in Ezekiel 47 appears to follow quite a different course. Joel spoke of the Lord dwelling in His holy mountain Zion, when "a fountain shall come forth of the house of the Lord, and shall water the valley of Shittim", 3. 17-18; some expositors have suggested that this valley is the Cedron valley. But Zechariah 14. 4-8 informs us that, when the Lord's feet touch the mount of Olives in that future day, the mount shall split into two parts, with "a very great valley" directed eastwards, along which "living waters shall go out from Jerusalem", half of which shall flow eastwards towards the Dead Sea. Certainly, when Jerusalem shall be named "The Lord is there", Ezek. 48. 35, these great geological changes will have taken place. These waters expand outwards, first rising to the ankles, then to the knees, and the loins, and finally out of a man's depth, 47. 3-5. Moreover, the desert will yield "many trees" on the banks of the river, while the Dead Sea will produce fish "exceeding many". Truly the desert will blossom as a rose, as the garden of Eden, in the last one thousand years of the earth's existence.

In the N.T., living water is a prominent spiritual theme. The Lord Jesus promised "water that . . .shall be in him a well of water springing up into everlasting life", John 4. 14. He also promised that from the believer's inner being "shall flow rivers of living water", 7. 38, referring to the Holy Spirit. Finally, in Revelation 22. 1-2, the "pure river of water of life" arises from the throne of God and of the Lamb — not on earth but in heaven — yet reaching to earth, producing fruit and leaves for the healing of the millennial nations; see Ezek. 47. 12.

Introducing Daniel

THE OBJECT of the book of Daniel is to show that captivity, persecution, and suffering ultimately come to an end in God's timetable. This assurance brings hope and encouragement to God's people who, at different times, have to endure such afflictions. Usually in such cases as illness, imprisonment for Christ's sake, warfare and political uncertainty, we do not know when or what the end will be; we await God's time. But after the Church will have been taken, and when God's people of future days have to pass through the great tribulation, the exact end of this period of suffering should be known to them. The Book of Daniel, which provides this information, is divided into three sections.

(i) *Daniel the Man*, ch. 1. As a youth fresh from Jerusalem, he was educated both in the school of men, and in the school of God. He came through with flying colours, and was thereby prepared for a long life in the service of God.

(ii) *Daniel the Interpreter*, chs. 2-6. From his youth up to his eighties, God used Daniel to interpret divinely given messages to kings, in the form, usually, of dreams, but once of writing on the wall. He and his companions suffered for their faith in chapters 3 and 6, but there was almost immediate deliverance by God from the burning fiery furnace and the den of lions. In chapter 2, the dream-image depicts the panorama of the "times of the Gentiles", Luke 21. 24, showing the Babylonian, Medo-Persian, Grecian and Roman kingdoms up to the time of the advent of the Messiah in glory to establish His everlasting kingdom. Political, military, and religious power amongst men will be shattered, when Divine rule pervades the earth.

(iii) *Daniel the Seer*, chs. 7-12. As an old man, Daniel had dreams that needed angelic interpretation. In chapter 7, the four kingdoms of chapter 2 are now seen from God's point of view. They are represented as beasts — beasts to be destroyed, particularly the fourth, taking us up to the last times. Chapter 8 introduces two more beasts, leading to the evil Syrian king Antiochus Epiphanes, a pointer to evil leaders in the great tribulation. Chapters 10-12 also have the same objective. Chapter 9, after Daniel's intercession, gives Gabriel's prophecy of the 70 weeks, leading to Israel's national blessings.

Nov. 18th

READING : Daniel 1. 1-21

THE EDUCATION OF A SERVANT OF GOD

THE UNIVERSITY IN CAPTIVITY, vv. 1-5. Daniel's original schooling had been in Jerusalem, since he had been born in the reign of the last good king, Josiah. His faithfulness to God commenced then, and in that city of evil and idolatry he remained undeflected during the few following years. He and his fellows could not choose the place of their higher education at the hands of men. His captivity in Babylon commenced at about the age of 16, and in a heathen land he determined to remain steadfast for God, with divine teaching forming him in his youthful days, and influencing him until the end of his long life. He knew that holy things from the temple had been deported to Babylon, to be used in unholy ceremonies in idols' temples, but Daniel remained separated from all such evil.

Faithful Students, vv. 6-16. Nebuchadnezzar's intention was that these new students from Jerusalem should quickly imbibe Babylonian culture and idolatry, but Daniel could have said, "I have more understanding than all my teachers", Psa. 119. 99. Their four Hebrew names in verse 7 (all containing the name of their God) were changed to heathen names (all containing the names of Babylonian gods). Yet Daniel remembered his God until the end. The danger of compromise with the king's food (perhaps offered to idols, or unclean, or still containing blood) was completely avoided, v. 8; both physically and spiritually the young men prospered in their separation to God.

A First Class Degree, vv. 17-21. Although they had to learn much that was contrary to their faith, their true education came from God, v. 17. Daniel's subsequent service derived from the skill and ability that God granted him. These four young men had to pass an oral examination conducted by the king himself, vv. 19-20; they all passed with highest honours at about the age of 19. Young believers today should ensure that they are primarily educated in the school of God, whatever teaching they may acquire from men; service will then open up in God's will. All God's servants should "purchase to themselves *a good degree*", 1 Tim. 3. 13. Again using the terminology of school examinations, we can say that Demetrius obtained a "*good report* of all men", 3 John 12; see Acts 16. 2 (Timothy); 22. 12 (Ananias).

Nov. 19th

READING : Daniel 2. 31-49

NEBUCHADNEZZAR'S DREAM-IMAGE

THE DICTATOR'S PROBLEM, vv. 1-30. Daniel was now equipped to serve God as an interpreter of dreams. Quite near the beginning of the Babylonian kingdom, with all its power and splendour residing in the efforts of an absolute monarch, the king was musing on what would be the future of his kingdom after his death, v. 29. To show that the Divine will would ultimately be done, God granted him the dream of the metallic colossus which was suddenly smitten to the ground. The king knew that his wise men had methods of interpreting any dream; distrusting these, he insisted that they inform him of the dream as well as its interpretation. It does not seem that he had forgotten the dream; he merely gave this impression to his wise men. He wanted to see whether their description of the dream was correct, that he might be able to trust in their interpretation. But the flesh was impotent before a divinely-given dream. Only Daniel could make it known. The four young men spent the night in prayer, praise and thanksgiving, vv. 18-23, when the matter was revealed to Daniel.

The Dream, vv. 31-55. Such huge images were not unknown in Egypt and Babylon (see 3. 1). The gold and series of inferior metals did not excite fear in the king's heart; rather the fear was caused by the sudden destruction of the image by a stone which then grew and filled the whole earth.

The Interpretation, vv. 36-49. The king was where he wanted to be in his wishful musing state — at the top, as valuable as gold. The other three subsequent kingdoms (the Medo-Persian, the Grecian and the Roman) would all be inferior. But man's vain glory cannot last for ever. The degradation of political power is worthy only of Divine judgment. Three kingdoms passed away in due time, but the apex of political power is ripe for future judgment by the Stone, the Lord Jesus coming in power and glory to establish His everlasting kingdom, and to reign on earth. Nebuchadnezzar confessed God as "a God of gods", v. 47, namely One of many, but this was only a vain pronouncement. The blessed consummation beyond the "times of the Gentiles" should give encouragement to believers today, as they view the growing darkness of the nations, knowing God's great purpose for the future.

Nov. 20th
READING : Daniel 3. 1-30
DELIVERANCE FROM THE FIERY FURNACE

THE IMAGE OF GOLD, vv. 1-7. The pride of the king as the "head of gold" caused him to depart from the interpretation of the dream-image, and he visualized the glories of his own kingdom as lasting for ever. He therefore erected this image all of gold. Gold at the head and gold at the feet — a rejection of the iron-clay mixture of the toes, and a vile unwitting imitation of the testimony of the bride concerning her beloved, *"His head* is as the most *fine gold* . . . His legs are . . . set upon *sockets* of *fine gold"*, Song of Songs 5. 11-15. For ourselves, is Christ pre-eminent, or do the politics of the world engage our affections also? How quickly duped were the conquered peoples under Nebuchadnezzar's sway — they immediately worshipped at the sound of music, merely adding another god to the ones they served already, 1 Cor. 8. 5-7.

The Means of Divine Deliverance, vv. 8-27. Daniel's three companions remained faithful to God, bringing about the king's "rage and fury", v. 13, denoting the worst of the flesh that would maintain at all costs the rights that the king arrogated to himself. The three men trusted in God, vv. 17-18, but did not know what God's will was in the matter. Yet, upon being cast in the fire, they quenched the violence of it by faith, Heb. 11. 34, this being accomplished by a fourth man: "the form of the fourth is like the Son of God", Dan. 3. 25. We believe that this was an O.T. Christophany — a manifestation of Christ before His advent in the flesh. No doubt the king thought this was merely one of his gods, but since these had no power, we perceive this was genuinely "the Son of God".

Nebuchadnezzar's Confession, vv. 28-30. Upon emerging, the clothes and hair of these men gave no sign that they had been in the fire, v. 27. Such deliverance stands as a picture of Israel's future deliverance from the great tribulation, and indeed gives encouragement to saints at all times. These three men were saved, but the men who cast them into the furnace were themselves slain, v. 22, as the beast will be at the end of the great tribulation, Rev. 19. 20. Nebuchadnezzar's confession "Blessed be the God of Shadrach . . ." stands half way between the first confession, Dan. 2. 47, and his last one, 4. 2-3; an improvement occurs at each stage.

Nov. 21st
READING : Daniel 4. 1-37
THE EDUCATION OF AN UNBELIEVING KING

NEBUCHADNEZZAR'S TESTIMONY, vv. 1-9. Education is received either willingly or unwillingly. In both cases there will be results, but very evidently distinguished the one from the other. Daniel learnt willingly as a youth, ch. 1, and was therefore a servant of God throughout life. Nebuchadnezzar had not learnt through his experiences in chapters 2-3, so God's education was forced upon him. Eight years are described in chapter 4, at the end of which a humbled Nebuchadnezzar related what had happened. (Verses 19, 28-33 are written in the *third person,* as if too dreadful for the king to relate personally, so another speaker held forth for him.)

The Dream and Interpretation, vv. 10-27. The dream in verses 10-17 commences in symbolic form — a tree being cut down, but with a stump left in the field. However, the last two verses of the dream are personalized so as to refer to a man. The king was troubled, as in chapter 2, but trusted in his wise men before he called Daniel in, vv. 6-7; the lesson of chapter 2 had not been learnt. The interpretation was so awful, that Daniel found great difficulty in explaining it to the king, and even then he repeated the whole dream as if to delay coming to the point, vv. 19-23. The interpretation referred to a seven-year period of insanity, that would force the king to own that "the most High ruleth in the kingdom of men", v. 25. But an offer of repentance was held out to the king, v. 17.

The Accomplishment and its Effects, vv. 28-37. The opportunity for repentance lasted for a year, but was rejected. The king looked over Babylon, his heart filled with pride, and "*while* the word was in the king's mouth", judgment fell, vv. 29-33. Truly, "it is a fearful thing to fall into the hands of the living God", Heb. 10. 31. The king was insane for seven years ("seven times"), vv. 16, 23, 32, after which he owned the status of the most High and of His everlasting kingdom, v. 34. Yet "*my* power" and "*my* majesty" *prior to* his insanity, v. 30, seem to be exceeded *afterwards* by his glorying in his own status and possessions, v. 36. He was "converted" in one sense, but though he was humbled he still exalted himself in *this* life. Believers should humble themselves in *this* life, that they may be exalted — not in this life — but in the *next.*

Nov. 22nd

READING : Daniel 5. 1-31

VENGEANCE ON THEM THAT KNOW NOT GOD

THE LAST NIGHT OF THE FIRST KINGDOM, vv. 1-9. The Neo-Babylonian kingdom lasted for 66 years; Daniel lived throughout, and was over 80 when Belshazzar was slain, and when Darius the Mede took the kingdom. Although Babylon was surrounded by enemies, Belshazzar must have felt absolutely secure within a city which he thought was impregnable. So he engaged in idolatrous feasting with 1,000 of his subjects. In God's plan, the kingdom would be changed, with the silver Medo-Persian coming to dominate the times of the Gentiles. God chose to act when a new peak of idolatry brought out the vessels of God's house from the Babylonian temple, v. 2, to be used for godless revelry and drunkenness. The writing on the wall caused consternation in the palace.

Recognition of Daniel's Ability, vv. 10-16. It appears that Daniel's fame had disappeared from public view when Nebuchadnezzar died. The king's recourse to his astrologers merely showed up their incompetence; truly, "the flesh profiteth nothing", John 6. 63. Only the queen (perhaps the queen mother) recalled the ability of Daniel, who was quickly brought in. The promise of high office was given, but even today this can only be accepted by a believer if it is God's will.

Daniel's Last Interpretation, vv. 23-31. No one else could read or interpret the writing on the wall, which was *"mn, mn, tql, prs"*. As enabled by God, Daniel read it as *"mene, mene, tekel, upharsin"*, and interpreted it as (i) "numbered": the Babylonian kingdom had a divinely determined span of existence, and its end had come; (ii) "weighed": Belshazzar's life and policy were deficient in God's scales that measured righteousness; "By him actions are weighed", 1 Sam. 2. 3; (iii) "divided": Daniel dropped the *"u"* meaning "and", and detected a play on the plural and singular forms of *"peres"*. The kingdom was to be divided (singular) between the Medes and the Persians — the plural consonants *"prsn"* indicating the Medes with the "Persians". Daniel was immediately given high honours, since it was God's will for him to carry them into the following kingdom. But the king was slain and Babylon taken by the enemies walking along the dried-up bed of the Euphrates that passed through the fortified city.

Nov. 23rd

READING : **Daniel 6. 1-28**

DANIEL IN THE DEN OF LIONS

DANIEL'S HIGH OFFICE, vv. 1-3. When over 80 years of age, Daniel was given high office as soon as the Medes and Persians established their kingdom. This empire was divided into 120 provinces, each administered by a "prince", or a satrap. There were also three "presidents", to ensure that the satraps obtained the appropriate taxes for the king, so that the king should suffer no loss financially. The relationship between honesty in the affairs of this world, and faithfulness in the service of God are very closely linked, as seen in Luke 16. 10-12. "He that is faithful in that which is least is faithful also in much", Luke 16. 10.

Trickery against Faithful Daniel, vv. 4-17. The other two presidents, and the 120 satraps, were jealous of Daniel because he was "set . . . over the whole earth". They could not attack his *honesty*, but they could exploit his *faithfulness* to his God. His consistent prayer life would form the basis of their attack, and using the fact that Persian kings were regarded as representatives of the gods, they tricked Darius into signing a decree that prayer was to be made only through him. Believers should always assess the consequences of any legal document which they sign! Yet Daniel continued faithfully; "Evening, and morning, and at noon, will I pray", Psa. 55. 17. The conspirators immediately went into action; the king realized the disastrous effects of the decree he had authorized, and in spite of legal efforts all day, the king could not deliver Daniel, who was then cast into the den of lions. The stone and the seal remind us of the Lord's burial, Matt. 27. 60-66. In Daniel's case, it was to keep him in with no possibility of rescue *alive*; in the Lord's case, it was to keep His body safe *in death*.

Deliverance and Opportunity for Testimony, vv. 18-28. In verse 18, no natural means as fasting, and no artificial means as music, could give the king relief. Only when he saw Daniel alive, and heard his testimony, did the king obtain immediate relief. He then gave his own testimony concerning "the God of Daniel: for he is the living God", v. 26. Thus the *first* Medo-Persian king believed in the living God. The *second* king, Cyrus, was charged in Divine service, God calling him "my shepherd" and "his anointed", Ezra 1. 2; Isa. 44. 28; 45. 1.

Nov. 24th

READING : **Daniel 7. 1-28**

DANIEL'S FIRST VISION OF THE FOUR BEASTS

GOD'S VIEW OF THE NATIONS AS BEASTS, vv. 1-8. Daniel started to have visions in his old age, and they required angelic interpreters. Just before the end of the Babylonian kingdom, God allowed His servant to view the nations from His point of view. We believe that the four beasts answer to the four metals in the dream-image given in chapter 2. The lion stands for Babylon, the bear for Medo-Persia, the leopard for Greece, and the last nameless beast for Rome. The characteristics of these animals answer to features of the four kingdoms. In particular, *all* these features are seen in the last beast, Rev. 13. 2. The age of the Church is not a subject of prophecy, so the Roman empire in Daniel 7. 7-8 stretches from the time before the Lord was here (passing over the "prophetic gap" of the Church age) up to the future seven years prior to the Lord's kingdom in glory. This answers to Revelation 17. 8, "the beast that was (when the Lord was here), and is not (when the Church is here), and yet is (the little horn, after the rapture)".

The Beast Slain, and God's Kingdom Established, vv. 9-14. Daniel sees a throne in heaven, a fiery chariot prepared for judgment, occupied by One Divine in absolute purity, and surrounded by multitudes of attendants, reminding us of Revelation 4-5. The little horn, and the political system over which it ruled, are swept away — the little horn to "the burning flame"; cf. Rev. 19. 20. The kingdom of God in glory and display is then established, with all that offends being rooted out and destroyed, Matt. 13. 41-43. False teachers avoid the subject of judgment on this scale, rather speaking of a pervading love to transform the world; but Scripture is full of the subject of Divine worldwide judgment. The Son of man is subsequently given "dominion, glory, and a kingdom".

Nature of the Fourth Kingdom, vv. 15-28. Daniel had to ask for the interpretation of the fourth beast and the little horn, vv. 19-20. The description given refers to the time of the great tribulation after the rapture, when the last political power will be at its most abominable climax, vv. 24-26, and ripe for immediate judgment. Concerning any religious or political system, God would say to us today, "Come out of her, my people, that ye be not partakers of her sins", Rev. 18. 4.

Nov. 25th

READING : **Daniel 8. 1-27**

DANIEL'S SECOND VISION OF THE TWO BEASTS

PRINCIPLES OF PROPHETIC INTERPRETATION. In this chapter, another "little horn" makes its appearance, v. 9. Historically, this referred to the Syrian king Antiochus Epiphanes, who reigned from B.C. 175 to 164, committing abominable deeds against the Jews and the temple. Prophetically, expositors differ in their interpretation of this, some saying that he was a type of the coming anti-Christ, while others say that he was a type of the coming "king of the north", Dan. 11. 40. Certainly, events that were future for Daniel, but relatively near at hand, were used by God as a pointer to events that are still future from today's standpoint. Such an approach was used by the Lord in Matthew 24. 2-3, where the destruction of the temple in A.D. 70 was used as a pointer to "the end of the world". In Daniel 8, this "little horn" is active in two ways (religious and military) against God's people in the coming day.

The Dream, and Religious Activity, vv. 1-12. The ram stands for Medo-Persia, and the he goat stands for Greece; see vv. 20-21. The "notable horn", v. 5, or the "great horn", v. 21, denotes Alexander the Great (not named in Scripture) as the first king, who conquered territory from Greece to North India. After his death, these lands were divided between four generals, and in particular the territory of Syria ultimately gave rise to the "little horn", Antiochus Epiphanes. In the dream, symbolism gives place to reality in verses 9-12, where evil *religious* exploits are described against the temple in Jerusalem. Hence these evils of Antiochus (well documented in the Apocrypha and profane history) are a pointer to the evils of the anti-Christ, described in 2 Thess. 2. 3-12 and Rev. 13. 11-18.

The Interpretation, and Military Activity, vv. 19-27. Gabriel interpreted the dream for Daniel, but the description of this "king of fierce countenance" in the interpretation is *rather different* from that in the dream. Verses 24-25 describe a man of *military* might motivated by Satan, "not by his own power". In local prophecy, this was Antiochus, a man of military activity (described in 11. 21-32). In this sense he answers to the future "king of the north", a man seeking the military destruction of the Jews in the coming day. But Antiochus' reign of terror came to an end, and so will that of the king of the north.

Nov. 26th

READING : Daniel 9. 1-27

DANIEL'S THIRD VISION—THE SEVENTY WEEKS

DANIEL'S INTERCESSION FOR IMMEDIATE RESTORATION, vv. 1-20. Daniel had lived in captivity throughout the whole period of 70 years foretold by Jeremiah, Jer. 25. 12. This period was nearing its end when Darius was king, so Daniel anticipated restoration. Believing in the promises of God, he knew God would intervene, so that Jerusalem could be reinhabited and the temple rebuilt. Yet all that the prophet could do was to set his face to God, by prayer, supplications, fasting and confession not only of his own sins but those of his people, the Jews. He confessed that the nation had not taken heed to the prophets, v. 6; that "mercies and forgivenesses" belong to the Lord, v. 9; that the curse upon them was justified in keeping with the law of Moses, vv. 11, 13. Confession concludes in verse 15, while prayer commences in verse 16; stress is laid on "thy" city, "thy" mountain, "thy" sanctuary, "thy" name.

The Immediate Answer, vv. 21-23. God's intervention was not delayed; "whiles I was speaking, and praying . . . the man Gabriel . . . touched me". How typical of Divine mercy and grace! God *starts* to answer at the *beginning* of our prayers. God even promised, "before they call, I will answer; and while they are yet speaking, I will hear", Isa. 65. 24. Daniel was "greatly beloved", or "greatly desired"; Daniel's life and faithfulness were such that God desired his prayers and service.

The Ultimate Restoration, vv. 24-27. The local event (the end of the 70 years) was transformed into prophecy concerning the end of 70 weeks or groups of seven years, making 490 years in total. The blessings are listed in verse 24, and must be understood as referring to the Jews as they enter into the Messianic kingdom. Before that event, 69 weeks (483 years) had to elapse between the command to rebuild Jerusalem, Neh. 2. 1-11, and the time when the Lord was crucified. In verse 26, "the people" who destroyed the sanctuary were the Romans in A.D. 70, but then the prophecy leaps over the "gap" of the Church age, up to the end times when "the prince that shall come" refers to the emperor of the revived Roman empire, the beast of Revelation 13. 1-8. The 70th week is described in verse 27, the second half being taken up with idolatry and tribulation until the desolator is destroyed.

Nov. 27th

READING : **Daniel 10. 1-21**

DANIEL'S PREPARATION FOR THE LAST VISION

THE THEOPHANY, vv. 1-9. Chapters 10-12 form one connected narrative, the vision taking place in the third year of Cyrus, namely, after the Jews had returned to Jerusalem to rebuild the temple. Daniel was in mental and spiritual trouble, no doubt concerning the terrors of the last days as made known to him, but also due to the fact that the rebuilding of the temple was being met with resistance and enmity, Ezra 4. 4-6. After three weeks, Daniel saw "a certain man clothed in linen", Dan. 10. 5. The description of this "certain man" in verse 6 far outweighs that given to any angel, and the graphic description "fine gold, beryl, lightning, lamps of fire, polished brass" uniquely suggests the Lord Jesus prior to His incarnation. Only Daniel saw this vision, leading to physical weakness, to show that help and strength come only from heaven.

Angelic Strengthening, vv. 10, 16, 18. Three times Daniel was touched by an angel (not by the man clothed in linen, and we suggest that it was by Gabriel). When the Lord was here, He touched men directly, but one function of the angels is that they are "all ministering spirits, sent forth to minister for them who shall be heirs of salvation", Heb. 1. 14.

Satanic Opposition amongst the Nations, vv. 13-14, 20-21. Daniel had chastened himself before God for three weeks, and he may have wondered why there was a delay in the Divine answer; cf. 9. 20-21. There had been resistance by "the prince of the kingdom of Persia". This could not refer to a mere man, since one angel could deal with 185,000 Syrians, 2 Kings 19. 35. Rather, this "prince" originated from Satan's domain. Michael the archangel, Jude 9, comes to help, as he will help when he appears as head of the angelic forces directed against Satan himself, Rev. 12. 7. Later, "the prince of Grecia" is mentioned, Dan. 10. 20, Satan being the prince of the power of the air, and having his agents everywhere over the nations. Yet God rules over all, and His angels keep the power of the enemy sufficiently at bay so that God's will shall be done constantly. By this vision, Daniel was prepared to receive the details of chapters 11-12, encouraged by the fact that God was in control, in spite of apparently adverse circumstances. This passage will provide encouragement during the great tribulation.

Nov. 28th

READING : Daniel 12. 1-13

THE GREAT TRIBULATION: ITS DETERMINED END

TODAY, when tribulation and suffering come the way of men, they know not when it will end. The commencement of war, the common pursuit of so many national leaders over the centuries, provides no clue as to its end, whether it be short or long.

Chapter 11. 1-20 traces from verse 4 the historical intrigues and warfare of "the king of the south" (Egypt) and "the king of the north" (Syria), parts of the Grecian empire, up to the Syrian king, "a vile person", namely Antiochus Epiphanes. Historians tell us that these prophetical details fit in exactly with the outworking of history during those centuries. Then verses 21-32 treat of the activity of Antiochus, but this came to an end, bringing liberty to God's people again; cf. ch. 8. All this is a pointer to verses 36-45, dealing with the end times, when the anti-Christ, vv. 36-39, falls after warfare conducted between the north and the south across "the glorious land".

This period (the last three and a half years) will be "a time of trouble", 12. 1, and the elect will only be saved when Michael stands up to protect them. But this tribulation has its determined end; resurrection is promised, v. 2. Some say this refers to the national rebirth of Israel, as in the vision of the valley of dry bones, Ezek. 37. 1-14. But the "first resurrection" takes place at the end of this tribulation with the glorious advent of Christ, Rev. 20. 5-6, when the martyrs of that period will be raised. We prefer to relate Daniel 12. 2 to this event.

The Period Involved, vv. 5-13. Daniel saw "the man clothed in linen" for the last time — Christ revealed to His servant. This Man "sware by him that liveth for ever" that the duration of this tribulation would be specifically for a "time, times, and an half ", namely 3½ years. After that, "all these things shall be finished", v. 7. The Babylonian captivity had its end, and Daniel lived to realize this. Similarly the greatest tribulation of all time will have its end, when the overcomers will enter into blessing. Verses 11 and 12 add 30 and a further 45 days to the 1,260 days (3½ years). The reason is not stated; it may be a time to cleanse the earth of the effects of judgment, Rev. 14. 18-20; 19. 21, when "all the fowls were filled with their flesh", and to prepare the world for millennial administration.

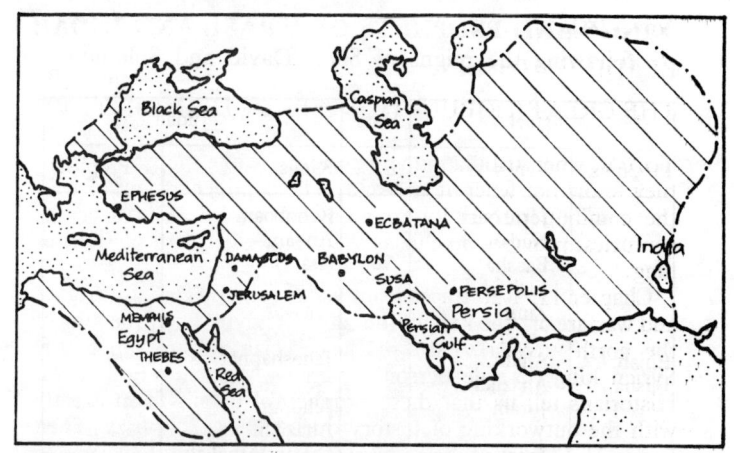

The Persian Empire

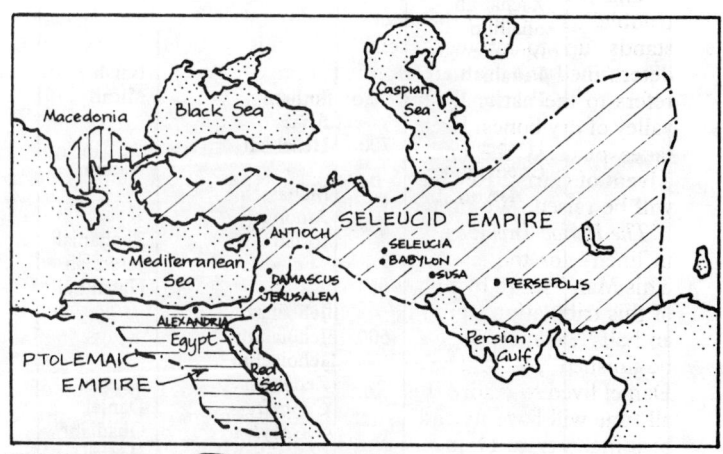

The Greek Empire

ALEXANDER THE GREAT CONQUERED THE PERSIAN EMPIRE (SEE MAP AT TOP OF PAGE) AND SET UP THE GREEK EMPIRE. THE MAP SHOWS THE DIVISION OF THE EMPIRE AT THE TIME OF ANTIOCHUS IV EPIPHANES

KINGS AND PROPHETS OF ISRAEL AND JUDAH
following the reigns of Saul, David and Solomon

Israel		Date	Judah	
Prophets	Kings	B.C.	Kings	Prophets
	Jeroboam I Nadab Baasha Elah Zimri Omri	900	Rehoboam Abijam Asa	
Elijah Elisha	Ahab Ahaziah Joram		Jehoshaphat Jehoram Ahaziah	
 Jonah Amos Hosea	Jehu Jehoahaz Jehoash Jeroboam II	800	Queen Athaliah Jehoash (Joash) Amaziah Uzziah (Azariah)	Joel*
	Zachariah Shallum Menahem Pekahiah Pekah		 Jotham Ahaz	Isaiah Micah
	Hoshea *Captivity—* *Assyria*	700	Hezekiah Manasseh Amon Josiah	Nahum* Zephaniah Jeremiah Habakkuk*
		600	Jehoahaz Jehoiakim Jehoiachin Zedekiah *Captivity—* *Babylon* (Zerubbabel)	Ezekiel Daniel Obadiah* Haggai Zechariah
		500	(Ezra) (Nehemiah)	Malachi

* Date uncertain

Introducing Hosea and Amos

Hosea's ministry extended over a long period. He served during the reign of four kings of Judah and one king of Israel. He was sometime a contemporary of Isaiah, Amos and Micah. The days of Jeroboam II in Israel and Uzziah in Judah were days of *economic prosperity, agricultural productivity* and *military security*, 2 Kings 14. 23-29; 2 Chron. 26. This apparent "golden age" soon lost its glitter in the spiritual departure and moral decay of the nation. The beneficence of God did not lead them to repentance. Rather, they turned from God to idols, and attributed the bounty of the land to Baal, Hos. 2. 5-8. God considered this to be spiritual harlotry with its inevitable alienation and judgment.

Jehovah's suffering love however would not utterly forsake them. He would allure them back to Himself, but through a long wilderness experience. At last they will return to their first love, and openly declare their relationship and loyalty to the true God they have so grieved.

Hosea was to bring this message to them first as a living parable. The first three chapters present this, and the rest of the book is the exposition and application of it.

While the message is for Israel, there are principles that might well be applied to Christendom in this day.

Amos lived in the same period as Hosea, but he had a different message. Israel is not viewed by him as an unfaithful wife, but as one nation among many, 9. 7. Amos shows that all nations are answerable to God and He will judge them, 1. 3 to 2. 16. If Israel rejoiced in this judgment of her enemies, that joy was shortlived, for the prophet startles the people by declaring that since they were specially privileged they would be heavily punished, having sinned against the light, 3. 1.f.

National sins bring national calamities, not only future judgment. These distresses are "the roar of the lion" to awaken the nation to impending judgment and to call them to repentance. That repentance must be genuine. Empty rituals cannot avert the judgment. This is the message of Amos, revealing *Jehovah's inflexible and universally applied righteousness*. But it is not without hope. At the last, the Lord will turn the captivity of Israel and they will never go out again.

Nov. 29th

READING : **Hosea 1. 1 to 3. 5**

A PAINFUL PARABLE

ISRAEL in her prosperity so violated her unique relationship with God that she attributed His blessings to Baal and worshipped him, 2. 5, 8, 12, 13. God calls this spiritual adultery, and commands Hosea to present a living parable of this to the nation, 1. 2. This was a solemn message to the people, and to the prophet it would reflect the sorrow of God's heart. Here we learn a principle. *The Lord will not sit idly by and watch the departure of His beloved without intervening.*

Gomer, Hosea's wife, bare *him* a son named Jezreel in view of coming judgment against the throne of Israel, 1. 4. That would remind Israel of the rough zeal of Jehu. While he did right and was rewarded in his family, it was not with a pure heart, 2 Kings 10. 29-31. Here is another principle; *the Lord will reward obedience, but will always judge motives.* In prospect "Jezreel" spoke of a future breaking of Israel's military power.

Gomer bore two more children, but not to Hosea, 1. 6-8. These were the evidence of unfaithfulness. So she became a living parable of Israel's departure from God. Their names express God's discipline, 1. 6, 9. He would withdraw mercy from Israel (preserving Judah for a time, 1. 6-7). He would no longer identify Himself as their God. They would be without His continuing protection and presence, 1. 9-10. Yet they would be multiplied, unified and identified with their God again, 1. 10-11. In her distress, all forsake her; still God speaks, 2. 1-7. He seeks to win her back through the wilderness experience, 2. 14. Then in the valley of troubling (Achor) she will learn that there is hope, for *the Lord's discipline is not for destruction but instruction*, 2. 14-15. *He still speaks to our heart*, 2. 14 marg.

Israel will sing again the song of the Lord, 2. 15. She will proclaim her covenant relationship with the Lord, 2. 16-23. Until that day however, she is set aside in isolation, without a Sovereign, a Saviour, a Sacrifice and a true Service for God, 3. 1-5. All this until God's glorious "afterward" when the peaceable fruit of righteousness will burst forth. They will seek the Lord and the One whom they pierced, Zech. 12. 10. Then she will follow the Lord, fear the Lord and enjoy the favour of the Lord "in the latter days". *He will never abandon His own.*

Nov. 30th

READING : **Hosea 4. 1 to 5. 15**

THE FRUIT OF FOLLY

HERE BEGINS the declaration of the Lord's message, 4.1. **The Controversy** of the Lord. They had violated the truth and mercy of His character. As a result, they violated the trust and morals of His people, v. 2. This led them to violate the treasures and munificence of His provision in nature, v. 3. *Sin is never static. It is an ever degenerating process*; see James 1. 14-15. **The Cause** of their separation from God was spiritual ignorance — not the absence of knowledge but the rejection of it. It was the wilful forgetting of the law they had well known, v. 6. *Before the act of sin in the life there is always the fact of sin in the will*; see Matt. 5. 28. **The Charge** was laid most heavily upon the spiritual leaders. The prophets brought no light of God. The priests led not in the ways of God. Instead they conformed to the misbehaviour of the people, vv. 7-11. *The servant of God is never neutral. He either leads to God or away from Him*; see Matt. 12. 30. **The Crime** at its ultimate depth became spiritual harlotry. Their adultery betrayed idolatry. This unholy union was an insult in the face of the God who loved them, vv. 12-16. God's solemn word concerning Ephraim, the representative tribe, was "let him alone", v. 17. Once inscribed and clasped on the breast of the high priest in the sanctuary, now he lurks in the shadows of reeking altars clutching his idols to his heart, vv. 13-17. What backsliding, v. 16! What bitterness, v. 18! What blame, v. 18! *Backsliding, permitted and unconfessed, can carry God's people from the delights of the sanctuary to the devices of Satan*; see Eph. 6. 11. **The Consequence.** (1) Instead of the Lord in the midst, a spirit of evil, 5. 4. (2) Ignorance of God, v. 4b. (3) Inevitable collapse, v. 5. (4) The withdrawal of God's presence, v. 6. (5) Desolation, v. 9. (6) Oppression and brokenness, v. 11. (7) Erosion of their treasures, v. 12. (8) Betrayal by their allies, vv. 13-14. (9) The silence of God, v. 15. Here is the law of retribution in effect. *What we sow, of that same kind we reap unless God in His mercy withholds the harvest*; see Gal. 6. 7-9. **The Closing Gleam** shines in 5. 15. Israel will yet seek the Lord, but through much affliction. God is waiting in His place until that glad day. *God's sovereign purposes shall be fulfilled*, 3. 5; see Rom. 11. 26-27.

Dec. 1st

READING : Hosea 6. 1 to 9. 17

SOWING AND REAPING

The People's Cry: 6. 1-3 is the cry of the returning people. Torn and smitten, the world has been her cemetery. Nevertheless the dry bones will be revived again, Ezek. 37. **The Plaintive Call:** twice in verse 4 the Lord cries, "what shall I do unto thee?". Neither His goodness nor His glory had led them to repentance, vv. 4-5. Their goodness was but a fleeting philanthropy and a false formality devoid of compassion and the knowledge of God, vv. 4-6. **Their Picture:** in chapter 7 four pictures present the people as they appeared to the eye of God. (1) *A hot oven*, vv. 4, 6, 7. Not heated to provide bread, Isa. 58. 7, but burning with lust and illicit appetites. (2) *An unturned cake*, v. 8. One side overdone, the other underdone. Their creed was correct but their conduct was corrupt. (3) *A silly dove without a heart*, v. 11. Defective in love and loyalty, they flitted from one alliance to another. God Himself binds their wings lest they fly even farther from Him, v. 12. What a lesson to all who long to flee their circumstance but cannot! The constrictions are but God's net for preservation and instruction. (4) *A deceitful bow*, v. 16. There was an inbuilt deflection, a moral twist, that meant they would always miss the mark and be a derision to their enemies, v. 16; cf. Rom. 3. 10, 23. **Their Public Condemnation:** chapter 8 opens with the alarm. The enemy swoops upon them as a scourge of God for their transgression, v. 1. When in trouble, like so many, they cry to God, but all is hypocrisy, v. 2. They turned from faith in an invisible Sovereign to the earthly pomp of human rulers. Trust in an unseen Majesty was exchanged for the trinkets of home-made gods, vv. 4-6. Thus they set in motion a law over which they have no control, v. 7. Chapter 8 ends with a solemn charge, "Israel hath forgotten his Maker", v. 14. **The Pathetic Consequences:** in chapter 9 the sad results of their infidelity are recorded. Joyless days, v. 1. Foodless stores, v. 2. Meaningless offerings, v. 4. Distracted leaders, v. 7. Depleted population, vv. 11-14. Thus Israel reaps the bitter fruits of her national sins as she wanders among the peoples of the earth, hated and decimated, 9. 17. Surely there is a solemn lesson for all in this. *The law of God cannot be violated with impunity, and the law of sin cannot be activated without responsibility.*

Dec. 2nd

READING : **Hosea 10. 1 to 12. 14**

UNREQUITED LOVE

The Degenerate Vine: 10. 1. God had planted Israel as a vine to bear fruit to Himself, and the nations, Psa. 80. 8-12. She perverted this purpose by self-indulgence, and used God's bounty to further her idolatry. One day the True Vine would appear to fulfil the Divine purpose, John 15. 1. *God's ultimate purpose cannot be thwarted!* **Divided Devotions:** 10. 2. Israel had tried to compromise by worshipping idols, and professing to know God, 8. 2. *God and evil however are mutually exclusive!*, 1 Cor. 10. 21. **Departed Deities:** 10. 5. They turned to "no gods", but when they needed help they feared for the safety of their supposed protectors! **The Desolate Land:** 10. 8. The Assyrian would come and strip them. Despair would be theirs and they would cry for sudden death rather than endure protracted captivity; cf. Rev. 6. 15-17. *God always had a better alternative than despair!* **The Definite Hope:** 10. 12. All is not lost! The prophet calls for the plough of self-judgment to open up the conscience, for the Word of God to enter while there is time; cf. Psa. 32. 6. *God's judgment may be averted by self-judgment!*, 1 Cor. 11. 31. **The Day of Battle:** 10. 14-15. The thunder of the approaching Assyrian army is heard with alarm. *God's mercy gives time to repent, but if despised, the wages of sin are inevitable!* **The Divine Choice:** 11. 1-4. Jehovah now speaks as a father, loving but unloved. Gently He had upheld them as an infant nation while they took their first tottering steps, v. 3. Yet, for all this love, they were bent on backsliding. **The Divine Love:** 11. 8. *God's justice demands punishment, but His love longs to save them!* He would purge them, but not annihilate them as the cities of the plains. He would discipline, but not destroy, v. 9. **Divine Intervention:** 11. 10-11. Israel will yet hear the compelling call of the Lord. He will yet deliver them from their enemies and their exile. *God will not utterly forsake His own!* **Their Deceit:** 11. 12 to 12. 14. Marked by dishonesty, futility and disloyalty, 11. 12; 12. 1, they took up the ways of Canaan, v. 7. God's dealings with Jacob are the basis of an appeal to return, vv. 2-13. In spite of this example they bitterly provoked Jehovah, even with blood-guiltiness, v. 14. Therefore He would leave that guilt upon them. Herein is another lesson. *God will not relieve the unrepentant!*

Dec. 3rd

READING : Hosea 13. 1 to 14. 9

TRANSGRESSION AND RESTORATION

A Sad Transition, from the place of distinction to the place of death, took place when Ephraim as a leader went over to the worship of Baal, 13. 1. As his gods were but the transitory work of his own hands, v. 2, so Ephraim, the representative tribe, would pass away, v. 3. *Men become like the object of their worship!*; cf. 2 Cor. 3. 18. **A Solemn Warning** is presented to them, vv. 4-5. No sooner did they enter into the beneficence of God than they forgot Him, v. 6. Thus they brought judgment upon themselves. Silently, suddenly, and savagely it would break upon them, vv. 7-8. They must learn that the *rejection of God brings retribution from God!* This judgment is really **Self-Destruction**, v. 9. Yet there is help and hope in Jehovah, if only they would bow to His sovereign rule, v. 10. The charge has been laid, the case is closed, all the evidence is in, and the crime is on record!, v. 12. **The Sorrows of Death** are as certain as a travailing woman trying to deliver a child that will not naturally come forth, v. 13. **A Sudden Declaration** bursts forth from the heart of Jehovah, not now as a judge, but as a deliverer. Death will be robbed of its prey. The Lord will bring the nation forth as newly born, even from the place of death, and of this purpose He will not repent, v. 14; cf. Isa. 25. 8; 1 Cor. 15. 55. **The Savage Desolation** of Israel and Samaria is predicted in their near future, because of rebellion against God, vv. 15-16. When Jacob, renamed Israel, returned, "the sun rose upon him", Gen. 32. 31. So, when at last the nation returns, they will walk in **The Sunshine of His Love**. If they will return, repent and repeat honestly, acceptable words of confession, commitment and confidence, 14. 2-3, 8, then the Lord will respond in healing, in love, and in bountiful blessing, vv. 4-7. Then Ephraim ("double-fruit") will know *the rooting of stability*, v. 5, *the spreading of fertility*, v. 6, *the shining of beauty*, v. 6, and *the rejoicing of fragrant acceptability* among the nations, vv. 6b, 7b. **The Summary** of the whole prophecy is contained in the last verse. The ways of the Lord are right. The just obediently walk wisely and prudently in them, and are blessed, ever growing in the knowledge of them. The transgressor will find the way hard and God's retribution heavy. *Shun the wrong way and love the true God.*

Introducing Joel and Micah

JOEL's name means "Jehovah is God", and lends some character to his prophecy. No date is given, but internal evidence suggests that he is one of the earliest of the twelve. He ministered to Judah, probably during the reign of Joash. From the references to the house of the Lord, he probably prophesied in Jerusalem. The burden of his message is "The day of the Lord", which was prefigured for him by a devastating plague of locusts. Jehovah is presented as the God of government. This is not all, however, for the prophet goes on to present Jehovah as the God of grace, restoring and bountifully providing for His people. Remarkably, the dispensation of the Holy Spirit is anticipated. It is from this prophecy that Peter quotes on the day of Pentecost, Acts 2. 16-21. The prophet however sweeps on beyond Pentecost, beyond the day of grace to the final intervention of Jehovah on behalf of His people by crushing the gathered armies of their enemies. He Himself will be their refuge and refreshing. Their beloved city will be holy. The Lord will dwell in Zion and they will abide His people forever.

MICAH, like Joel, was an early prophet. The period of his ministry is given in 1. 1. He was sometime contemporary with Isaiah and Hosea, and ministered to both Israel and Judah. However, he directed his prophecy especially to the capital cities of Samaria in Israel, and Jerusalem in Judah. These centres influenced the whole nation, and must bear that responsibility. The prophet came from a town about ten miles south west of Jerusalem. His name means "Who is like Jehovah", and throughout the prophecy the singular glory of God is seen in authority and power, in holiness and judgment, in grace and mercy. The prophecy takes the form of three addresses. Each begins "Hear", 1. 2; 3. 1; 6. 1. In each there is a rebuke for sin, warning of judgment for sin, and the promise of pardon for sin with future blessing. Micah lived in a day of arrogant rulers, of oppression of the poor, of social evils and immoral living. While the message is for Israel and Judah, there are some words of prophecy that relate to the opening of the day of grace, by the coming of the Promised One into the human race at Bethlehem, who is yet to be ruler in Israel, 5. 2.

Dec. 4th

READING : **Joel 1. 1 to 2. 17**

DESOLATION

THE VOICE OF THE LORD is to be heard in national disasters. The prophet vividly describes the invasion of a vast army of locusts that stripped the land bare. Not one, but four kinds of locusts follow each other as the very "incarnation of hunger". The words used in 1. 4 may be translated "the shearer", "the swarmer", "the licker" and "the finisher". The prophet sees in this desolation a vast object lesson he wants no one to miss. He knows it is a message from God, for "the word of the Lord . . . came" to him, 1. 1. Everyone is affected. Those that have seen God's provision, the elders, 1. 2. Those that have perverted God's provision, the drunkards, 1. 5. Those that reap God's provision, the farmers, 1. 11. Those that offer back God's provision, the priests, 1. 13. Joel wants the people to know that whatever they think of their God, *his* God has spoken by this plague. He sees in this tragedy "the day of the Lord", 1. 15. The day of the Lord, viewed generally, is a period when He is manifestly in control. It is peculiarly His day when His will is carried out, especially in judgment. Viewed specifically, it is that day, after the rapture, when the Lord will intervene for Israel, and destroy their enemies. The locusts were not just a misery, they were a message! So even today, *national disasters are a voice from God, calling for repentance, and are the harbinger of the day of the Lord yet to come.*

The Trumpet of Alarm is sounded in 2. 1. In view of what the locusts prefigured, a day would come when, not insects, but a great military invasion would sweep the land. Unnatural darkness, 2. 2, 10, unquenchable fire, 2. 3, and irresistible force would accompany that destruction. These forces are called "his army", 2. 11, for "Jehovah is God" (Jo-el). He uses nature and nation *to chasten* His people for their treatment of Him. He will lead His armies of heaven, *to judge* the nations for their treatment of His people Israel, Rev. 19. 11-16.

The Trumpet of Repentance calls, 2. 15, not to mourning and lamenting alone, but to true contrition and supplication, 2. 12-13. The very character of Jehovah encourages this humble response, for still "Jehovah is God" (Jo-el), but such a God of grace and mercy, patience and kindness, that, *while He must judge sin, it is His delight to show mercy,* 2. 13.

Dec. 5th

READING : **Joel 2. 18 to 3. 21**

RESTORATION

The Silence of the Centuries will be Broken, 2. 18-19. For so long have the heavens been silent for Israel. But the day will come, and "Then" the Lord will answer the long crying of His people. There will be a *removing* of their proud and boastful enemy, the great northern army, 2. 20. Primarily, of course, we have an answer to the prayers of the priests in 2. 17, for relief from the locusts. But, by the law of prophetic perspective, it relates to their national enemy Assyria. If this enemy boasted great things, 2. 20, the Lord will accomplish great things for the land and the people, 2. 21. There will be *rejoicing and gladness*, 2. 23. There will be *refreshing and fulness*, 2. 23-24. There will be *restoration and acceptance*, with the presence of the Lord in the midst. So they will no longer be viewed as a poor people whose God is either unable or unwilling to help them, 2. 27. **The "Afterward" of God's Purposes Will Come,** 2. 28-32. For God's people the chastening of the present will pass, and He will introduce His "afterward" when the peaceable fruit of righteousness will abound as a result of the ministry and power of the Holy Spirit, 2. 28. In the Hebrew text, 2. 28-32 is a distinct section. Thus we see its significance, for it speaks of the dispensation of the Holy Spirit. Peter refers to this at Pentecost in Acts 2. 16-21, not as the consummation of the prophecy, but as an evidence to the Jews that what God had begun He would complete. **The Judgment of the Nations Will be Certain,** 3. 1-21. A two-fold gathering is seen in 3. 1-21. The Lord will gather His people back to their land again from their scattering among the nations. Also "in those days" another vast gathering will take place. The gathering of the nations into the valley of Jehoshaphat, "the Lord judges", 3. 2. These are the enemies of Israel that have spoiled them, sold them, and slaughtered them. *War is declared*! The nations "sanctify" it as a holy war, 3. 9. But the battle is the Lord's. The Judge of the whole earth takes His seat. The battle is in array! By the word of His mouth He smites the nations, Rev. 19. 15. Then they will learn that "Jehovah is God", and Israel will acknowledge Him as their covenant God, 3. 17. We may learn from all this, *He is over all, blessed forever! A God of government, and a God of grace!*

Dec. 6th

READING : Amos 1. 1 to 2. 16

THE ROAR OF THE LION

The days of Amos were days of affluence, 3.15. The rich shamelessly exploited the poor, 2. 6, etc. The empty form of religion was meticulously observed, 4. 4. Into this scene came Amos, the herdman of Tekoa with a message to Israel, *the uncompromising righteousness of God against sin*! The word of the Lord was first directed to six nations that surrounded Israel and Judah. They were without special revelation, but they were not without responsibility, Rom. 1. 19-20. The repeated expression "For three transgressions . . . and for four" did not mean *only* three or four, but that their transgression was full, and that God had waited in patient mercy for their repentance. Now it was not the request of the patient Lord, but the roar of the pouncing lion, 1. 2; 3. 8. *Damascus and Gaza* were guilty of gross cruelty and slave trading, 1. 3-5, 6-8. *Tyrus and Edom* despised the brotherly covenant between Hiram and David and Solomon, 1 Kings 5. 1, etc. *Ammon and Moab*, in a delirium of savagery, sought to destroy the hope of the future (the unborn child), and to desecrate the sacred emblems of the past (the bones of the dead), 2. 1. Those six nations violated the basic principles of human conduct, man to man, brother to brother, the strong to the weak, the innocent and the helpless. Whoever violates these sacred principles, without repentance, can be sure of the devouring judgment, 1. 2; 4. 7, etc. For all national leaders the lesson is clear, *God is watching*!

Now the Lord moves closer. *Judah* comes under judgment, God's people! They had despised His law, disobeyed His commandment, and committed the sins of their father, 2. 4-5. The same fire will fall upon them. Finally, *Israel* is the target, 2. 6. Sadly, she is judged for the treatment of her own people, 2. 6-8. The debtor they sold like merchandise to the creditor, 2. 6. They longed to bring the poor down in despair, 2. 7. They engaged in incestuous depravity, and despised the pledges of the poor, 2. 8; Deut. 24. 12-13. They violated God's Word, God's people, and God's grace, 2. 10. So judgment was inescapable, neither by ability, 2. 14, skill, 2. 15, nor courage, 2. 16. *Sin is never more abhorred by God than when commited by His own people, who have enjoyed His grace, who have known His work, and who have tasted His abundant blessings.*

Dec. 7th

READING : **Amos 3. 1 to 4. 13**

HIGHLY PRIVILEGED—HEAVILY PUNISHED!

AMOS NOW brings the word of the Lord to Judah and Israel together, as a family so highly privileged, 3. 1. They had a unique relationship, a great redempion, and a gracious election, 3. 2. God's knowledge of them includes His choosing; cf. Jer. 1. 5; Rom. 8. 28-30. With man, intimacy often means permissiveness, but *with God, privilege increases responsibility,* Jude 5-11. Seven rhetorical questions are asked, to show that in God's dealings there is always cause and effect, 3. 3-6. *God's warnings precede His judgments*, 3. 7. The very fact of Amos prophesying was an evidence that Jehovah was going to act. It was no idle threat. If they had not sinned, the prophet would not be crying against them, 3. 8. Amos is now commanded to call upon Ashdod and Egypt, 3. 9. Ashdod had witnessed the deliverance of the ark of God, 1 Sam. 5. Egypt had witnessed the deliverance of the people of God, Exod. 14. 30. Now they are called to be witnesses that the presence of the Lord was not with them, 3. 3, and that they would be carried away captive, only a ragged remnant escaping, 3. 11-13. *What a tragedy when the outsider is called to testify against the highly privileged*!; cf. Matt. 12. 41. From this judgment there will be no escape in their degenerate religion, 3. 14, nor their luxuriant materialism, 3. 15. A word is now given to the typical women of the day, called "cattle" because they lived by the instincts of the flesh, by oppression, arrogance, and impudence, 4. 1. They would lose their liberty and their luxury. Amos ironically calls them to pursue their empty religion and pretended piety. They mixed some truth with great error, as to place, 1 Kings. 2. 28-30, as to practice, Lev. 2. 11, and proclamation, Lev. 22. 18-19. This only added to their guilt, 4. 4. Judgment had already begun in their circumstances; famine and drought, 4. 6-8, blight and pestilence, 4. 9-10, war and destruction, 4. 10-11. The Lord now calls His people to meet Him in grace, while there is time; cf. Exod. 5. 3, etc. The preparation is to be that true repentance required of God. Only thus can they escape the otherwise inevitable judgment. The final doxology affirms that it is futile to think of escape, for *the One they must deal with is no golden calf at Bethel, but "The Lord, The God of hosts"*, *omnipotent, omniscient, and omnipresent*, 4. 12-13.

Dec. 8th

READING : **Amos 5. 1 to 6. 14**

SEEK THE LORD!

AMOS LAMENTS the demise of Israel. Pictured as a virgin, she has never entered the full purpose of Jehovah, 5. 1-2. She is *fallen in death, forsaken by dispossession,* and *finished through defeat,* 5. 3. The people are warned not to seek help in their religious centres, Beth-el, Gilgal and Beer-sheba, 5. 5. Beth-el was where Jacob received the promise of the land as *a possession,* Gen. 28. 11-19. Gilgal was the place where the people left the tokens of their *deliverance,* Josh. 4. 19-24, and the tokens of the covenant, Josh. 5. 2-3; Gen. 17. 4-11. Beer-sheba was the place where Abraham, having made an oath, called on the name of Jehovah as *the God who can never die,* Gen. 21. 33. How incongruous that those three sacred places could offer no hope against death, dispossession and defeat! They were to seek Jehovah. Only in Him is life, 5. 6, hope, 5. 8, and victory against impossible odds, 5. 9. *These blessings cannot be found in holy places nor holy things alone, but only in the Lord*! They despised righteous judgment, and faithful witnesses, 5. 10. Oppression, 5. 11a, presumption, 5. 11b, affliction, corruption, 5. 12, and suppression of the truth, 5. 13, marked out their evil ways. Yet the Lord, the God of hosts, is willing to be gracious, if they will but give evidence of changed lives, 5. 14-15. Otherwise it will be wailing and woe everywhere, 5. 16-18. Judgment will be inescapable, 5. 19, with no flicker of hope, 5. 20. The Lord rejected their dead religious forms, since they did not result in judgment and righteousness, 5. 21-24. They engaged in idolatry, 5. 26, and for this would go into captivity, 5. 27. Amazingly, they are at ease in their sin, and the prophet's "Woe" is to awaken them, 6. 1-6. They would suffer captivity, 6. 7, plunder, 6. 8. slaughter, 6. 9, destruction, 6. 11, and affliction, 6. 14. This would be as impossible to escape as it is for horses to run up a rocky cliff, or for oxen to plough there. Well may we hear the echo of this woe today! Affluence, ease, empty religion, and condoning of evil, wound our nations. The weak and innocent are violated, and justice is scorned. While these words were for Israel, it would be wisdom to heed the warning, that God cannot excuse unrepentant sinners. *National disasters are God's warnings that no spiritual, social, or moral evil will go unpunished.*

Dec. 9th

READING : **Amos 7. 1 to 9. 15**

DIVINE REPENTANCE

FIVE VISIONS are given to Amos. **The First Two Visions** are literal, and speak of total destruction, 7. 1-6. The prophet, moved in pity, beseeches Jehovah for mercy, 7. 2, 5. *In answer to prayer God brings sovereign purposes to pass*!, Dan. 9. 2-3; Matt. 9. 38; Luke 1. 13; Rev. 22. 20, etc. God's sovereignty allows for the repentance and prayers of His creatures. His repentance is not so much a change of decision, but a change of dispensation. In 7. 3, 6 He turns from wrath to mercy. **The Third Vision** is spiritual. The plumbline is emblematic of the Divine test, 7. 7-9; Deut. 4. 7-8. The Lord calls them "my people Israel", affirming that *special relationship involves special responsibility*. Amos does not pray now. The plumbline has shown the structure dangerously out of line, cf. Isa. 30. 13, and it must come down. The first to fall are their holy places, for judgment must begin there, Ezek. 9. 6. Next is the house of the ruler, 7. 9. He had violated the conditions of his rule, 1 Kings 11. 38; 2 Kings 14. 24. Amaziah attacks Amos for his message, Amos 7. 10-17, by misrepresentation, v. 11, by rejection, v. 12, and confrontation, v. 13; cf. Acts 5. 28-29. The prophet's credentials were simple, "The Lord said. . .Go, prophesy". Amaziah learns that individual as well as national sins must be judged, 7. 17. **The Fourth Vision,** 8. 1, portrays Israel as ripe for judgment; cf. Jer. 8. 20. When it falls they are told to stop howling and be silent, 8. 3. Their lust for gain destroyed their love for God, and respect for human dignity, 8. 4-6. They despised His light, they would dwell in darkness, 8. 9. They rejected His Word, they would famish for it, 8. 11-14. **The Fifth Vision** was of the Lord Himself, 9. 1. He is going to smash their idolatry, and for the idolaters there is no refuge, neither out of time, 9. 2, nor out of sight, 9. 3-6. The Lord God of hosts is over all, and will pursue sinners relentlessly, sparing only a faithful remnant, 9. 5-10. *But after the sin, the sorrow and the sword, the sun will shine again for Israel*! The fallen will be *raised*, the ruins *restored*, and the glory *revived*, 9. 11-12. The land will be *repossessed* in luxuriant bounty, 9. 13. They will reap, rest, and be refreshed, and never go out again. Amos exults in his closing words of hope. *Their land! Their liberty! Their life! The Lord their God*!, 9. 14-15.

Dec. 10th

READING : Obadiah 1-21

DIVINE RETRIBUTION

EDOM IS the target of the prophet's message of judgment. Shortest of all the O.T. books, it contains no relief nor hope for this implacable foe of God's people, Ezek. 35. 5. Yet their father was Esau, twin brother of Jacob, Gen. 25. 25; 27. 41. The date of the prophecy is not certain. Whether given in prospect, or in retrospect, of the fall of Jerusalem we cannot be sure; cf. Jer. 49. 9, 14-16. Nevertheless, the cause of Edom's judgment is clear. Their pride, self-assurance, and shameful indifference, bring upon them utter desolation, Obad. 3-6. No one would escape. God would use their neighbours and allies to drive them out of their land (N.T.=Idumea). The Lord Himself would destroy their worldly wisdom, and dismay their mighty men, vv. 8-9. Their reputation as "wise" would pass away. Details of their cold-hearted attitude follows, vv. 10-14. When Jerusalem was besieged and sacked by Nebuchadnezzar, Edom goaded on the attackers, Psa. 137. 7. Indifferent to Israel's grief, they gambled for the spoil, Obad. 11. They gloated over the people's calamity, v. 12, and took sadistic pleasure in being spectators to their grief, v. 13. Their heartless obstruction, to prevent the escape of the populace and assuring their capture, was despicable malice, 2 Kings 25. 4-6. They, and all nations, shall be judged for their treatment of God's people, Obad. 15; Matt. 25. 31-46; Zech. 2. 8. Edom would permit Israel neither passage nor water, Num. 20. 14-21. They will drink the cup of God's wrath and pass from the earth, Obad. 16; Jer. 25. 15-16. For Edom there was no escape. But a remnant of God's people will finally escape the time of great tribulation, Obad. 17. The evil purposes of the Hamans, the Herods, and the Hitlers, will always be frustrated. God will preserve a remnant from the gallows, the sword, and the ovens, and bring them at last into their possession, v. 17. Then the kingdom, long divided, will be one again. Burning with holy zeal, they will devour the last remaining opposition, v. 18. The Word of the Lord ensures it. All territory will be reclaimed and possessed, vv. 19-20. Divinely appointed "Joshuas" will administer the nation under God; cf. Jud. 3. 9; 2 Kings 13. 5. Israel alone, as a nation, can trace its source and consummation, with Jehovah Himself as Possessor and Potentate!

Introducing Jonah and Nahum

THESE TWO prophets were commissioned to minister regarding the same Gentile people, the Assyrians. They lived over a century apart, and while their messages both dealt with judgment they had quite different objectives. Jonah's message produced results that revealed *the extent of God's grace* to repentant sinners. Nahum's message portrayed *the execution of God's judgment* on the unrepentant. In Jonah, then, we see the grace of God, and in Nahum, His government. For the Nineveh of Jonah's day there was space for repentance. In Nahum's day it is too late, so the prophet is not sent to warn Nineveh as was Jonah, but he is sent to console Judah by the declaration of their enemy's inevitable downfall. In Jonah, it is the word of warning. In Nahum, it is the word of woe. In Jonah, God speaks of pity. In Nahum, He speaks of punishment. To Jonah, the Lord speaks of the greatness and influence of Nineveh, "that great city", 1. 2. Through Nahum He speaks of its guilt and iniquity, "the bloody city", 3. 1. In Jonah the Lord vindicates His mercy; in Nahum He vindicates His vengeance. In Jonah we read mostly about the prophet and his experience, and of the Lord's sovereignty in power and salvation. In Nahum we read mostly about the prophecy, and of the Lord's sovereignty in power and condemnation. Jonah becomes himself a living prophecy, typically presenting Israel as the vehicle of the oracle of Jehovah for the whole world. Failing in her mission by outright disobedience, she is swallowed up in the place of death, and carried away into the sea of the nations. Then, by God's grace and power, she is brought forth again and recommissioned to fulfil the Divine will, and in doing so to discover the heart of God. Jonah is also a unique sign of the Lord Jesus in His substitutionary death, burial and resurrection, Matt. 12. 39f. Nahum ("consolation") has no comfort for the enemies of Judah, but by his message he would bring comfort to God's people. While Jonah experienced the power of God in nature, Nahum declared it. Jonah may also reflect the day of God's grace when the Word of the Lord goes out to all, and God is "ready to pardon". Nahum may reflect the day of the Lord when the wrath of God comes upon all His enemies because of their treatment of His own.

Dec. 11th

READING : **Jonah 1. 1-16**

THE WORD AND THE WIND

JONAH is another of the earlier prophets, 2 Kings 14. 25. He likely was an old man when commissioned to go to Nineveh, the capital city of the Assyrians, whose cruel hordes were the avowed enemies of Israel. Jonah knew his God, and that He delighted in mercy, 4. 2. So, when given the word of the Lord to cry against the wickedness of "that great city", he decided to resign his commission, 1. 3. Being well acquainted with the Psalms, he knew he could not escape the omnipresence of God; cf. Psa. 139. He thought, however, to escape his obligation as a servant in the presence of the Lord. If the Ninevites repented at his preaching he knew that the Lord would turn away His anger from them, and he did not really want that enemy of his people to be saved. Thus he fled the work, found a way of escape, and "paid the fare", little realizing the true cost of his disobedience. Now begins a series of miracles performed by the Lord to effect the recovery of His disobedient servant. It is not quite so easy to "retire" from the Royal Service, especially by disobedience. *The Lord will not sit idly by and watch the departure of one of His own without intervening.* The Lord "sent out a great wind into the sea", 1. 4. The resulting storm filled even those seasoned sailors (*lit.*, "old salts") with fear, and incited them to cry to their various heathen gods, 1. 5. Jonah is below deck in a deep sleep. Not by indifference surely but another escape, a withdrawal from reality. Awakened by the call of the ungodly to pray (sad state!), lots are cast and by another miracle, the lot exposed Jonah, 1. 7. Thoroughly questioned, the silent servant testifies at last to his faith, 1. 8-9. He knew now he had not escaped the hand of the Lord, and confesses he deserved to die. Judging himself, he passes the sentence of death. Nevertheless, those noble men of the sea do all to save themselves and Jonah. Their attitude was yet another rebuke to Jonah. The heathen sailors appreciated the value of human life, and that man's blood was precious to the Lord, 1. 14. When all else failed, they threw Jonah overboard. The ensuing calm assured them they had done well, and the fear of the Lord inspired their sacrifice and submission. *It is a solemn thing for the Lord's servant to shirk his task. Sad too when there is deep sleep, guilty silence, and noble sinners who rebuke.*

Dec. 12th

READING : **Jonah 1. 17 to 3. 10**

THE WHALE AND THE WARNING

AS THE SAILORS saw Jonah disappear in the raging sea, they would assume, that was the sad end of him. The Lord, however had "appointed" the means of his recovery, whether a whale or a shark it matters not. *The Lord is never taken by surprise, but He has a provision for every exigency.* All things are under His control, the wind, the lot, the fish, its capacity and location. *God's purposes shall be fulfilled.* Jonah becomes a picture of Israel, failing by disobedience to fulfil her obligations to the world as the true witnesses of Jehovah, Isa. 43. 10. As a result, she has been scattered among the nations, Deut. 4. 27. Yet miraculously preserved there, she will come forth again and fulfil her calling, Jer. 30. 11; Isa. 60. 1-3, etc. Jonah represents a deeper truth however. The Lord Jesus referred to him as the only sign given to the unbelieving scribes and Pharisees, of His death, burial and resurrection, Matt. 12. 38-40. Thus in Jonah 2 we catch a glimpse of the deep sufferings of the Saviour beneath the waves and billows of the wrath of God. Jonah, in echoes of the Psalms, acknowledges that behind the hand of man is the hand of God: "*thou*" cast me . . ., "*thy* billows . . . *thy* waves", 2. 3. So with the Lord Jesus, He well knew that behind the smiting hand of man was the hand of Divine justice; cf. Mark 4. 41; Zech. 13. 7; Matt. 27. 46. While Jonah must pay the price for his own sins, 2. 9, our Beloved Lord, the Obedient Servant, paid the price for ours, freely, 1 Pet. 1. 18-19 etc. When the Divine purpose was fulfilled, the Lord caused the fish to disgorge Jonah on dry land, 2. 10. Recommissioned, Jonah becomes a sign to the Ninevites, Luke 11. 30, and his message stirs them to repentance. Brief, bold, blunt, and urgent, it was hardly a gospel of good news, 3. 4. Yet it had the desired effect. The whole city repented. The repentance of sinners is not just remorse, nor reconsideration; it involves a change of direction in life, 3. 10; cf. 1 Thess. 1. 9. Jonah repented and brought God's message. Nineveh repented and brought down God's mercy. We read too that "God repented", 3. 10. That is, He turned from judgment to mercy. Jonah learned that *God is neither parochial nor national. He is the God "of the Gentiles also"*, Rom. 3. 29. He loves the world of sinners.

Dec. 13th

READING : **Jonah 4. 1-11**

THE WEED AND THE WORM

JONAH was not happy that God was so good! Apart from the fact that his own reputation as a prophet was at stake, Deut. 18. 22, the cruel enemy of his people had been preserved, 3. 10. That very possibility had been weighed by Jonah before the Lord at his first call, 4. 2. Perhaps the prophet was seeking to vindicate his voyage. He could have rationalized that if God really meant to destroy Nineveh, then the way to ensure that was to avoid warning them. "Therefore" he says to God, "I fled". Because of God's change of dispensation towards Nineveh, Jonah was angry. He seemed to forget for the moment that his own preservation and deliverance was because of the very nature of God he outlined, 4. 2. Deeply vexed that God had spared the city, in despair he wished to die. *While anger in itself is not sinful, for man it is a dangerous emotion*, Eph. 4. 26. Jonah needs further instruction on the true nature of God's love and mercy. The Lord God "appointed" a fast growing plant to provide shade for him. Not just to save him from the heat, but to deliver him from his "evil", as the word is, 4. 6. The booth provided shade, the plant insulated him from the heat, and he rejoiced in this. Next, God appointed a worm to puncture the weed, so it withered. Then God appointed a sultry wind, full of moisture from the Caspian sea and the intervening forests, making the heat unbearable, so Jonah wished to die. Now he was angry because he was suffering from the death of the plant.

God is ready to teach Jonah a great lesson. In 4. 4 it is Jehovah speaking. This is the covenant God who requires righteousness, and must judge evil even though He Himself suffers with His creature in the judgment. In 4. 6 it is Jehovah Elohim appointing the gourd, and in 4. 7 it is Elohim acting. Elohim is the triune mighty God whose covenant is as Creator of all, working to bring all things to their consummate purpose. Jonah was vexed because he was suffering by the death of a weed which grew in a night and perished in a night. Now he must learn how much more Jehovah Elohim would suffer if that great city should be destroyed including six score thousand infants and imbeciles, and the multitude of the cattle; the helpless and the guiltless. *What suffering love!*

Dec. 14th

READING : **Micah 1. 1 to 2. 13**

RETRIBUTION AND RESTORATION

MICAH'S message is directed to the capitals of Israel and Judah, Samaria and Jerusalem, as the centres of influence. He gives three calls to be heard. The first is **against the apostasy of the people**, 1. 2, to 2. 13. All nations are called to pay attention, 1. 2. God is presented to them as *Adonai Jehovah*. This great ascription first occurs when the Lord gives Abram the promise of a seed and a land, Gen. 15. This sovereign Lord of relationship and righteousness calls out of the sanctuary; cf. Lev. 1. 1. His people violated that relationship, offended that righteousness, and despised the holy place with their idolatry, Mic. 1. 5. First the Lord *calls* from the sanctuary, then He *comes forth* from the sanctuary in judgment. That is the Divine order. The result is cataclysmic, 1. 3-4. In 1. 5 we see the nation ripe for judgment because of their iniquity. The Lord's anger is *against it*, 1. 3-7, the prophet's lamentation is *because of it*, 1. 8, and the people's shame is as *a result of it*, 1. 16. From 1. 9-15 follows a unique expression of grief. Micah mingles sorrow and satire, agony and anger, as he plays word against word. "In the house of dust roll in the dust", 1. 10 *lit*. etc. This national distress would spread until an invader would inherit the rule by their default, 1. 15. For all this, mourning is the only logical response, 1. 16. Further reasons for this judgment are given. Social evil is perpetrated by the rich, 2. 1. Premeditated evil quickly is translated into action. Covetousness soon erupts into rapacity and oppression, 2. 2. Corresponding retribution would be theirs, 2. 3-5. The people wish to silence Micah's unpalatable truth, 2. 6. He assures them that the Lord is not characterized by judgment, but is ever ready to bless the upright, 2. 7. Nevertheless *sins against God's people are sins against the Lord*, 2. 8; Acts 9. 5. Micah calls the people to flee the folly of self-destruction, 2. 10, but they prefer their prophets who are blown along by current fads, and condone earthly pleasure and sensual gratification, 2. 11. Yet there is forgiveness and a future for Jacob, 2. 12. As a Shepherd, the Lord will gather His flock as one. The "Wall-Breaker" will destroy every obstacle to His grand purpose, 2. 13; cf. Eph. 2. 14. Triumphantly led by their Lord and King, they shall be regathered in their land.

Dec. 15th

READING : **Micah 3. 1 to 5. 15**

PEACE IN A PERSON

THE PROPHET'S second call is **against the avarice of the rulers**. The princes ruled unrighteously. They dispossessed the poor, 3. 1-3. *They showed no mercy, they would receive none*, 3. 4. The prophets degraded their ministry into professionalism. They preached what the paying people wished to hear, and attacked all who would not contribute, 3. 5. *They dispensed darkness, they would dwell in darkness*, 3. 6-7. Micah was not so, 3. 8. The priests shared the avarice, so would share in the judgment, 3. 11. These leaders greatly erred. Their building programme was funded with ill-gotten gain, 3. 10. They pretended to serve the people for God, but really served for gain, 3. 11. They presumed the presence of the Lord while His face was averted, 3. 4, 11. They assumed immunity from judgment while destruction was on the way, 3. 11-12. "But" there is hope, 4. 1. The kingdom shall come, 4. 8. Then the nation will enjoy *recognition internationally*, 4. 2, *peace nationally*, 4. 3, *security domestically*, 4. 4-5, and a *renewed fellowship with God spiritually*, 4. 6-8. "Now" however they would know inevitable sorrow, 4. 9-11. "But" God's thoughts are different from their enemy's. He has determined a glorious future, 4. 12-13. First they must prepare for a siege culminating in the humiliation of their ruler, 5. 1; 2 Kings 25. "But" there will come a Ruler for them out of the eternal days, Mic. 5. 2. Because that Ruler would come by way of little Bethlehem and not Jerusalem, that could only mean that then the house of David had fallen upon hard times, having been given up to the rule of another power. That wondrous birth, prophesied before, Isa. 7. 14, would activate the programme whereby the scattered remnant of Judah will one day be joined again with Israel in the land, Isa. 11. 12. He will govern, be glorified, and be great, Mic. 5. 4. He is peace personified, Isa. 9. 6. He will *defend* and *deliver* Israel, and make her a *delight* among the nations as *the dew* is to the thirsty soil, and a terror to her enemies as a lion among the flocks, Mic. 5. 5-9. When at last her enemies are cut off there will be a final disarmament, 5. 10-11, a final purging of every vestige of idolatry, 5. 12-14; cf. Col. 3. 5, and a final judgment on the heathen. Nothing again will ever spoil the glorious reign of the Prince of Peace over His people.

Dec. 16th

READING : **Micah 6. 1 to 7. 20**

THE DARKNESS AND THE DAWN

MICAH'S final call is **against the attitude of the people.** Its form is as a legal suit, 6. 1. They were wearied with God! Yet He had delivered them, redeemed them, provided for them, 6. 4, and protected them, 6. 5. He called them to recall the evil counsel of Balaam, and the resulting trespass at Shittim, Num. 25; 31. 16. Then to remember His great grace at Gilgal, Josh. 5. 9. Thus He had displayed many righteous acts on their behalf, Mic. 6. 5b. Whether 6. 6-7 is the query of His people or of Balak, the error and the principle remain. The error was in assuming that God was impressed, and His anger appeased, by the quantity and the quality of their offerings. But *religious observance cannot replace obedience*, 6. 8. The Divine requirements are universal ("O man"). In relation to self, *a dutiful righteousness*. In relation to others, *a generous mercy*. In relation to God, *a genuine and humble piety*, 6. 8. This is only possible when the heart is right with God, Deut. 10. 12-16. The natural man cannot produce these. They are the fruit of the obedience of faith, Rom. 3. 10-12, 20-24. Micah cries to Jerusalem to be exercised about the appointed chastening, 6. 9. *The Lord is auditing the books*! They sought profit; they would suffer loss of health and wealth, 6. 13, of satisfaction and savings, 6. 14, of harvest and happiness, 6. 15. All because they had adopted Baalism and avarice as a way of life, 6. 16; cf. 1 Kings 16. Micah laments the emptiness in every strata of his society, 7. 1-6. Hope and help could only come from the Lord, 7. 7. *Calamities cannot destroy true confidence, the darkness cannot delay the dawn*!, 7. 8. After the discipline comes the daybreak, 7. 9; cf. Gen. 32. 31. The mocking enemy will be silenced, Mic. 7. 10. God's people will be vindicated. A great rebuilding will take place, 7. 11. From far and near many will come to view it after the great desolation, 7. 13. Micah prays that the Shepherd of Israel will rule His flock, 7. 14. The Lord assures the prophet of a marvellous and mighty deliverance, 7. 15. The nations are in shock, and will come crawling to Israel in the dust of submission, and in the fear of the God of Israel, 7. 16-17. Micah concludes, praising God for His singular glory displayed in grace and mercy, compassion and power, and for His faithfulness in keeping His covenant, 7. 18-20.

Dec. 17th

READING : **Nahum 1. 1 to 3. 19**

VENGEANCE VINDICATED

THIS PROPHECY is a supplement to Jonah's of over a century before. Sins then repented from, were perpetrated later without repentance. Nahum is given a message for Judah concerning her great enemy. It presses as a burden, and is permanent as a book being a revelation of Jehovah who must judge sin, 1. 1. The prophet begins by presenting the character of God. He is "jealous", that is, "full of burning zeal", Deut. 6. 15. The threefold reference to vengeance affirms it is settled, Nah. 1. 2. He waited long years to administer judgment, showing He is slow to anger. When He is angry the forces of nature are moved, 1. 3-6. *Man cannot sin with impunity, the day of reckoning will surely come*. He will preserve His own but punish the evil doer, 1. 7-8. Judah is assured her enemy is doomed, 1. 9-10. Though cruelly assailed, Jehovah would end their affliction, and their vile enemy would perish, 1. 11-14; cf. 2 Kings 18. 30-35. Since the gospel of their peace was on the way, they should resume their spiritual ministries and fulfil their commitments, Nah. 1. 15; cf. Rom. 10. 15. Nineveh's downfall is graphically portrayed. As a vine, Israel had been stripped, 2. 2, but glory would be restored. The spearhead of Nineveh's attackers reach the outskirts, 2. 3-4. The defenders, in confusion, retreat to the defence of the inner city, but the foe opens the sluice gates and the city is inundated, 2. 5-6. The populace flees ignoring the commands of the military to stand fast, and are taken captive, 2. 7-8. The city is sacked. The people are in terror, 2. 9-10. As the Assyrians had torn like lions, young lions would eat the bodies of their dead, 2. 11-12. They had opposed the Lord, now He takes His stand against them. The battle is over. The fire and the flood have devastated. All is mud, ashes, death and silence, 2. 13. This Divine vengeance is vindicated by the depth of their wickedness. Nineveh was built with the spoils of war, 3. 1-3. Defiled, it would be exposed in shame to the nations, 3. 5-7. A city without hope. Its numbers, defences, and allies together could not save it, 3. 8-10. Stripped, slaughtered, betrayed, and scattered, they became anathema among the nations, 3. 11-19. Take heed all ye nations who forget God! *"Ill fares the land, to hastening ills a prey, where wealth accumulates, and men decay"*.

Introducing Habakkuk, Zephaniah and Obadiah

HABAKKUK, "the Embracer", embraced by faith what he could not understand. He was a contemporary of Zephaniah and Jeremiah. His message is in the form of a dialogue between himself and the Lord concerning his deep perplexities. The prophecy is in two parts. Chapters 1 and 2 record the dialogue. Chapter 3 is a prayer in the form of a Psalm. It is an eleventh-hour document, and can bring assurance even in our day. We can learn from it that behind even the most perplexing circumstances is the hand of a sovereign God. In it the Lord lays down the great principle for living, which is taken up in the New Testament for our instruction. Embracing this principle enabled the prophet to sing again, and to sing with words of trust and triumph.

ZEPHANIAH, "he whom God hides", lived about the same time. While Habakkuk speaks of *the Way of the Lord*, Zephaniah speaks of *the Day of the Lord*. He refers to that day more often than any other Old Testament writer. At times he is almost apocalyptic in his language. A descendant of king Hezekiah, he was of the blood royal. In chapter 1 he speaks of a universal judgment, when the forces of nature are affected. In chapter 2 he speaks of judgment on the nations, when all the heathen will be affected. In chapter 3 he speaks of a judgment on Jerusalem, when all Judah will be affected. Nevertheless the nation will be restored and Jehovah will find joy in her again.

OBADIAH, "the servant of Jehovah", brings a message down for Edom, Israel's neighbour and enemy. As descendants of Esau, they were related to Israel, the descendants of Jacob. They were hateful towards God's people Israel. They became increasingly antagonistic. At first they were passively indifferent to Israel's urgent need on the wilderness journey. Then they rejoiced at being spectators of Israel's distress. They gambled for and gathered up their goods as spoils of war, and ultimately they intervened actively to prevent their escape from their enemy. This cold hearted hatred for God's people is not unnoticed by God, and He assures them He has not forgotten. They shall reap in anguish what they sowed in arrogance. The Lord will frustrate their evil purpose by gathering Israel into their possession at last.

Dec. 18th

READING : **Habakkuk 1. 1 to 2. 20**

FROM FEAR TO FAITH

HABAKKUK is perplexed by unanswered prayer, 1. 2. He just cannot understand how the Lord can allow evil amongst His people without intervening, 1. 3. Furthermore, the law is relaxed, and the wicked are not judged. The ungodly feel immune to arrest and punishment, and threaten the righteous. The victims suffer, and the criminals go free, 1. 4. The prophet's problem is deepened when Jehovah answers him, 1. 5-11. His silence was because of the people's incredulity. "Seeing is believing", they would say. They shall see more than they expected, 1. 5. The Lord will raise up the Chaldeans to come against them as a scourge, 1. 6-10. In their offensiveness the Chaldeans worshipped power as a god, 1. 11. How many of God's people have likewise been perplexed through the ages? The flood of evil, the weakness of the law, the suffering innocents, and arrogant criminals have perplexed many. Not to speak of godless governments persecuting God's people. Above all this, a silent heaven! *In all these perplexities there is a Rock, the Lord God, changeless, holy, righteous and mighty*. Upon this covenant keeping God Habakkuk depends, that His people, while chastened, will not be destroyed, 1. 12. Yet this adds another problem. How can a holy God use an unholy instrument for His purposes?, 1. 13-17. The prophet knows the wise thing to do. *It is better to commit the whole matter to the Lord and to wait on Him, than to fret and faint*, 2. 1; Phil. 4. 6-7. The answer comes as a command to write for all to see the Divine purpose in its certainty, 2. 2-3. The Lord now gives the prophet a firm assurance and a great principle, 2. 4. *The proud will perish by their folly, but the just shall live by his faithfulness*. Faithfulness to God implies faith in God. Note the N.T. emphasis varies: the just, Rom. 1. 17, the life, Gal. 3. 11, the faith, Heb. 10. 38. Five woes are called on the Chaldeans: (1) for their lust for conquest, 2. 5-8; (2) for their coveting the place of power, 2. 9-11; (3) for their use of slave labour, 2. 12-13; (4) for their immorality in victory, 2. 15-17; (5) for their idolatry, 2. 18-19. Two great affirmations are given. The earth will acknowledge the glory of the Lord, 2. 14, and the earth will acknowledge in silence the holiness of the Lord, 2. 20; cf. Zeph. 1. 7. *His ways will be vindicated at last.*

Dec. 19th
READING : Habakkuk 3. 1-19

FROM JUDGMENT TO JOY

HAVING KEPT silent and listened for the Lord, the prophet now engages in a prayerful Psalm, "upon Shigionoth", a kind of reeling, exulting musical accompaniment, 3. 1. There is no questioning of God's ways now. The prophet has accepted the word of the Lord, though with amazement, 3. 2a; not for fear of impending trouble, but fear of the Lord. *In our day of easy familiarity, we surely need a revival of "reverence and godly fear: for our God is a consuming fire"*, Heb. 12. 28-29. Habakkuk rises to great heights here. He has caught the vision of the sovereign Lord, far above and beyond his own perplexities. He desires now the prosperity of the Lord's work, for Him to restore life to and keep alive His work even in the midst of the years of their loss and suffering, Hab. 3. 2b. This may be a preview of the remnant in great tribulation rising above her own sorrow to desire the fulfilling of the Divine purpose, the Lord showing mercy by shortening the days; cf. Matt. 24. 22. This glorious Lord has intervened for His people in the past, so He would also in the future, 3. 3. Habakkuk echoes Moses' last words, Deut. 33. 2, and the song of Deborah, Jud. 5. 4-5, but changes the tense to the future. He sees the glory of Eloah radiating throughout the universe in rays of light emanating from His person, though veiling His power, Hab. 3. 3-4. He comes first in judgment. The plague precedes Him, and the burning fever follows, 3. 5. The earth and the nations tremble, the primeval mountains disintegrate, 3. 6; cf. Psa. 97. Neighbouring nations are put in fear, Hab. 3. 7. The prophet now addresses the Lord in terms of praise for His power over the nations, the waters, the mountains, the heavens and the wicked, 3. 8-15. The God-fearing man trembles at such majesty and manifest holiness as he considers the approaching distresses, 3. 16. Yet in spite of the danger and deprivation he anticipates fragrance, fruit, food, and fold, 3. 17; by faith he is enabled to exult in the salvation of his God, 3. 18, and the God of his salvation, who is the Source and Sphere of his joy, 3. 19. So it is in every age, *faith in God enables the believer to walk faithfully and to rejoice in spite of his sorrows. Rising above his circumstances, he can see beyond to the ultimate purposes in glory.*

Dec. 20th

READING : **Zephaniah 1. 1 to 3. 20**

THE DAY OF THE LORD

ZEPHANIAH'S great theme is "the day of the Lord". He begins with a description of universal judgment, 1. 2-3; cf. Rom. 8. 20. "Also" the Lord will deal with Judah, judging the Baal worshippers that remain after the revival of Josiah, with their idolatrous priests, 1. 4; cf. 2 Kings 23. 5. The star-worshippers, and those that mixed God-worship with emperor-worship, will feel His fury, 1. 5. The despisers and the indifferent shall not escape, 1. 6. Silence in the court! The Judge of the whole earth is about to appear. His people are to be offered on the altar of the nations again, as they gather around for the kill, 1. 7. Still, judgment must begin with His own people for their sins against Him. All will be judged within the nation; princes, foreigners and those that dress like them, cultists, 1. 8-9, the merchants, and the irreligious, all will be judged, 1. 11-13. The prophet sees beyond to the end time. He senses its imminence, and hears its approach, 1. 14. Distress, desolation, darkness and dust, and the devouring fire dramatically describe "the day of the Lord's wrath", 1. 15-18. *This inevitable judgment reveals God's holy hatred against sin, in every form, and in every place.* High privilege means heavy punishment. Judah and Jerusalem, so blessed with Divine revelation, must in their shameless sin suffer Divine retribution, 2. 1. *The Lord's mercy gives space for repentance*, 2. 2-3; cf. Psa. 32. 6; Rev. 2. 21, etc. No repentance, no escape, Rev. 2. 16. Next, judgment falls on the nations for their sins against God's people, Zeph. 2. 4-15. By natural disaster and military invasion they will be reduced to ruins, overgrown with weeds and inhabited by wild beasts and birds. Then impenitent Jerusalem becomes the focus of fury for her faithless filth, 3. 1. Ignoring past lessons, the leaders violated God's holy law, 3. 2-4. The Lord had subdued her enemies, but they used the peace to sin the more, 3. 5-7. Thus with all nations, they must endure His fire, 3. 8. But *the fire will pass, and out of the silent ashes the Lord will bring forth the green shoot of new life.* Babel will be reversed, and worship will be spoken with pure lips, 3. 9. Israel will exult and Jehovah will own them, joy in them with silent love and singing joy, and they will never leave His heart again, 3. 10-20. *Hallelujah! What a Saviour!*

Introducing Haggai, Zechariah, and Malachi

WHEN CYRUS, king of Persia, took over the Babylonian Empire, he would have been busy establishing his rule. Yet, in the very first year of his reign, God moved him to allow, and assist, a remnant of the Jews to return to Jerusalem. This was in fulfilment of the prophetic word, Jer. 25. 12; 29. 10; Isa. 45; 2 Chron. 36. 22; Ezra 1. What a mighty and a saving God providentially to incline a pagan despot to favour a despised group of captives! Surely, such a God could be counted upon to complete His purposes.

After the remnant had returned to their homeland, they set up the altar, and laid the foundation of the temple in Jerusalem, Ezra 3. The work was stopped through opposition, Ezra 4. Significantly, at that very time aged Daniel in Babylonia sensed a great need for prayer. Satan was active to hinder prayer, and the work, Dan. 10.

About 14 years later, the first of the post-captivity prophets, Haggai and Zechariah, were sent by God. They came with "good and comfortable words", to bestir Zerubbabel (of the house of David), and Joshua (the high priest), to restart the work, Ezra 5. The temple was completed in 516 B.C., Ezra 6.

About a century later, Malachi speaks the message of the Lord. His name means "my messenger". His Book historically rounded off the canon of O. T. Scripture. No addition was made to this authoritative volume until the appearance of the first of the N.T. Scriptures over 400 years later.

As the Spirit of inspiration had spoken through the earlier writings, so He continues to do in these three closing prophets. The coming Messiah, the Lord Jesus, is prophetically referred to as, for example, the desire of all nations, Hag. 2. 6, 7; the sent One, Zech. 2. 8, 11; My servant the Branch, 3. 8; the man the Branch, 6. 11; the stone, 3. 9; the priest-king, 6. 13; the king, lowly yet having world-wide dominion, 9. 9, 10; the pierced One, 12. 10; the Lord who is coming to Olivet, 14. 4; the messenger of the covenant, and the Sun, Mal. 3. 1; 4. 2.

Haggai's five messages were delivered over a few months, though he worked with the people over some four years. Zechariah's dated ministry extends over two years, though chapters 9-14 may have been delivered much later.

Dec. 21st

READING : **Haggai 1. 1 to 2. 9**

REVIVING A REVIVAL

THE REMNANT of Jews, some 42,000, who left the relative comfort and stability of life in Babylon to return to Jerusalem, purposed to re-establish God's testimony there. They set up the altar of burnt-offering, laid the foundation of the temple, and by faith observed the Feast of Ingathering of the fruit of the land, Ezra 3. The proffered help of the semi-pagan Samaritans was refused, and they, with others, became open enemies. The work of rebuilding ceased for fourteen years.

Haggai, the Lord's messenger in the Lord's message, brought a message of rebuke and encouragement. He rebuked their materialism, and their seeking their own comforts. Their priorities were wrong. At such a time it was not fitting. Excuse was ready at hand: "the time is not come . . . that the Lord's house should be built", said they. To which the pertinent reply was "Is it a time for you, O ye, to dwell in your ceiled (panelled) houses?", Hag. 1. 2, 4. God's house was lying waste!

The drought that was afflicting them was in fulfilment of the threat of Leviticus 26. 19. It should have exercised their hearts. Their selfishness proved as foolish as putting wages into a bag with holes, 1. 6. The wise one will provide a bag which waxes not old, a treasure in the heavens, Luke 12. 33.

The rebukes are accepted, and encouragements follow. God remained faithful to His covenant, Hag. 2. 5; Deut. 30. 3. Count on Him! God's Spirit remained among them, Hag. 2. 4f.

They were to see their work as part of a movement of God. They were preparing the way to a glorious future. This gives a new dimension to present responsibility. The Desire of all nations shall come after the shaking of things that can be moved. Then, the kingdom that cannot be shaken will be established, Hag. 2. 6, 7; cf. vv. 21-22. It is by apprehending that to which grace has brought us, as also the certain future of glory that is before us, that we are motivated the more to serve God acceptably with reverence and godly fear, Heb. 12. 28.

Outwardly their temple would be inferior. There would not be a cloud of glory, there was no ark, miracles would not be as of old, leaders like Moses would not be among them. But their work would show faith in God, Hag. 1. 8.

"Consider" 1. 5, 7; 2. 15, 18, and "work", 1. 14; 2. 4.

Dec. 22nd
READING : Zechariah 1. 1-21

VISIONS THAT VIVIFY

ZECHARIAH WAS contemporary with Haggai. By their teaching and prophecies they urged on the builders with "good words and comfortable words", 1. 13. Among other things, they caused the glories of Christ's person, the depths of His sufferings, and the glories that should follow, to add significance and value to the present work for Him. The people prospered under such ministry, Ezra 6. 14.

God was faithful, but the practical enjoyment of His blessing was conditioned by their turning to Him, vv. 3, 4, 6. He would then turn to them, vv. 3, 16; cf. 9. 12; Mal. 3. 7, 18; 4. 6; Isa. 30. 15; Luke 17. 18; Acts 11. 21; 26. 18; 1 Thess. 1. 9.

In one night eight visions are given to Zechariah, 1. 7 to 6. 8, progressively unfolding the purpose of God.

Vision One. The lowly, but fragrant, myrtle trees represent the people of God at that time. They were in the valley of humiliation, dwarfed by the tall cedars, their Gentile rulers, 1. 8; Isa. 37. 24. But the Lord of hosts (armies) had over-all control universally, Zech. 1. 10. The leader of these hosts was the Captain of the hosts, even our Lord, Josh. 5. 13-15. Are not the angels ministering spirits sent forth to minister to the heirs of salvation?, Heb. 1. 14; Gen. 32. 1; Exod. 23. 23. The Lord open our eyes to those that are with us, 2 Kings 6. 17!

The Lord's intense love for His people makes Him greatly jealous for them, assuring them that His purposes for them must be fulfilled, Zech. 1. 14, 17; Isa. 9. 7.

Vision Two. God had permitted Gentile nations to conquer Israel. They were indifferent to the land and its people, v. 15. But God had a "carpenter" for each oppressor. He would terrify (fray) the offending empire by another empire. Assyrian, Babylonian, Persian, Grecian in their turn were dealt with by the succeeding empire. Men should know that "the Most High (God) ruleth in the kingdom of men", Dan. 4. 17; 5. 21 R.V., for He is "Lord of the whole earth", Zech. 4. 14.

God is determined to return to Jerusalem with mercies. His house will be built, the cities will spread abroad.

Deep in unfathomable mines of never failing skill.

He treasures up His bright designs, and works His sovereign will.

Dec. 23rd

READING : Zechariah 2. 1-13

MEASURING AND REBUILDING

THIS CHAPTER unfolds *Vision three*. The remnant who returned to Jerusalem from Babylon were busy rebuilding the temple. Now the promise is given that the city shall be measured for rebuilding, vv. 1-4, and the population shall be multiplied, so that it shall spread beyond the city walls, v. 4. Other cities, too, would prosper, 1. 17. To accomplish this, those who tarried in Babylon should deliver themselves from its attractions and false security, making their way back to their Zion, vv. 6, 7. "And be not conformed to this world: but be ye transformed by the renewing of your mind" is apposite, for our faces should be Zion-ward, Rom. 12. 2; Jer. 50. 5; Isa. 48. 20.

But was there not a great risk, seeing the city-walls would not be built for many years ahead?, Neh. 6. Count on God's promised presence, is the inferential reply. He will be the unseen wall about you, and the glory in the midst of you, Zech. 2. 5. Our God guarantees present safety, and future splendour, and the faith that grasps this gives another dimension to circumstances.

The Lord was extremely sensitive to their enemies' cruelties, for they that touched His people with evil intent touched the apple of His eye, v. 8. They were very precious to Him; cf. Deut. 32. 10; Psa. 17. 8; Prov. 7. 2. They had been Babylon's spoil of war, yet Babylon would become the slave, vv. 8, 9.

Looking beyond the present, Zechariah makes the ultimate to impinge upon the present. The Lord will come, and will dwell in the midst of regathered Israel, v. 10. They shall then know that He was the Sent-One, vv. 8, 11. The Father sent the Son to be the propitiation, to be the Saviour of the world, and that we might live through Him, 1 John 4. 9, 10, 14.

The Sent One said "Lo, I come . . . to do thy will". That refers to His coming in grace at His *incarnation*, Psa. 40. 7-8; Heb. 10. 7. He also says "behold, I come quickly; and 'my reward is with me". There is a grand day of *compensation* ahead for the faithful and diligent believer, when the Lord comes into the air, Rev. 22. 12. Yet again He says "lo, I come, and I will dwell in the midst of thee". This is in connection with the Lord's second advent to earth, when He shall reign. That will be in the day of His manifest *glorification*, Zech. 2. 10.

Dec. 24th
READING : Zechariah 3. 1-10
THE ANSWER TO ALL ACCUSATIONS

VISION FOUR is taken up with the cleansing of the people that have been delivered. The high priest was representative of the people, for example, when he confessed their sins on the Day of Atonement, Lev. 16. Here Joshua the high priest represents the people, and Jerusalem, in their natural state, v. 2. All their righteousness was as filthy rags, v. 3. Only God's sovereign grace saved them from fiery judgment. God *chose* them whilst they were worthless branches, and, based on His satisfied righteousness, redeemed and justified them. He does this for a remnant of Israel today, and will soon save the whole nation, Rom. 11. 5, 26-28.

The accuser was standing in the customary place when so engaged. This position is soon to be denied him for ever, Psa. 109. 6; Rev. 12. 7-10. The judge was the Angel of the Lord, also stated to be the Lord, v. 2. Yet, in the miracle of grace, the judge answers every accusation! "Who shall lay anything to the charge of God's elect? . . . God that justifieth? . . . Christ that died . . . who is at the right hand of God, who also maketh intercession for us?", Rom. 8. 33, 34 R.V. marg.

O.T. priests were to "stand before" the Lord in holy service, Deut. 10. 8; Jud. 20. 28; 2 Chron. 29. 11, as they are yet to do, Ezek. 44. 15. But in this vision the priesthood and people were not in the practical holiness becoming their position in electing grace, v. 3. Upon confession, God would be faithful and just to forgive. Reclothed and walking in God's ways, they would keep their charge, and they would then be among those "standing by" Him in service, v. 7.

Believers today are an holy priesthood, even a royal priesthood, a *chosen* generation, a people for God's own possession, that we might offer spiritual sacrifices, and show forth the praises of Him who has called us in holiness, 1 Pet. 1. 15, 16; 2. 5, 9.

The vision goes further: Joshua and the priests were men symbolic of things to come, Zech. 3. 8. When Israel in the future is cleansed, it will be a nation of priests, Isa. 61. 6; Exod. 19. 6. Everyone shall then enjoy his lost patrimony, Zech. 3. 9, 10; Lev. 25. 10, for the Lord of hosts "will remove the iniquity of that land in one day", Zech. 3. 9.

Dec. 25th

READING : Zechariah 4. 1-14

THE GOLDEN LAMPSTAND

VISION FIVE is designed to encourage the prince, as the fourth lifted up the priest. Israel was established to be God's light-bearer amid Gentile idolatry and darkness, Isa. 43. 10. Their enlightenment by grace was never to lead to self-satisfaction.

The remnant now restored to Judaea are reminded of this high calling by this vision of the golden lampstand. The churches, too, are alerted in Revelation 2 and 3 to the fact that they are lights in the world's night. We are a city set on a hill. Our light must not be hidden under a bushel of self-interest, or under a bed of indolence, Matt. 5. 14, 15; Luke 11. 33. Let your light so shine that your Father may be glorified!

In the vision the two olive trees, which supply the oil to the lamp, represent Joshua the high priest, and Zerubbabel the prince of the house of David (though he functioned only as the civil leader). These two were to empty themselves for bright testimony and in sacrificial leadership, vv. 3, 11-14. Their work was truly royal and priestly. In the future, too, there are to be two special witnesses in Jerusalem, who shall prophesy and be given power from God throughout the great tribulation period, Rev. 11. 3-12.

Before such testimony the mountain of enemy opposition (Ezra 5 and 6) would be removed, and the temple completed with triumph, v. 7. The eyes of the Lord run to and fro to show Himself strong on their behalf, v. 10; 2 Chron. 16. 9. They were to know that it was "not by might (i.e. armies), nor by power (individual), but by my spirit" it should be done, so that "the excellency of the power may be of God", v. 6; 2 Cor. 4. 7. "For it is nothing with thee to help . . . help us, O Lord our God; for we rest on thee", 2 Chron. 14. 11.

The Lord of the whole earth desired Israel's testimony to be to all nations. Even when they crossed Jordan, the ark that led them was "the ark of the Lord of all the earth", Josh. 3. 11. The temple was to be "a house of prayer for all the nations".

We do well to ask our hearts as to our personal and corporate witnessing to the nations. Do we empty the golden oil of witness, being spent for the Gospel's sake? Do we sense that we are "anointed" ones in this service?, v. 14; 2 Cor. 1. 21.

Dec. 26th

READING : Zechariah 5. 1-11

FLYING SCROLL AND WOMAN IN THE EPHAH

IN VISION SIX, the flying scroll, vv. 1-4, represents the law of God, and its curse when broken. The two tablets given on mount Sinai were commandments concerning both God and man. Here the two sides of the scroll envisage the same division, a commandment from each of the two tablets being selected, v. 3. Our Lord spoke of the commandment to love God, and of the commandment to love man, as being those on which the whole law depends, Matt. 22. 37-40. The measurements of the scroll were those of the holy place in the tabernacle, and of the porch of the temple. This could point to both the demands, and the application to the nation, of God's holiness — "the vengeance of his temple", Jer. 50. 28. As they were building the temple they are reminded of the ethical demands which the temple would indicate, for they had vainly trusted in the former temple, Jer. 7. 4.

Ritualists, such as Paul once was, can fail to sense the searching character of the law in which they boast. Paul considered himself blameless until the law came in its inherent power. It slew him, for by it came the full-knowledge of sin's sinfulness. "For as many as are of the works of the law are under the curse". But "Christ hath redeemed us from the curse of the law, being made a curse for us", Gal. 3. 10, 13; Rom. 7. 7, 9, 10, 24. The believer is not justified by law-obedience. Yet he is not without law, being enslaved to Christ, whose commandments he will keep, for they are written on the tablets of his heart, John 14. 15, 23; 15. 14; 1 Cor. 9. 21; 2 Cor. 3. 3. So it is to be with Israel, when at last, by grace, in the good of the new covenant, Jer. 31. 31-34.

In *Vision Seven*, the woman in the ephah, vv. 5-11, belonged to Babylon, from whence the people had returned, v. 11. A remnant of the nation had returned from Babylon, but Babylon was not completely out of them! Grave clothes of the past life must be put off, and the wardrobe of the new life be put on, Col. 3. 8-14. Babylon has allured men from the beginning, Gen. 11. 1-9. She is aptly described as "the mother of harlots". Zechariah anticipates phase one in her destruction, which is fully documented in Revelation 17. "Come out of her my people", Rev. 18. 4; "Deliver thyself ", Zech. 2. 7.

Dec. 27th

READING : Zechariah 6. 1-15

A VISION AND A PARABLE

VISION EIGHT, vv. 1-8, completes the octave of visions given the prophet in one night. The first vision had portrayed the armies of heaven. This last one shows "the spirits of the heavens" which are God's providences among the nations, controlling evil agencies and powers for the good of His people. What consolation this could bring to the builders at that time! We too can find encouragement in such messages, for God is still on the throne. He is yet to crush the northerner, and deliver Israel, v. 8; Dan. 11. 40-45; Joel 2. 20.

The Symbolic Crowning of the High Priest, vv. 9-15. This is an enacted parable not a vision. A delegation of Jews came from Babylon, bringing silver and gold for the temple. They were staying with the hospitable Josiah, v. 10. He is eternally rewarded by the prophecy regarding Christ being uttered in his house. How often the Spirit shows the value of hospitality among believers: "pursuing hospitality", Rom. 12. 13 R.V. marg; "the house of Stephanas . . . addicted themselves" to it, 1 Cor. 16. 15.

Zechariah took the precious metals and made a royal crown, v. 11 R.V. marg. He then placed it on the head of the high priest, and not on the head of Zerubbabel, the prince of the house of David. Thus an high priest was made a king in symbol and prophetically. This had never been so in the history of Jewish royalty. King Saul and king Uzziah had attempted to unite the two offices, but were immediately rejected by God.

Our Lord's kingship is based on His being the Son of David. He is also a Great High Priest following His Divine appointment and His perfect sacrifice. Thus, He is an High Priest after the order of Melchisedec, who was both king of Salem, and priest of the Most High God.

"Behold the man", said the prophecy, v. 12. Unwittingly, Pilate uttered the same statement as he brought forth Christ *crowned* with thorns, John 19. 5. The crowning day is coming, but in the meantime the crown is reserved, v. 14. It is to be worn no more "until he come whose right it is", Ezek. 21. 27. Then the Christ shall be a priest upon His royal throne.

We see Jesus even now crowned. One day the whole universe will recognize Him, when "he shall bear the glory".

Dec. 28th

READING : **Zechariah 9. 1-12; 10. 4-6**

TWO KINGS IN CONTRAST

THE FIRST eight verses of chapter 9 form a prophetic oracle of judgment ("burden"), depicting the swift and victorious progress of Alexander's Grecian forces many years later. This terror is seen as coming from the north to Syria, vv. 1, 2a, then southward to Tyre and Sidon, vv. 2b, 3, 4, then further south to Phoenicia, and thence to Jerusalem, v. 8. But it shall not enter Jerusalem, but pass by it, sparing the city! Moreover, this it would do again on its return journey from Egypt, v. 8. What miraculous overruling by God!

Then, the prophecy provides *a twofold prediction*. First it describes a kindly, humble king, riding upon an ass (not upon a war horse). He will not "pass by" Jerusalem, but enter for their good, bringing peace and blessing if they knew the things that belong to their peace, v. 9. He wept over the city that He fain would gather under His wings, but they knew not the time of their visitation. So He foretold the future destruction of the city by the Romans, Luke 19. 41-44; Matt. 23. 37.

Secondly, it speaks of the Lord's coming in power. Then the battle horses and chariots of war will be eliminated, for He will speak peace to the nations and His dominion will be acknowledged, v. 10. Nations shall learn war no more, Isa. 2. 4; Mic. 4. 3. Notice how only a full stop separates the predictions of the first and second advents of our Lord.

Zechariah 10. 4 is one of the richest verses in the O.T. Scriptures, for in a succinct and beautiful manner it gives *a fourfold description of our Lord:*

1. The Corner Stone, R.V. At that time the foundation of the second temple had been laid. He calls the people to remember the One who would build His temple. He would be both foundation and capstone of it, 6. 12f; 4. 7; Psa. 118. 22.

2. The Nail. Upon this the vessels of worth in house or tent were hung, and thus kept safe and ready for the master's use. In the "sure place" of victory and glory our Lord is set. Blessed are the vessels that hang on Him!, Isa. 22. 23, 24.

3. The Battle Bow. In His victory He needs no second fight.

4. The Ruler of all rulers (see R.V. margin). The perfect Servant becomes the perfect Ruler; ct. Prov. 19. 10; cf. Isa. 52. 13-15.

Dec. 29th
READING : Zechariah 11. 1-17
TWO SHEPHERDS IN CONTRAST

THE GOOD SHEPHERD, vv. 4-14. The prophet is bidden to become a shepherd to a flock. So he took the usual two implements of a shepherd, the rod and the staff. One of these he named "Beauty" (i.e., Favour), the other he named "Bands" (i.e., Union). The flock represented the Jews as they would be when our Lord was among them. The prophet represented the true Messiah as the Good Shepherd, John 10. 1-18. Their leaders, who should have been under-shepherds, sought their own profit, and at the same time their Gentile rulers assumed the role of benefactors whilst oppressing them, v. 5; Luke 22. 25.

The Shepherd was sold for a contemptuous price of thirty pieces of silver, fit only to be cast to poor potters, vv. 12, 13; Exod. 21. 32. This was the price put upon the One who sought their good!, Matt. 26. 14-16; 27. 3-10; Mark 14. 10, 11; Luke 22. 3-6; John 13. 2, 27, 30.

Israel under the Romans, as previously under other Gentile powers, had been privileged, for God had covenanted to incline the ruling power to show some *grace*. But after the rejection of the Good Shepherd, the staff "Grace", as it were, was broken. They would find no grace from the Romans. "We have no king but Caesar", they insisted. They were delivered into their chosen king's hand, v. 6; John 19. 15.

The other implement called "Union" was broken, as it were, resulting in internecine strife among the Jews at the time of Jerusalem's destruction (A.D. 70), vv. 6, 9.

Yet among the people there was a remnant of grace, who waited upon the Lord. They were "the poor of the flock", but rich in faith, v. 11; Rom. 11. 5; James 1. 1; 2. 5.

The Idol Shepherd, vv. 15-17. In a future day, a shepherd that leads the nation into idolatry will be king in the land of Israel, Dan. 11. 36-39. He will come in his own name, not the Father's, John 5. 43. Israel's last state will be worse than their first, Luke 11. 26.

But the true Shepherd-King will come to deal with this, and all iniquity. Then there shall be one Shepherd over them, Ezek. 34. 23, even the smitten Shepherd of the cross, Zech. 13. 7. May we now know the comfort of His rod and staff!

Dec. 30th

READING : **Zechariah 12. 1 to 14. 9**

THE DAY OF THE LORD

OUR PRESENT time is called "man's day", 1 Cor. 4. 3 marg. It is the day when man makes his own carnal judgment of Divine matters. For believers of the present calling, the *"day of Christ"* will be when they will stand before the Judgment Seat of Christ, after the rapture of the Church, there to receive reward or loss, Phil. 1. 10; 1 Cor. 4. 4, 5; 2 Cor. 5. 10. The *day of the Lord*, Zech. 14. 1, will be the time of the Lord's dealing in judgment with the nations, and His manifestation in power and great glory to deliver Israel. The expression "in that day" refers to this period, and is found sixteen times in our section.

Chapter 11 prophesied of the seige of Jerusalem in A.D. 70, whilst chapter 12 speaks of the same city being beseiged in the coming great crisis. The Lord effects its deliverance, v. 9, its establishment in safety, and in real blessing, vv. 6, 8. It will then be the "city of righteousness", Isa. 1. 26, the "holy city", 52. 1, the "city of the Lord", 60. 14, the "city of God", Psa. 46. 4, and the "city of truth", Zech. 8. 3.

Then Israel will mourn for the One whom they pierced, 12. 10. It truly will be a Day of Atonement, when they afflict their souls, Lev. 23. 27, 28, and "look" believingly to the One who was lifted up on the cross, v. 10; Num. 21. 9; John 3. 14, 15.

Cleansing follows, Zech. 13. 1. The *separating* power of the cross is then known, 13. 1 marg., for conversion always brings practical separation to God. The language is that of Numbers 19; Isaiah 52. 15; 4. 4; Ezekiel 36. 25.

The presence of the Lord is then known, Zech. 14. 4. "And his feet shall stand in that day upon the mount of Olives", will be the fulfilment of the promise given at His ascension from that same mountain, Acts. 1. 11. This leads to His being "king over all the earth", Zech. 14. 9. Then, the feast of tabernacles, which will have found its prophetic fulfilment, will be the occasion, annually, for the nations to come up to Jerusalem, and "worship the King", v. 16.

Believers are even now come to the city of God, the heavenly Jerusalem. They, too, have looked to the Pierced One, John 3. 14, for they know that the sword of judgment came down upon Jehovah's Fellow, Zech. 13. 7, that they might be cleansed. Is every bell and pot holiness to the Lord with you?

Dec. 31st
READING : Malachi 1. 1-14; 3. 8-17
GOD'S GRACIOUS ANSWERS

THE REVIVING stimulated through Haggai and Zechariah was weakening in the days of Nehemiah. Whereupon God graciously sent His word through Malachi. The message is one of expostulation. What grace from an offended God! By challenging questions He sought to awaken their response, but, alas, their thirteen replies (the number of rebellion) evidenced a hardness of heart, feigned innocence, and arrogance.

The basic statement is of His electing love, that has purposed them for Himself and His glory. In contrast, He had not chosen Esau (although twin brother to Jacob their forefather), or his descendants Edom, vv. 1-3; Deut. 7. 7, 8; Rom. 9. 10-13.

Their carping reply was "Wherein hast thou loved us?". Their whole history, and His present patient dealings, showed the evil of their retort. With us now how could *we* ever doubt His love, since He spared not His own Son, but delivered Him up for us all? "*As* the Father hath loved me, *so* have I loved you" states our Lord, John 15. 9.

Who would not give due honour to a father, or a master? Yet the Lord's name was dishonoured, and that by priests. They had become familiar with holy things, so that which they would not presume to offer to superiors, they brazenly presented to the great King, Mal. 1. 14. Such perfunctory ritual caused God to exclaim "Oh that there were one among you that would shut the doors, that ye might not kindle fire on mine altar in vain!", v. 10 R.V. What a weariness it had become to them, v. 13! Serving is to be done fervently, Rom. 12. 11; acts of mercy are to be done cheerfully (lit., with hilarity), 12. 8, as is giving, 2 Cor. 9. 7; obedience is to be with alacrity, James 1. 19. In fact "whatsoever ye do, do it heartily, as to the Lord".

But there was a remnant who feared the Lord. They had sweet fellowship together, and seemed never to part, Mal. 3. 16 R.V.; Psa. 119. 63. They thought upon His name. He *was theirs*, in all that He had revealed Himself to be. Their holy contemplation kept them from robbing God of His due, 3. 8. The Lord hearkened, thrilled with their response to Him, and His book of remembrance was written. In the day of glory and reward, He would say "*they are mine*"!

Pentateuch Law Books (5)

JANUARY			FEBRUARY			MARCH		
1	Genesis	1-2	1	Exodus	15.22-17.27	1	Numbers	7-8
2	Genesis	3-4	2	Exodus	18-20	2	Numbers	9-10
3	Genesis	5-6	3	Exodus	21-22	3	Numbers	11-12
4	Genesis	7-9	4	Exodus	23-24	4	Numbers	13-14
5	Genesis	10-11	5	Exodus	25	5	Numbers	15
6	Genesis	12-14	6	Exodus	26-27	6	Numbers	16-17
7	Genesis	15-17	7	Exodus	28-29	7	Numbers	18-19
8	Genesis	18-19	8	Exodus	30-31	8	Numbers	20-21
9	Genesis	20-21	9	Exodus	32-34	9	Numbers	22
10	Genesis	22-23	10	Exodus	35-36	10	Numbers	23-25
11	Genesis	24	11	Exodus	37-38	11	Numbers	26
12	Genesis	25-26	12	Exodus	39-40	12	Numbers	27-28
13	Genesis	27-28	13	Leviticus	1-3	13	Numbers	29-30
14	Genesis	29-30	14	Leviticus	4-5	14	Numbers	31
15	Genesis	31	15	Leviticus	6-7	15	Numbers	32
16	Genesis	32-33	16	Leviticus	8-10	16	Numbers	33
17	Genesis	34-35	17	Leviticus	11-12	17	Numbers	34-36
18	Genesis	36-37	18	Leviticus	13-14	18	Deuteronomy	1-2
19	Genesis	38-40	19	Leviticus	15-17	19	Deuteronomy	3-4
20	Genesis	41	20	Leviticus	18-19	20	Deuteronomy	5-7
21	Genesis	42-43	21	Leviticus	20-22	21	Deuteronomy	8-10
22	Genesis	44-45	22	Leviticus	23-24	22	Deuteronomy	11-13
23	Genesis	46-47	23	Leviticus	25	23	Deuteronomy	14-16
24	Genesis	48-50	24	Leviticus	26-27	24	Deuteronomy	17-19
25	Exodus	1-3	25	Numbers	1	25	Deuteronomy	20-22
26	Exodus	4-5	26	Numbers	2-3	26	Deuteronomy	23-25
27	Exodus	6-7	27	Numbers	4	27	Deuteronomy	26-27
28	Exodus	8-9	28	Numbers	5-6	28	Deuteronomy	28
29	Exodus	10-11				29	Deuteronomy	29-30
30	Exodus	12				30	Deuteronomy	31-32
31	Exodus	13.1-15.21				31	Deuteronomy	33-34

History Books (12)

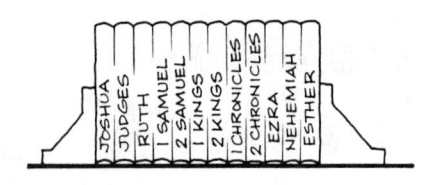

APRIL			MAY			JUNE		
1	Joshua	1-4	1	1 Samuel	25-28	1	2 Kings	21-23
2	Joshua	5-8	2	1 Samuel	29-31	2	2 Kings	24-25
3	Joshua	9-10	3	2 Samuel	1-2	3	1 Chronicles	1-2
4	Joshua	11-12	4	2 Samuel	3-5	4	1 Chronicles	3-4
5	Joshua	13-14	5	2 Samuel	6-9	5	1 Chronicles	5-6
6	Joshua	15	6	2 Samuel	10-12	6	1 Chronicles	7-8
7	Joshua	16-18	7	2 Samuel	13-14	7	1 Chronicles	9-10
8	Joshua	19-21	8	2 Samuel	15-16	8	1 Chronicles	11-12
9	Joshua	22-24	9	2 Samuel	17-18	9	1 Chronicles	13-15
10	Judges	1	10	2 Samuel	19-20	10	1 Chronicles	16-17
11	Judges	2-3	11	2 Samuel	21-22	11	1 Chronicles	18-21
12	Judges	4-5	12	2 Samuel	23-24	12	1 Chronicles	22-23
13	Judges	6	13	1 Kings	1-2	13	1 Chronicles	24-25
14	Judges	7-8	14	1 Kings	3-4	14	1 Chronicles	26-27
15	Judges	9	15	1 Kings	5-6	15	1 Chronicles	28-29
16	Judges	10-12	16	1 Kings	7	16	2 Chronicles	1-4
17	Judges	13-14	17	1 Kings	8-9.9	17	2 Chronicles	5-6
18	Judges	15-16	18	1 Kings	9.10-11.43	18	2 Chronicles	7-9
19	Judges	17-18	19	1 Kings	12-14	19	2 Chronicles	10-12
20	Judges	19	20	1 Kings	15-17	20	2 Chronicles	13-16
21	Judges	20-21	21	1 Kings	18-19	21	2 Chronicles	17-18
22	Ruth	1-4	22	1 Kings	20-21	22	2 Chronicles	19-20
23	1 Samuel	1-3	23	1 Kings 22-2 Kings 1		23	2 Chronicles	21-24
24	1 Samuel	4-7	24	2 Kings	2-4	24	2 Chronicles	25-26
25	1 Samuel	8-10	25	2 Kings	5-7	25	2 Chronicles	27-28
26	1 Samuel	11-13	26	2 Kings	8-9	26	2 Chronicles	29-30
27	1 Samuel	14-15	27	2 Kings	10-12	27	2 Chronicles	31-33
28	1 Samuel	16-17	28	2 Kings	13-14	28	2 Chronicles	34-36
29	1 Samuel	18-20	29	2 Kings	15-16	29	Ezra	1-3
30	1 Samuel	21-24	30	2 Kings 17.1-18.12		30	Ezra	4-6
			31	2 Kings 18.13-20.21				

Poetical Books (5)

	JULY			AUGUST			SEPTEMBER	
1	Ezra	7-8	1	Psalms	25-28	1	Psalms	119.57-112
2	Ezra	9-10	2	Psalms	29-32	2	Psalms	119.113-176
3	Nehemiah	1-3	3	Psalms	33-35	3	Psalms	120-127
4	Nehemiah	4-6	4	Psalms	36-37	4	Psalms	128-134
5	Nehemiah	7-8	5	Psalms	38-41	5	Psalms	135-136
6	Nehemiah	9-10	6	Psalms	42-45	6	Psalms	137-139
7	Nehemiah	11-13	7	Psalms	46-49	7	Psalms	140-143
8	Esther	1-3	8	Psalms	50-51	8	Psalms	144-146
9	Esther	4-7	9	Psalms	52-55	9	Psalms	147-150
10	Esther	8-10	10	Psalms	56-59	10	Proverbs	1-3
11	Job	1-3	11	Psalms	60-64	11	Proverbs	4-6
12	Job	4-7	12	Psalms	65-67	12	Proverbs	7-9
13	Job	8-10	13	Psalms	68-69	13	Proverbs	10-11
14	Job	11-14	14	Psalms	70-72	14	Proverbs	12-13
15	Job	15-17	15	Psalms	73-74	15	Proverbs	14-15
16	Job	18-19	16	Psalms	75-77	16	Proverbs	16-17
17	Job	20-21	17	Psalms	78	17	Proverbs	18-20
18	Job	22-24	18	Psalms	79-80	18	Proverbs	21-23
19	Job	25-28	19	Psalms	81-83	19	Proverbs	24-26
20	Job	29-31	20	Psalms	84-87	20	Proverbs	27-29
21	Job	32-34	21	Psalms	88-89	21	Proverbs	30-31
22	Job	35-37	22	Psalms	90-93	22	Ecclesiastes	1-4
23	Job	38-39	23	Psalms	94-96	23	Ecclesiastes	5-8
24	Job	40-42	24	Psalms	97-100	24	Ecclesiastes	9-12
25	Psalms	1-4	25	Psalms	101-103	25	Song of Songs 1.1-5.1	
26	Psalms	5-8	26	Psalms	104	26	Song of Songs 5.2-8.14	
27	Psalms	9-12	27	Psalms	105-106	27	Isaiah	1-3
28	Psalms	13-17	28	Psalms	107-108	28	Isaiah	4-6
29	Psalms	18	29	Psalms	109-112	29	Isaiah	7-8
30	Psalms	19-21	30	Psalms	113-118	30	Isaiah	9-12
31	Psalms	22-24	31	Psalms	119.1-56			

Prophetical Books (17)

ISAIAH, JEREMIAH, LAMENTATIONS, EZEKIEL, DANIEL, HOSEA, JOEL, AMOS, OBADIAH, JONAH, MICAH, NAHUM, HABAKKUK, ZEPHANIAH, HAGGAI, ZECHARIAH, MALACHI

OCTOBER			NOVEMBER			DECEMBER	
1	Isaiah	13-14	1	Jeremiah	30-31	1	Ezekiel	38-39
2	Isaiah	15-18	2	Jeremiah	32-33	2	Ezekiel	40-41
3	Isaiah	19-21	3	Jeremiah	34-36	3	Ezekiel	42-43
4	Isaiah	22-23	4	Jeremiah	37-39	4	Ezekiel	44-45
5	Isaiah	24-27	5	Jeremiah	40-42	5	Ezekiel	46-48
6	Isaiah	28-29	6	Jeremiah	43-45	6	Daniel	1-2
7	Isaiah	30-32	7	Jeremiah	46-48	7	Daniel	3-4
8	Isaiah	33-35	8	Jeremiah	49	8	Daniel	5-6
9	Isaiah	36-39	9	Jeremiah	50	9	Daniel	7-8
10	Isaiah	40-41	10	Jeremiah	51	10	Daniel	9-10
11	Isaiah	42-43	11	Jeremiah	52	11	Daniel	11-12
12	Isaiah	44-45	12	Lamentations	1-2	12	Hosea	1-3
13	Isaiah	46-48	13	Lamentations	3	13	Hosea	4-6
14	Isaiah	49.1-52.12	14	Lamentations	4-5	14	Hosea	7-10
15	Isaiah	52.13-54.17	15	Ezekiel	1-3	15	Hosea	11-14
16	Isaiah	55-57	16	Ezekiel	4-6	16	Joel	1-3
17	Isaiah	58-60	17	Ezekiel	7-9	17	Amos	1-3
18	Isaiah	61-64	18	Ezekiel	10-11	18	Amos	4-6
19	Isaiah	65-66	19	Ezekiel	12-14	19	Amos	7-9
20	Jeremiah	1-2	20	Ezekiel	15-16	20	Obadiah + Jonah	1-4
21	Jeremiah	3-4	21	Ezekiel	17-18	21	Micah	1-4
22	Jeremiah	5-6	22	Ezekiel	19-20	22	Micah	5-7
23	Jeremiah	7-8	23	Ezekiel	21-22	23	Nahum	1-3
24	Jeremiah	9-10	24	Ezekiel	23	24	Habakkuk	1-3
25	Jeremiah	11-13	25	Ezekiel	24-25	25	Zephaniah	1-3
26	Jeremiah	14-16	26	Ezekiel	26.1-28.19	26	Haggai	1-2
27	Jeremiah	17-19	27	Ezekiel	28.20-30.26	27	Zechariah	1-4
28	Jeremiah	20-22	28	Ezekiel	31-32	28	Zechariah	5-8
29	Jeremiah	23-24	29	Ezekiel	33-34	29	Zechariah	9-11
30	Jeremiah	25-26	30	Ezekiel	35-37	30	Zechariah	12-14
31	Jeremiah	27-29				31	Malachi	1-4

Index of Passages Treated

Pages are indicated by numbers in bold type

GENESIS							
1.1	**13**	19.1-25	**53**	4.1-13	**96**	1 SAMUEL	
1.26-31	**13**	20.1-26	**54**	4.32-40	**96**	1.1-28	**135**
2.1-3	**13**	25.1-40	**55**	5.1-21	**97**	2.1-11	**135**
2.16-17	**15**	26.31-37	**56**	6.1-15	**97**	3.1-21	**136**
2.18-25	**14**	27.1-8	**56**	7.1-26	**98**	4.1	**136**
3.1-6	**15**	28.1-43	**57**	8.1-20	**99**	7.1-17	**137**
3.7-24	**16**	30.1-38	**58**	9.1-29	**100**	8.1-22	**138**
4.1-16	**16**	31.1-18	**59**	10.12-22	**100**	12.1-25	**139**
4.17-24	**18**	32.1-35	**60**	12.1-32	**101**	15.1-35	**140**
4.25-26	**17**	33.1-23	**61**	15.1-23	**102**	16.1-23	**141**
5.1-6	**18**	34.1-7	**61**	16.1-22	**103**	17.1-54	**142**
5.21-24	**18**	35.20-29	**62**	17.14-20	**104**	17.55-58	**143**
6.5-14	**19**	36.1-8	**62**	18.1-22	**104**	18.1-30	**143**
7.1	**19**	40.1-38	**63**	19.1-21	**105**	20.1-42	**144**
8.1-5	**19**			22.1-8	**106**	21.1-15	**145**
8.20-22	**20**	LEVITICUS		24.10-22	**106**	22.1-5	**145**
9.18-29	**20**	1.1-17	**65**	25.1-3	**106**	25.2-44	**146**
11.1-9	**21**	4.1-35	**66**	26.16-19	**106**	26.1-25	**147**
11.26-32	**21**	6.8-30	**67**	27.1-13	**107**	30.1-31	**148**
12.1-3	**21**	7.37-38	**67**	28.1-19	**107**	31.1-13	**149**
12.1-9	**22**	8.1-36	**68**	31.1-6	**108**		
12.10-17	**23**	9.1-24	**69**	32.1-6	**108**	2 SAMUEL	
12.18-20	**23**	10.1-20	**70**	33.1-5	**108**	1.1-27	**149**
13.1-4	**24**	11.1-47	**71**	34.1-12	**108**	1.17-27	**150**
13.5-18	**25**	14.1-20	**72**			2.1-7	**151**
14.1-24	**26**	16.1-34	**73**	JOSHUA		4.4	**155**
17.1-8	**27**	21.1-24	**74**	1.1-18	**110**	5.1-16	**151**
18.9-15	**27**	23.1-44	**75**	2.1-24	**111**	6.12-23	**152**
22.1-12	**28**	24.1-23	**76**	3.1-17	**112**	7.1-17	**153**
24.1-27	**29**	25.1-24	**77**	4.1-9	**112**	7.18-29	**154**
24.12-52	**30**	26.1-13	**78**	5.13-15	**113**	9.1-13	**155**
25.19-34	**31**	26.27-46	**78**	6.1-27	**113**	12.1-25	**156**
26.1-33	**32**	27.1-34	**79**	7.1-26	**114**	15.1-37	**157**
28.10-22	**33**			9.1-27	**115**	16.1-4	**158**
32.1-32	**34**	NUMBERS		20.1-9	**116**	19.24-30	**158**
33.1-4	**34**	3.5-39	**81**	24.1-33	**117**	22.1-51	**159**
37.1-36	**35**	4.1-33	**82**			23.1-7	**160**
39.1-23	**36**	8.5-26	**83**	JUDGES		24.1-25	**161**
40.1-23	**37**	10.11-36	**84**	1.1-36	**120**		
41.14-46	**38**	11.1-9	**85**	3.7-31	**121**	1 KINGS	
42.18-23	**39**	11.10-35	**86**	4.1-24	**122**	1.1-48	**165**
44.1-34	**39**	13.1-33	**87**	6.11-32	**123**	3.1-15	**166**
45.1-11	**40**	14.1-45	**88**	6.33-40	**124**	6.1-14	**167**
48.1-22	**41**	16.1-40	**89**	7.1-25	**124**	6.15-38	**168**
50.14-26	**42**	16.41-50	**90**	9.1-22	**125**	7.1-12	**169**
		17.1-13	**90**	11.1-40	**126**	8.31-50	**170**
EXODUS		20.1-22	**91**	13.1-25	**127**	8.54-66	**171**
1.6-14	**44**	22.41	**92**	16.1-31	**128**	11.1-13	**172**
2.11-25	**44**	23.1-30	**92**	17.1-13	**129**	12.25-33	**173**
4.1-31	**45**	24.1-25	**92**			13.1-32	**174**
6.1-30	**46**			RUTH		14.21-31	**175**
10.1-29	**47**	DEUTER-		1.1-22	**130**	18.21-46	**176**
12.1-20	**48**	ONOMY		2.1-23	**131**	21.1-29	**177**
14.1-31	**49**	1.1-8	**94**	3.1-18	**132**		
15.1-27	**50**	1.19-46	**94**	4.10-13	**132**	2 KINGS	
16.1-36	**51**	2.1-7	**95**	4.17	**132**	2.1-17	**178**
17.1-16	**52**	2.24-31	**95**			6.8-23	**179**
		3.21-29	**95**			6.24-33	**180**

7.1-20	**180**		
9.1-37	**181**		
10.1-36	**182**		
11.21	**183**		
12.1-21	**183**		
14.1-20	**184**		
16.1-20	**185**		
17.1-23	**186**		
19.14-34	**187**		
22.8-20	**188**		
23.1-25	**188**		
24.8-20	**189**		
25.1-30	**189**		
1 CHRONICLES			
1.1-7	**192**		
2.1-7	**192**		
4.9-10	**193**		
9.1	**192, 194**		
9.10-27	**194**		
11.1-25	**195**		
13.1-14	**196**		
15.1-29	**197**		
16.1-36	**198**		
16.23-36	**199**		
23.1-32	**200**		
27.1-15	**201**		
28.1-10	**202**		
28.11-21	**203**		
29.1-30	**204**		
2 CHRONICLES			
3.14	**206**		
4.1	**206**		
5.1-14	**206**		
6.12-25	**207**		
7.1-3	**207**		
10.1-19	**208**		
15.1-19	**209**		
16.1-14	**209**		
17.1-10	**210**		
18.1-34	**211**		
19.1-3	**211**		
19.4-11	**210**		
20.1-30	**212**		
21.1-30	**213**		
22.1-12	**214**		
23.1-15	**214**		
26.1-23	**215**		
29.1-29	**216**		
30.1-27	**217**		
31.1	**217**		
32.24-31	**218**		
33.1-25	**219**		
34.1-21	**220**		
35.1-26	**221**		
36.1-23	**222**		

EZRA			118.1-29	272	15.1-9	308	38.1-28	344	5.1-27	384
1.1-11	224		119.1-24	273	16.1-14	308	51.1-26	345	6.1-14	384
3.1-13	225		120.1-7	274	17.1-14	309			7.1-17	385
4.1-24	226		121.1-8	274	18.1-7	309	**LAMENTA-**		8.1-14	385
7.1-28	227		122.1-9	274	19.1-25	309	**TIONS**		9.1-15	385
8.1-36	228		126.1-6	275	20.1-6	309	1.7-12	346		
			127.1-5	275	21.1-17	309	3.19-32	346	**OBADIAH**	
NEHEMIAH			128.1-6	275	22.1-25	310			1-21	386
2.1-20	230		132.1-18	276	23.1-18	310	**EZEKIEL**			
3.1-32	231		133.1-3	276	24.1-23	311	1.1-28	348	**JONAH**	
4.1-23	232		134.1-3	276	25.1-12	311	8.1-18	349	1.1-16	388
6.1-19	233		146.1-10	277	26.1-21	311	9.1-11	350	1.17	389
8.1-18	234		147.1-20	277	27.1-13	311	10.1-22	351	2.1-10	389
13.1-31	235		148.1-14	277	28.1-29	312	11.1-25	352	3.1-10	389
			149.1-9	277	29.1-24	312	16.1-34	353	4.1-11	390
ESTHER			150.1-6	277	30.1-33	312	28.1-19	354		
2.2-11	237				31.1-9	312	33.1-21	355	**MICAH**	
2.21-23	237		**PROVERBS**		32.1-20	312	37.1-28	356	1.1-16	391
3.1-6	237		1.1-7	279	33.1-24	312	43.1-12	357	2.1-13	391
4.1-17	238		3.1-10	280	34.1-17	313	47.1-12	358	3.1-12	392
6.1-14	239		4.10-19	281	35.1-10	313			4.1-13	392
			5.1-23	282	36.1-22	314	**DANIEL**		5.1-15	392
JOB			6.1-19	283	37.1-38	314	1.1-21	360	6.1-16	393
1.1-22	241		7.1-24	284	38.1-22	315	2.31-49	361	7.1-20	393
2.1-10	241		8.1-36	285	39.1-8	315	3.1-30	362		
2.11-13	242		13.1-25	286	40.1-11	316	4.1-37	363	**NAHUM**	
9.1-35	242		15.1-24	287	40.12-31	317	5.1-31	364	1.1-15	394
19.1-29	243		21.1-31	288	42.1-12	318	6.1-28	365	2.1-13	394
33.6-30	244		24.10-12	289	44.28	319	7.1-28	366	3.1-19	394
38.1-11	245		31.10-31	290	45.1-25	319	8.1-27	367		
40.1-5	245				49.1-26	320	9.1-27	368	**HABAKKUK**	
42.1-6	245		**ECCLESIASTES**		50.1-11	321	10.1-21	369	1.1-17	396
42.7-17	246		1.1-18	292	52.13-15	322	12.1-13	370	2.1-20	396
			5.1-7	293	53.1-6	322			3.1-19	397
PSALMS			12.1-7	294	53.7-12	323	**HOSEA**			
1.1-6	248				54.1-17	324	1.1-11	374	**ZEPHANIAH**	
2.1-12	249		**SONG**		55.1-13	325	2.1-23	374	1.1-18	398
8.1-9	250		1.1-17	295	59.20-21	326	3.1-5	374	2.1-15	398
16.1-11	251		2.1-7	295	60.1-22	326	4.1-19	375	3.1-20	398
19.1-14	252		2.8-17	296	61.1-11	327	5.1-15	375		
22.1-31	253		3.1-5	297	62.1-12	328	6.1-11	376	**HAGGAI**	
23.1-6	254		5.2-16	298	63.1-19	329	7.1-16	376	1.1-15	400
24.1-10	255		6.1-3	298	65.17-25	330	8.1-14	376	2.1-9	400
32.1-11	256		8.5-14	299	66.22-24	330	9.1-17	376		
40.1-17	257						10.1-15	377	**ZECHARIAH**	
45.1-17	258		**ISAIAH**		**JEREMIAH**		11.1-12	377	1.1-21	401
46.1-11	259		1.1-31	301	1.1-19	332	12.1-14	377	2.1-13	402
68.1-35	260		2.1-22	302	2.1-19	333	13.1-16	378	3.1-10	403
69.1-36	261		3.1-26	302	7.1-34	334	14.1-9	378	4.1-14	404
73.1-28	262		4.1-6	302	8.1-3	334			5.1-11	405
78.1-20	263		5.1-30	303	9.23-26	335	**JOEL**		6.1-15	406
78.59-72	263		6.1-13	304	10.1-25	335	1.1-20	380	9.1-12	407
80.1-19	264		7.1-25	305	15.1-21	336	2.1-17	380	10.4-6	407
84.1-12	265		8.1-22	305	17.1-27	337	2.18-32	381	11.1-17	408
89.1-37	266		9.1-7	305	23.1-32	338	3.1-21	381	12.1-14	409
90.1-17	267		9.8-21	306	26.1-24	339			13.1-9	409
91.1-16	267		10.1-34	306	28.1-17	340	**AMOS**		14.1-9	409
102.1-28	268		11.1-16	307	31.1-40	341	1.1-15	382		
103.1-22	269		12.1-6	307	32.1-15	342	2.1-16	382	**MALACHI**	
107.1-43	270		13.1-22	308	33.1-11	342	3.1-15	383	1.1-14	410
110.1-7	271		14.1-32	308	36.1-32	343	4.1-13	383	3.8-17	410